LINGUISTICS ISSUES IN LANGUAC

LINGUISTIC ISSUES IN LANGUAGE TECHNOLOGY

VOLUME 9

PERSPECTIVES ON SEMANTIC REPRESENTATIONS FOR TEXTUAL INFERENCE

edited by
Cleo Condoravdi, Valeria de Paiva
and Annie Zaenen

CSLI
PUBLICATIONS
Center for the Study of
Language and Information
Stanford, California

LiLT Volume 9

ISBN: 9781575868448 (pbk)
ISSN: 1945-3604

∞ The acid-free paper used in this book meets the minimum requirements
of the American National Standard for Information Sciences—Permanence
of Paper for Printed Library Materials, ANSI Z39.48-1984.

CSLI was founded in 1983 by researchers from Stanford University, SRI
International, and Xerox PARC to further the research and development of
integrated theories of language, information, and computation. CSLI headquarters
and CSLI Publications are located on the campus of Stanford University.

An online version of this journal is available at CSLI Publications
http://cslipublications.stanford.edu/

Contents

Acknowledgments

We would like to thank the contributors to the workshops that this volume is based on, the authors of the articles and our dedicated reviewers:

Danny Bobrow	Larry Moss
Robin Cooper	Charles Ortiz
Jan Van Eijck	Stephen Pulman
Nissim Francez	Stephen Read
David Israel	Mark Sammons
Bill MacCartney	Hinrich Schütze
Wei Lu	Mark Steedman
Gerard de Melo	Alessandra Zarcone

We also thank the staff of CSLI and especially Emma Pease for the help in producing this volume.

Introduction

ANNIE ZAENEN, CLEO CONDORAVDI, VALERIA DE PAIVA

The introduction of the RTE (Recognizing Textual Entailment) paradigm in 2004 constituted a turning point in computational work on inference in natural language. That paradigm sees the task of determining the relation between two texts as one where assuming the truth of the first text, T, the thesis, leads to concluding to the (likely) truth or falsity of the other text, called H, the hypothesis. Later variants extended the relation also to contradictions. It has focused work on textual inference on tasks that are on the one hand feasible and on the other hand based on real texts. In this volume we present some of the work that arose from this conceptualization of the task, mostly but not only focussing on methods that involve logical formalizations. The volume is based on three workshops that we organized in 2011 and 2012: the *CSLI Workshop on Natural Logic, Proof Theory, and Computational Semantics* on April 8 and 9, 2011 at Stanford,[1] *Semantics for textual inference* on July 9/10, 2011 at the University of Colorado at Boulder,[2] and the CSLI workshop on *Semantic Representations for Textual Inference* on March 9 and 10, 2012 at Stanford.[3]

The first paper in this volume, "The BIUTEE Research Platform for Transformation-based Textual Entailment Recognition" by Asher Stern and Ido Dagan, is from the lab that introduced the current textual inference paradigm, RTE. The paper is an interim report on BIUTEE, an open source and open architecture platform that allows users to develop components for textual inference systems. The system consists of a preprocessing module that does parsing, named en-

[1]http://www.stanford.edu/~icard/logic&language/
[2]http://www.stanford.edu/~cleoc/Sem-Text-Inf/
[3]http://semanticrepresentation.stanford.edu

LiLT Volume 9
Perspectives on Semantic Representations for Textual Inference.
Copyright © 2014, CSLI Publications.

tity recognition and coreference resolution and several modules that do inference recognition. The architecture allows the user to insert different lexical/knowledge resources (e.g. DIRT, WordNet, Wikipedia) and to add his/her own modules. The inference recognition engine itself is transformation-based, constructing derivations that go from text to hypothesis via rewrite rules. This procedure that can be seen as an instance of a proof, with the difference from traditional formal proofs being that the procedure allows for conclusions to likely true (false) instead of aiming for certainty. The system presented in this paper has meanwhile been integrated in an wider platform, EXCITEMENT, that allows more flexibility.[4] The hope is that ultimately the community interested in textual inference will have a platform comparable to that provided to the (statistical) translation community by MOSES.[5]

There are two other papers describing full systems. They concentrate on building systems that allow true textual entailments and are not geared to allowing conclusions that are only *likely* to be drawn by native speakers.

The first paper "Is there a place for logic in recognizing textual entailment" by Johan Bos describes Nutcracker, a system that integrates Combinatory Categorial Grammar, Discourse Representation Theory (translated into first-order formulas through the reification of modality) and first order theorem proving. It argues that the main problem for such systems is the acquisition of the relevant *background knowledge* and shows how axioms deriving synonyms and hyponyms relations can be automatically derived from WordNet information. It proposes axioms for verbs of 'saying' that allow one to conclude that a reported event holds in the real world assuming one trusts the source and axioms learned from the RTE sets themselves. Several different theorem provers can be plugged into the system as well as different model builders that search for models up to a specified domain size. The analysis terminate either with (i) a proof, (ii) a finite counter model of size n, or (iii) neither. The system has, as expected, high precision but low recall as the knowledge acquisition problem is only partially solved.

Another take on textual inference is provided in the paper by Lenhart Schubert "NLog-like Inference and Commonsense Reasoning". The paper describes the key properties of the Epilog system, an implementation of Episodic Logic, whose language is meant to provide a target representation for natural language. Epilog performs Natural Logic kind of inferences, but it goes beyond them in two ways: it can

---

[4]http://www.excitement-project.eu
[5]http://www.statmt.org/moses/

perform goal-directed and forward inferences, not just inferences with known premises and conclusions, as well as inferences based on lexical knowledge and language-independent world knowledge. Moving beyond narrow textual inference to common sense inference, essential to natural language understanding, requires addressing the problem of the "knowledge acquisition bottleneck". The paper describes various under way and potential efforts for gathering knowledge from texts. These are based on the idea that one can recover some of the background knowledge assumed in one text from what is stated in another. In addition to lexical knowledge, necessary for inferences based on meaning, and world/common sense knowledge, necessary for general reasoning and true understanding, it recognizes semantic pattern knowledge. This knowledge comprises general 'factoids' that guide parsing and interpretation. Such factoids can also be used to acquire world knowledge via factoid strengthening and factoid sharpening as defined in the contribution.

The RTE challenge stressed the importance of working on real text and to take into account all the phenomena that contribute to making an inference valid or not. In this it is contrasted with earlier approaches that would concentrate on getting inferences involving specific semantic phenomena, e.g. quantifiers (Cooper et al. 1996, 1994) but after several years, the need to decompose the TE task into basic phenomena and the way these basic phenomena interact. Two papers address that issue.

Elena Cabrio and Bernardo Magnini in "Decomposing Semantic Inferences" look at the problem from an empirical angle. They analyze a TE data set looking at the nature of the inference (deductive, inductive, adductive) and the linguistic phenomena involved (e.g. synonymy, coreference, negation, active/passive alternation). Their results show that a huge amount of background information is required to approach the TE task. They also decompose the inferences of the thesis-hypothesis TH pairs into smaller atomic inference pairs consisting of a linguistic and an inference pattern. They conclude that "the polarity of most of the phenomena is not predictable for the logical judgments" and point out the consequences for attempts to learn from the annotated RTE data sets.

Assaf Toledo et al., in "Towards a Semantic Model for Textual Entailment Annotation", develop a theoretical model of entailment recognition. The main idea consists in providing an interpreted lexicon, which specifies the semantic types and denotations of content and function words, and which ultimately serves as a target canonical representation for constructions in Text and Hypothesis sentences. After "binding to" an interpreted lexicon, an inferential relation can be proven between T and H using predicate calculus and lambda calculus reduction, or disproven by the construction of a countermodel. Starting from the assumption that the model can incrementally incorporate increasingly complex phenomena, the authors concentrate on three prevalent inferential phenomena in the RTE data bases: intersective, restrictive, and appositive modification. At the same time, they acknowledge that interaction between phenomena might significantly complicate scaling up their model. The contrast between intersective vs. restrictive modification provides a nice illustration of how expressions with the same syntactic structure can have radically different inferential properties and how "binding to" an interpreted lexicon can model the difference.

Four of the remaining papers focus on logic more traditionally construed.

Alex Djalali's "Synthetic Logic" reminds us that derivability plays as central a role in NL semantics as that of entailment and that it makes sense to develop a more proof-based approach to the logic of Natural Language, where one tries to capture the sorts of inferences speakers make in practice. Djalali considers MacCartney and Manning's model of Natural Logic (MacCartney and Manning 2009; MacCartney 2009) as a kind of generalized transitive reasoning system and makes it, in the process, much easier to understand as a system of logic than the original system. His proof rules in Gentzen-style sequent calculus are divided into M-rules (which explain the composition of MacCartney and Manning relations) and D-rules, which correspond to structural properties of the MacCartney relations themselves. Djalali's soundness and completeness proofs are crisp and enlightening, despite, like MacCartney and Manning, dealing only with a fragment of the algorithm developed for the implemented system NatLog.

The paper by Icard and Moss summarizes classic as well as more recent work on monotonicity reasoning in natural language. They first offer an informal overview of work on the Monotonicity Calculus, beginning with van Benthem and Sánchez-Valencia in the late 1980s, and continuing on to the present day, including extensions, variations, and applications. Alongside examples from natural language, they also present analogous examples from elementary algebra, illustrating the fact that the Monotonicity Calculus makes sense as a more general system for reasoning about monotone and antitone functions over (pre)ordered sets. Following a discussion of current logical, computational, and psychological work on monotonicity in natural language, they develop a fully explicit Monotonicity Calculus using markings on simple types, with a well-defined language, semantics, and proof system, and culminating in an overview of soundness and completeness results, pointing to recent and forthcoming work by the authors.

The paper by Ian Pratt-Hartman, "The Relational Syllogistic Revisited" is part of the tradition of extending the original syllogistic calculus. In previous work Moss and Pratt-Hartman introduced the relational syllogistic, an extension of the language of classical syllogisms in which predicates are allowed to feature transitive verbs with quantified objects. They showed that this relational syllogistic does not admit a finite set of rules whose associated direct derivation relation is sound and complete. Thus for the relational syllogistic, indirect reasoning, in the form of *reduction ad absurdum* is essential. Pratt-Hartmann's paper in this volume presents a modest extension of the relational syllogistic language which is sound and complete, as desired for direct proofs. This shows that the impossibility of providing a finite rule-set for the relational syllogistic can be overcome by a modest increase in expressive power. The proof is quite complicated. Still one important conclusion from the existence of a sound and complete proof system defined by a finite set of syllogism-like rules such as the ones here is that adding relations (as transitive verbs) to a basic syllogistic logic does not represent a logical 'boundary' with respect to the expressiveness of fragments of natural language. From the previous result of Moss and Pratt-Hartmann one could get the (wrong) impression that syllogistic extensions could not be provided for transitive verbs while keeping the system sound and complete. The system RE introduced shows that this is not the case, soundness and completeness are within reach.

In "Intensions as Computable Functions", Shallom Lappin deals with an long standing problem of intensional logic, proposing a type theoretical solution. Classical intensional semantic representation languages, like Montague's Intensional Logic do not accommodate fine-grained intensionality well. In the traditional work intensional identity is reduced to equivalence of denotation across possible worlds and logically equivalent expressions are semantically indistinguishable. Thus not only all mathematical truths are the same, but also the denotations of belief statements are all logically equivalent. Lappin's paper shows that terms in the type theory PTCT (Property Theory with Curry Typing) proposed by Fox and Lappin (to appear) constitute an alternative intensional semantic representation framework. PTCT uses two notions of equality: intensional identity and extensional equivalence, and while intensional identity implies extensional equivalence, the converse is not true. Their fine-grained notions allow PTCT to prove the equivalence of mathematical truths, while allowing the non-equivalence of all belief statements. Here, Lappin proposes to characterize the distinction between intensional identity and provable equivalence *computationally* by invoking the contrast between operational and denotational semantics in programming language. Since the terms of PTCT are lambda-expressions that encode computable functions and since Lappin has identified these with the intensions of words and phrases in natural language, given the distinction between denotational and operational meaning, he can interpret the non-identity of terms in the representation language as an operational difference in the functions that these terms express. In other words if the terms compute the same result set through different sets of procedures, they are different. This approach factors modality and possible worlds out of the specification of intensions.

While the series of conferences this volume is based on had several talks on machine learning approaches to semantics, none of the authors could find the time to write up their work in a way to that would have fitted it. But "Frege in Space", the contribution of Marco Baroni, Raffaella Bernardi and Roberto Zamparelli, fills the gap with an extensive discussion of distributional semantics and its relation to traditional compositional semantics. One of the problems of classical approaches to semantics is that most lexical items are unanalyzed ('prime semantics'). Distributional semantics proposes a way to handle this through a 'the meaning of a word, is the company it keeps' approach. The approach has shown to deliver interesting results for noun and noun adjective combinations. It is less clear how to extend it to argument taking predicates and how to handle compositionality. "Frege in Space" proposes an ambitious program to do so and shows the way for a synthesis between both approaches.

We would like to dedicate the volume to our colleagues of the now defunct PARC NLTT group, especially Danny Bobrow, Dick Crouch, Lauri Karttunen, Ron Kaplan, Martin Kay, Tracy King and John Maxwell. They kindled our interest in the problems of the relation between logic, computation and natural language understanding that the volume aims to be a contribution to.

References

Cooper, R., R. Crouch, J. van Eijck, C. Fox, J. van Genabith, J. Jaspars, H. Kamp, D. Milward, M. Pinkal, M. Poesio, and S. Pulman. 1996. Using the framework. Technical Report LRE 62-051 D-16, The FraCaS Consortium.

Cooper, R., R. Crouch, J. van Eijck, C. Fox, J. van Genabith, J. Jaspars, H. Kamp, M. Pinkal, M. Poesio, S. Pulman, and E. Vestre. 1994. Describing the approaches.

Fox, C. and S. Lappin. to appear. *Formal Foundations of Intensional Semantics*. Blackwell.

MacCartney, B. 2009. *Natural Language Inference*. Ph.D. thesis, Stanford University.

MacCartney, Bill and Christopher Manning. 2009. An extended model of natural logic. In *The Eighth International Conference on Computational Semantics (IWCS-8)*.

The BIUTEE Research Platform for Transformation-based Textual Entailment Recognition

ASHER STERN AND IDO DAGAN[1]

Recent progress in research of the Recognizing Textual Entailment (RTE) task shows a constantly-increasing level of complexity in this research field. A way to avoid having this complexity becoming a barrier for researchers, especially for new-comers in the field, is to provide a freely available RTE system with a high level of flexibility and extensibility. In this paper, we introduce our RTE system, BIUTEE[2], and suggest it as an effective research framework for RTE. In particular, BIUTEE follows the prominent transformation-based paradigm for RTE, and offers an accessible platform for research within this approach. We describe each of BIUTEE's components and point out the mechanisms and properties which directly support adaptations and integration of new components. In addition, we describe BIUTEE's visual tracing tool, which provides notable assistance for researchers in refining and "debugging" their knowledge resources and inference components.

1 Introduction and Background

Textual inference (the ability to automatically find conclusions that can be inferred from a natural language text) is a capability required for many tasks at the semantic level of *Natural Language Processing (NLP)*. For example, a typical *Information Extraction (IE)* task may be to extract, from a natural language text, the employer-employee

---

[1]Bar-Ilan University, Ramat-Gan, Israel

[2]BIUTEE: **B**ar **I**lan **U**niversity **T**extual **E**ntailment **E**ngine. It is freely available at http://www.cs.biu.ac.il/~nlp/downloads/biutee/

LiLT Volume 9
Perspectives on Semantic Representations for Textual Inference.
Copyright © 2014, CSLI Publications.

relationship. Such a task can be formalized as the task of identifying text fragments from which it can be concluded that "X is employed by Y" for some entities X and Y. Similarly, a typical *Question Answering (QA)* task might be the task of finding answers to the question "By whom X is employed", for some entity X (a person, in this case). Addressing both these examples requires a mechanism that recognizes that the text fragment "X is employed by Y" can be inferred from a given text. *Recognizing Textual Entailment (RTE)* unifies this concept, and aims to serve as a common paradigm for textual inference. By adopting the RTE paradigm, the efforts required to solve the problem of textual inference need not to be duplicated for multiple NLP tasks which require this capability. Rather, the aim is to develop a generic solver for the RTE task, which can then be used as an inference component in task-specific systems.

The formal definition of the *Recognizing Textual Entailment* task is as follows. Given two text fragments, one termed *text* and the other *hypothesis*, the task is to recognize whether the hypothesis can be inferred from the text (Dagan et al. 2006a).

Since first introduced, several approaches have been proposed for this task, ranging from shallow lexical similarity methods (e.g., Clark and Harrison 2010; MacKinlay and Baldwin 2009), to complex linguistically-motivated methods, which incorporate extensive linguistic analysis (syntactic parsing, coreference resolution, semantic role labelling, etc.) and a rich inventory of linguistic and world-knowledge resources (e.g., Iftene 2008; de Salvo Braz et al. 2005; Bar-Haim et al. 2007). The latter methods convert the text and the hypothesis into rich representation levels, like syntactic parse-trees, semantic-role graph, or even a logical representation in which the text is converted into a collection of logical formulas. The next step is the entailment recognition itself in which the available knowledge resources are utilized.

Building such complex systems requires substantial development efforts, which might become a barrier for new-comers to RTE research. Thus, flexible and extensible publicly available RTE systems are expected to significantly facilitate research in this field. More concretely, two major research communities would benefit from a publicly available RTE system:

1. End application developers, who would use an RTE system to solve inference tasks within their application. RTE systems utilized by this type of researchers should be adaptable for the application specific data: they should be configurable, trainable, and extensible with inference knowledge that captures application-

specific phenomena.

2. Researchers in the RTE community, who would not need to build from scratch a complete RTE system for their research, but could integrate their novel research components into an existing open-source system. Such research efforts might include developing knowledge resources, developing inference components for specific phenomena such as temporal inference (see, for example, (Wang and Zhang 2008)), or extending RTE to different languages. A flexible and extensible RTE system is expected to encourage researchers to create and share their textual-inference components. A good example from another research area is the *Moses* system for *Statistical Machine Translation (SMT)* (Koehn et al. 2007), which provides the core SMT components while being extended with new research components by a large scientific community.

Until now rather few and quite limited RTE systems were made publicly available. These systems are quite restricted in the types of knowledge resources which they can utilize, and in the scope of their inference algorithms. For example, *EDITS*[3] (Kouylekov and Negri 2010) is a distance-based RTE system, which can exploit only lexical knowledge resources. *NutCracker*[4] (Bos and Markert 2005) is a system based on logical representation and automatic theorem proving, but utilizes only WordNet (Fellbaum 1998) as a lexical knowledge resource.

To address the above needs, we provide our open-source textual-entailment system, BiuTee.[5] Our system provides state-of-the-art linguistic analysis tools and exploits various types of manually built and automatically acquired knowledge resources, including lexical, lexical-syntactic and syntactic rewrite rules. Furthermore, the system components, including pre-processing utilities, knowledge resources, and even the steps of the inference algorithm, are modular, and can be replaced or extended easily with new components. Extensibility and flexibility are also supported by a *plug-in mechanism*, by which new inference components can be integrated without changing existing code.

Notable support for researchers is provided by *a visual tracing tool, Tracer*, which visualizes every step of the inference process as shown in Figures 5 and 6, in Section 4.

This paper is organized as follows: A review of the main algorithmic components of BiuTee is given in Section 2, followed by the system architecture description in Section 3. The visual tracing tool and its

---

[3]http://edits.fbk.eu/
[4]http://svn.ask.it.usyd.edu.au/trac/candc/wiki/nutcracker
[5]See footnote 2 above.

TABLE 1: A sequence of transformations that transform the text *"He received the letter from the secretary."* into the hypothesis *"The secretary delivered the message to the employee."*. The knowledge required for such transformations is often obtained from available knowledge resources and NLP tools.

#	Operation	Generated text
0	-	He received the letter from the secretary.
1	Coreference substitution	The employee received the letter from the secretary.
2	X received Y from Z → Y was sent to X by Z	The letter was sent to the employee by the secretary.
3	Y [verb-passive] by X → X [verb-active] Y	The secretary sent the letter to the employee.
4	X send Y → X deliver Y	The secretary delivered the letter to the employee.
5	letter → message	The secretary delivered the message to the employee.

typical use cases are described in Section 4, while in Section 5 we present experimental results. Conclusions, as well as suggestions for future work are given in Section 6.

2 Algorithms and Components

In this section we describe BIUTEE's main algorithms and components. This description is given at a high-level, while more details of individual components are available in the papers cited along this section.

BIUTEE (Stern and Dagan 2011) is a *transformation-based* inference system, in the sense that it transforms the text, T, into the hypothesis, H. Transforming T into H is done by applying a *sequence* of transformations, such that after applying the last transformation, the resulting text is identical to the hypothesis.[6] In this paper we use the term *proof* to refer to such a sequence of transformations. Table 1 demonstrates a proof for a typical (T,H) pair. The transformation-based paradigm requires three main design decisions:

1. How to represent the text and the hypothesis?
2. Which transformations to apply?
3. How to estimate whether a sequence of transformation preserves entailment?

In the following subsections we discuss each of these aspects. Finally, we deal with another crucial issue, namely:

---

[6]In practice, this goal is heuristically relaxed in the current version of BIUTEE to having the hypothesis embedded in the obtained transformed text.

4. How to *find* automatically an "optimal" sequence of transformations that transforms T into H?

2.1 Representation level

There are several levels on which the text and the hypothesis can be represented. The simplest level of representation is the lexical level (e.g. bag of words) (see, for example, (Shnarch et al. 2011; Clark and Harrison 2010)). While this level has some advantages, for example, it can be easily implemented for languages that lack linguistic processing tools, it cannot handle structural differences of T and H. Consider, for example, the text "The first chapter of the book was written yesterday" and the hypothesis "The book was written yesterday". Though the hypothesis words are embedded in the text in the same order, the text does not entail the hypothesis. A common representation level of sentence structure is the syntactic representation, given as parse trees (See Figure 1). This level of representation was adopted by the vast majority of RTE systems (e.g., Iftene 2008; Cabrio et al. 2008; Wang and Neumann 2008). A deeper representation is the logical form level, which represents T and H as logical clauses, extracted from the syntactic representation. Typical examples are Tatu and Moldovan (2006), Raina et al. (2005) and Clark and Harrison (2010)

While deep logical representations may capture additional aspects of the meaning of the text, their much higher complexity makes them more vulnerable to inaccuracies and errors involved in their generation. Moreover, most of the structural information required for inference can be found in the syntactic representation, which was therefore chosen for BIUTEE. However, since syntax does not capture some key semantic properties (e.g., the truth-value of predicates), we enrich the syntactic parse trees with additional annotations, as described later (Subsection 2.3).

2.2 Transformations

The second aspect in transformation-based inference is the type of transformations that can be applied by the system. Our goal is to apply transformations, such that each of them preserves the meaning of the text, as follows. When a transformation is applied on a text t, it transforms it into a new text, t'. The goal is that the meaning of t' will be entailed from t.

We apply many types of transformations, that are derived from many knowledge and linguistic resources. These transformations are relatively reliable, in most cases. In addition, we allow less reliable transformations, to be utilized when no prior knowledge of reliable transformations

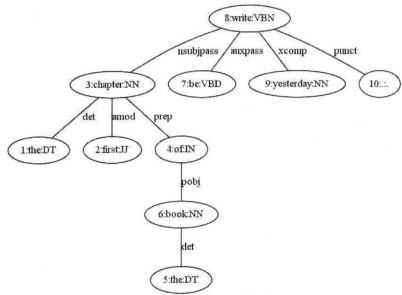

The first chapter of the book was written Yesterday.

FIGURE 1: A parse tree, parsed by Easy-First parser (Goldberg and Elhadad 2010).

is available. Then, we estimate the validity of every transformation, and consequently of every *sequence* of transformations, and decide whether the text entails the hypothesis based on this estimation.

In the rest of this subsection we describe the transformations allowed by BIUTEE, and in the next subsection we describe the model by which transformation reliability is estimated.

Entailment rules

The main type of transformations, and the most reliable one, is the application of *entailment-rules* (Bar-Haim et al. 2007), which are available from various knowledge resources. An entailment rule is composed of two sub-trees, termed *left-hand-side* and *right-hand-side*. It is *applied* on a parse-tree fragment that matches its left-hand-side, by substituting the left-hand-side with the right-hand-side. Figure 2 demonstrates a rule and its application. The complete formalism of entailment rules, adopted by our system, is described in (Bar-Haim et al. 2007; Stern and Dagan 2011).

The entailment rules formalism is simple yet powerful, and captures many types of knowledge. The simplest type of rules is *lexical rules*, like

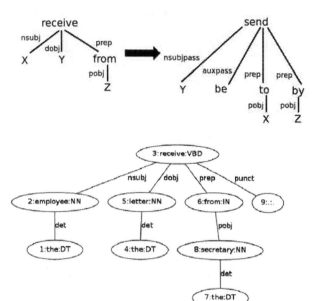

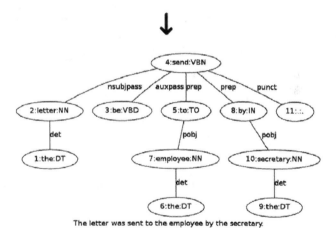

FIGURE 2: An entailment rule and its application. The rule "X received Y from Z → Y was sent to X by Z" is applied on the sentence "The employee received the letter from the secretary.", resulting in "The letter was sent to the employee by the secretary."

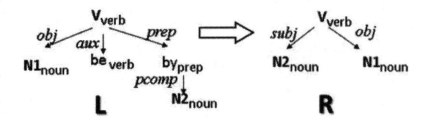

FIGURE 3: A syntactic entailment rule that converts passive form into active form.

car → vehicle. More complicated rules capture the entailment relation between predicate-argument structures, like X receive Y from Z → Y was sent to X by Z.

Entailment rules can also encode syntactic phenomena like the semantic equivalence of active and passive structures (X Verb[active] Y ↔ Y is Verb[passive] by X). See illustration in Figure 3.

BIUTEE incorporates a comprehensive set of knowledge resources, which are represented as entailment-rules. Lexical knowledge resources within BIUTEE include:

- WordNet (Fellbaum 1998) – a large database of English words, which are interconnected by means of conceptual-semantic and lexical relations. We used the following WordNet relations: *synonym, derivationally-related, hypernym, instance-hypernym, part-holonym, member-holonym, substance-meronym* and *verb-entailment.*

- Wikipedia – Wikipedia-based entailment-rules (Shnarch et al. 2009) which contain background knowledge about various entities and concepts, e.g., Einstein is a Scientist.

- GEO – a geographical knowledge resource (Mirkin et al. 2009) which contains information like New-York is in United States.

- CatVar – English derivations (Habash and Dorr 2003). For example motivation (noun) is derived from motivate (verb).

- DIRECT – directional distributional similarity (Kotlerman et al. 2010).

- Distributional-similarity-based entailment rules by Lin (1998a), as well as a reimplementation of the Lin-Similarity algorithm on the Reuters-corpus.[7]

---

[7]http://trec.nist.gov/data/reuters/reuters.html

- VerbOcean (Chklovski and Pantel 2004). – A broad-coverage semantic network of verbs. The used VerbOcean relations are configurable in BIUTEE's configuration file. We achieved the best results when using only the "stronger than" relation.

Lexical-Syntactic knowledge resources, which capture entailment between predicate-argument structures within BIUTEE include:

- DIRT (Lin and Pantel 2001)
- REVERB (Berant 2012)
- FrameNet-based entailment-rules (Ben-Aharon et al. 2010)

As for entailment-rules that capture syntactic phenomena, we use the freely available collection of rules by Lotan (2012).

Discourse phenomena

Other phenomena that must be handled by textual entailment systems are discourse phenomena, by which the desired information, expressed within a single sentence hypothesis, can be spread over several sentences of the text. The importance of this type of phenomena was investigated in (Mirkin et al. 2010), along with several proposals for ways to handle it by utilizing coreference information. In BIUTEE, we utilize coference resolution information by defining two types of transformations: coreference substitution and Is-A coreference. We obtain the coreference information from an off-the-shelf coreference resolution system, ArkRef (see Subsection 3.1).

Coreference substitution is implemented as follows: one mention of an entity is replaced by another mention of the same entity, based on a coreference relation between them. Consider, for example, the following text-hypothesis pair:

Text: ... Obasanjo invited him to step down as president ... and accept political asylum in Nigeria.

Hypothesis: Charles G. Taylor was offered asylum in Nigeria.

In this example it is required to apply such a transformation to substitute "him" with "Charles G. Taylor" (which is mentioned earlier in the document).

The Is-A coreference transformation creates a new parse-tree of the form "X is Y" for each two coreferring mentions X and Y. Consider the following hypothesis:

The Irish Republican Army is a paramilitary group.

and consider the following text:

Northern Ireland's peace process would receive a major boost if the Irish Republican Army responds positively to appeals to embrace political methods, a leading figure in the paramilitary group's political wing said Friday.

Given that "Irish Republican Army" corefers to "paramilitary group", the Is-A coreference transformation can construct the desired hypothesis.

On the fly transformations

Since applications of entailment rules from available knowledge resources and coreference substitutions are, in most cases, insufficient for completely transforming T into H, our system allows *on-the-fly* parse-tree transformations. These transformations include insertions of missing nodes, flipping parts-of-speech, moving sub-trees, etc. (see (Stern and Dagan 2011) for a complete list of these transformations). Since these transformations are not justified by given knowledge resources, we use linguistically-motivated features to estimate their validity. For example, for on-the-fly lexical insertions we consider as features the named-entity annotation of the inserted word, and its probability estimation according to a unigram language model, which yields lower costs (higher confidence) for more frequent words (with similar rationale to that of the Inverse Document Frequency (IDF) heuristic in Information Retrieval). The usage of such features is described in Subsection 2.4.

Plug-ins

BiuTee is designed as an open system, which can serve as a research platform for the RTE community. As such, it is not limited to the aforementioned transformations. Easy integration of additional types of transformations is supported by BiuTee's *plug-in* mechanism, described in Subsection 3.2.

2.3 Truth-value annotations

As mentioned above, BiuTee transforms T's parse tree into H's parse tree. This requires a well defined criterion for determining that nodes and edges in T are identical to corresponding nodes and edges in H. The natural criterion is that nodes are identical if they contain the same lemma and the same part-of-speech, while edges are identical if they have the same relation (edge label). This criterion, however, might lead to an error when a predicate is negated in T, but not in H, or vice versa. More generally, such inconsistencies might arise not only due to negations, but also due to other natural language constructions that change the *truth-value* of a predicate. For example, given a text "The computer failed to calculate the equation.", the truth-value of "calculate" is negative, since it can be inferred that the computer did not calculate the equation (See (Karttunen 1971)). Thus, we should not treat the predicate "calculate" in a hypothesis "The computer calculated the equation." as identical to "calculate" in the text.

Handling such cases is performed by the integration of *Truth-Teller* (Lotan 2012; Lotan et al. 2013), which annotates truth-values of all the predicates in a given sentence, by utilizing several mechanisms. Given a sentence, *Truth-Teller* begins by annotating some of its clauses with a polarity of positive, negative, or unknown. This is done by identifying pre-suppositions, which are marked as positive-polarity clauses, as well as the main clause of the sentence, which is always marked as positive. In addition, it annotates the predicates of the annotated clauses with a positive, negative or unknown polarity. This annotation is based on the clause annotation along with identification of negation and modality expressions (e.g. "not", "never"). Then, the annotation process proceeds to annotate all remaining clauses and predicates by utilizing a recursive algebra which makes use of the implicativity and factivity signatures of the predicates.

A parse-tree node that corresponds to a predicate in the text is considered identical to a corresponding node in the hypothesis only if these two nodes have the same predicate-truth annotation, as well as the same lemma and part-of-speech. A new transformation, *change predicate-truth value*, has been added to BIUTEE. This transformation flips the truth-value annotation of a predicate in the text, such that it becomes identical to a predicate in the hypothesis. Like all other transformations (see Subsection 2.4), a cost is learned for this transformation. Following the high reliability of Truth-Teller, the learned cost is usually high. Hence, proofs which require a flip in a truth-value annotation are usually considered incorrect proofs.

2.4   Cost model

Given a (T,H) pair, the system has to find a sequence of transformations (a *proof*) that transforms T into H. Next, the system calculates how likely it is that the proof preserves entailment. This calculation is performed by a *cost model*, similar to the one defined in (Raina et al. 2005), as follows. First, we define features which characterize transformations (see below). A single transformation, o, can then be characterized by a *feature-vector*, $f(o)$, which contains values for all of these features. We use this feature vector to define a *cost* for each transformation, such that reliable transformations are assigned low costs, while transformations that are less likely to be reliable are assigned high costs. This cost is calculated using a *weight vector*, w, learned automatically over a training-data. Formally, the cost of a transformation o is defined as:

$$(1) \qquad c(o) = w \cdot f(o) = \sum_{i=1}^{m} w_i \cdot f_i(o)$$

where m is the number of features, and $f_i(o)$ is the value of of the ith feature of transformation o.

Next, we define the cost of the proof as the sum of the costs of all its transformations. Formally, a proof $O = (o_1, o_2 \ldots o_n)$ is assigned the cost $c(O) = \sum_{j=1}^n c(o_j)$. By defining $f(O) = \sum_{j=1}^n f(o_j)$, the last equation can be algebraically manipulated as follows:

$$(2) \quad c(O) = \sum_{j=1}^n c(o_j) = \sum_{j=1}^n \sum_{i=1}^m w_i \cdot f_i(o_j) = \sum_{i=1}^m w_i \cdot f_i(O) = w \cdot f(O)$$

The last equation suggests a typical linear learning paradigm, in which the training data is represented as a collection of feature vectors, and the goal is to find two parameters: a weight vector, w, and a threshold b, for which $w \cdot f(O) \leq b$ for positive examples (i.e. T entails H), while $w \cdot f(O) > b$ for negative ones. The learning scheme details are described in (Stern and Dagan 2011).

For the transformations described above (Subsection 2.2) we defined the features as follows. First, a feature has been defined for each knowledge resource. For some knowledge resources, the feature is assigned a constant value of 1 for each rule-application based on this resources. For example, let us assume that feature number 10 is the WordNet feature, and that we are given a transformation which substitutes "dog" by "pet" based on a WordNet hypernym relation. The feature-vector for this transformation then has 1 as the value of the 10th feature, while all other features are assigned 0. Other knowledge resources (e.g. DIRT) provide a score for each rule. For these knowledge resources we use the log of that score as the value for the corresponding feature.

For on-the-fly insertion transformations we defined several features that describe whether the inserted word is a content word, whether it is a named entity, etc. In all cases, the feature value is the probability of the inserted word to appear in an English text, according to a Unigram language model based on the Reuters corpus[8].

For on-the-fly move transformations we defined features that quantify how much the move transformation changed the context of the moved node. The feature-value is the path-length between the original and the new parents of the moved node.

We also defined features for other on-the-fly transformations, like flip-part-of-speech, splitting a multi-word-expression, etc.

As for plug-ins, the plug-in mechanism allows every plug-in to define its own features, which get their values by the plug-in when applied, as described below (Subsection 3.2).

---

[8]http://trec.nist.gov/data/reuters/reuters.html

2.5 Search challenge

Given a text-hypothesis pair, there might be many proofs by which the text can be transformed into the hypothesis. For example, a syntactic manipulation can be performed by applying a syntactic rule. However, the same manipulation might be achieved by applying several "on-the-fly move sub-tree" transformations. Another example is when the same knowledge exists in two different knowledge-resources, but one of them is more reliable than the other.

Since the decision whether the text entails the hypothesis is determined by the cost of the proof, the system has to find the proof with the lowest cost. Finding that proof is a non-trivial challenge since, in general, there are many transformations that can be applied to a given parse-tree, and thus the number of possible *sequences* of transformation is exponential in the size of the proof.

BIUTEE provides implementations of several search algorithms, which differ from one another in their speed and proof quality (measured by the cost of the proofs they find). A novel improved search algorithm that directly utilizes characteristics of the textual-inference domain was recently developed and integrated into BIUTEE. This algorithm iteratively generates limited-length subsequences of transformations. In each iteration it measures the quality-cost ratio of each generated subsequence, and chooses the one with the best ratio. The full details are described in (Stern et al. 2012).

3 System Architecture

The input of BIUTEE is a collection of (T,H) pairs, and the output is an entailment / non-entailment classification for each pair. To determine these classifications, each (T,H) pair is pipe-lined in several processing phases which (1) generate the appropriate representations, (2) find a sequence of transformations (a proof) which transforms the text into the hypothesis, (3) classify these proofs. During training, the last step, *classification* of proofs, is replaced by *learning* a classification model.

We note that in phase (2) we start with inference-related calculations that are not part of the proof construction, but add additional annotations which are required for entailment recognition, and are used during the proof construction. Currently, the *Truth-Teller* annotations (see Subsection 2.3) take place here. In the future we plan to add other types of annotations, like recognizing temporal relations between T and H (see, for example, (Wang and Zhang 2008)).

BIUTEE's processing flow is illustrated in Figure 4, and is described in the reminder of this section.

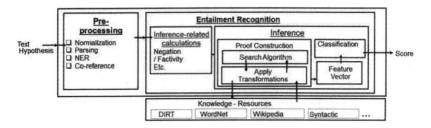

FIGURE 4: System architecture

3.1 Linguistic analysis processing

The target representation of T and H is a parse-tree representation. We generate dependency parse trees, in which each node corresponds to exactly one token of a sentence, and contains its lemma and part-of-speech. In addition, it contains named-entity annotation, integrated into parse-tree nodes. In addition, we build a data-structure for coreference information. This data-structure is a collection of coreference chains of the text's parse trees nodes.

To build this representation, each text fragment (which may be either T or H) is processed through the following steps.

1. Text normalization
2. Sentence splitter
3. Tokenizer
4. Part-of-speech tagger
5. Parser
6. Coreference resolver

Text normalization is done through a collection of text modifications that are performed over the raw text, prior to any linguistic analysis. Mainly, we perform number normalization,[9] and heuristically add missing punctuations when necessary.

Then, BIUTEE proceeds to linguistic processing, using state-of-the-art utilities: Tokenization and part-of-speech-tagging are performed by *Stanford* utilities (Toutanova et al. 2003), parsing is performed by *Easy-First parser* (Goldberg and Elhadad 2010), named-entity recognition is done by *Stanford named-entity-recognizer* (Finkel et al. 2005) and coreference resolution is performed by *ArkRef coreference resolver*.[10]

---

[9] Available to download as a stand-alone utility at http://www.cs.biu.ac.il/~nlp/downloads/normalizer.html

[10] This tool is a reimplementation of (Haghighi and Klein 2009), and is downloadable from http://www.ark.cs.cmu.edu/ARKref/.

As a flexible system, BIUTEE provides simple interfaces for each type of linguistic analysis utility. This way, replacing the above-mentioned utilities can be done by merely implementing the relevant interfaces.

3.2 Proof construction

Entailment recognition begins with *inference-related calculations*. As mentioned above, the Truth-Teller annotations are added at this phase.

Next, the system constructs a proof comprising of a sequence of transformations that transform the text into the hypothesis. Finding such a proof is a sequential process, conducted by the search algorithm (see Subsection 2.5). In each step of the proof construction the system examines all possible transformations that can be applied, generates new trees by applying these transformations, and calculates their accumulated proof costs by constructing appropriate feature-vectors for them.

BIUTEE provides unified interfaces for all types of transformations, making the addition of new types of transformations straightforward. The interfaces are:

1. *Finder* which gets a parse tree, and finds the transformations that can be applied on that tree.
2. *Operation* which gets a parse tree and a transformation (found by the *Finder*), and applies this transformation on the given parse tree. The result is a new parse tree.
3. *Feature-Vector Updater* which gets a parse-tree, a feature-vector and a transformation, and updates this feature-vector with new values that correspond to the given transformation. This updated feature-vector represents the new parse-tree that was generated by applying the given transformation.

BIUTEE contains a collection of implementation steps for these interfaces for each type of transformation and for each knowledge resource. For example, for the WordNet lexical resource that is used with lexical entailment rules, the implementation is as follows: the *Finder* gets a parse-tree, and finds for each parse-tree node (when applicable) a lexical rule from WordNet which changes its lemma to another lemma, entailed by the original one.[11]

The *Operation* then takes the parse-tree and generates a new parse tree in which the original lemma is replaced by the entailed lemma. The *Feature-Vector Updater* adds 1 to the WordNet feature in the feature vector.

---

[11]This *Finder* is actually shared among all the lexical resources, as they all share the same interface for querying lexical entailment rules.

When a (T, H) pair is given to the system, it is first processed in the inference-related calculations phase. Then, the system iteratively runs all of the implementation steps of the above mentioned interfaces (*Finder*, *Operation* and *Feature-Vector Updater*). Thus, in each iteration several new parse-trees, along with their corresponding feature-vectors, are generated. Since the number of generated trees increases exponentially, the system must prune the set of the generated trees after few iterations, and maintain only those which are most likely to be part of the best (i.e., cheapest) proof. The policy of which trees to prune is determined by the search algorithm.

Extension mechanism

The goal of BIUTEE is not only to apply its own built-in transformations, but also to be a framework for transformation-based inference, into which additional types of transformations can be integrated and applied. This is achieved by the *plug-in* mechanism. Using plug-ins, new types of transformations can be integrated and applied, without the need to change the current system code. For example, imagine a researcher applying BIUTEE in the medical domain, say, over prescription texts. There might be some well-known domain knowledge and some re-writing rules that every medical person knows. Integrating such new rules is directly supported by the plug-in mechanism.

Basically, adding a new type of transformation can be done by implementing the above mentioned interfaces. Thus, the plug-in developer has to implement *Finder*, *Operation* and *Feature-Vector Updater*. A factory of these implementations, called *Plugin*, has to be developed as well, and be integrated into the system. BIUTEE has a smart mechanism, which safely utilizes Java reflection capabilities, by which this integration is performed with no changes of existing code.

In addition, BIUTEE provides a more advanced type of plug-in that is able to perform its own calculations in the *inference-related calculations phase*, in addition to integrating the new transformations. Such plug-ins have to implement a method which gets the parsed text and the hypothesis, as well as other auxiliary parameters, as input. This method is called by the system for each (T, H) pair right before starting the proof construction phase. The results of a plug-in's global calculation can be stored in the plug-in's internal data-structures, and be forwarded to the actual instances of its corresponding *Finder*, *Operation* and *Feature-Vector Updater*. By implementing such a plug-in, the user can incorporate new types of inference-oriented annotations, which can then be utilized by new types of transformations.

3.3 Learning and classification

The final processing phase is to classify the constructed proof as reliable or not. The proof, represented as a feature vector, is assigned a cost, as described in Subsection 2.4. The proof is classified as reliable if its cost is lower than a threshold. The system also provides the result as a numerical value in the $[0, 1]$ range by using the *sigmoid* function: the return value is $\frac{1}{1+e^{-z}}$ where z is the cost minus the threshold. This value is interpreted as "positive" (T entails H) if it is higher than 0.5, and "negative" otherwise.

This final phase has a different role during training. In training we are not interested in classifying the proof, but in learning the cost model parameters: the weight vector, w, and the threshold b. These parameters can be learned by any linear learning algorithm. The input for the learning algorithm is a collection of feature-vectors that represent the proofs of a collection of (T, H) pairs (i.e., an RTE dataset). We use a *Logistic-Regression* learning algorithm, but, similar to other components, alternative learning-algorithms can be integrated easily by implementing an appropriate interface.

Note that for the last two RTE datasets of 2010 and 2011 (RTE-6 and RTE-7), the goal is to optimize the F1 measure[12] of the positive entailments, while in the older datasets, the goal is to optimize the accuracy measure. We implemented the logistic regression classifier to optimize each of these measures. The accuracy-optimized classifier is the standard logistic-regression classifier, while the F1-optimized classifier was implemented according to (Jansche 2005). The appropriate classifier is automatically chosen by the system, based on the given dataset.

We note that the weight vector, w, has a dual role. One is to assign a cost to the constructed proof. The other role is to be used by the search algorithm. As described above, the search algorithm prunes some of the intermediate trees that are generated during the proof construction, and it favours trees that are more likely to be part of the best (cheapest) proof. One of the parameters by which the search algorithm estimates this likelihood is the current cost of the generated tree. If that cost is higher than that of other generated trees, it is less likely that it will be part of the best proof. This dual role raises a new problem: the only way to learn the weight vector is by considering the proofs that

---

[12]F1 measure is a success-rate estimation which takes both the recall (how many positive instances have been detected by the system) and precision (how many of the positively classified instances are indeed positive) into consideration. Formally, it is defined as $2 \cdot \frac{\text{Recall} \cdot \text{Precision}}{\text{Recall} + \text{Rrecision}}$

have already been constructed for a complete (T, H) pairs dataset. However, to construct these proofs, a weight vector is needed for the search algorithm.

We solve this problem by an *iterative learning* scheme. In this scheme we initialize w with a reasonable guess vector, and iteratively process the whole dataset, such that in each iteration w is improved. More information about the learning scheme can be found in (Stern and Dagan 2011).

3.4 Configuration, adaptation and extension

BiuTee supports all of the RTE datasets that have been published so far (Dagan et al. 2006b; Bar-Haim et al. 2006; Giampiccolo et al. 2007, 2008; Bentivogli et al. 2009, 2010, 2011).

Controlling the system behaviour, adapting it to specific needs as well as extending it, can be done at various levels. First, many of the system parameters are controlled by a configuration file, as follows:

1. Parser: the user can choose to use either easy-first parser (Goldberg and Elhadad 2010) or Minipar parser (Lin 1998b).

2. Coreference resolver: The user can choose the coreference resolver to be either ArkRef[13] or Bart (Versley et al. 2008). A third option is to configure the system to skip coreference resolution.

3. Knowledge Resources: The user can provide a list of knowledge resources to be used for the proof construction. Using many knowledge resources often increases the system performance, but also increases its runtime.

4. Multi-threading: The number of concurrent threads used by the system is a configurable parameter.

5. Plug-ins: If the user writes a plug-in, it can be integrated into the system through configuration file parameters.

Beyond configuration, the system can be extended by the plug-in mechanism, described in Subsection 3.2.

More advanced adaptations and extensions can be performed by changing the system's source code, as all of BiuTee's source code is freely available. The code is modular so that changing one module does not affect the others. Further support is given by an extensive documentation, both code-level documentation as well as a developer guide that describes the details of the system flow and its components.

---

[13]See footnote 10.

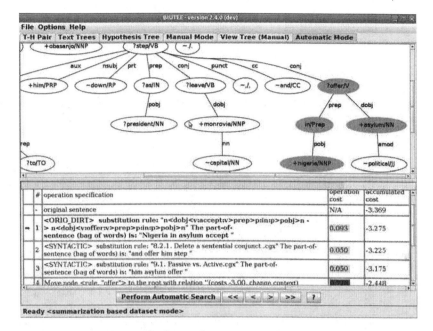

FIGURE 5: Entailment Rule application visualized in the tracing tool. The upper pane displays the parse-tree generated by applying the rule. The rule description, highlighted in bold, is the first transformation of the proof, shown in the lower pane. The rule is "X (is) accepted in Y" → "X (is) offered in Y", and captures, for example, that if someone accepted asylum in Nigeria, than it is also known that he was offered asylum in Nigeria. This rule application is followed by transformations 2 and 3, which are syntactic rewrite rules.

4 Visual Tracing Tool

The final score provided as output, as well as the system's detailed logging information, do not expose all the decisions and calculations performed by the system. In particular, they do not show all the potential transformations that could have been applied, but were rejected by the search algorithm. However, such information is crucial for researchers, who need to observe the use and the potential impact of each component of the system.

We address this need by providing an interactive *visual tracing tool*, *Tracer*, which presents detailed information for each proof step, including the ability to force potential inference steps that were not included in the automatically-constructed proof.

4.1 Modes

Tracer provides two modes for tracing proof construction: *automatic mode* and *manual mode*. In the automatic mode, shown in Figure 5, the tool presents the complete process of inference, as conducted by the system's search: the parse trees, the proof steps, the cost of each step and the final score. For each transformation the tool presents the parse tree before and after applying the transformation, highlighting the impact of this transformation.

In manual mode, the user can invoke specific transformations pro-actively, including transformations rejected by the search algorithm. As shown in Figure 6, the tool provides a list of transformations that match the given parse-tree, from which the user can choose to apply a single transformation at each step. Similar to automatic mode, the impact on the parse tree is shown visually.

		BIUTEE - version 2.4.0 (dev)									
File Options Help											
T-H Pair	**Text Trees**	**Hypothesis Tree**	**Manual Mode**	**View Tree (Manual)**	**Automatic Mode**						
O... ID	Last Operation			Original Sentence	Classific. Score	Proof Cost	Operation Cost	Iteration	Missing Relations	Predicti. Score	
10	Coreference substitution: replace subtree			1	1.000	-3.272	0.097	1	9	1.000	
11	Coreference substitution: replace subtree			1	1.000	-3.272	0.097	1	9	1.000	
12	Insert <5, "offer", VBN, >			1	0.999	-2.335	1.034	1	8	1.000	
13	SYNTACTIC substitution			1	1.000	-3.319	0.050	1	9	1.000	
14	SYNTACTIC substitution			1	1.000	-3.319	0.050	1	9	1.000	
15	SYNTACTIC substitution			1	1.000	-3.319	0.050	1	9	1.000	
<SYNTACTIC> substitution rule: "8.3.2. Swap Conjuncts - with subj.cgx" The part-of-sentence (bag of words) is: "him leave an											
17	SYNTACTIC substitution			1	1.000	-3.319	0.050	1	9	1.000	
18	SYNTACTIC substitution			1	1.000	-3.319	0.050	1	9	1.000	
19	SYNTACTIC substitution			1	1.000	-3.319	0.050	1	9	1.000	
20	SYNTACTIC substitution			1	1.000	-3.319	0.050	1	9	1.000	
21	ORIG_DIRT substitution			1	1.000	-3.275	0.093	1	8	1.000	
22	ORIG_DIRT substitution			1	1.000	-3.275	0.093	1	8	1.000	
		□ Display Only Last Generated Trees	Display Selected Tree	?							
Ready <summarization based dataset mode>											

FIGURE 6: List of available transformations, provided by *Tracer* in the manual mode. The user can manually choose and apply each of these transformations, and observe their impact on the parse-tree.

4.2 Typical Use cases

Developers of knowledge resources and other types of transformations can use *Tracer* as follows. Applying an entailment rule is a process of first *matching* the rule's left-hand-side to the text parse-tree (or to any tree along the proof), and then substituting it by the rule's right-hand-side. To test a rule, the user can provide a text for which the rule is supposed to match, examine the list of potential transformations that can be performed on the text's parse tree, as shown in Figure 6, and verify that the examined rule has been matched as expected. Next, the user can apply the rule, visually examine its impact on the parse-tree,

TABLE 2: Performance (accuracy) of an earlier version of BIUTEE on RTE challenges, compared to other systems participated in these challenges. *Median* and *Best* indicate the median score and the highest score of all submissions, respectively.

RTE challenge	Median %	Best %	BIUTEE %
RTE-1	55.20	58.60	57.13
RTE-2	58.13	75.30	61.63
RTE-3	61.75	80.00	67.13
RTE-5	61.00	73.50	63.50

as in Figure 5, and validate that it operates as intended and does not cause undesired side-effects.

Researchers of proof construction and classification algorithms can also make use of *Tracer*. As described above, the complete inference process depends on the parameters learned in the training phase, as well as on the search algorithm which looks for a lowest-cost proof from T to H. For a given (T,H) pair, the automatic mode provides the complete proof found by the system. Then, in the manual mode the researcher can try to construct alternative proofs. If a proof with a lower cost can be constructed manually it signals a limitation of the search algorithm. In contrast, if the user can manually construct a better linguistically motivated proof, but it turns out that this proof has higher cost than the one found by the system, it signals a limitation of the learning phase which may be caused either by a limitation of the learning method, or due to insufficient training data.

5 Experimental Results

In this section we briefly overview BIUTEE's performance on the RTE challenges. We omit RTE-4 (2008) since it does not contain training data. Table 2 shows results of an earlier version of BIUTEE on RTE 1,2,3 and 5 (Dagan et al. 2006b; Bar-Haim et al. 2006; Giampiccolo et al. 2007; Bentivogli et al. 2009). This earlier version does not contain many components that were described in this paper, e.g., it does not contain the syntactic rules, the Truth-Teller, the logistic-regression classifier, and uses an older parser, an older coreference resolver and an older scheme for the search algorithm. It can be seen, however, that even the earlier version achieved better results than the median of all submitted results to these challenges.

BIUTEE's performance on the more recent RTE-6 and RTE-7 (Bentivogli et al. 2010, 2011) challenges is presented in Table 3: BIUTEE is better than the median of all submitted results, and in RTE-6 it

TABLE 3: Performance (F1) of BiuTee on RTE challenges, compared to other systems participated in these challenges. *Median* and *Best* indicate the median score and the highest score of all submissions, respectively.

RTE challenge	Median %	Best %	BiuTee %
RTE-6	33.72	48.01	49.09
RTE-7	39.89	48.00	42.93

outperforms all other systems.

6 Conclusions and Future Work

In this paper we described BiuTee, an open-source textual-inference system, and suggested it as a research platform in the RTE field in general, and within the transformation-based paradigm in particular. Such a platform is needed in this complex research area, in which a lot of linguistic analysis utilities, extensive usage of knowledge resources, and sophisticated entailment recognition components are needed.

From this perspective, we highlighted the following key advantages of our system: (a) modularity and extensibility, (b) a plug-in mechanism, (c) utilization of entailment rules that can capture diverse types of knowledge, and (d) a tracing tool that visualizes every detail of the inference process.

We suggest several directions for future work. First, as described above, BiuTee can be extended with additional types of transformations. One example is arithmetic transformations, as in the following example:

Text: *Two men and three women were wounded in the accident.*

Hypothesis: *Three people were wounded in the accident.*

Such example requires a complex transformation which first identifies that men, as well as women, entail people, and then makes the arithmetic calculation of $2 + 3 = 5$.

Another suggested extension is temporal entailment, like:

Text: *In 2004 the Olympic games took place in Athens, and four years later in Beijing*

Hypothesis: *In 2008 the Olympic games took place in Beijing.*

This example requires a transformation of "four years later" into "2008", followed by the introduction of the implicit sentence "the Olympic games took place in Beijing" by generic-syntactic rewrite rules.

Another direction for future work is in improving the on-the-fly transformations and their features. For example, the current feature-values for on-the-fly insertion are based on a Unigram language model. However, this model is limited, as it does not consider the context of the given text. A better model would calculate for each inserted word how likely it is that this word is entailed by the given text, thus improving the overall cost estimation of proofs that contain the insertion on-the-fly transformation.

More broadly, an appealing property of BIUTEE's inference model and architecture is the ability to easily integrate various types of linguistically-motivated inferences. For example, one can easily integrate additional linguistic processing levels, such as semantic role labelling,discourse analysis and temporal analysis as additional annotation levels, which can then be leveraged by appropriate transformations with their reliability being assessed by corresponding features. Thus, we believe that BIUTEE provides a suitable platform for investigating the incorporation of various advanced annotations and inference types within textual entailment recognition.

Acknowledgments

We thank Amnon Lotan for contributing and integrating the Truth-Teller component, and for enhancing the visual tracing tool. This work was partially supported by the Israel Science Foundation grant 1112/08, the PASCAL-2 Network of Excellence of the European Community FP7-ICT-2007-1-216886, and the European Community's Seventh Framework Programme (FP7/2007-2013) under grant agreement no. 287923 (EXCITEMENT).

References

Bar-Haim, Roy, Ido Dagan, Bill Dolan, Lisa Ferro, Danilo Giampiccolo, Bernardo Magnini, and Idan Szpektor. 2006. The second PASCAL recognising textual entailment challenge. In *Proceedings of the Second PASCAL Challenges Workshop on Recognising Textual Entailment*.

Bar-Haim, Roy, Ido Dagan, Iddo Greental, and Eyal Shnarch. 2007. Semantic inference at the lexical-syntactic level. In *Proceedings of AAAI*.

Ben-Aharon, Roni, Idan Szpektor, and Ido Dagan. 2010. Generating entailment rules from framenet. In *Proceedings of ACL*.

Bentivogli, Luisa, Peter Clark, Ido Dagan, Hoa Trang Dang, and Danilo Giampiccolo. 2010. The sixth PASCAL recognizing textual entailment challenge. In *Proceedings of TAC*.

Bentivogli, Luisa, Peter Clark, Ido Dagan, Hoa Trang Dang, and Danilo Giampiccolo. 2011. The seventh PASCAL recognizing textual entailment challenge. In *Proceedings of TAC*.

Bentivogli, Luisa, Ido Dagan, Hoa Trang Dang, Danilo Giampiccolo, and Bernardo Magnini. 2009. The fifth PASCAL recognizing textual entailment challenge. In *Proceedings of TAC*.

Berant, Jonathan. 2012. *Global Learning of Textual Entailment Graphs (submitted)*. Ph.D. thesis, Tel Aviv University.

Bos, Johan and Katja Markert. 2005. Recognising textual entailment with logical inference. In *Proceedings of EMNLP*.

Cabrio, Elena, Milen Kouylekov, and Bernardo Magnini. 2008. Combining specialized entailment engines for RTE-4. In *Proceedings of TAC*. Gaithersburg, Maryland.

Chklovski, Timothy and Patrick Pantel. 2004. Verbocean: Mining the web for fine-grained semantic verb relations. In *Proceedings of EMNLP*.

Clark, Peter and Phil Harrison. 2010. Blue-lite: a knowledge-based lexical entailment system for rte6. In *Proceedings of TAC*.

Dagan, Ido, Oren Glickman, and Bernardo Magnini. 2006a. The PASCAL recognising textual entailment challenge. In *Quiñonero-Candela, J.; Dagan, I.; Magnini, B.; d'Alché-Buc, F. (Eds.) Machine Learning Challenges. Lecture Notes in Computer Science*.

Dagan, I., O. Glickman, and B. Magnini. 2006b. The pascal recognising textual entailment challenge. *Machine Learning Challenges. Evaluating Predictive Uncertainty, Visual Object Classification, and Recognising Tectual Entailment* .

de Salvo Braz, Rodrigo, Roxana Girju, Vasin Punyakanok, Dan Roth, and Mark Sammons. 2005. An inference model for semantic entailment in natural language. In *Proceedings of AAAI*.

Fellbaum, Christiane, ed. 1998. *WordNet An Electronic Lexical Database*. The MIT Press.

Finkel, Jenny Rose, Trond Grenager, and Christopher Manning. 2005. Incorporating non-local information into information extraction systems by gibbs sampling. In *Proceedings of ACL*.

Giampiccolo, Danilo, Hoa Trang Dang, Bernardo Magnini, Ido Dagan, Elena Cabrio, and Bill Dolan. 2008. The fourth PASCAL recognizing textual entailment challenge. In *Proceedings of TAC*.

Giampiccolo, Danilo, Bernardo Magnini, Ido Dagan, and Bill Dolan. 2007. The third PASCAL recognizing textual entailment challenge. In *Proceedings of the ACL-PASCAL Workshop on Textual Entailment and Paraphrasing*.

Goldberg, Yoav and Michael Elhadad. 2010. An efficient algorithm for easy-first non-directional dependency parsing. In *Proceedings of NAACL*.

Habash, Nizar and Bonnie Dorr. 2003. A categorial variation database for english. In *Proceedings of NAACL*.

Haghighi, Aria and Dan Klein. 2009. Simple coreference resolution with rich syntactic and semantic features. In *Proceedings of EMNLP*.

Iftene, Adrian. 2008. Uaic participation at RTE4. In *Proceedings of TAC*.

Jansche, Martin. 2005. Maximum expected f-measure training of logistic regression models. In *Proceedings of EMNLP*.

Karttunen, Lauri. 1971. Implicative verbs. *Language* .

Koehn, Philipp, Hieu Hoang, Alexandra Birch, Chris Callison-Burch, Marcello Federico, Nicola Bertoldi, Brooke Cowan, Wade Shen, Christine Moran, Richard Zens, Chris Dyer, Ondrej Bojar, Alexandra Constantin, and Evan Herbst. 2007. Moses: Open source toolkit for statistical machine translation. In *Proceedings of ACL*.

Kotlerman, Lili, Ido Dagan, Idan Szpektor, and Maayan Zhitomirsky-geffet. 2010. Directional distributional similarity for lexical inference. *Natural Language Engineering* .

Kouylekov, Milen and Matteo Negri. 2010. An open-source package for recognizing textual entailment. In *Proceedings of ACL Demo*.

Lin, Dekang. 1998a. Automatic retrieval and clustering of similar words. In *Proceedings of COLING*.

Lin, Dekang. 1998b. Dependency-based evaluation of minipar. In *Proceedings of the Workshop on Evaluation of Parsing Systems at LREC 1998*.

Lin, Dekang and Patrick Pantel. 2001. DIRT - discovery of inference rules from text. In *Proceedings of ACM SIGKDD Conference on Knowledge Discovery and Data Mining*.

Lotan, Amnon. 2012. *A Syntax-based Rule-base for Textual Entailment and a Semantic Truth Value Annotator*. Master's thesis, Bar Ilan University.

Lotan, Amnon, Asher Stern, and Ido Dagan. 2013. Truthteller: Annotating predicate truth. In *Proceedings of NAACL*.

MacKinlay, Andrew and Timothy Baldwin. 2009. A baseline approach to the RTE5 search pilot. In *Proceedings of TAC*.

Mirkin, Shachar, Roy Bar-Haim, Jonathan Berant, Ido Dagan, Eyal Shnarch, Asher Stern, and Idan Szpektor. 2009. Addressing discourse and document structure in the RTE search task. In *Proceedings of TAC*. Gaithersburg, Maryland.

Mirkin, Shachar, Ido Dagan, and Sebastian Pado. 2010. Assessing the role of discourse references in entailment inference. In *Proceedings of ACL*.

Raina, Rajat, Andrew Y. Ng, and Christopher D. Manning. 2005. Robust textual inference via learning and abductive reasoning. In *Proceedings of AAAI*.

Shnarch, Eyal, Libby Barak, and Ido Dagan. 2009. Extracting lexical reference rules from Wikipedia. In *Proceedings of ACL-IJCNLP*.

Shnarch, Eyal, Jacob Goldberger, and Ido Dagan. 2011. A probabilistic modeling framework for lexical entailment. In *Proceedings of ACL*.

Stern, Asher and Ido Dagan. 2011. A confidence model for syntactically-motivated entailment proofs. In *Proceedings of RANLP*.

Stern, Asher, Roni Stern, Ido Dagan, and Ariel Felner. 2012. Efficient search for transformation-based inference. In *Proceedings of ACL*.

Tatu, Marta and Dan Moldovan. 2006. A logic-based semantic approach to recognizing textual entailment. In *Proceedings of ACL*.

Toutanova, Kristina, Dan Klein, Christopher Manning, and Yoram Singer. 2003. Feature-rich part-of-speech tagging with a cyclic dependency network. In *Proceedings of NAACL*.

Versley, Yannick, Simone Paolo Ponzetto, Massimo Poesio, Vladimir Eidelman, Alan Jern, Jason Smith, Xiaofeng Yang, and Ro Moschitti. 2008. Bart: A modular toolkit for coreference resolution. In *Proceedings of ACL, Demo Session*.

Wang, Rui and Guenter Neumann. 2008. An divide-and-conquer strategy for recognizing textual entailment. In *Proceedings of TAC*. Gaithersburg, Maryland.

Wang, Rui and Yajing Zhang. 2008. Recognizing textual entailment with temporal expressions in natural language texts. In *Proceedings of IEEE*.

Is there a place for logic in recognizing textual entailment?

JOHAN BOS[1]

From a purely theoretical point of view, it makes sense to approach recognizing textual entailment (RTE) with the help of logic. After all, entailment matters are all about logic. In practice, only few RTE systems follow the bumpy road from words to logic. This is probably because it requires a combination of robust, deep semantic analysis and logical inference—and why develop something with this complexity if you perhaps can get away with something simpler? In this article, with the help of an RTE system based on Combinatory Categorial Grammar, Discourse Representation Theory, and first-order theorem proving, we make an empirical assessment of the logic-based approach. High precision paired with low recall is a key characteristic of this system. The bottleneck in achieving high recall is the lack of a systematic way to produce relevant background knowledge. There is a place for logic in RTE, but it is (still) overshadowed by the knowledge acquisition problem.

1 Introduction

Recognizing textual entailment—predicting whether one text entails another—is a task that embraces everything that needs to be accomplished in natural language understanding. In the past, textual entailment was limited to the domain of formal semanticists, who used it as an illustrative device to show that certain natural language inferences hold or not (Gamut 1991; Chierchia and McConnell-Ginet 1991; Kamp and Reyle 1993; Heim and Kratzer 1998). By now, however, recognizing textual entailment (RTE, henceforth) is viewed by many as a key task in the area of natural language processing (Dagan et al. 2006).

---

[1]University of Groningen

LiLT Volume 9
Perspectives on Semantic Representations for Textual Inference.
Copyright © 2014, CSLI Publications.

In the early developments of approaches to RTE it soon became clear that RTE is an extremely difficult task: simple baseline systems based on textual surface features are hard to outperform by more sophisticated systems. Not only does one need a robust component that gives an accurate analysis of text, the use of external resources to inform the inference process are also essential to achieve a good performance on the standard RTE data sets.

Various approaches to RTE have been proposed, ranging from "shallow" methods working directly on the surface features of texts, to "deep" methods using sophisticated linguistic analyses. The formalism proposed in this article belongs in the latter category, and works by determining textual inferences on the basis of deductive logical inference. The idea is simple and rooted in the formal approaches to natural language semantics mentioned before: we translate the texts into logical formulas, and then use (classical) logical inference to find out whether one text entails the other or the other way around, whether they are consistent or contradictory, and so on.

Even though this idea itself sounds simple, its execution is not. In this article we describe a framework for textual inference based on first-order logic and formal theory. It comprises a system for RTE, Nutcracker, developed by myself over the years since the start of the RTE challenge (Bos and Markert 2005).[2] The input of this system is a text, and an hypothesis (another text). The output of the system is an entailment prediction for the hypothesis given the text. The system makes use of external theorem provers to calculate its predictions.

Performance on RTE data sets is measured in terms of recall (the number of correctly predicted entailments divided by the total number of text–hypothesis pairs given to a system) and precision (the number of correctly predicted entailments divided by the number of predictions made by the system). RTE systems based on logical inference tend to be low in recall and high in precision. This means that, currently, such systems ideally can play an important role in ensemble-based architectures of RTE systems, because they could complement simpler surface-based systems performing with higher recall and low precision.

The logical inference approach for RTE has been criticized by other RTE practitioners with respect to its low recall. However, in doing so, not always the correct explanation is given. MacCartney et al. (2006), for instance, write "few problem sentences can be accurately translated to logical form" when discussing Bos and Markert (2005), and al-

---

[2]The Nutcracker system has been briefly described by others (Balduccini et al. 2008), but never been the focus of publication itself. The source code of the system can be downloaded via the website of the C&C tools (Curran et al. 2007).

though one could debate the notion of accurate translation, it is doubtful whether this is the main reason for the lack of recall in RTE systems using deductive inference. In fact, one of the aims of this article is to show that logical inference is a promising approach to RTE, despite its limitations.

The rest of this article is organized as follows. First we explain what we mean by semantic interpretation in the context of RTE, and what formalism is useful for doing so, both from a theoretical and practical perspective. Then we make the link to (modal) first-order logic, in preparation for the inference tasks required for RTE. We then show which inference tasks are useful for the RTE task, and point out that supplementary background knowledge is required to increase recall. Finally we present the details of the Nutcracker system, a complete implementation of an RTE system based on logical reasoning, and will return to address the issue why RTE systems based on logical inference show low recall, and what can be done about it.

2 Semantic Interpretation

The challenge of translating ambiguous text into unambiguous logical formulas is usually performed by a detailed syntactic analysis (with the help of a parser) followed by a semantic analysis that produces a logical form based on the output of the syntactic parser. For the purposes of RTE based on logical inference, the linguistic analysis needs to be reasonably sophisticated and at the same time offer high coverage. Its analysis needs to be sophisticated because a shallow analysis would not support the required logical inferences and hence sacrifice precision in performance. It needs to be robust and offer wide coverage to achieve a high recall in performance. As a practical rule of thumb, the loss in coverage should outweigh the gain in performance using deep linguistic analysis.

Due to the development of tree-banks in the past decades, many high-performing statistical parsers are available that offer broad coverage syntactic analysis for open-domain texts. The parser employed in our RTE system, the C&C parser (Clark and Curran 2004), combines speed and robustness with detailed syntactic analyses in the form of derivations of categorial grammar (Steedman 2001). Categorial grammar offers a neat way to construct formal meaning representations with the help of the λ-calculus (Bos 2008). Each basic syntactic category is associated with a basic semantic type, and using the recursive definition of categories and types, this also fixes the semantic types of complex syntactic categories. This results in a strongly lexically-driven approach, where only the semantic representations have to be provided for the lexical categories. Function application will take care of the rest and produce meaning representations for phrases beyond the token level, and eventually a complete meaning representation for the entire sentence will be produced.

Next we arrive at the choice of meaning representation language. This language needs to be capable of supporting logical inference, as well as being able to adequately describe natural language meaning. There is an uneasy and unsolved tension between expressiveness on the one hand and efficiency on the other. The formalisms proposed by linguists and philosophers are usually not computationally attractive— most of them are based on higher-order formalisms and exceed the expressive power of first-order logic, and theorem proving for first-order logic is already undecidable (more precisely, first-order logic is known to be semi-decidable). Nevertheless, there are powerful theorem provers for first-order logic available developed by the automated deduction research community. Hence, given the state-of-the-art in automated reasoning, the choice of first-order logic as representation language seems a good compromise between the ability to perform logical inferences and the expressive power for representing meaning.[3]

The standard first-order formula syntax is not a convenient format for meaning analysis. Instead we use a variant of Discourse Representation Theory's DRSs, Discourse Representation Structures, graphically visualized as boxes (Kamp and Reyle 1993). DRT offers a representational way to deal with many linguistic phenomena in a principled way, including quantifiers, pronouns, negation, presupposition and events. Diverging from standard DRT, we adopt a neo-Davidsonian way for describing events, because this results in a lower number of background knowledge rules (meaning postulates) required to draw correct inferences.

Another issue worth emphasizing is that we work with fully specified logical forms, despite many efforts in the past twenty years to produce underspecified semantic interpretations, in particular with respect to scope of quantifiers and other scope-bearing operators. Semantic underspecification is not a feasible option, because it is unclear how theorem provers would work with underspecified representations — they expect ordinary first-order formulas as input. Even when scope is resolved with a "naive" algorithm following mostly the surface order of scope-bearing

---

[3]Note that, in our framework, λ-calculus, a higher-order logic, only plays a role in meaning composition, and is not used for the inference tasks required for textual entailment prediction. This is basically the same strategy as put forward by Blackburn and Bos (2005).

operators, no harm seems to be done to the performance of RTE tasks. In fact, we have never encountered an example in the existing RTE data sets where correct scope resolution mattered for making a correct textual entailment prediction.

In sum: categorial grammar gives us a systematic and robust way to produce semantic representations from text; fully resolved first-order representations are a good practical choice for the basis of logical inference. In the next section we present how we produce such logical forms.

3 Semantic Representations and First-Order Logic

The RTE data sets consists of pairs of texts, and once we have established a method to produce semantic representations (DRSs in our case) for such pairs, we arrive at the problem of translating such DRSs into formulas of first-order logic (FOL). The result from this translation, FOL formulas, are given to a theorem prover to perform various inference tasks. One of them, the most important one, is to find out whether the text (T) entails the hypothesis (H). If the theorem prover then succeeds in finding a proof, we predict an entailment for this RTE pair. In this section we will discuss this translation, motivate the choice of theorem provers, and present basic results.

The standard translation from DRS to FOL (Muskens 1996, Kamp and Reyle 1993) is not suitable to RTE because it does not take modalities and embedded propositions into account. We will explain why this is a problem with the help of some examples. In Ex. 1, H is not entailed, because if John *thinks* that Mary smokes, it does not follow from this information that Mary does in fact smoke. Put differently, H contains new information, namely the fact that Mary smokes, which is information that cannot be deduced from T.

Example 1: H is informative wrt T

T: John thinks that Mary smokes.
....
H: Mary smokes.

A more general observation for attitude verbs like *think* and *believe* is: if X thinks/believes that P, then it doesn't mean that P. In contrast, factive verbs like *regret* and *know* result in an entailment of their propositional complement (Ex. 2).

These are hand-crafted examples to illustrate the point, but note that real-world examples of modal contexts are abundant. Ex. 3 below shows an example from the RTE data set in which the modal construc-

---

Example 2: H is entailed from T

T: John knows that Mary smokes.
....
H: Mary smokes.

---

tion in T blocks the inference hypothesized in H. Ex. 4 below shows a T–H pair with a subordinated clause introduced by *when*.

Example 3: H is informative wrt T

T: Leakey believed Kenya's wildlife, which underpins a tourist industry worth Dollars 450m a year, could be managed in a profitable and sustainable manner.
....
H: Kenya's wildlife is managed in a profitable manner.

Example 4: H is entailed from T

T: When an earthquake rumbled off the coast of Hokkaido in Japan in July of 1993, the resulting tsunami hit just three to five minutes later, killing 202 people who were trying to flee for higher ground.
....
H: An earthquake occurred on the coast of Hokkaido, Japan.

In order to predict correct entailments for modal contexts, one needs lexical information about which verbs and adverbs entail their complements and which do not. In addition, one needs an adequate semantic interpretation of modal contexts – an issue to which we turn now.

In the standard translation, it is impossible to connect the embedded proposition to a belief report or other propositional attitude or modal operator, because first-order terms cannot be formulas. The modal translation, that we adopt, is based on a technique called reification, as proposed for DRSs in Bos (2004). It translates a basic DRS condition with n terms into a first-order formula with $n+1$ arguments, where the added term is a first-order variable ranging over (a particular kind of) entities. One could imagine these entities as ranging over "possible worlds" or simply "propositions". This extension in notation makes it possible to connect embedded propositions to attitudinal verbs or modal operators. We will not give the full translation from DRSs to modal FOL here (the interested reader is referred to Bos (2004)), but instead give an example translation of the DRS and first-order logic formulas for Ex. 1 to illustrate the approach.

x y e p
john(x)
mary(y)
think(e)
agent(e,x)
theme(e,p)

$$\exists w\exists x\exists y\exists e\exists p(john(w,x) \land$$
$$mary(w,y) \land$$
$$think(w,e) \land$$
$$agent(w,e,x) \land$$
$$theme(w,e,p) \land$$
$$smoke(p,e) \land$$
$$agent(p,e,y))$$

e
smoke(e)
agent(e,y)

p:

The modal first-order translation above does not admit that Mary smokes, because the event where Mary smokes is established in connection with possible world p, which is not necessary the same as w, the actual world. But for certain verbs or other syntactic constructions we will add background knowledge axioms that force to make the actual world identical with a subordinated situation. We show how to do so in Section 5, but first we discuss how first-order theorem proving is integrated in our RTE framework.

4 Theorem Proving

In this section we show how to use off-the-shelf theorem provers for the task of recognizing textual entailment. Apart from checking whether there is an entailment between T and H, they can also be used for checking whether T or H contains contradictions or tautologies, or whether T and H together are contradictory or not. Such tests are also important in RTE, and we will discuss them first. We refer to them as consistency checking.

Consistency checking is important, because without doing so we might predict false entailments. In logic, anything follows from a contradiction. Hence, if T is inconsistent, H would automatically follow. It is questionable whether this is a desired outcome in the context of RTE. Consider the following example:

Example 5: Word Sense Ambiguity

T: A fan is a useful instrument.
....
H: The workers used a fan to prevent overheating.

In Ex. 5, the text T contains the ambiguous noun *fan*. Word sense disambiguation is a hard task and an RTE system might make the mistake of assigning the sense of *sports fan* or *admirer* to the noun *fan*, instead of the device sense. Together with the knowledge that people (sports fans, admirers) are disjoint from artifacts (instruments, devices), this would lead to an inconsistent T. As a result, the RTE system would predict an entailment for Ex. 5.

Clearly, it would help an RTE system if such situations could be detected automatically. For instance, detection of a contradiction in T could give the RTE system reason to revise its background knowledge, even though as far as we know such systems have not been realized yet. Similarly, a clever RTE system would detect that the semantically ill-formed T in Ex. 6 is inconsistent, because an event cannot happen in the past as well as in the future. Examples of this kind do not occur in the current RTE data sets, but in real-world applications noisy data could yield such ill-formed texts.

Example 6: Inconsistent T

T: David Beckham had a tendon rupture tomorrow.
....
H: David Beckham was fortunate.

For similar, logical reasons, we need to verify whether H is consistent or not. Because if H turns out to be inconsistent, checking whether T entails H boils down to verifying whether T is inconsistent, which is not the original goal of the inference task. Furthermore, we want to check whether T and H taken together are inconsistent. If this is so, we want to predict a non-entailment (for a two-way classification of entailment prediction), or report a contradiction between T and H (in the case of a three-way classification of entailment prediction).

In sum, we need to check whether T is consistent, H is consistent, and T∧H is consistent. We do this by translating them to modal first-order logic, and trying to prove their negation. At the same time we attempt to find a counter-model by using a finite model builder. If a counter-model is found, the theorem prover can be halted, which is a way to save valuable resources (time and memory). In addition, we try to find a proof for T → H (or the logically equivalent ¬(T ∧ ¬H). Table 1 summarizes the situation.[4]

5 Adding Background Knowledge

For a good performance on RTE examples not only translations of T and H in (modal) first-order logic are required—what is crucial for an increase in recall is a set of background knowledge axioms. Such axioms

---

[4]One could also extend the inference tasks by explicitly verifying whether T and H are tautologies or not. If T is logically valid (i.e. a tautology), then it would not make sense to test whether T entails H. Similarly, if H is a validity, T would always entail it.

TABLE 1: Inference Tasks for RTE and corresponding predictions based on proofs or countermodels.

Input	Output				
¬ T	proof	model	model	model	model
¬ H	–	proof	model	model	model
¬(T ∧ H)	–	–	proof	model	model
¬(T ∧ ¬H)	–	–	–	proof	model
Prediction	unknown	unknown	contradiction	entailment	informative

need to be stated in modal first-order logic too, and can be added to the inference requests, simply as additional background theory. In the inference examples above, this can be achieved by replacing T by (BK ∧ T). This is one of the attractive sides of a logic-based approach: background knowledge can be supplied in a modular way.

Axioms are generally of the form $\forall w \forall x (\phi(w,x) \rightarrow \psi(w,x))$, where ϕ and ψ denote first-order formulas. Here we discuss three types of background knowledge axioms:

1. Axioms automatically derived from synonym and hyponym relations between WordNet synsets;

2. Manually encoded axioms for propositional embeddings;

3. Complex axioms automatically derived from positive RTE pairs.

The number of general background knowledge axioms can be very large. But given a textual entailment problem, we do not want to give irrelevant background knowledge to the theorem prover and waste its resources. It remains an interesting research challenge to select appropriate axioms—axioms that are likely to increase the chance of finding a proof.

A simple way to solve this problem is to associate *triggers* with axioms (Blackburn and Bos 2005). The non-logical symbols in meaning representations are useful triggers for many types of axioms, as long as axioms themselves are not able to initiate the triggering of new axioms, thereby risking a chain reaction resulting in the selection of the entire knowledge base. Following this approach, each type of axiom is illustrated by a T–H pair that triggers it.

Axioms derived from WordNet

Let us start with axioms derived from the WordNet relations. Consider Ex. 7. In WordNet (Fellbaum 1998), the first sense of the noun *role* is a hyponym of the second sense of *duty*, which in turn is a hyponym of the first sense of *activity*. Similarly, *murder* is a hyponym of *kill* in WordNet, enabling a proof for Ex. 8. We note in passing that this example also demonstrates the benefits from a deep linguistic analysis that assigns syntactically equivalent meaning representations to active and passive forms, as our system does.

Example 7: T entails H, hyponymy

T: The World Bank has also been criticized for its role in financing projects.
....
H: The World Bank is criticized for its activities.

Example 8: T entails H, active-passive alternation

T: Lennon was murdered by Mark David Chapman outside the Dakota on Dec. 8, 1980.
....
H: Mark David Chapman killed Lennon.

Example 9: T entails H, synonymy

T: The two presidents, Bush and Chirac, were honored with a 21-gun salute.
....
H: The two presidents, Bush and Chirac, were honoured with a 21-gun salute.

The WordNet hyponym relation is translated into first-order logic as an implication. As we use the modal translation, we need to include possible worlds in the generated background knowledge. As a consequence, we end up with the following set of axioms for the examples above:

$\forall w(\text{possible-world}(w) \to \forall x(\text{n1role}(w,x) \to \text{n2duty}(w,x)))$
$\forall w(\text{possible-world}(w) \to \forall x(\text{n2duty}(w,x) \to \text{n1work}(w,x)))$
$\forall w(\text{possible-world}(w) \to \forall x(\text{n1work}(w,x) \to \text{n1activity}(w,x)))$
$\forall w(\text{possible-world}(w) \to \forall x(\text{v1murder}(w,x) \to \text{v1kill}(w,x)))$

It is easy to see that such axioms can be systematically generated from WordNet.[5] Apart from hyponyms, we can also explore synonyms

---

[5]Note that the non-logical symbols are composed using part-of-speech information (noun, verb, modifier) and a sense number, to avoid unwanted clashes of symbols derived from the same words with different meanings. That is, we want to have different non-logical symbols for the noun *fly*, the verb *fly*, and the adjective *fly*, because they mean different things. Similarly, we would like to distinguish

stored in WordNet. In WordNet, synset members are considered to correspond to equivalent concepts. A case in point is Ex. 9, where we can observe that *honor* and *honour* are members of the same synset in WordNet. Members of the same synset are translated into axioms with a bi-implication. Returning to Ex. 9, we trigger the following axiom:

$\forall w(\text{possible-world}(w) \rightarrow \forall x(\text{v1honor}(w,x) \leftrightarrow \text{v1honour}(w,x)))$

There is more information in WordNet that could form the basis for background knowledge axioms. The antonymy relation found between adjectives is a good candidate. But other lexical resources could supply useful information too. The NomLex database (Meyers et al. 1998) provides information about normalizations, thereby making it possible to compute background knowledge axioms that relate concepts and events.

Axioms for embedded contexts

The axioms for embedded contexts all follow the same pattern. They are manually picked for sentential complement verbs like *know*, *regret*, *say*, *report*, *tell*, *reveal*, as well as for sentential adverbs such as *because*, *although* and *when*, that presuppose their subordinated sentential argument. They are manually selected because existing lexical resources such as WordNet do not contain this information. Ex. 10 illustrates the idea behind this type of axioms:

Example 10: T entails H, sentential complement

T: Authorities say Monica Meadows, who has appeared in catalogs and magazines, is in stable condition.

H: Monica Meadows is in stable condition.

The required background knowledge is that the information of the theme of a *saying* event also holds in the world in which this event was expressed. The relevant axiom is the following.

$\forall w(\text{possible-world}(w) \rightarrow \forall x \forall y(\text{v1say}(w,x) \wedge \text{r1theme}(w,x,y) \leftrightarrow w = y))$

This axiom template is accurate for factive verbs, but in general not for reporting verbs.[6] All what is said is not necessarily true, and we would like to exclude, for instance, liars. In Ex. 10, it is the source of

---

between the different senses of words. For example, n2duty is the symbol for the second noun sense of the word *duty*.

[6]There is also a connection with presupposition projection here (Beaver 1997). Factive verbs such as *regret* presuppose their propositional complement. If presupposition projection is implemented by the semantic formalism, then these axioms would not be needed.

the information, the *authorities*, that cause the textual entailment of H with respect to T. In fact, in most newspaper examples reporting verbs entail the content of their propositional complement. In general however, one wants to strengthen the axioms of reporting verbs, by including a constraint on the reliability of the agent of the reporting event.

Automatically learned axioms

The third type of axiom can be automatically learned from positive T–H pairs of the available RTE data sets (Ihsani 2012). The idea here is to identify a pattern between two entities that appear both in T and H. If the same pattern is observed in different T–H pairs, then this indicates that it might be a valid and useful background knowledge axiom. In Ex. 11, the complex relations between *Tilda Swinton* and *White Witch* in T and H suggest the axiom that "X playing a role as Y implies that X plays the part of Y".

Example 11: T entails H, complex axiom

T: Tilda Swinton has a prominent role as the White Witch in The Chronicles of Narnia: The Lion, The Witch and The Wardrobe, coming out in December.

H: Tilda Swinton plays the part of the White Witch.

Ihsani (2012) presents a method to automatically generate such axioms from positive T–H pairs, and tested on negative T–H pairs (inclusion of a learned axiom should not result in a proof). The axiom automatically generated for the above example is:

$$\forall w(\text{possible-world}(w) \rightarrow$$
$$\forall x \forall y \forall z (\exists e (have(w,e) \wedge \text{agent}(w,e,x) \wedge \text{theme}(w,e,y) \wedge$$
$$\text{role}(w,y) \wedge \text{as}(w,y,z)) \rightarrow$$
$$\exists e(\text{play}(w,e) \wedge \text{agent}(w,e,x) \wedge \text{theme}(w,e,y) \wedge \text{part}(w,y) \wedge \text{of}(w,y,z))))$$

Lin and Pantel (2001) present an unsupervised algorithm, DIRT, for discovering inference rules, such as *X is the author of Y* $\approx$ *X writes Y*, by applying the distributional hypothesis to syntactic dependency analysis. The method of Ihsani (2012) could be viewed as a variation of this, but differs in the level of supervision during learning (DIRT is unsupervised). The level of linguistic analysis is also different, as DIRT produces (non-directional) surface string paraphrases, and Ihsani's method yields (directional) first-order axioms. In general, Ihsani's method produces axioms with high precision and low recall, while DIRT tends to yield opposite results (Szpektor et al. 2007).

6   Implementation and Evaluation

The framework presented before has been implemented in a complete RTE system known as Nutcracker. The system (including source code) is distributed as part of the C&C tools (Clark and Curran 2004). A description of the most important components of this complex system follows below.

The Nutcracker system has a traditional pipeline architecture of components, starting with a tokenizer, POS tagger, lemmatizer (Minnen et al. 2001) and named entity recognizer. This is followed by syntactic and semantic parsing. The meaning representations are produced by the semantic interpreter Boxer (Bos 2008), which works on the output of the C&C parser, based on Combinatory Categorial Grammar. Boxer performs pronoun resolution, presupposition projection, thematic role labeling and assigns scope to quantifiers, negation and modal operators.

The coverage of the pipeline—meaning the percentage of examples for which a semantic representation could be produced—on RTE examples is high, reaching nearly 98% on the examples of the RTE data sets. Remember that the parser's statistical model is not specifically trained on examples of these data sets. The NLP pipeline formed by the C&C tools and Boxer is therefore suitable for a task such as RTE, contrary to what MacCartney et al. (2006) suggest. Note however, that high coverage does not always mean high correctness, but at present no corpora with gold-standard annotated semantic representations are available to measure accuracy.

The end of the pipeline is formed by a theorem provers and model builders. Any theorem prover for first-order logic could be used, in theory. In practice, there is quite a lot of choice, thanks to the active area of automated deduction that offers various efficient state-of-the-art provers for research purposes. The Nutcracker systems allows us to plug in several different provers, among them Vampire (Riazanov and Voronkov 2002), Otter (McCune and Padmanabhan 1996), and Bliksem (De Nivelle 1998). Vampire is currently the highest-ranked prover in CASC, the annual competition for inference engines (Sutcliffe and Suttner 1997), and it also gives the best results on RTE examples.

In addition to a theorem prover, a model builder is needed to find counter-models. Again, various model builders can be used with Nutcracker, including Mace (McCune 1998) and Paradox (Claessen and Sörensson 2003). Following Blackburn and Bos (2005), for each inference problem the theorem prover and model builder work in parallel, where the model builder gets the negated input of the theorem prover. If a proof is found for problem $\neg\phi$, the model builder is halted because it would never be able to find a model for ϕ—if a model is found for ϕ, the theorem prover is halted because it would never be able to find a proof for $\neg\phi$.

The model builder searches for models up to a specified domain size n, and terminates if it cannot construct a model for sizes $1 - n$. In theory, because first-order logic is semi-decidable, the combination of theorem proving and finite model building always terminates with one of three results: (i) proof found, (ii) no proof but finite counter-model found of size n, or (iii) no proof and no model for size n (for instance for inputs that have non-finite counter-models). Case (i) succeeds if we give enough resources (time and space) to the theorem prover, but in practice we use a time-out. For case (ii) by specifying the maximum domain size as high as possible while maintaining reasonable response times. Case (iii) is one that we wish to avoid in practice.

The performance of Nutcracker, without supplying background knowledge axioms, on the RTE data sets shows that only few proofs are found (61 for all the 3,200 examples RTE-2 and RTE-3 data sets) but with high precision (54 correct, yielding 88.5%). This shows that, without appealing to further background knowledge, a high-precision performance paired with a low recall is achieved. This is not a big surprise. Many of the examples from the RTE data sets require additional information to draw the wanted inferences. Ihsani (2012) shows that some of these background knowledge axioms can be retrieved using supervised learning. Axioms based on synonym and hyponym relations extracted from WordNet give only a small increase of recall (12 extra proofs found, of which 11 correct). WordNet relations combined with modality axioms gives a further increase in recall (21 extra proofs found, of which 18 correct). Adding automatically generated axioms based on positive T–H pairs yields 52 extra proofs, of which 46 correct (Ihsani 2012). These numbers indicate that recall can be increased without a loss of precision, when appropriate background knowledge can be selected.

7 Related Work

Compared to other RTE approaches, closely related to the "logical approach" are systems based on Natural Logic. The Natural Logic approach is an interesting alternative to logical inference because it is more flexible (resulting in more robust systems) yet based on local logical inferences. The best known example (and implementation) in this tradition is NatLog (MacCartney 2009), which we will compare to our Nutcracker system.

Given an RTE pair T–H, NatLog works by a sequence of components, to wit (1) parsing T and H; (2) aligning T and H with a sequence of local edit operations turning T into H; (3) predicting entailment relations for each of these local edit operations; (4) joining the local entailment relations to produce an entailment prediction for the entire T–H pair. The NatLog system uses lexical resources (including Word-Net and NomBank) and also information on string similarity to predict local entailments, with the help of a statistical classifier.

The Natural Logic approach is interesting because it does not use the full power of FOL (in fact, as MacCartney (2009) shows, it is incomplete), yet it makes use of (local) logical inference and performs well on tasks such as RTE, with a lower precision than Nutcracker, but with a much higher recall (MacCartney 2009). A disadvantage of the approach is that the alignment procedure excludes texts consisting out of more than one sentence.

Like the background knowledge axioms for the Nutcracker system, the NatLog system has to get the local entailment predictions from external resources, and for an informative comparison it would be interesting to see how well NatLog would perform without appealing to lexical resources and similarity measurements. Equally interesting, it would be an informative exercise to translate the local inference rules obtained by the NatLog system, transform them into first-order axioms, and feed them into the Nutcracker system, and measure performance differences.

8 Conclusion

The logical approach to RTE is costly—one needs to perform all steps of linguistic analysis ranging including detailed syntactic and semantic analysis. Current semantic parsers reach high coverage and are able to produce reasonably adequate semantic representations for RTE. This is at least what the available data sets for RTE suggest. Translating T–H pairs into first-order formulas result in input that state-of-the-art theorem provers can easily digest most of the time, reaching high precision. Nonetheless, without additional background knowledge, recall is low. Such background knowledge can be provided as additional first-order axioms, but they are hard to generate in a domain-independent manner. Experiments shows however that such additional background knowledge raises recall without a (big) loss in precision. The bottleneck of logical inference in RTE is not the inability to translate text to logical formulas as; it is not the performance of theorem provers; but it is the lack of a systematic way to produce relevant background knowledge.

References

Balduccini, M., C. Baral, and Y. Lierler. 2008. Knowledge representation and question answering. In V. Lifschitz, F. van Harmelen, and B. Porter, eds., *Handbook of Knowledge Representation*, pages 779–819. Elsevier.

Beaver, David Ian. 1997. Presupposition. In J. Van Benthem and A. Ter Meulen, eds., *Handbook of Logic and Language*, chap. 17, pages 939–1008. Elsevier, MIT.

Blackburn, P. and J. Bos. 2005. *Representation and Inference for Natural Language. A First Course in Computational Semantics*. CSLI.

Bos, Johan. 2004. Computational semantics in discourse: Underspecification, resolution, and inference. *Journal of Logic, Language and Information* 13(2):139–157.

Bos, Johan. 2008. Wide-Coverage Semantic Analysis with Boxer. In J. Bos and R. Delmonte, eds., *Semantics in Text Processing. STEP 2008 Conference Proceedings*, vol. 1 of *Research in Computational Semantics*, pages 277–286. College Publications.

Bos, Johan and Katja Markert. 2005. Recognising textual entailment with logical inference. In *Proceedings of the Conference on Empirical Methods in Natural Language Processing*, pages 628–635.

Chierchia, Gennaro and Sally McConnell-Ginet. 1991. *Meaning and Grammar. An Introduction to Semantics*. The MIT Press.

Claessen, K. and N. Sörensson. 2003. New techniques that improve mace-style model finding. In P. Baumgartner and C. Fermüller, eds., *Model Computation – Principles, Algorithms, Applications (Cade-19 Workshop)*, pages 11–27. Miami, Florida, USA.

Clark, Stephen and James R. Curran. 2004. Parsing the WSJ using CCG and Log-Linear Models. In *Proceedings of the 42nd Annual Meeting of the Association for Computational Linguistics (ACL '04)*, pages 104–111. Barcelona, Spain.

Curran, James, Stephen Clark, and Johan Bos. 2007. Linguistically Motivated Large-Scale NLP with C&C and Boxer. In *Proceedings of the 45th Annual Meeting of the Association for Computational Linguistics Companion Volume Proceedings of the Demo and Poster Sessions*, pages 33–36. Prague, Czech Republic.

Dagan, Ido, Oren Glickman, and Bernardo Magnini. 2006. The PASCAL recognising textual entailment challenge. In *Lecture Notes in Computer Science*, vol. 3944, pages 177–190.

De Nivelle, Hans. 1998. A Resolution Decision Procedure for the Guarded Fragment. In *Automated Deduction - CADE-15. 15th International Conference on Automated Deduction*, pages 191–204. Springer-Verlag Berlin Heidelberg.

Fellbaum, Christiane, ed. 1998. *WordNet. An Electronic Lexical Database*. The MIT Press.

Gamut, L.T.F. 1991. *Logic, Language, and Meaning. Volume II. Intensional Logic and Logical Grammar*. Chicago and London: The University of Chicago Press.

Heim, Irene and Angelika Kratzer. 1998. *Semantics in Generative Grammar*. Malden and Oxford: Blackwell.

Ihsani, Annisa. 2012. *Automatic Induction of Background Knowledge Axioms for Recognising Textual Entailment*. Master's thesis, University of Groningen.

Kamp, Hans and Uwe Reyle. 1993. *From Discourse to Logic; An Introduction to Modeltheoretic Semantics of Natural Language, Formal Logic and DRT*. Dordrecht: Kluwer.

Lin, Dekang and Patrick Pantel. 2001. DIRT—discovery of inference rules from text. In *Proceedings of the ACM SIGKDD Conference on Knowledge Discovery and Data Mining*, pages 323–328.

MacCartney, Bill. 2009. *Natural Language Inference*. Ph.D. thesis, Stanford University.

MacCartney, Bill, Trond Grenager, Marie-Catherine de Marneffe, Daniel Cer, and Christopher D. Manning. 2006. Learning to recognize features of valid textual entailments. In *Proceedings of the main conference on Human Language Technology Conference of the North American Chapter of the Association of Computational Linguistics*, HLT-NAACL '06, pages 41–48. Stroudsburg, PA, USA: Association for Computational Linguistics.

McCune, W. 1998. Automatic Proofs and Counterexamples for Some Ortholattice Identities. *Information Processing Letters* 65(6):285–291.

McCune, W. and R. Padmanabhan. 1996. *Automated Deduction in Equational Logic and Cubic Curves*. No. 1095 in Lecture Notes in Computer Science (AI subseries). Springer-Verlag.

Meyers, A., C. Macleod, R. Yangarber, R. Grishman, L. Barrett, and R. Reeves. 1998. Using nomlex to produce nominalization patterns for information extraction. In *Coling-ACL98 workshop Proceedings, The Computational Treatment of Nominals*, pages 25–32. Montreal, Canada.

Minnen, Guido, John Carroll, and Darren Pearce. 2001. Applied morphological processing of english. *Journal of Natural Language Engineering* 7(3):207–223.

Muskens, Reinhard. 1996. Combining Montague Semantics and Discourse Representation. *Linguistics and Philosophy* 19:143–186.

Riazanov, A. and A. Voronkov. 2002. The Design and Implementation of Vampire. *AI Communications* 15(2–3):91–110.

Steedman, Mark. 2001. *The Syntactic Process*. The MIT Press.

Sutcliffe, Geoff and Christian Suttner. 1997. The results of the cade-13 atp system competition. *Journal of Automated Reasoning* 18(2):259–264. Special Issue on the CADE-13 Automated Theorem Proving System Competition.

Szpektor, Idan, Eyal Shnarch, and Ido Dagan. 2007. Instance-based evaluation of entailment rule acquisition. In *Proceedings of the 45th Annual Meeting of the Association of Computational Linguistics*, pages 456–463. Prague, Czech Republic: Association for Computational Linguistics.

NLog-like Inference and Commonsense Reasoning

LENHART SCHUBERT[1]

Recent implementations of Natural Logic (NLog) have shown that NLog provides a quite direct means of going from sentences in ordinary language to many of the obvious entailments of those sentences. We show here that Episodic Logic (EL) and its EPILOG implementation are well-adapted to capturing NLog-like inferences, but beyond that, also support inferences that require a combination of lexical knowledge and world knowledge. However, broad language understanding and commonsense reasoning are still thwarted by the "knowledge acquisition bottleneck", and we summarize some of our ongoing and contemplated attacks on that persistent difficulty.

1 Introduction: Natural Logic, Episodic Logic, and EPILOG

Natural Logic (NLog, as we will abbreviate it) provides an attractive framework for implementing many "obvious" entailment inferences, starting with little more than a syntactically analyzed sentence (e.g., MacCartney and Manning 2008). But in itself, NLog is certainly insufficient for language understanding or commonsense inference. We advocate here a formalized (not necessarily fully disambiguated) representation that is very close to language, along with an inference methodology that easily accommodates NLog inferences, but beyond that enables more general reasoning based on both lexical knowledge and world knowledge. This approach to representation and inference has been pursued by our group at the University of Rochester (and

---

[1]University of Rochester

LiLT Volume 9
Perspectives on Semantic Representations for Textual Inference.
Copyright © 2014, CSLI Publications.

prior to that, at the University of Alberta) for over two decades, and the outcome so far is the Episodic Logic (EL) representation and its implementation in EPILOG systems 1 and 2. We have also built up very substantial amounts of general knowledge,[2] much of it rough, but a good deal of it precise enough for EPILOG-based inference.

In the next section we review the EL representation and the EPILOG inference architecture. In section 3 we illustrate NLog-like inferences in EPILOG, and touch on some evaluation results for such inferences. Section 4 provides examples of commonsense inferences performed by EPILOG that lie beyond the capabilities of NLog, in part because they involve radical differences in phrase structure between the premises and the conclusion and in part because they draw on world knowledge as well as lexical semantic knowledge. However, enhanced inference capabilities alone cannot take us very far towards achieving broad understanding and commonsense reasoning: We still face the knowledge acquisition bottleneck, and in section 5 we discuss multiple facets of our efforts to provide broad knowledge to EPILOG. In section 6 we assess the prospects for general knowledge acquisition through genuine understanding of WordNet glosses, Simple Wikipedia entries, or the Open Mind collection of general statements. We sum up the relationship between NLog and EPILOG in section 7, also briefly reiterating the status of our knowledge acquisition efforts and the prospects for moving beyond them through deeper understanding of general statements.

2   EL and EPILOG

Figure 1 provides a glimpse of the EL representation and the EPILOG architecture. Note the infixing of predicates like *car* and *crash-into* in formulas, used for readability.[3]

Note also the association of an episodic variable *e* with the subformula [*x crash-into y*], via the operator '**'. Intuitively, the operator expresses that the sentence *characterizes* episode *e* as a whole (rather than merely some temporal portion or aspect of it). (Schubert and Hwang 2000) provides a general explanation of EL, and (Schubert 2000) explicates the logic of '**' viewed as an extension of first-order logic (FOL), relating this aspect of EL to various extant theories of events and situations (such as those of Davidson, Reichenbach, and Barwise & Perry). Given an input such as is shown in the figure, and a general

---

[2]Browsable at http://www.cs.rochester.edu/research/knext/browse

[3]As a further aid to readability, printed EL infix formulas are often written with square brackets (while prefix expressions use round brackets), and restricted quantification is indicated with a colon after the variable. In the "computerized" version, all brackets are round and there are no colons preceding restrictors.

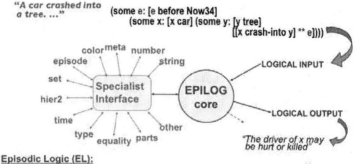

FIGURE 1: Episodic Logic and the EPILOG system

axiom that if a car crashes into a tree, its driver may be hurt or killed, EPILOG would draw the expected conclusion. This is of course an inference based on world knowledge, not one feasible in NLog systems, at least as so far developed.

EPILOG 1 performs forward (input-driven) as well as backward (goal-driven) inference, and is fully integrated with the indicated specialist modules. However, its selective knowledge retrieval method and somewhat patchwork construction (driven by a succession of contracts) leave it with certain hard-to-predict blind spots in its backward inference, and these are remedied in the more recent EPILOG 2 version.[4]

The EL language is Montague-inspired and is structurally and semantically very close to natural language (NL). We might say that it is scope-resolved, partially disambiguated NL with variables, including explicit episodic (i.e., event and situation) variables. Historically, most research on NL understanding and dialogue has taken a depth-first approach, creating end-to-end systems for highly focused problem solving or text understanding domains, and trying to build "outward" from these. We have instead pursued a breadth-first approach, attempting

---

[4]Implemented by University of Rochester PhD graduate Fabrizio Morbini, now at the Institute for Creative Technologies in California. Forward inference is only partially implemented in EPILOG 2 at this point, and the specialists are not yet re-integrated.

to build general frameworks for representing knowledge (especially verbalizable knowledge), semantic interpretation, and inference; we wished to avoid the temptations and pressures that arise in specialized applications to use domain-specific representations and interpretive heuristics that are unusable outside the chosen domain.

There are various considerations that make the idea of a language-like internal ("Mentalese") meaning representations plausible:

- A common conjecture in anthropology and cognitive science is that language and thought appeared more or less concurrently, perhaps some 200,000 years ago.[5] This makes it likely that they are variants of the same basic symbolism; after all, language serves to communicate thoughts.

- The assumption that what comes out of our mouths closely resembles what is in our heads (at an appropriately abstract level of analysis, and allowing for time-saving abbreviations, omissions, and other "telegraphic" devices) is prima facie simpler than the assumption that the two representational systems diverge radically; especially so if we keep in mind that NL understanding is incremental, requiring that fragmentary interpretations be brought into inferential contact with stored knowledge.

- All our symbolic representations, at least those based on tree-structured expressions, are derivative from language; this includes logics, programming languages, semantic nets, and other AI-oriented knowledge representations. This suggests a language-like substrate in our higher-level thinking.

- Surely, it cannot be a mere coincidence that, as shown by Montague, entailment can be understood in terms of semantic entities corresponding one-to-one with syntactic phrases.

- Recent successes in applying NLog to entailment inference underscore the advantages of working directly with (structurally analyzed) NL.

These considerations may strike many linguistic semanticists (and perhaps cognitive scientists and anthropologists) as belaboring the familiar idea of "language as a mirror of mind". But in AI there is strong resistance among many researchers to extending the expressivity of knowledge representations to full first-order logic, let alone *beyond* FOL

---

[5]Preceded, perhaps, by around 2 million years of evolution of the mirror neuron system and Broca's area, allowing imitation of the actions and gestures of others, and grasp of their intentions (Fadiga et al. 2006). Recent fMRI studies suggest that a distinct portion of Broca's area is devoted to cognitively hard tasks such as arithmetic (Fedorenko et al. 2012).

– despite the difficulty of mapping many easily verbalized ideas into FOL, frames, or description logics. The argument made is that expressivity must be reined in to achieve inferential efficiency and completeness. Though we won't elaborate here, this seems to us a false trade-off, much like denying programmers the ability to use recursion or looping (with the number of iterations as a run-time variable), to prevent them from writing inefficient programs. Greater expressivity allows not only greater coverage of ideas expressible in language but also more efficient inference in cases where weakly expressive representations would require complex work-arounds, if feasible at all.

The goal in the design of EL was to match the expressive devices shared by all human languages. These include the following:

- Ways of naming things
- Boolean connectives: and, or, not, if-then, ...
- Basic quantifiers: every, some, no, ...
- Ways of ascribing properties and relationships to entities
- Identity

These items alone already imply the expressivity of FOL, at least if we do not impose arbitrary restrictions, for instance, on quantifier embedding or predicate adicity. But natural languages allow more than that:

- Generalized quantifiers (Most women who smoke)
- Intensionality (is planning a heist; resembles a Wookiee)
- Event reference (Members of the crowd hooted and shouted insults; *this* went on for minutes)
- Modification of predicates and sentences (*barely* alive, dances *gracefully*, *Perhaps* it will rain)
- Reification of predicates and sentences (*Xeroxing money* is illegal; *That there is water on the Moon* is surprising)
- Uncertainty (It will *probably* rain tomorrow; The more you smoke, the greater *your risk of developing lung cancer*)
- Quotation and meta-knowledge (Say "cheese"; How much do you know about description logics?)

All of these devices are directly enabled in EL. Here are some illustrative examples of logical forms:

- Restricted quantifiers
  "Most laptops are PCs or MACs"
  ```
  [<Most laptop> <or PC MAC>]              {unscoped LF}
  (Most x: [x laptop] [[x PC] or [x MAC]]) {scoped LF}
  ```

- Event relations

  "If a car hits a tree, the driver is often hurt or killed"

  ```
  (Many-cases e:
    (some x: [x car] (some y: [y tree] [[x hits y] ** e]))
    [[[(driver-of x) (pasv hurt)] or
      [(driver-of x) (pasv kill)]] @ e])
  ```

  The episodic operator '@' is a variant of '**', expressing that a sentence characterizes some episode *concurrent with* a given episode *e*.

- Modification and reification

  "He firmly maintains that aardvarks are nearly extinct"

  ```
  (Some e: [e at-about Now17]
           [[He (firmly (maintain
                         (that [(K (plur aardvark))
                                (nearly extinct)])))] ** e])
  ```

Note the predicate modifiers *firmly, plur,* and *nearly,* and the reifying operators *that* and *K; that* maps sentence intensions (partial functions from possible episodes to truth values) to individuals, and *K* maps predicate intensions to individuals, namely *kinds* in the sense of (Carlson 1977). Further features are the allowance for quoted syntactic expressions as terms, and substitutional quantification over expressions of all sorts. In this way EPILOG can entertain propositions about syntactic entities such as names and other linguistic expressions, telephone numbers, mathematical expressions, Lisp programs, or its own internal formulas, and can use formalized axiom schemas for inference – a crucial capability for reasoning with general meaning postulates in NLog-like manner, as we will see. The following example illustrates the use of substitutional quantification and (quasi)quotation to express two claims about name-knowledge:

"I know the names of all CSC faculty members"

```
(all x: [x member-of CSC-faculty]
        (all_subst y: ['y name-of x]
                      [ME know (that ['y name-of x])])))
```

"There is no CSC faculty member whose name I know to be 'Alan Turing'."

```
(no x: [x member-of CSC-faculty]
       [ME know (that ['(Alan Turing) name-of x])])
```

From this EPILOG would easily infer that there is no member of the CSC faculty named Alan Turing. Incidentally, contrary to the notion that high expressivity entails low efficiency, experimental application of EPILOG to large-scale theorem proving in first-order logic showed it to be competitive with the best theorem provers, especially for relatively large axiom bases (Morbini and Schubert 2009).

3 NLog-like inference in EPILOG

The essential ideas behind NLog are the following (e.g., van Benthem 1991, 2007; Valencia 1991; van Eijck 2005; Nairn et al. 2006; MacCartney and Manning 2008):

1. Starting with a syntactically structured natural language sentence, we can replace phrases by more general [more specific] ones in positive- [negative-] polarity environments; identity or equivalence replacements are permissible in both types of environments as well as in (transparent) environments that are neither upward nor downward entailing;

   e.g., *Several trucks are on their way* →
          Several vehicles are on their way;
          If a vehicle is on its way, turn it back →
          If a truck is on its way, turn it back

2. We exploit implicatives/factives;

   e.g., X *manages to do* Y → X *do* Y;
          X *doesn't manage to do* Y ⤳ X *doesn't do* Y;
          X *knows that* Y → Y
          X *doesn't know that* Y → Y;

3. Full disambiguation is not required; e.g., *several* and *on their way* in (1) above can remain vague and ambiguous without disabling the indicated inferences.

Like NLog inference, inference in EPILOG is *polarity-based*. In essence, it consists of replacing subformulas in arbitrarily complex formulas by consequences or anticonsequences in positive and negative polarity environments, respectively (and using identity or equivalence substitutions much as in NLog).

The equivalents of Nlog inferences are readily encoded via axioms and rules in EPILOG 2. For example, we have duplicated MacCartney and Manning's illustrative example,

    Jimmy Dean refused to move without his jeans
      → *James Dean didn't dance without pants*

However, in EPILOG the (anti)consequences may depend on world knowledge as well as lexical knowledge; also polarity-based inference is supplemented with natural deduction rules, such as assumption of the antecedent in proving a conditional, or reasoning by cases in proving a disjunction.

A restriction in EPILOG is that it replaces only sentential parts of larger formulas, while NLog can replace fragments of arbitrary types.

However, this makes little practical difference. For example, NLog might replace *truck* by *vehicle* in a positive environment, while EPILOG would replace a formula of form [τ *truck*] by [τ *vehicle*]. The result is the same, at least when τ is unaltered. (An example where both the predicate and its argument are altered would be in the replacement of [*Sky overcast*] by [*Weather cloudy*].) Another example would be the replacement of *many* by *some* in NLog, while EPILOG would replace a sentence of form (*many* α: φ ψ) by one of form (*some* α: φ ψ). Again, the effect is the same in cases where the operands of the quantifier are unaltered. Note that the *truck/vehicle* example above would depend in EPILOG on an ordinary axiom, (*all x*: [*x truck*] [*x vehicle*]), while the *many/some* example would depend on an axiom *schema*, i.e., one that quantifies susbstitutionally over formulas (in the restrictor and nuclear scope).

The replacements effectuated by EPILOG in performing NLog-like inferences based on implicatives also typically depend on axiom schemas. The following pair of schemas for the implicative *dare* illustrate this point:

```
(all_pred p (all x [[x dare (Ka p)] => [x p]])),
(all_pred p (all x [(not [x dare (Ka p)]) => (not [x p])))
```

These schemas capture the fact that if someone dared to do something, they did it, and if they didn't dare do something, they didn't do it. We can say that the *signature* of *dare* is of type +/−, to indicate its positive entailment in a positive environment and its negative entailment in a negative environment. Here *Ka*, the logical counterpart of the infinitive particle *to*, is another predicate reifying operator, forming a *kind of action or attribute* when applied to verbal predicates. (Actions are treated in EL as consisting of an individual – the agent or subject of the predication – and an episode. *Ka* is definable in terms of *K* and the episodic operator '**'.)

Similar axiom schemas can be provided for other implicatives, such as the following (in stylized rather than precise form):

> X decline to P => X not P
> X not decline to P => (probably) X P[6]
> X agrees to P => (probably) X P
> X does not agree to P => (probably) not X P
> X doubts that W => X believes probably not W.

The signatures here are −/(+) and (+)/(−) for *decline* and *agree* respectively. Note that some entailments are weakened to implicatures, e.g., it is possible that Bob did not decline to review a certain paper,

---

[6]Whether the qualifier *probably* should be present or not is debatable

yet failed to review it. The example of *doubt* is included here to indicate that certain attitudinal entailments not normally regarded as falling under the implicative or NLog motif can be captured via axiom schemas like those supporting NLog inference.

Besides various axiom schemas, matching the capabilities of NLog also requires special inference rules. (These are formalized in EPILOG much like axiom schemas.) In particular, *factive (presuppositional)* verbs such as *know* and *realize*, with $+/+$ signatures in simple assertional contexts, can be partially handled with rules such as

```
(all_wff w (all_term x ((x know (that w)) ---> w))),
(all_wff w (all_term x ((not (x know (that w))) ---> w))),
```

where the long arrow indicates inferrability. Clearly we could not use axiomatic versions of these rules, since by the law of excluded middle, either x knows that w or x does not know that w, regardless of x and w, and so axioms stating that w holds in either case would lead us to conclude that w holds, regardless of its content. However, these rules only address part of the "projection problem" for presuppositions. For example, they cannot be applied to the consequent clause of a sentence such as *"If Bob was telling the truth, then Alice knows that he was telling the truth"*, which does not entail that Bob was telling the truth. A full treatment of presuppositional clauses, whether in NLog, EPILOG or any other framework, would need to take account of the context established by prior clauses in the discourse. In the preceding example, the *if*-clause establishes a context where it is an open question whether Bob was telling the truth, blocking presupposition projection from the *then*-clause.[7]

The following examples are some (rather eye-catching) headlines collected by Karl Stratos, and rendered into EL by him to demonstrate inferences based on implicatives. A significant point to note is that human readers seem to (unconsciously) generate and internalize the corresponding inferences; this point stands in contrast with the current emphasis in NLP on *recognizing* textual entailment, i.e., on making boolean judgements where both the premise and the hypothetical conclusion are at hand, so that piecemeal alignments and transformations as well as statistical guesswork can be employed in the task.

---

[7]As we noted in (Stratos et al. 2011), Clausen and Manning (2009) proposed a way of projecting presuppositions in NLog in accord with the plug-hole-filter scheme of Karttunen (1973). In this scheme, plugs (e.g., 'say') block all projections, filters (e.g., 'if-then') allow only certain ones, and holes (e.g., 'probably') allow all. But the approach does not fully handle the effects of discourse context.

- *Vatican refused to engage with child sex abuse inquiry* (The Guardian: Dec 11, 2010).
- *A homeless Irish man was forced to eat part of his ear* (The Huffington Post: Feb 18, 2011).
- *Oprah is shocked that President Obama gets no respect* (Fox News: Feb 15, 2011).
- *Meza Lopez confessed to dissolving 300 bodies in acid* (Examiner: Feb 22, 2011)

Corresponding EL representations for EPILOG inference are the following (with various contractions for readability, and neglecting tense and thus episodes; (*l y* ...) indicates lambda-abstraction):

```
[Vatican refuse (Ka (engage-with Child-sex-abuse-inquiry))]
(some x: [x (attr homeless (attr Irish man))]
        [x (pasv force)
           (Ka (l y (some r: [r ear-of y]
                       (some s: [s part-of r] [y eat s]))))])
[Oprah (pasv shock) (that (not [Obama get (K respect)]))]
[Meza-Lopez confess
       (Ka (l x (some y: [y ((num 300) (plur body))] [x dissolve y])))].
```

Obvious inferences confirmed by EPILOG using implicative axiom schemas (in fractions of a second) were the following (returned in English):

The Vatican did not engage with child sex abuse inquiry.
An Irish man did eat part of his ear,
President Obama gets no respect, and
Meza Lopez dissolved 300 bodies in acid.

In addition to treating these illustrative examples, Stratos also extracted a random test set of 108 sentences from the Brown corpus, restricting these to ones containing any of the 250 verbs (including some short phrases) covered by an axiomatic knowledge base. The knowledge base comprised a superset of the collections of implicative and factive verbs obtained from (Nairn et al. 2006), (Danescu-Niculescu-Mizil et al. 2009), and Cleo Condoravdi (personal communication), and also included axioms for separately collected attitudinal verbs, for testing inference of beliefs and desires. Two sample sentences, along with the conclusions drawn from their logical forms, are the following:

I know that you wrote this in a hurry.
→ *You wrote this in a hurry.*

They say that our steeple is 162ft high.
→ *Probably they believe that our steeple is 162ft high.*

Note that the latter inference falls outside the scope of standard NLog inference, since it involves not only a substitution (of *believe* for *say*) but also a simultaneous premodifier insertion (*probably*). The logical forms of the 108 sentences (obtained by manual correction of flawed outputs from the current NL-to-EL interpreter) led to 141 inferences rendered automatically into English, which were rated by multiple judges. They were predominantly judged to be good (75%) or fairly good (17%). Lower ratings were due mostly to incomprehensibility or vacuity of the conclusion, as in *"The little problems help me to do so"* → *"I do so"*. Further details can be found in (Stratos et al. 2011).

Our conclusion is that NLog inferences are readily implemented within the EL-Epilog framework, though further work on the NL-to-EL interface is needed for full automation. (The errors come mostly from faulty parses, which are certainly an issue in automating NLog as well.)

4 Commonsense inferences beyond the scope of NLog

Not all lexical entailments and implicatures are as simple as those we have focused on so far. For example, asking someone to do something entails conveying to them that one wants them to do it. This is expressed in EL with the schema

```
(all_pred p
 (all x
  (all y
   (all e1: [[x ask-of.v y (Ka p)] ** e1]
    [[x convey-info-to.v y
      (that [[x want-tbt.v
              (that (some e2: [e2 right-after.p e1]
                      [[y p] ** e2]))] @ e1])] * e1])))))
```

(Here '*' is weakening of '**' from characterization to partial description – see Schubert 2000.) Thus, given that *"John asked Mary to sing"*,

```
[[John.name ask-of.v Mary.name (Ka sing.v)] ** E1],
```

the question *"Did John convey to Mary that he wanted her to sing?"*,

```
[[John.name convey-info-to.v Mary.name
  (that [[John.name want-tbt.v
          (that (some e2: [e2 right-after.p E1]
                  [[Mary.name sing.v] ** e2]))] @ E1])] * E1],
```

is immediately answered in the affirmative by the Epilog system.

Even further removed from the current reach of NLog are inferences dependent on world knowledge along with lexical knowledge. The premises in the following desired inference are based on a (human-to-human) dialogue excerpt from James Allen's and George Ferguson's Monroe domain (Stent 2000), where the dialogue participants are considering what resources are available for removing rubble from a collapsed building. The first premise is presumed background knowledge, and the second premise reflects an indirect suggestion by one of the participants:

Every available crane can be used to hoist rubble onto a truck.
The small crane, which is on Clinton Ave, is not in use.
→ *The small crane can be used to hoist rubble from the collapsed building on Penfield Rd onto a truck.*

The two premises are expressed in EL as follows:

```
(all x: [x ((attr available) crane)]
  (all r: [r rubble]
    [(that (some y: [y person]
              (some z: [z truck]
                [y (adv-a (for-purpose (Ka (adv-a (onto z) (hoist r))))
                       (use x))])))) possible]))

(the x: [x ((attr small) crane)]
   [[x on Clinton-Ave] and (not [x in-use])])
```

We also need to make a connection between the notion of a device not being in use and being available, [8] and affirm that cranes are devices:

```
(all x: [[x device] and (not [x in-use])] [x available])
(all x: [x crane] [x device])
```

If we now pose the desired inference as the question, *"Can the small crane be used to hoist rubble from the collapsed building on Penfield Rd onto a truck?"*,

```
(the x: [x ((attr small) crane)]
  (some r: [[r rubble] and
            (the s: [[s (attr collapsed building)] and
                     [s on Penfield-Rd]] [r from s])]
    [(that (some y: [y person]
              (some z: [z truck]
                [y (adv-a (for-purpose (Ka (adv-a (onto z) (hoist r))))
                       (use x))])))) possible]))
```

an affirmative answer is produced by EPILOG (in about 1/8 sec on a Dell workstation with an Intel dual core CPU @ 2GHz; however, the time would go up with a larger knowledge base). Such inferences are made by humans just as quickly (and unconsciously) as those based on implicatives, but they are not possible in NLog as currently understood.

Two related inference examples from the same domain are the following.

Most of the heavy Monroe resources are located in Monroe-east.
→ *Few heavy resources are located in Monroe-west.*
→ *Not all Monroe resources are located in Monroe-west.*

---

[8] In the Monroe domain, and perhaps in task-oriented dialogues more broadly, the phrase *not in use* (applied to equipment) pretty reliably indicates *available for use*.

These depend on knowledge about the meanings of vague quantifiers, and on knowledge about the way in which we often conceptually partition geographical regions into disjoint eastern, western, northern, and southern parts. The following are some natural lexical schemas and geographical axioms:

- *If most P are not Q, then few P are Q*:
  ```
  (all_pred P
    (all_pred Q
      [(most x: [x P] (not [x Q])) => (few x: [x P] [x Q])]))
  ```
- *"Heavy" in premodifying position is subsective*:
  ```
  (all_pred P (all x: [x ((attr heavy) P)] [x P]))
  ```
- *If most P are Q, then some P are Q* (existential import of "most"):
  ```
  (all_pred P
    (all_pred Q
      [(most x: [x P] [x Q]) => (some x: [x P] [x Q])]))
  ```
- *All Monroe resources are in Monroe. A thing is in Monroe iff it is in Monroe-east or Monroe-west; and iff it is in Monroe-north or Monroe-south; nothing is in both Monroe-east and Monroe-west; or in both Monroe-north and Monroe-south*:
  ```
  (all x: [x Monroe-resources] [x loc-in Monroe])
  (all x: [[x loc-in Monroe] <=>
      [[x loc-in Monroe-east] or [x loc-in Monroe-west]]])
  (all x: [[x loc-in Monroe] <=>
      [[x loc-in Monroe-north] or [x loc-in Monroe-south]]])
  (all x: [(not [x loc-in Monroe-east]) or (not [x loc-in Monroe-west])])
  (all x: [(not [x loc-in Monroe-north]) or (not [x loc-in Monroe-south])])
  ```
- *There are some heavy Monroe resources; most of the heavy Monroe resources are located in Monroe-east*:
  ```
  (some x [x ((attr heavy) Monroe-resources)])
  (most x: [x ((attr heavy) Monroe-resources)] [x loc-in Monroe-east])
  ```

Some questions that can now be tackled are the following (with a *yes* and *no* answer respectively):

Are few heavy resources in Monroe-west?

```
(few x: [x ((attr heavy) Monroe-resources)] [x loc-in Monroe-west])
```

Are all Monroe resources in Monroe-west?

```
(all x: [x Monroe-resources] [x loc-in Monroe-west])
```

The reasoning behind the *no* answer to the latter question is this: Most heavy resources, hence some heavy resources, hence some resources, are in Monroe-east; but whatever is in Monroe-east is not in Monroe-west, hence not all resources are in Monroe-west. These reasoning examples took a few seconds, probably because EPILOG 2's limited form of input-driven inference did not fire in this case. But one may also speculate that a spatial reasoning specialist could accelerate inference here – people seem to build or access a mental model of the spatial layout alluded to in such examples, and "read off" the answers.

5   Tackling the knowledge acquisition bottleneck

As long as our knowledge bases are small, or restricted to approximate relations between pairs of lexical items, we cannot hope to achieve broad language understanding in machines, or come anywhere close to matching the human capacity for spontaneously generating commonsense inferences upon receipt of new inputs. Therefore, we now turn to the long-standing issue of scaling up a general knowledge base to enable understanding and inference for miscellaneous texts.

We divide the knowledge we are seeking into three general sorts: (a) *lexical knowledge* (for NLog-like and other meaning-based inference); (b) *semantic pattern knowledge* (which we have come to regard as a separate category needed to guide parsing and interpretation, and as a starting point for formulating deeper knowledge); and (c) *world knowledge*, essential to our comprehension of and reasoning about everyday entities and events.

While our methods of mining textual resources for general knowledge, and methods of knowledge accumulation pursued by others, have yielded millions of items of formal knowledge, many of them inference-enabling, these methods still seem far too weak to capture the breadth and richness of human commonsense knowledge. We believe that knowledge bootstrapping ultimately must be grounded in actual, deep understanding of a limited, but ever-growing range of sentences. The most direct method of bootstrapping would be to supply large numbers of explicitly stated generalizations to a system, where these generalizations are presented in the form of relatively simple, relatively self-contained statements. Such generalizations should provide much of the "glue" that binds together sentences in coherent discourse, and should allow generation of expectations and explanations. Thus we will follow our discussion of our efforts to acquire knowledge of types (a-c) with a commentary on the remaining hurdles in deriving deep, logically defensible representations of the content of generic sentences in such sources as WordNet glosses, Simple Wikipedia entries, and Open Mind factoids.

5.1   Acquiring lexical semantic knowledge

Our several approaches to acquiring lexical meaning postulates have been motivated by the availablity of several resources, namely distributional similarity clusters, WordNet hierarchies, collections of implicative and factive verbs, and VerbNet classes. In particular we have pursued the following strategies.

Finding relations among similar words: Starting with distributional similarity clusters (made available to us by Patrick Pantel), we used supervised machine learning techniques to identify entailment, synonymy, and exclusion relations among pairs of words in a cluster, using features borrowed from (MacCartney and Manning 2009) such as WordNet distance, the DLin feature based on Dekang Lin's thesaurus, and morphosyntactic features. After transitivity pruning, we formalized these relations as quantified axioms. Accuracies ranging from 65% to over 90% (depending on word class and relation) were attained (Schubert et al. 2010). While this sort of accuracy may be sufficient for statistical entailment judgements, it falls short of the kind of accuracy we are trying to achieve for reasoning purposes. Indeed, the "gold standard" examples used in training were only as reliable as the judgements of the humans responsible for the labeling, and we have come to the conclusion that such judgements need to be refined before they can be usefully deployed for axiom generation. For example, a lexicographer or graduate student in NLP may well judge that *cognition* entails ("isa") *psychological feature*, yet on careful consideration, it makes little sense to say that "*Every entity with the property of being (a?) cognition has the property of being a psychological feature*". Rather, cognition, as a *kind* of activity performed *by some entity* could be said to be a psychological feature *of* that entity. Similarly, while we might casually judge each link in a hypernym chain such as *ellipse* → *conic section* → *shape* → *attribute* to correspond to an entailment, the conclusion that every ellipse is an attribute is unacceptable.

Thus in current work we are focusing on formulating hypotheses concerning the features of synset pairs classified as hyponym-hypernym pairs in WordNet that are indicative of a specific type of logical relation. For example, whereas a hyponym-hypernym transition from (some sense of) a count noun to (some sense of) another count noun is typically (though by no means always) an entailment transition, and similarly for mass-mass transitions, in the case of a mass-count transition we are more likely confronted with an *instance* relation between a *kind* derived from a mass predicate and a count predicate applicable to kinds. For example, in the hypernym chain *gold dust* → *gold* → *noble metal* → *metallic element* → *element* we can perfectly well infer that every entity with the property of being gold dust has the property of being gold; or, that every entity with the property of being a noble metal has the property of being a metallic element; however, we should not conclude (transitively) that every entity with the property of being gold dust has the property of being a metallic element. The breakdown occurs at the mass-count boundary between *gold* and *noble metal*: The correct reading of the transition here is not as one from property to property, but as a predication about a kind, viz., the kind, *gold*, is a noble metal. We are currently able to generate axioms from the majority of direct hypernym relations in WordNet, but our casual observation that the great majority of these axioms are tenable awaits formal confirmation.

Unfortunately, hierarchy relations for nouns, though fundamentally important, do not go very far towards capturing their meanings. For example, in the case of gold it is essential to know not only that it is a noble metal, but also that it is mined, that it is of high density and malleable, that it melts at sufficiently high temperatures, that it is prized as material for jewelry, and so on. This observation ties in with our comments below on the need for "object-oriented" knowledge in verb-based inference.

Axiomatizing implicative verbs: As already noted in our reference to Karl Stratos' work, we have undertaken a knowledge engineering effort to collect factive and implicative verbal predicates (along with some antifactive and belief- or want-implying ones) and axiomatize them for use in EPILOG. The 250 entries were gleaned from various sources and expanded via VerbNet, thesauri, etc. But as pointed out by Karttunen (2012), there are also numerous *phrasal implicatives*, such as *make a futile attempt to, make no effort to, take the trouble to, use the opportunity to*, or *fulfill one's duty to*. It is doubtful that such cases can be adequately treated by an enumerative approach; rather it appears that multiple items of lexical knowledge will need to be used in concert to derive the desired entailments or implicatures.

Axiomatizing Verbnet classes: After an initial attempt to directly render VerbNet semantic annotations into EPILOG axioms, which led to generally weak and often flawed axioms, we switched to a more meticulous approach to acquiring formal verb semantics (as first sketched in (Schubert et al. 2011)). We have been tackling one verb class at a time, typically formulating an axiom schema for the class (or two or three schemas for subsets of the class), and instantiating the parameters of these schemas with particular predicates or modifiers for particular verbs. For example, the VerbNet change-of-state class *other_cos-45.4*, which includes such verbs as *clean, darken, defrost, open, sharpen,* and *wake*, can be partially characterized in terms of an axiom schema that states that in an event e characterized by an animate agent X acting on a physical entity Y in accord with one of these verbs, Y will have a certain property P at the beginning of the event and a (contrasting) property Q at the end. P and Q might be the (adjectival) predicates *dirty.a* and *clean.a* for verbal predicate *clean*, *light.a* and *dark.a* for *darken*, *frozen.a* and *unfrozen.a* for *defrost*, and so on. (However, quite a few of the 384 verbs, such as *abbreviate, brighten, dilute, improve,* and *soften* require axiomatization in terms of a change on a scale, rather than an absolute transition.) For many classes, the axiom schemas make use of separately axiomatized *primitive* verbal predicates; these number about 150, and were chosen for their prevalence in language, early acquisition by children, inclusion in primitive vocabularies by others, and utility in capturing meanings of other verbs.

This is decidedly still work in progress, with 116 axioms for primitives and 246 for verbs (in 15 VerbNet classes) in the lexical knowledge base so far. A related ongoing project is aimed at evaluation of the axiom base via human judgements of forward inferences based on the axioms. But even completion of these projects will leave untouched most of the verb semantic knowledge ultimately required. Our current axioms are "generic", but we will require much more specific ones. For example, the exact entailments of the verb *open* depend very much on what is being opened – a door, a book, a wine bottle, a mouth, a briefcase, a store, a festive event, etc. Our assumption is that capturing such entailments will require an "object-oriented" approach, i.e., one that draws upon the properties and methods associated with particular object types. We know the physical form, kinematics, dynamics, and function of doors, books, wine bottles, and so forth, and the use of a verb like *open* with a particular type of object seems to align the entailments of the verb with the known potentialities for that type of object. The work of James Pustejovsky and his collaborators on the Generative Lexicon (Pustejovsky 1991) is clearly relevant here. For example, he points out the different interpretations of the verb *use* in phrases such as *use the new knife (on the turkey), use soft contact lenses, use unleaded gasoline (in a car), use the subway,* etc., where these interpretations depend on the "telic qualia" of the artifacts referred to, i.e., their purpose and function.

5.2 Acquiring pattern-like world knowledge

A project we initiated more than 10 years ago is dubbed KNEXT (General **KN**owledge **EX**traction from **T**ext). Unlike KE efforts that glean specific facts about named entities from textual data – birth dates, occupations, geographic locations, company headquarters, product lines, etc. – our goal from the outset was the acquisition of simple *general* facts. The underlying idea was that sentences of miscellaneous texts, including realistic fiction, indicate common patterns of relationships and events in the world, once inessential modifiers have been stripped away and specific entities have been generalized to entity types.

For example, consider the following sentence (from James Joyce's *Ulysses*):

> *Mr Bloom stood at the corner, his eyes wandering over the multicoloured hoardings.*

Using the Charniak parse

```
(S1 (S (NP (NNP Mr) (NNP Bloom))
       (VP (VBD stood)
           (PP (IN at)
               (NP (DT the) (NN corner)))
           (, ,)
           (S (NP (PRP$ his) (NNS eyes))
              (VP (VBG wandering)
                  (PP (IN over)
                      (NP (DT the) (JJ multicoloured) (NNS hoardings)))
                  (. .)))))))
```

KNEXT applies compositional interpretive rules to obtain abstracted logical forms for several parts of the sentence that directly or implicitly provide propositional content. These propositional components are separately returned and automatically verbalized in English. The results are[9]

```
(:i <det man*.n> stand.v (:p at.p <the corner.n>))
A man may stand at a corner

(:i <the (plur eye.n)> wander.v (:p over.p <the (plur hoarding.n)>))
Eyes may wander over hoardings

(:i <det (plur eye.n)> pertain-to.v <det male*.n>)
Eyes may pertain-to a male

(:i <det (plur hoarding.n)> multicoloured.a)
Hoardings can be multicoloured
```

Note that in the first of the four factoids, *Mr Bloom* has been generalized to *a man*, and the modifying clause has been omitted. However, that clause itself gives rise to the second factoid, from which the possessive relation and the modifer *multicoloured* have been omitted. These modifiers in turn provide the remaining two factoids (where *pertain-to* is used as a noncommittal initial interpretation of the possessive). In the next subsection we mention some methods for partially disam-

---

[9] In preliminary logical forms, the ':i' keyword indicates an infix formula, and angle brackets indicate *unscoped* quantifiers. Determiner 'det' is used for an indefinite determiner; definites such as *the corner* are ultimately converted to indefinites as well, except in the case of ever-present "local entities" such as *the weather* or *the police*.

biguating factoids and introducing quantifiers. In particular, we will show "sharpened", quantified formulas that are derived automatically from the first and third factoids.[10]

In this way we typically obtain two or more general factoids per sentence in miscellaneous texts such as those comprising the Brown Corpus, The British National Corpus, Wikipedia, and weblog corpora. The first two of these sources provided several million factoids, and the latter two about 200 million (Gordon et al. 2010b). As some indication of the variety of factoids obtained, here is a small selection of some of the more interesting ones:

```
A bird may have feathers
A person may see with binoculars
Cats may meow
A cat may be chased by a dog
A baby may be vulnerable to infections
People may wish to be rid of a dictator
A male may refuse to believe a proposition
A female may tell a person to put_down a phone
A pen may be clipped to a top of a breast pocket
Factoids can be arcane
```

Generally above 80% of the factoids are rated by human judges as reasonable, potentially useful general claims. Among the publications on this work detailing the extraction methodology, filtering, refinement, and evaluation, the earliest was (Schubert 2002); a more recent one focusing on comparison with related work was (Van Durme and Schubert 2008).

As indicated at the beginning of the section, we have come to view such factoids as a separate but important knowledge category. One of the potential applications is in guiding a parser. For example, it is easy to see how the first two factoids in the above list could help select the correct attachments in the two versions of the sentence

He saw the bird with {binoculars, yellow tail feathers}.

In general, we believe that accurate parsing will require guidance by a multitude of syntactic and semantic patterns, where matches to a pattern "reinforce" particular combinatory choices (Schubert 1984, 2009).

---

[10]Concerning the apparent ambiguity of *wander* in the second factoid, a theoretical position one might take is that the meaning of this verb is actually the same whether the wandering is done by persons, eyes, or minds – but the *entailments* of this verb (and of verbal predicates more generally) depend on the types of the arguments. When persons wander, they physically move about; when eyes wander, it is the target of the gaze that shifts; when minds wander, it is the subject matter contemplated that shifts. An alternative to this position is that argument patterns, potentially in combination with other contextual cues, disambiguate the sense of the verb, and it is the disambiguated senses that carry the preceding entailments.

(This view seems in principle compatible with feature-based discriminative parsing models such as in (Huang 2008), though the features in the latter involve specific word and structural patterns, rather than any meaningful semantic patterns.) From this perspective, conformity with a particular abstract syntax is just one factor in the final analysis of a sentence; recognition of stock phrases, idioms, and patterns of predication and modifications are powerfully influential as well.

The second application of general factoids, which we have been actively exploring, is as a starting point for generating inference-enabling, quantified knowledge, as discussed in the following subsection.

5.3 Acquiring inference-enabling world knowledge

Statements such as that "*A bird may have feathers*" and "*Cats may meow*", though indicative of relationships and events apt to be encountered in the world, do not directly enable usefully strong inferences. For example, we cannot conclude that a particular bird named Tweety is likely to have feathers, only that this is a possibility. In order to obtain inference-enabling knowledge, we have sought to strengthen KNEXT factoids into quantified formulas in two different ways. One is aimed at inference of argument types, given certain relationships or events, while the other is aimed at inferring relationships or events, given certain argument types. A simple example of these alternative ways of strengthening a factoid would be to strengthen "*A bird may have feathers*" into

If something has feathers, it is most likely a bird,

and

All (or at least most) birds have feathers.

Our methodology for the first type of strengthening involves collecting argument types for a given verbal predicate, and seeking a small set of Wordnet hypernyms that cover those types. In the case of the factoid above we would collect factoids matching the pattern "*A(n) ?P may have feathers*", and then look for a WordNet hypernym that covers (some senses of) the nominals matching *?P* (or at least a majority of them). In the present case, we would obtain (the primary senses of) *bird* and *person* as a covering set, and hence derive the quantified claim that "*most things that have feathers are either birds or persons.* (Persons unfortunately cannot easily be eliminated because of such locutions as "ruffled his feathers", and also because of default assumptions that, e.g., *their feathers* refers to human possessors.)

This method turned out to be quite effective (Van Durme et al. 2009), and – serendipidously – provided a method of disambiguating the senses of nominal argument types. For example, the capitalized types in the following factoids were disambiguated to their literary communication senses, thanks to their subsumption under a common *communication* hypernym,

A child may write a LETTER
A journalist may write an ARTICLE,

thereby excluding such senses as alphabetic letters, varsity letters, grammatical articles, and articles of merchandise. However, while we have demonstrated the efficacy of the method on limited samples, we have not yet applied it to the full KNEXT factoid base. The problem is that the requisite WordNet searches for a small (not too general, not too specific) set of covering hypernyms can be very expensive. For example, the search for a set of hypernyms covering a majority of types matching *?P* in *"A person may get a(n) ?P"* would be quite time-consuming, in view of the many complement types allowed by *get*: *chance, babysitter, doctor, checkup, pizza, newspaper, break, idea, job, feeling, point, message, impression, kick, look, ticket, etc.*

We refer to the second type of strengthening, aimed at finding probable relationships and action/event types for given types of individuals, as *factoid sharpening* (Gordon and Schubert 2010). This method is not dependent on abstraction from groups of factoids, but rather strengthens individual factoids (except that we favor factoids that have been abstracted several times from different sources). This may at first seem suspect: A factoid says what it says – how can it be coerced into saying more? The answer lies in the semantic categories of the predicates involved. For example, a factoid like *"A bird may have feathers"* instantiates the predicate pattern '*A(n)* ANIMAL *may have* ANIMAL-PART". Since we know that part-of relationships are typically uniform across living species, and permanent, we can fairly safely sharpen the factoid to a quantified fomula asserting that *all or most birds permanently have some feathers as a part.* Note that just like the first method of strengthening factoids, the sharpening process can also lead to predicate disambiguation; in the present example, uncommon senses of *bird* and *feather* are eliminated, and *have* is specialized to *have-as-part.*

The following are the sharpened formulas automatically derived from two of the factoids displayed earlier (obtained from the James Joyce sentence). The expression [x | e] in the last formula denotes the ordered pair (or list) consisting of the semantic values of x and e; such agent-episode pairs represent specific, temporally located actions or attributes of an agent in EL.

```
(:i <det man*.n> stand.v (:p at.p <the corner.n>))
```

```
A man may stand at a corner

(:i <det (plur eye.n)> pertain-to.v <det male*.n>)
Eyes may pertain-to a male

  (many x: [x man.n]
     (occasional e
        (some y: [y corner.n]
           [[x stand-at.v y] ** e]))))

Many men occasionally stand at a corner.

(all-or-most x: [x male.n]
   (some e: [[x | e] enduring]
      (some y: [y eye.n]
         [[x have-as-part.v y] ** e]))))

All or most males have an eye as a part.
```

We take such formulas as justifying inferences such as that if John is a man, then it is rather likely that he occasionally stands at some corner, and very likely that he has an eye as a part. (The probabilistic qualifiers are presumed to apply in the absence of other knowledge bearing on the conclusions.)

Of course, obtaining such results requires rules that match various patterns of predication against factoids, and generate appropriate sharpened formulas corresponding to successful matches. This has been facilitated by two broadly useful devices: predicate classification with the aid of programs that make use of WordNet relations and VerbNet classes; and a template-to-template transduction system called TTT (Purtee and Schubert 2012). Some subject and object types that are important in transducing factoids into sharpened formulas are ones with WordNet hypernyms *causal agent, body part, professional, food, artifact, event, state, psychological feature*, and several others. Properties of sentential predicates that are important include repeatability (contrast *swim, marry*, and *die*), stativity (contrast *swim, believe*, and *lawyer*), and ones headed by special verbs such as copular *be* and relational *have*. Small sets of VerbNet classes and WordNet relations often enable identification of the relevant properties.

We have produced more than 6 million sharpened formulas, and evaluated the quality of samples by human judgement. When the factoids supplied as inputs to the sharpening process were restricted to ones assessed as being of good quality, about 55.4% of the resulting formulas were judged to be of good quality (for details see Gordon and Schubert 2010); unsurprisingly, for unscreened factoids the percentage of good sharpened formulas was lower, 36.8%. Though the results are encouraging, clearly much remains to be done both in screening or improving input factoids and doing so for resultant sharpened formulas. One possible approach is use of Amazon's Mechanical Turk (see Gordon et al. 2010a). For some further refinements of the sharpening work, aimed at refining event frequencies in general claims (e.g., *"If a person drives taxis regularly, he or she is apt to do so daily or multiple times a week"*), see (Gordon and Schubert 2012).

Finally, we have also begun to extract "if-then" knowledge from text based on discourse cues, in particular, on locutions that indicate failed expectations, expected or hoped-for results, or "good-bad" contrasts (Gordon and Schubert 2011). For example, from the sentence

> The ship weighed anchor and ran out her big guns,
> but did not fire a shot,

it can be plausibly conjectured that

> If a ship weighs anchor and runs out her big guns,
> then it may fire a shot.

However, this work to date generates hypotheses in English only; logical formulation of these hypotheses is left to future work.

6 Can we acquire knowledge by direct interpretation of general statements?

None of the above approaches to acquiring lexical and world knowledge are dependent on genuine understanding of even a limited range of ordinary language. This fact testifies to the elusiveness of a long-standing AI dream: to develop a NLU system stocked with just enough linguistic and world knowledge to be able to learn from lexical glosses, encyclopedias and other textual knowledge repositories, and in this way achieve human-like, or even trans-human, competence in language understanding and commonsense reasoning.

We will not attempt here to survey work to date towards achieving this dream. Rather, we will outline some of the challenges confronting such an enterprise, from an Episodic Logic/ EPILOG perspective. After all, EL is close in its form and semantic types to ordinary language, so that transduction from surface language to an EL meaning representations ought to be relatively easy; easier, for instance, than mapping English to CycL (Lenat 1995), whose representations of linguistic content, though logically framed, bear little resemblance to the source text.[11]

---

[11]Without belittling this important effort, we should add that the Cyc project has not yet gathered nearly enough knowledge for general language understanding and commonsense reasoning; based on our perusal of KNEXT factoids, and on knowledge

Computing initial logical forms in Episodic Logic is in fact fairly straightforward – a refinement of the compositional methods used in Knext. Some issues we should note before moving on to the more formidable challenges in fully interpreting sentences intended to express general knowledge are the following:

- word sense ambiguity (e.g., *crown* in the WordNet gloss for *tree*, which is not disambiguated in the "glosstag" data provided for WordNet (http://wordnet.princeton.edu/glosstag.shtml);

- distinguishing between verb complements and adjuncts, such as the two PPs in *communicating with someone with hand signals*;

- identifying the syntactic/semantic role of "SBAR" constituents, which can be relative clauses, clausal adverbials, or clausal nominals; for example, note the ambiguity of *"There are many villages where there is no source of clean water"*;

- attachment decisions, for PPs and other phrases (e.g., The Open Mind sentence *"Sometimes writing causes your hand to cramp up"* is parsed by our off-the-shelf parser with a subject *sometimes writing*, viewed as an adverb modifying a progressive participle);

- coordinator scope (e.g., the WordNet gloss for *desk* is *"a piece of furniture with a writing surface and usually drawers or other compartments"*, which our parser mangles rather badly, forming a conjunction *"with a writing surface **and** usually"* and a disjunction *"furniture ... **or** other compartments"*);

- ellipsis (this is more important in discourse than in statements of general knowledge);

- anaphora (e.g., from Simple Wikipedia, *"The roots of a tree are usually under the ground. One case for which **this** is not true are the roots of the mangrove tree"*; as noted below, such complexities contraindicate reliance on this source).

Assuming that many of these problems can be overcome using syntactic and semantic pattern knowledge, can we then obtain inference-enabling knowledge of the sort needed for language understanding and commonsense reasoning from the sources we have mentioned?

There are two sorts of challenges: challenges inherent in the kinds of knowledge provided by the targeted sources and the way the knowledge is presented, and challenges in interpreting generic sentences. The primary sources we are considering are WordNet glosses, Simple Wikipedia entries, and Open Mind factoids.

---

gaps observed when posing questions to ResearchCyc, we conjecture that at least tens of millions of individual knowledge items will be required.

6.1 Problems with the sources

One problem with WordNet is that glosses for verbs resolutely refrain from mentioning verb objects, let alone their types. For example, the glosses for the verbs *saw* and *lisp* are *cut with a saw* and *speak with a lisp*, respectively, leaving any automated system guessing as to whether either of these verbs requires an object, and if so, what kind. Consultation of the examples, such as *"saw wood for the fireplace"* can sometimes resolve the ambiguity, but there may be no examples (as in the case of *lisp*), or parsing the examples may itself be problematic.

The descriptions of physical objects in WordNet provides very few constraints on the typical structure and appearance of the objects. For example, the description of a tree as (in part) *"a tall perennial woody plant having a main trunk and branches ..."* does not distinguish the height of a tree from other tall plants, such as sunflowers, or provide a clear picture of the verticality of the trunk and configuration of branches relative to it.[12] It seems that a few internal geometric prototypes (representing, say, a deciduous tree, an evergreen and a palm), traversable by property abstraction algorithms, would be worth a thousand words in this regard. (For a recent paper on the computational learnability of geometric prototypes, and their utility in vision and tactile sensing, see (Yildirim and Jacobs in press).)

A more serious problem from an NLU and commonsense reasoning perspective is that the gloss is silent on the roles trees play in our world and in our stories – providing shade, shelter, fruits, a pleasing sight, a climbing opportunity, a habitat for birds and other creatures, wood for buildings, etc. Can these gaps be filled in from sources like Simple Wikipedia? The initial 240-word summary in the entry for *tree* unfortunately contains few of the generalities we are looking for, while the 2700-word entry taken in its entirety touches on more of them (though still not mentioning shade, fruits, birds, or building materials), but these are scattered amidst many less relevant items, such as the aerial roots of the Banyan tree, the xylem and phloem cells comprising wood, the significance of growth rings, and so on. Consequently, gaining basic knowledge from such entries already presupposes a far more sophisticated language understanding system than we can currently envisage.

The Open Mind Common Sense project at MIT (Singh 2002; Singh et al. 2002) comes much closer to providing the kinds of knowledge we are seeking (e.g., the various roles of trees mentioned above), cast in the form of simple, separately interpretable statements. The kinds of

---

[12]The definition as a *tall* plant does not directly entail a vertical trunk; consider a *windjammer* described as a *tall sailing ship having a steel hull.*

statements obtained are constrained by the way information is solicited from contributors. Consequently, many of the more subtle kinds of factoids obtained by KNEXT are unlikely to show up in Open Mind (e.g., the earlier example, *"A baby may be vulnerable to infections"*, or *"A pen may be clipped to the top of a breast pocket"*). But on the other hand, the Open Mind factoids (exclusive of Verbosity-derived ones) seem more reliable at this point, as we have not yet used filtering of KNEXT factoids by crowd-sourcing on a large scale. Also, Open Mind factoids often include desires, propensities, uses, and locales that are much rarer in KNEXT, such as *"A baby likes to suck on a pacifier"*, *"Pens can be used to write words"*, or *"You are likely to find a pen in an office supply store"*.

However, many of the statements are awkwardly phrased as a result of the particular 20 questions posed to contributors, and for our interpretive purposes would require either a specially adapted parser or preliminary rule-based transformations into more natural English. For example,

Somewhere a bird can be is on a tree

would be more readily interpretable as

A bird can be on a tree.

(Jonathan Gordon at the University of Rochester has implemented a few such transformations based on the previously mentioned tree-to-tree transduction tool TTT.) Also, many of the statements (including the above) share a weakness with our KNEXT factoids in that they express mere possibilities, providing little support for inference. We would expect to apply our sharpening methods in many such cases.

In addition, some of the Open Mind statements reflect the hazards of crowdsourcing. Integration of Verbosity data into Open Mind, in particular, seems to have contributed a fair share of fractured-English examples, such as *"Coat is looks lot"*, *"Chicken is a saying"*, and *"Car is broom-broom"*. Also, some statements blend myth and reality. An example is *"Something you find under a tree is a troll"*, which is annotated with the same degree of support as, for instance, *"A tree can produce fruit"*. Fortunately, however, Open Mind also contains the statement that *"A troll is a mythical creature"*.

Perhaps the most serious problem (also shared with many KNEXT factoids) is the radically underspecified nature of many claims, such as that *"Cars can kill people"*, *"Fire can kill"*, *"A knife is used for butter"*, or *"Milk is used for cream"*; these give no indication of the agent, patient, or event structure involved, and as such could be quite misleading. While we can imagine filtering out many such terse statements in favor of more elaborate ones, such as *"A knife is used for spreading butter"* and *"Knives can butter bread"* (also found in Open Mind), ultimately we need to confront the fact that generic statements are almost invariably underspecified in various ways. This relates to the observations in the following subsection.

6.2 Problems with interpretation of generics

There are subtle interpretive issues, familiar in the literature on generic sentences, that would need to be addressed (e.g., Carlson and Pelletier 1995). For example, *"A tree can grow"* should not be interpreted as referring to a particular tree, but rather to trees in general. Contrast the sentence with *"An asteroid can hit the Earth"*, which is unlikely to be understood as a generalization about asteroids. Moreover, while we would regard *"A tree can grow"* as essentially equivalent to *"Trees can grow"*, where on G. Carlson's analysis, *trees* denotes the *kind, trees,* the singular indefinite subject in the first version cannot be so viewed, as is clear from the contrast between *"Trees are widespread"* and #*"A tree is widespread"*.

A general approach to computing the logical forms of generic (as well as habitual) sentences, covering the above phenomena and others, appears to require the introduction of various syntactically null constituents, including kind-forming operators, quantifying adverbials, and presupposed material, all under various soft constraints dependent on such features as telicity and the sortal categories of predicates (e.g., individual-level vs. stage-level, and object-level vs. kind-level). For example, consider the generic sentence

Dogs bark.

As a preliminary logical form, abiding by Carlson's analysis of bare plurals, we would obtain

    [(K (plur dog)) bark].

However, this is sortally inconsistent, since *bark* is a predicate applicable to objects, rather than kinds (in contrast with predicates like *evolve* or *are widespread*). Thus we would elaborate the LF to

    [(K (plur dog)) (generally bark)],

where *generally P* is understood as something like *"is a kind such that all or most of its realizations have property P"*. In other words, the quantifying adverbial (Q-adverbial) *generally* in effect type-shifts[13] an object-level predicate to a kind-level predicate. However, this is still sortally faulty, because *bark* is not an individual-level predicate (one

---

[13]More accurately, sortally shifts.

simply true or false of an individual viewed as space-time entity spanning its entire existence), but rather an episodic predicate (true or false of an individual *at* a particular temporally bounded episode). Therefore, a further operator is called for, one that converts an episodic predicate into an individual-level predicate. A natural choice here seems to be a *habitual* operator expressing *(at least) occasionally*:

```
[(K (plur dog)) (generally (occasionally bark))]
```

This corresponds to the quite natural reading of the original sentence, expressing that dogs *in general* bark *(at least) occasionally*. EL and Epilog allow us to work directly with such logical forms, but we can also easily use them, in conjunction with meaning postulates about *K*, *generally*, and *occasionally* to derive representations closer to FOL-like ones (though with loss of the law-like content of the original version):

```
(all-or-most x: [x dog]
  (exist-occasional e [[x bark] ** e])).
```

There is a plausible alternative to the operator *occasionally*, namely *can*, expressing an ability or propensity; this also converts an episodic predicate into an individual-level predicate. After conversion to the explicit quantified form, we would have

```
(all-or-most x: [x dog] [x (can bark)])
```

We note that the Open Mind instructions requesting input from contributors preclude simple habitual generics such as *"Dogs bark"*, favoring ability-generics instead. Indeed the highest-rated entry for *dog* is

An activity a dog can do is bark,

whose phrasing we would simplify to *"A dog can bark"*.

Without going into additional details, we note some further issues that arise in the interpretation of generics, as illustrated by the following sentences.

Dogs are occasionally vicious
Dogs can mother puppies
Dogs often chase mailmen

Note that the first sentence is ambiguous between a reading that quantifies over dogs (*"The occasional dog is vicious"*) and one that ascribes a habitual behavior (occasional episodes of viciousness) to dogs in general. These alternatives seem to arise from a basic atemporal/temporal ambiguity that Q-adverbs are subject to; in the present case, *occasionally* can mean either *"is a kind some of whose realizations ..."*, or *"at some times ..."*, where in the latter case we would also assume an implicit *generally*, i.e., the sentence expresses that *"Dogs in general are at some times vicious*". Which reading comes to the fore in a given generic sentence depends on whether the sentential predicate is itself individual-level or episodic, or ambiguous between these, as in the case of *vicious*. The second sentence (from Open Mind) illustrates the fact that a proper understanding of a generic sentence often requires imposition of constraints on the kind in subject position, based on common knowledge; i.e., here we need to restrict the kind under consideration to *female* dogs. The third sentence (also from Open Mind) illustrates that in addition, we may need to bring into play presuppositions based on world knowledge. We know that mailmen are not perpetually available for chasing by a given dog, but only when delivering mail in the immediate vicinity of the dog's abode. So in effect we understand the sentence as saying something like

> *When a mailman delivers mail in the vicinity of a dog's abode, the dog often chases the mailman.*

Arriving at such interpretations automatically seems further out of reach than in the case of the earlier examples – we would have to use general facts about mailmen, and about mail delivery to homes, and about the presence of dogs in and around homes, to reach the desired interpretation of the sentence in question.

7 Concluding remarks

We showed that the representational and inferential style of Episodic Logic and the EPILOG system are close to those of Natural Logic. But we also gave ample evidence showing that our approach and system allow for a broader range of inferences, dependent on world knowledge as well as lexical knowledge. Moreover, EPILOG performs goal-directed inference without being told from what specific premises to draw its conclusion (as in recognizing textual entailment), and can also perform some forward inferences.

It is sometimes assumed that Natural Logic has an advantage over symbolic logic in that it is tolerant of ambiguity, vagueness, and indexicality. However, EPILOG also tolerates ambiguous, vague or indexical input, as was seen in the examples concerning the availability of a *small crane* for rubble removal, and the location of *most of the heavy equipment* in a part of Monroe county. At the same time, we need to recognize that there are limits to how much vagueness of ambiguity can be tolerated in a knowledge-based system, lest it be led astray. For example, a system with common sense should not conclude from "*Bob had gerbils as a child*" that Bob consumed, or gave birth to, small rodents as a child (as a method based on alignment, polarity and word-level editing might well conclude).

We argued that the greatest challenge in achieving deeper under-standing and reasoning in machines is (still) the knowledge acquisition bottleneck, and outlined our multiple lines of attack, all with some de-gree of success, on lexical and world knowledge acquisition. The meth-ods for lexical knowledge acquisition have relied on sources such as dis-tributional similarity data, WordNet hierarchies, VerbNet classes, and collections of implicative and other verbs that can easily be mapped to axioms supporting NLog-like inferences. Our approach to general knowledge extraction from text has delivered many millions of simple general factoids, which we suggested were potentially useful for guid-ing parsers, and which we showed to be capable of yielding inference-enabling quantified formulas through techniques based on groups of factoids with shared verbal predicates, or based on *sharpening* of indi-vidual factoids with the help of additional knowledge sources.

But the knowledge procurable in these ways provides only a fraction of the kinds of general knowledge people appear to employ in language understanding and reasoning, and we are therefore committed in fu-ture work to continuing the development of interpretive methods that can produce generally accurate, logically defensible, inference-enabling interpretations of verbally expressed general knowledge in such sources as WordNet glosses and Open Mind. The challenges that we outlined in considering such an enterprise are certainly formidable but seem to us ones that can be met, using the NLP resources already at hand along with pattern-based parser guidance, and methods for interpreting generic sentences grounded in linguistic semantics.

Acknowledgments

As indicated by the various citations, much of the work surveyed here was carried out by the author's student collaborators, including Ben Van Durme (now at JHU), Ting Qian, Jonathan Gordon, Karl Stratos, and Adina Rubinoff. The paper owes its existence to the organization of the LSA Workshop on Semantics for Textual Inference and follow-up work by Cleo Condoravdi and Annie Zaenen, and benefited from their editorial comments and the comments of the anonymous referee. The work was supported by NSF Grants IIS-1016735 and IIS-0916599, and ONR STTR N00014-10-M-0297.

References

Carlson, G.N. 1977. A unified analysis of the English bare plural. *Linguistics and Philosophy* 1(3):413–456.

Carlson, G.N. and F.J. Pelletier, eds. 1995. *The Generic Book*. Chicago and London: Univ. of Chicago Press.

Clausen, David and Christopher D. Manning. 2009. Presupposed content and entailments in natural language inference. In *ACL-IJCNLP Workshop on Applied Textual Inference*.

Danescu-Niculescu-Mizil, C., L. Lee, and R. Ducott. 2009. Without a 'doubt'? Unsupervised discovery of downward-entailing operators. In *Proc. of NAACL HLT*, pages 137–145.

Fadiga, L., L. Craighero, M. Fabbri Destro, L. Finos, N. Cotilon-Williams, A.T. Smith, and U. Castiello. 2006. Language in shadow. *Social Neuroscience* 1(2):77–89.

Fedorenko, E., J. Duncan, and N. Kanwisher. 2012. Language-selective and domain-general regions lie side-by-side within Broca's area. *Current Biology* 22:1–4.

Gordon, J. and L.K. Schubert. 2012. Using textual patterns to learn expected event frequencies. In *NAACL-HLT Joint Workshop on Automatic Knowledge Base Construction and Web-scale Knowledge Extraction (AKBC-WEKEX)*. Montreal, Canada.

Gordon, Jonathan and Lenhart K. Schubert. 2010. Quantificational sharpening of commonsense knowledge. In *Proc. of the AAAI 2010 Fall Symposium on Commonsense Knowledge*.

Gordon, Jonathan and Lenhart K. Schubert. 2011. Discovering commonsense entailment rules implicit in sentences. In *Proc. of the EMNLP Workshop on Textual Entailment (TextInfer 2011)*.

Gordon, Jonathan, Benjamin Van Durme, and Lenhart K. Schubert. 2010a. Evaluation of commonsense knowledge with Mechanical Turk. In *Proc. of the NAACL Workshop on Creating Speech and Language Data with Amazon's Mechanical Turk*. Los Angeles, CA.

Gordon, Jonathan, Benjamin Van Durme, and Lenhart K. Schubert. 2010b. Learning from the Web: Extracting general world knowledge from noisy text. In *Proc. of the AAAI 2010 Workshop on Collaboratively-built Knowledge Sources and Artificial Intelligence (WikiAI)*. Atlanta, GA.

Huang, Liang. 2008. Forest reranking: Discriminative parsing with non-local features. In *Proc. of ACL-08: HLT*, pages 586–594. Columbus, OH.

Karttunen, Lauri. 1973. Presuppositions of compound sentences. *Linguistic Inquiry* 4:167–193.

Karttunen, Lauri. 2012. Simple and phrasal implicatives. In *Proc. of *SEM: The First Joint Conf. on Lexical and Computational Semantics*, pages 124–131. Montréal, Canada.

Lenat, Doug. 1995. CYC: A large-scale investment in knowledge infrastructure. *Comm. of the ACM* 38(11):33–38.

MacCartney, Bill and Christopher D. Manning. 2008. Modeling semantic containment and exclusion in natural language inference. In *Proc. of the*

22nd Int. Conf. on Computational Linguistics (COLING '08), pages 521–528.

MacCartney, Bill and Christopher D. Manning. 2009. An extended model of natural logic. In *Proc. of IWCS-8*.

Morbini, Fabrizio and Lenhart K. Schubert. 2009. Evaluation of EPILOG: a reasoner for Episodic Logic. In *Commonsense 09*. Toronto, Canada.

Nairn, R., C. Condoravdi, and L. Karttunen. 2006. Computing relative polarity for textual inference. In *Inference in Computational Semantics (ICoS-5)*, pages 67–76.

Purtee, A. and L.K. Schubert. 2012. TTT: A tree transduction language for syntactic and semantic processing. In *EACL 2012 Workshop on Applications of Tree Automata Techniques in Natural Language Processing (ATANLP 2012)*. Avignon, France.

Pustejovsky, James. 1991. The generative lexicon. *Computational Linguistics* 17(4):409–441.

Schubert, L.K. 2009. Language understanding as recognition and transduction of numerous overlaid patterns. In *AAAI Spring Symposium on Learning by Reading and Learning to Read*, pages 94–96. Stanford, CA.

Schubert, L.K., J. Gordon, K. Stratos, and A. Rubinoff. 2011. Towards adequate knowledge and natural inference. In *AAAI Fall Symposium on Advances in Cognitive Systems*. Arlington, VA.

Schubert, Lenhart K. 1984. On parsing preferences. In *Proc. of the 10th Int. Conf. On Computational Linguistics (COLING-84)*, pages 247–250. Stanford Univ., Stanford, CA.

Schubert, Lenhart K. 2000. The situations we talk about. In J. Minker, ed., *Logic-Based Artificial Intelligence*, pages 407–439. Kluwer, Dortrecht.

Schubert, Lenhart K. 2002. Can we derive general world knowledge from texts? In *Proc. of HLT02*.

Schubert, Lenhart K. and Chung Hee Hwang. 2000. Episodic Logic Meets Little Red Riding Hood: A comprehensive, natural representation for language understanding. In L. Iwanska and S. Shapiro, eds., *Natural Language Processing and Knowledge Representation: Language for Knowledge and Knowledge for Language*. Menlo Park, CA, and Cambridge, MA: MIT/AAAI Press.

Schubert, Lenhart K., Benjamin Van Durme, and Marzieh Bazrafshan. 2010. Entailment inference in a natural logic–like general reasoner. In *Proc. of the AAAI 2010 Fall Symposium on Commonsense Knowledge*.

Singh, Push. 2002. The public acquisition of commonsense knowledge. In *Proc. of AAAI Spring Symposium on Acquiring (and Using) Linguistic (and World) Knowledge for Information Access*.

Singh, P., T. Lin, E.T. Mueller, G. Lim, T. Perkins, and W.L. Zhu. 2002. Open Mind Common Sense: Knowledge acquisition from the general public. In *Proc. of the Confederated Int. Conf. DOA, CoopIS and ODBASE*, pages 1223–1237. Irvine, CA.

Stent, Amanda. 2000. The Monroe Corpus, Tech. Rep. no. TR728 and TN99-2. Tech. rep., Dept. of Computer Science, Univ. of Rochester, Rochester, NY, USA.

Stratos, Karl, Lenhart Schubert, and Jonathan Gordon. 2011. Episodic Logic: Natural logic + reasoning. In *Int. Conf. on Knowledge Engineering and Ontology Development (KEOD)*. Paris, France. Available (with INSTIC/Primoris login) at http://www.scitepress.org/DigitalLibrary.

Valencia, V. Sánchez. 1991. *Studies on Natural Logic and Categorial Grammar*. Ph.D. thesis, University of Amsterdam.

van Benthem, J. 1991. *Language in Action: categories, lambdas and dynamic logic*, vol. 130. Amsterdam: Elsevier.

van Benthem, J. 2007. A brief history of natural logic. In *Int. Conf. on Logic, Navya-Nyāya & Applications: Homage to Bimal Krishna Matilal*.

Van Durme, Benjamin, Phillip Michalak, and Lenhart K. Schubert. 2009. Deriving generalized knowledge from corpora using WordNet abstraction. In *12th Conf. of the Eur. Chapter of the Assoc. for Computational Linguistics (EACL09)*. Athens, Greece.

Van Durme, B. and L.K. Schubert. 2008. Open knowledge extraction using compositional language processing. In *Symposium on Semantics in Systems for Text Processing (STEP 2008)*. Venice, Italy.

van Eijck, J. 2005. Natural Logic for Natural Language. http://homepages.cwi.nl/\verb+~+jve/papers/05/nlnl/NLNL.pdf.

Yildirim, I. and R.A. Jacobs. in press. Transfer of object category knowledge across visual and haptic modalities: 3 experimental and computational studies. *Cognition* .

Decomposing Semantic Inferences

Elena Cabrio[1] and Bernardo Magnini[2]

Beside formal approaches to semantic inference that rely on logical representation of meaning, the notion of Textual Entailment (TE) has been proposed as an applied framework to capture major semantic inference needs across applications in Computational Linguistics. Although several approaches have been tried and evaluation campaigns have shown improvements in TE, a renewed interest is rising in the research community towards a deeper and better understanding of the core phenomena involved in textual inference. Pursuing this direction, we are convinced that crucial progress will derive from a focus on decomposing the complexity of the TE task into basic phenomena and on their combination. In this paper, we carry out a deep analysis on TE data sets, investigating the relations among two relevant aspects of semantic inferences: the logical dimension, i.e. the capacity of the inference to prove the conclusion from its premises, and the linguistic dimension, i.e. the linguistic devices used to accomplish the goal of the inference. We propose a decomposition approach over TE pairs, where single linguistic phenomena are isolated in what we have called *atomic inference pairs*, and we show that at this granularity level the actual correlation between the linguistic and the logical dimensions of semantic inferences emerges and can be empirically observed.

1 Introduction

The ability to carry out semantic inferences is pervasive in our capacity to understand natural languages. In particular, we show a crucial skill in establishing meaningful relations among different pieces of text in order to reconstruct their connections: as an example, the meaning of one portion of text can be expressed by another portion of text (i.e. paraphrasing), it can be contained (i.e. entailed) by the other, it can

---

[1]INRIA Sophia Antipolis, France.
[2]Fondazione Bruno Kessler, Trento, Italy.

LiLT Volume 9
Perspectives on Semantic Representations for Textual Inference.
Copyright © 2014, CSLI Publications.

be interpreted as the cause or the effect, or it can express the fact that it temporally precedes or follows the other. From a computational perspective, it seems difficult for any automatic system not to aim at replicating some degree of human semantic inferencing.

While the logical nature of such semantic inferences has been the subject of a huge amount of literature in the area of Philosophy of Language, it is only in the recent years that this topic has produced new trends of investigation in Computational Linguistics. A relevant achievement has been the focus on automatically recognizing "textual inferences" as the main research goal, which has let to the set-up of a general framework of research, independent from the actual methods used to address the problem. Focusing on the discovery of semantic relations among two portions of text has in fact opened the way to a number of new approaches and techniques, as well as to the development of several annotated data sets.

The renaissance of interest around semantic inferences in Computational Linguistics is well shown by several initiatives. Among them, the Recognizing Textual Entailment initiative (RTE) (Dagan et al. 2009), started in 2005 with the organization of the RTE series of evaluation campaigns,[3] the semantic text similarity task at Semeval,[4] and the recognition of causal relations.[5] A common feature of the above mentioned initiatives is that they all define semantic inferences as a direct relation among two portions of text. This distinguishes them from several annotation tasks (e.g. Part of Speech Tagging, Named Entity Recognition, Semantic Role Labeling), where the goal is the detection of linguistic phenomena within a single portion of text. The text-based approach to inferences has also made it easier to integrate several current research tools for text annotation in the service of inference detection.

As mentioned, establishing the inference tasks at the level of text, thus independently from the actual method implemented, has opened the door to a new research stream. New initiatives are pursing this approach to create shared and open platforms.[6] A relevant effect of this text-based view on semantic inferences is that much more annotated material is currently available for investigating the linguistic phenomena underlying semantic inferences. In addition, several approaches are now using such data sets for training automatic systems based on machine learning algorithms.

While this paper takes advantage of the text-based framework in

---

[3]http://www.nist.gov/tac/2011/RTE/
[4]http://www.cs.york.ac.uk/semeval-2013/task6/
[5]http://www.cs.york.ac.uk/semeval-2012/task7/
[6]http://www.excitement-project.eu/

semantic inferences, and builds on top of the impressive progress in this area, we think that a deeper analysis of the current available data sets is still required, as it may bring new insight for further technological developments. Specifically, we notice that most of the current annotated data sets for the Textual Entailment task have been mainly developed according to applications criteria (e.g. in RTE-1-4 pairs are selected from relevant application domains; RTE-5-6 mainly serve summarization purposes; AVE[7] data sets (Peñas et al. 2008) come from Question Answering, etc.). Although this may serve the purpose of creating training material for specific application scenarios, overall, less attention has been paid to the analysis of the linguistic phenomena underlying textual inferences and the way they interact with different types of inferences. A consequence of the current lack of analysis is that it is not fully clear what a system can actually learn from the available data sets.

In the light of the above considerations, the purpose of this paper is to carry out a deep analysis of Textual Entailment (TE) data sets. We investigate the relations among two relevant aspects of semantic inferences: the *logical* dimension, i.e. the capacity of the inference to prove the conclusion from its premises, and the *linguistic* dimension, i.e. the linguistic devices that are used to accomplish the goal of the inference.

With respect to other studies - see, for instance, Garoufi (2007) and Sammons et al. (2010) - that have annotated and investigated TE datasets, we take a data oriented and neutral approach. As an example, we do not assign a polarity to single linguistic phenomena, and we do not impose specific categorizations on positive and negative entailment, rather we expect to derive such distinctions from observations.

According to this perspective, we aim at understanding whether there are regularities (i.e. relevant patterns) that might be learned combining the two dimensions. In the paper we show that the sparseness of the linguistic phenomena in current data sets and their distribution in positive and negative pairs, actually constitute an intrinsic limitation to supervised approaches to TE. Given this, we plead for a *decomposition framework* of semantic inferences in order to facilitate both a deeper understanding of the distribution of the phenomena that contribute to the inference, and to simplify the computational complexity of the problem. In this framework systems can learn from *specialized data sets*, covering both the most relevant phenomena underlying inferences and the different nature of the inferences.

---

[7] http://nlp.uned.es/clef-qa/ave/

In the paper we systematically analyze a data set of TE pairs according to two relevant dimensions: *(i)* the nature of the inference, using the traditional logical view on arguments (Section 3); *(ii)* the linguistic phenomena involved in the inference (Section 4). In both sections we first provide the necessary background, and then we apply the analysis to a TE data set that we use throughout the paper. Section 5 presents a novel approach aiming at producing inference data sets where single linguistic phenomena are isolated one at a time. Through the decomposition of an initial RTE pair we obtain all the *atomic* pairs involved in the inference process, each tagged with the corresponding phenomenon. We show that the fine-grained analysis allowed by atomic pairs is a powerful investigation tool, which sheds new light on the relations between the polarity of a certain linguistic phenomenon and the occurrence of that phenomenon in both positive and negative pairs. Such analysis provides evidence that current RTE data sets offer a limited capacity to discriminate features that may support learning algorithms, particularly because the polarity of several linguistic phenomena correlates poorly with their distribution in positive and negative pairs. Finally, we conclude the paper recommending a systematic development of *specialized* data sets of atomic pairs and learning approaches over them.

2   Inference data sets

This section first presents the current status of RTE data sets, then describes other data sets used by the community for semantic inferences, and finally introduces the data set we have used for the analysis carried out in this paper.

In 2005, the PASCAL Network of Excellence started an attempt to promote a generic evaluation framework covering semantic-oriented inferences needed for practical applications, launching the Recognizing Textual Entailment challenge (Dagan et al. 2005), (Dagan et al. 2006), (Dagan et al. 2009), with the aim of setting a unifying benchmark for the development and evaluation of methods that typically address similar problems in different, application-oriented, manners. As many of the needs of several Natural Language Processing (NLP) applications can be cast in terms of TE, the goal of the evaluation campaign is to promote the development of general entailment recognition engines, designed to provide generic modules across applications. Since 2005, such initiative has been repeated yearly,[8] asking the participants to develop a system that, given two text fragments (the *text* T and the *hypothesis*

---

[8]http://aclweb.org/aclwiki/index.php?title=Recognizing_Textual_
Entailment

H), can determine whether the meaning of one text is entailed, i.e. can be inferred, from the other. Example 1 represents a positive example pair (i.e. *entailment*), where the entailment relation holds between T and H (pair 10, RTE-4 test set). For pairs where the entailment relation does not hold between T and H, systems are required to make a further distinction between pairs where the entailment does not hold because the content of H is contradicted by the content of T (i.e. *contradiction*, see Example 2 - pair 6, RTE-4 test set), and pairs where the entailment cannot be determined because the truth of H cannot be verified on the basis of the content of T (i.e. *unknown*, see Example 3 - pair 699, RTE-4 test set).

(1) T: *In the end, defeated, Anthony committed suicide and so did Cleopatra, according to legend, by putting an asp to her breast.*

  H: *Cleopatra committed suicide.*

(2) T: *Reports from other developed nations were corroborating these findings. Europe, New Zealand and Australia were also beginning to report decreases in new HIV cases.*

  H: *AIDS victims increase in Europe.*

(3) T: *Proposals to extend the Dubai Metro to neighbouring Ajman are currently being discussed. The plans, still in the early stages, would be welcome news for investors who own properties in Ajman.*

  H: *Dubai Metro will be expanded.*

In line with the rationale underlying the RTE challenges, T-H pairs are collected from several application scenarios (e.g. Question Answering, Information Extraction, Information Retrieval, Summarization), reflecting the way by which the corresponding application could take advantage of automated entailment judgment. In the collection phase, each pair of the data set is judged by three annotators, and pairs on which the annotators disagree are discarded. The obtained data set is split into training and test data sets (note that most of the participating systems implement Machine Learning approaches requiring training data), containing on average about 1000 pairs each. The distribution according to the three-way annotation, both in the individual setting and in the overall data sets, is: 50% *entailment*, 35% *unknown*, and 15% *contradiction* pairs.[9]

---

[9]Since RTE-6, the task has been partially changed, and consists in finding all the sentences that entail a given H in a given set of documents about a topic (i.e.

Entailment in RTE pairs is defined as the inference a speaker with basic knowledge of the world would make. Entailments are therefore dependent on linguistic knowledge, and may also depend on some world knowledge - see the controversy between Zaenen et al. (2005) and Manning (2006). Partially guided by reasons of convenience for the task definition, some assumptions have been defined by the organizers of the challenge, for instance, the a priori truth of both T and H, and the sameness of meaning of entities mentioned in T and H. From a human perspective, the inference required are fairly superficial, since generally no long chains of reasoning are involved. However some pairs are designed to trick simplistic approaches.

Since the goal of RTE data sets is to collect inferences needed by NLP applications while processing real data, the example pairs are very different from a previous resource built to address natural language inference problems, i.e. the FraCas test suite (Cooper et al. 1996). This resource includes 346 problems, containing each one or more premises and one question (i.e. the goal of each problem is expressed as a question). With respect to RTE pairs, here the problems are designed to focus on a broader range of semantic and inferential phenomena, including quantifiers, plurals, anaphora, ellipsis and so on, as shown in Example 4 (fracas-022: monotonicity, upwards on second argument).[10]

(4) P1: *No delegate finished the report on time.*

Q: *Did no delegate finish the report?*

H: *No delegate finished the report.*

Answer: *unknown*

Why: *can't drop adjunct in negative context*

Even if the FraCas test suite is much smaller when compared to the number of annotated pairs in RTE data sets, and it is less natural-seeming (i.e. it provides textbook examples of semantic phenomena, quite different from the kind of inferences that can be found in real data), it is worth mentioned here.

---

the corpus). This task is situated in the summarization application setting, where *i)* H's are based on Summary Content Units (Nenkova et al. 2007) created from human-authored summaries for a corpus of documents about a common topic, and *ii)* the entailing sentences (T's), are to be retrieved in the same corpus from which the summaries were made. Data sets for this task are therefore very different from the previous edition of the challenge, since there are no predefined T-H pairs.

[10]In the example, P and Q are respectively the premises and the question from the original source problem. The H element contains a sentence which is, as nearly as possible, the declarative equivalent to the question posed in the Q element. B. MacCartney (Stanford University) converted FraCas questions into declarative hypothesis: http://www-nlp.stanford.edu/~wcmac/downloads/fracas.xml

Another available inference data set that we are aware of is the Microsoft Research Paraphrase Corpus[11], that contains 5800 pairs of sentences which have been extracted from news sources on the web, and then manually annotated as paraphrase/semantic equivalence. Moreover, other inference data sets have been built to train automatic systems in the following NLP challenges: *i)* for the Answer Validation Exercise (AVE) at the Cross-Language Evaluation Forum (CLEF), systems have to consider triplets (Question, Answer, Supporting Text) and decide whether the Answer to the Question is correct and supported or not according to the given Supporting Text. Resources containing such triplets have been built for training and testing the participating systems, both for Spanish and for English languages[12]; *ii)* for the Semantic Textual Similarity task at Semeval 2012[13], where systems are asked to examine the degree of semantic equivalence between two sentences, the data set comprises pairs of sentences drawn from the publicly available data sets used in training (e.g. Microsoft Paraphrase, WMT2008 development data set - Europarl section[14], pairs of sentences where the first comes from Ontonotes and the second from a WordNet definition, and so on). In both competitions, most of the approaches implement Machine Learning methods, that try to exploit training set data for learning.

Since the work we present in this paper focuses in particular on Textual Entailment, the data we consider for our analysis include a sample of pairs extracted from RTE-5 data set (Bentivogli et al. 2009b). More specifically, in order to compare our results with the literature, we created our reference data joining the data sets annotated by Sammons et al. (2010) (composed of 210 pairs from RTE-5 test set: 107 *entailment*, 37 *contradiction*, 66 *unknown*) and by Bentivogli et al. (2010) (composed of 90 pairs from RTE-5: 30 *entailment*, 30 *contradiction*, 30 *unknown*). Since the two data sets have a lot of pairs in common, joining the two results in 243 pairs, divided into 117 positive (i.e. *entailment*), and 126 negative (i.e. 51 *contradiction* and 75 *unknown*) pairs. With respect to RTE-5 sub tasks (IE, IR and QA), such pairs are distributed as follows: 91 QA, 74 IE and 75 IR. From now on, we consider this data set as the reference data for our study (we will refer to it as "RTE-5-SAMPLE"), on which the annotation and the experiments described in the next sections are carried out.

---

[11]http://research.microsoft.com/en-us/downloads/
607d14d9-20cd-47e3-85bc-a2f65cd28042/

[12]http://nlp.uned.es/clef-qa/ave/

[13]http://www.cs.york.ac.uk/semeval-2012/task6/

[14]http://www.statmt.org/wmt08/shared-evaluation-task.html

3 Analyzing semantic inferences by their logical nature

TE can be seen as the capacity to capture the strength of an inference (i.e. how much the conclusion can be inferred from the premises). We have found appropriate for our purposes the four validity criteria described in (Nolt et al. 1998): *truth of premises, validity and inductive probability, relevance, requirement of total evidence.* In our analysis, we apply such criteria to a sample of RTE pairs, aiming at understanding whether there are regularities (i.e. relevant patterns) that might be learned combining the *logical* dimension with the *linguistic* dimension of semantic inferences.

3.1 Semantic inferences as logical arguments

The main purpose of an argument is to demonstrate that a conclusion is true or at least likely to be true. It is therefore possible to judge an argument with respect to the fact that it accomplishes or fails to accomplish this purpose. In Nolt et al. (1998), four criteria for making such judgments are examined: *i)* whether the premises are true; *ii)* whether the conclusion is at least probable, given the truth of the premises; *iii)* whether the premises are relevant to the conclusion; and *iv)* whether the conclusion is vulnerable to new evidence.[15]

The motivations for criterion 1 (i.e. *truth of premises*) are related to the fact that if any of the premises of an argument is false, it is not possible to establish the truth of its conclusion. Often the truth or falsity of one or more premises is unknown, so that the argument fails to establish its conclusion "so far as we know". In such cases, we may suspend the judgment until relevant information that would allow us to correctly apply criterion 1 is acquired. Criterion 1 is a necessary - but not sufficient - condition for establishing the conclusion, i.e. the truth of the premise does not guarantee that the conclusion is also true.

In a good argument, the premises must adequately support the conclusion, and the second and third criteria (i.e. *validity and inductive probability*, and *relevance*, respectively) are thought to assess this aspect. In particular, the goal of criterion 2 is to evaluate the arguments with respect to the probability of the conclusion, given the truth of the premises. According to this parameter, arguments are classified into three categories:

- *deductive arguments*, whose conclusion follows *necessarily* from their basic premises (i.e. it is impossible for their conclusion to be false while the basic premises are true);

---

[15]In Section 3.2 examples for each criterion are presented and discussed.

- *inductive arguments*, whose conclusion does not necessarily follow from their basic premises (i.e. there is a certain probability that the conclusion is true if the premises are, but there is also a probability that it is false)[16];

- *abductive arguments*, where the reasoning goes from data description of something to a hypothesis that accounts for the reliable data and seeks to explain relevant evidence. From an observable Q and a general principle P ⊃ Q we conclude that P must be the underlying reason that Q is true. We assume P because Q is true (Hobbs 2008).

Given a set of premises, the probability of a conclusion is called *inductive probability*, and it is measured on a scale from 0 to 1. The inductive probability of a deductive argument is maximal, i.e. equal to 1, while the inductive probability of an inductive argument is (typically) less than 1. Although deductive arguments provide the greatest certainty (inductive probability = 1), in practice we must often settle for inductive reasoning, that allows for a range of inductive probabilities and varies widely in reliability. When the inductive probability of an argument is high, the reasoning of the argument is said to be *strong* or *strongly inductive*. On the contrary, it is said to be *weak* or *weakly inductive* when the inductive probability is low. There is no clear distinction line between strong and weak inductive reasoning, since these definitions can be context-dependent.

The inductive probability of an inductive argument depends on the relative strengths of its premises and conclusion. Nolt et al. (1998) claim that the strength of a statement is determined by what the statement says, i.e. the more it says, the stronger it is (regardless of the truth of its content). The truth of a strong statement is proved only under specific circumstances, while the truth of a weak statement can be verified under a wider variety of possible circumstances because its content is less specific.

For these reasons, the strength of a statement is approximately inversely related to its *a priori* probability, i.e. the probability prior or in the absence of evidence: the stronger the statement is, the less inherently likely it is to be true, while the weaker it is, the more probable it is. Inductive arguments can be divided into two types: *i)* the *Humeian* arguments (after the philosopher David Hume who was the first to study them) require the presupposition that the universe or some aspects of

---

[16]Nolt et al. (1998) highlight the fact that in the literature the distinction between inductive and deductive argument is not universal, and slightly different definitions can be found in some works.

it is or is likely to be uniform or law like (e.g. *generalization, analogy* and *causality*); and *ii)* the *statistical* arguments, which do not require this presupposition, and the conclusions are supported by the premises for statistical or mathematical reasons (e.g. *statistical syllogism* and *statistical generalization*).

Criterion 3 claims that any argument which lacks relevance (regardless of its inductive probability) is useless for demonstrating the truth of its conclusion (it is said to commit a *fallacy of relevance*).

One of the most important differences between inductive and deductive arguments concerns their vulnerability to new evidence, meaning that deductive arguments remain deductive when new premises are added, while the inductive probability of inductive arguments can be strengthened or weakened by the introduction of new information. For this reason, the criterion of *total evidence condition* stipulates that if an argument is inductive its premises must contain all known evidence that is relevant to the conclusion. Inductive arguments which fail to meet this requirement are said to commit the *fallacy of suppressed evidence*, that can be committed either intentionally or unintentionally.

3.2 Validation criteria applied to RTE pairs

In the light of the definitions provided in the previous section, we annotated our RTE-5-SAMPLE data set with respect to the argument evaluation criteria described in Section 3.1. In general, in TE we assume the fact that: *i)* if T and H refer to an entity x, the reference is the same (reinforcing the relevance criterion), and *ii)* T (i.e. the premise) is assumed to be true (criterion 1 is always satisfied).

According to the second evaluation criterion (i.e. validity and inductive probability), TE pairs are annotated as *deductive* (Example 5, pair id=414), *inductive* (Example 6, pair id=194), *abductive* (Example 7, pair id=224) or *not valid* (i.e. invalid argument, contradiction) (Example 8, pair id=11). Inductive arguments have also been annotated according to the subcategories of inductive reasoning following Nolt et al. (1998), i.e. *statistical syllogism, statistical generalization* (both statistical arguments), *inductive generalization, simple induction, analogy* and *causality* (i.e. Humeian arguments).

(5)   T: *On February 24th the Swedish Royal Court announced that the Crown Princess Victoria was to be married in 2010 to her boyfriend and former fitness trainer Daniel Westling. Victoria, 31, and Daniel, 35, have been in an relationship for 7 years. Since the wedding is to be held in the summer of 2010 [...]*

H: *Princess Victoria will get married in 2010.*

(6) T: *SEOUL, South Korea - North Korea's state news agency says that leader Kim Jong Il observed the launch of the country's satellite. The Korean Central News Agency says in a reported dated Sunday that Kim visited the General Satellite Control and Command Center and observed the liftoff. North Korea launched a rocket Sunday that flew over Japan. [...]*

H: *Kim Jong-il is the leader of North Korea.*

(7) T: *Secretary of State of the Vatican City, Cardinal Tarcisio said that the Pope apologized for the way his remarks made during a speech at the University of Regensburg in Germany on September 12 2006 were interpreted saying, "the Holy Father is very sorry that some passages of his speech may have appeared offensive to Muslims and were interpreted in a way he hadn't intended them to be. [...]"*

H: *The Pope works with Cardinal Tarcisio.*

(8) T: *A Soyuz capsule carrying a Russian cosmonaut, an American astronaut and U.S. billionaire tourist Charles Simonyi has docked at the international space station. Russian cosmonaut Gennady Padalka manually guided the capsule to a stop ahead of schedule Saturday two days after blasting off from the Baikonur cosmodrome in Kazakhstan. [...]*

H: *Charles Simonyi is a Russian cosmonaut.*

With respect to criterion 3, (i.e. relevance) a pair is annotated as *not relevant* when such criterion is not satisfied, meaning that the text does not contain enough information to infer the truth of the hypothesis (a *fallacy of relevance* is committed), as in Example 9 (pair id=100).

(9) T: *A South Korean official expressed doubts over United Nations Secretary-General Kofi Annan's apparent support for a permanent Security Council seat for Japan, and attention has been drawn to widespread mistrust of Japan by Chinese—although the Chinese government has not commented directly against Japan.*

H: *China won't receive money from Japan.*

With respect to criterion 4 (i.e. total evidence condition), a pair is annotated as *lack of total evidence* when it commits the *fallacy of suppressed evidence*, i.e. some information is omitted in the premises due to lack of knowledge (Example 10, pair id=49). When pairs are annotated as *deductive*, *inductive* and *abductive*, we verify that criteria 3 and 4 are satisfied.

(10)   T: *The earthquake happened at 0332 (0132 GMT), hours af-*
            ter a 4.6-magnitude tremor shook the area but caused no
            reported damage. Thousands of the city's 70,000 residents
            ran into the streets in panic during the 30 second tremor. A
            student dormitory was said to be one of the buildings badly
            damaged. [...] One student told Rai state TV that he man-
            aged to escape the building before the roof collapsed.

       H: *A powerful earthquake strikes central Italy.*

To assess the validity of the proposed annotation, a subset of RTE-5-SAMPLE (i.e. 90 pairs from RTE-5: 30 *entailment*, 30 *contradiction*, 30 *unknown*, Bentivogli et al. (2010)) has been independently annotated by another annotator with linguistic skills. To measure the inter-rater agreement we calculate the Cohen's kappa coefficient (Carletta 1996), that is generally thought to be a more robust measure than simple percent agreement calculation since κ takes into account the agreement occurring by chance. More specifically, Cohen's kappa measures the agreement between two raters who each classifies N items into C mutually exclusive categories. The equation for κ is:

(1) $$\kappa = \frac{\Pr(a) - \Pr(e)}{1 - \Pr(e)},$$

where Pr(a) is the relative observed agreement among raters, and Pr(e) is the hypothetical probability of chance agreement, using the observed data to calculate the probabilities of each observer randomly saying each category. If the raters are in complete agreement then $\kappa = 1$. If there is no agreement among the raters other than what would be expected by chance (as defined by Pr(e)), $\kappa = 0$. For NLP tasks, the inter-annotator agreement is considered as significant when $\kappa > 0.6$. We applied the formula 1 to our data considering the six possible annotation tags listed above (i.e. *deductive, inductive, abductive, not valid, not relevant, lack of total evidence*), and the inter-annotator agreement results in $\kappa = 0.75$. As a rule of thumb, this is a satisfactory agreement. A closer look at the annotations produced by the two raters brings to light that while annotating a pair as *deductive* is straightforward, tagging a pair with respect to criteria 3 and 4 (i.e. as either *not relevant* or *lack of total evidence*) is not trivial, resulting in the highest disagreement between the annotators. Table 1 provides the results of the annotation process, as resulting after a reconciliation phase carried

Table 1: Distribution of inferential phenomena in RTE-5-SAMPLE.

Argument types		RTE pairs			
		TOT	Ent	Contr	Unk
Deductive		86	86	0	0
Inductive	statistical syllogism	31	0	0	0
	statistical generalization		2	0	1
	inductive generalization		5	0	2
	simple induction		11	1	2
	analogy		1	0	3
	causality		2	0	1
Abductive		22	10	0	12
not valid		47	0	47	0
not relevant		21	0	0	21
lack of total evidence		36	0	3	33
TOTAL		**243**	**117**	**51**	**75**

out by the annotators.

The four criteria for argument evaluation that we have applied to TE pairs have highlighted that Textual Entailment involves both deductive, inductive and abductive arguments, the first ones prevailing numerically on the other two (as can be seen in Table 1, 73% of the positive entailment pairs are deductive arguments). In particular, positive *entailment* pairs can be deductive arguments, inductive arguments with a strong inductive probability or abductive arguments. On the contrary, (almost) all *contradiction* pairs are invalid arguments (the premises do not support the conclusion). *Unknown* pairs can be either inductive arguments with a low inductive probability (i.e. 12%), abductive arguments (i.e. 16%), arguments committing the fallacy of relevance (i.e. 28%), or arguments committing the fallacy of suppressed evidence (44%). In general, abductive arguments are very infrequent in RTE data set, and can result both in entailment or in unknown pairs.

As introduced in Section 3.1, relevance is an essential criterion, even if simplifying assumptions have been made by RTE organizers (i.e. the same meaning of entities mentioned in T and H is assumed). The criterion of total evidence relates to the problem of background knowledge, since incomplete arguments require new evidence both to validate or invalidate the conclusion. The motivation underlying the proposal of a generic framework to model language variability has been source of misunderstandings, since the definition of TE does not set a clear distinction line between linguistic knowledge and world knowledge that is involved in such kind of reasoning. In the Recognizing Textual Entailment challenge, strategies to deal with this issue have been outlined, partially guided by reasons of convenience for the task definition. They will be discussed in the next section.

4 Analyzing semantic inferences by linguistic and knowledge phenomena

This section analyses semantic inferences according to the linguistic and background knowledge phenomena present in both the premises and the conclusion of an argument, that are required to support the reasoning process. The goal is twofold: on one side, we aim at providing a fine-grained and data-driven classification of the linguistic and knowledge phenomena underlying the inference process. On the other hand, showing the distribution of such phenomena in real data gives indications on the expected capabilities of Textual Entailment systems.

4.1 Phenomena identification and classification

In line with the TE framework, addressing the inference task at a textual level opens different and new challenges from those encountered in formal deduction systems, where the arguments are already expressed in some formal meaning representation (e.g. first order logic) in the input. To identify implications in natural language sentences, automatic systems are therefore asked to deal with inductive reasoning, lexical semantic knowledge, and variability of linguistic expressions (Bos and Markert 2006). Indeed, language variability manifests itself at different levels of complexity, and involves almost all linguistic phenomena of natural languages, including lexical, syntactic and semantic variation.

Although different levels of granularity can be used to define the inference sub-problems, we decided to group the phenomena using both fine-grained categories and broader categories (Bentivogli et al. 2010). Macro categories are defined referring to widely accepted linguistic categories in the literature (Garoufi 2007), and to the inference types typically addressed in RTE systems: lexical, syntactic, lexical-syntactic, discourse and reasoning. Each macro category includes fine-grained phenomena, listed below. This list is not exhaustive and reflects the phenomena we detected in the sample of RTE-5 pairs we analyzed.[17]

- *lexical:* identity, format,[18] acronymy, demonymy, synonymy, semantic opposition, hyperonymy, geographical knowledge;
- *lexical-syntactic:* nominalization/verbalization, causative, paraphrase, transparent heads;
- *syntactic:* negation, modifier, argument realization, apposition, list, coordination, active/passive alternation;

---

[17] A definition of the listed phenomena, and examples for each category are available here: http://www-sop.inria.fr/members/Elena.Cabrio/resources.html

[18] Normalization of temporal or spatial expressions.

- *discourse:* coreference, apposition, zero anaphora, ellipsis, statements;
- *reasoning:* apposition, modifiers, genitive, relative clause, elliptic expressions, meronymy, metonymy, membership/representativeness, reasoning on quantities, temporal and spatial reasoning, all the general inferences using background knowledge.

Some phenomena (e.g. apposition) can be classified in more than one macro category, according to their specific occurrence in the text. For instance, in Example 11 the apposition is considered as syntactic, while in Example 12 the apposition is classified into the category reasoning.

(11) T: *The government of Niger and Tuareg rebels of the Movement of Niger People for Justice (MNJ) have agreed to end hostilities [...].*

  H: *MNJ is a group of rebels.*

(12) T: *Ernesto, now a tropical storm, made landfall along the coastline of the state of North Carolina [...].*

  H: *Ernesto is the name given to a tropical storm.*

World knowledge is an omni-pervasive phenomenon (as discussed in Section 3.2). It has not been categorized separately.

4.2 Empirical analysis on RTE-5-SAMPLE

In order to assess the feasibility of the proposed approach, we annotated RTE-5-SAMPLE (described in Section 2), with the categories of entailment phenomena described in Section 4.1. The annotation has been carried out by two annotators with linguistic skills and inter-annotator agreement has been calculated on a subset of the annotated pairs[19] (i.e. 90 pairs, randomly extracted from the sample, and balanced with respect to *entailment, contradiction* and *unknown* pairs). A first measure of *complete* agreement was considered, counting when judges agree on all phenomena present in a given original T-H pair. The complete agreement on the full sample amounts to 64.4% (58/90 pairs). In order to account for partial agreement on the set of phenomena present in the T-H-pairs, we used the *Dice coefficient* (Dice 1945).[20] The Dice

---

[19]Same sample used to calculate the inter annotator agreement in Section 3.2.

[20]The *Dice coefficient* is a typical measure used to compare sets in IR and is also used to calculate inter-annotator agreement in a number of tasks where an assessor is allowed to select a set of labels to apply to each observation. In fact, in these cases, and in ours as well, measures such as the widely used K are not good to calculate agreement. This is because K only offers a dichotomous distinction between agreement and disagreement, whereas what is needed is a coefficient that also allows for partial disagreement between judgments.

coefficient is computed as follows:

$$Dice = 2C/(A + B)$$

where C is the number of common phenomena chosen by the annotators, while A and B are respectively the number of phenomena detected by the first and the second annotator. Inter-annotator agreement on the whole sample amounts to 0.78. Overall, we consider this value high enough to demonstrate the stability of the (micro and macro) phenomena categories, thus validating their classification model. Table 2 shows inter-annotator agreement rates grouped according to the type of the original pairs, i.e. *entailment, contradiction* and *unknown* pairs.

The highest percentage of *complete* agreement is obtained on *unknown* pairs. This is due to the fact that since the H in *unknown* pairs typically contains information which is not present in (or inferable from) T, for 19 pairs out of 30 both the annotators agreed that no linguistic phenomena relating T to H could be detected.

TABLE 2: Agreement measures on linguistic phenomena per entailment type.

	Complete	Partial (Dice)
entailment	60%	0.86
contradiction	57%	0.75
unknown	76%	0.68

With respect to the Dice coefficient, the highest inter-annotator agreement can be seen for the *entailment* pairs, whereas the agreement rates are lower for *contradiction* and *unknown* pairs. This is due to the fact that for the *entailment* pairs, all the single phenomena are directly involved in the entailment relation, making their detection straightforward. On the contrary, in the original *contradiction* and *unknown* pairs not only the phenomena directly involved in the contradiction/unknown relation are to be detected, but also those preserving the entailment, which do not play a direct role on the relation under consideration (contradiction/unknown) and are thus more difficult to identify. To clarify this aspect, let's consider Example 13 (pair 125, marked as *contradiction*).

(13)   T: *Mexico's new president, Felipe Calderon, seems to be doing all the right things in cracking down on Mexico's drug traffickers. He's appointed new people to key military [...]*

        H: *Felipe Calderon is the outgoing President of Mexico.*

The phenomena that should be detected in order to correctly judge the pair are: *argument realization, apposition* and *semantic opposition.* While the phenomenon that triggers the contradiction is the semantic opposition, (*new ⇏ ongoing*) the other two phenomena contribute to the inference process, and should be taken into consideration to reach a decision about the entailment label. Contrary to the semantic opposition, in this example both the argument realization (*Mexico's new president ⇒ new president of Mexico*) and the apposition (*Mexico's new president Felipe Calderon ⇒ Felipe Calderon is Mexico's new president*) would support the entailment.

The distribution of the phenomena present in RTE-5-SAMPLE, as resulting after a reconciliation phase carried out by the annotators, is shown in Table 3. The total number of occurrences of each specific phenomenon is given in the Column *TOT*, while in the next columns we report the number of occurrences of each specific phenomenon in *entailment* pairs (Column *E*), and in negative examples, i.e. *contradiction* and *unknown* pairs (Columns *C* and *U*, respectively).

A number of remarks can be made on the data presented in Table 3. Both macro categories and fine-grained phenomena are well represented but show a different absolute frequency: some have a high number of occurrences, whereas some others occur very rarely. To highlight the main features and the points of strengths of our annotation strategy, we compare it with two relevant works in the literature, i.e. Garoufi (2007) and Sammons et al. (2010).

In Garoufi (2007), a scheme for manual annotation of textual entailment data sets (ARTE) is proposed, with the aim of highlighting a wide variety of entailment phenomena in the data. ARTE views the entailment task in relation to three levels, i.e. *Alignment, Context* and *Coreference*, according to which 23 different features for positive entailment annotation are extracted. Each level is explored in depth for the positive entailment cases, while for the negative pairs a more basic and elementary scheme is conceived. The ARTE scheme has been applied to the complete positive entailment RTE-2 test set (400 pairs, i.e. 100 pair of each task), and to a random 25% portion of the negative entailment test set, equally distributed among the four tasks (100 pairs, i.e. 25 pairs of each task). *Reasoning* is the most frequent feature appearing altogether in 65.75% of the annotated pairs: this indicates that a significant portion of the data involves deeper inferences. The combination of the entailment features is analyzed together with the entailment types and their distribution in the data.

More recently, Sammons et al. (2010) carried out an annotation work that is very similar in spirit to the approach proposed in Bentivogli et al.

TABLE 3: Distribution of linguistic phenomena in T-H original pairs (RTE-5-SAMPLE).

Phenomena	RTE Pairs			
	TOT	E	C	U
Lexical:	**60**	**38**	**18**	**4**
Identity/mismatch	8	2	6	0
Format	2	0	2	0
Acronymy	7	6	1	0
Demonymy	4	4	0	0
Synonymy	18	14	3	1
Semantic opposition	4	0	4	0
Hypernymy	13	9	1	3
Geographical knowledge	4	3	1	0
Lexical-syntactic:	**38**	**29**	**5**	**4**
Transparent head	4	2	1	1
Nominalization/verbalization	11	7	3	1
Causative	1	0	1	0
Paraphrase	22	20	0	2
Syntactic:	**133**	**98**	**28**	**7**
Negation	1	0	1	0
Modifier	31	24	3	4
Argument Realization	26	21	4	1
Apposition	55	40	15	0
List	1	1	0	0
Coordination	10	7	1	2
Active/Passive alternation	9	5	4	0
Discourse:	**108**	**72**	**26**	**10**
Coreference	64	43	15	6
Apposition	4	4	0	0
Anaphora Zero	26	17	5	4
Ellipsis	9	5	4	0
Statements	5	3	2	0
Reasoning:	**147**	**91**	**43**	**13**
Apposition	4	3	1	0
Modifier	4	4	0	0
Genitive	2	1	1	0
Relative Clause	2	1	1	0
Elliptic Expression	1	1	0	0
Meronymy	6	3	2	1
Metonymy	4	4	0	0
Membership/representative	2	2	0	0
Quantity	9	3	5	1
Temporal	5	2	1	2
Spatial	1	1	0	0
Common background/ general inferences	107	66	32	9
TOTAL	**486**	**328**	**120**	**38**

(2010), and that we extend in this work. Highlighting the need of resources for solving textual inference problems in the context of RTE, the authors challenge the NLP community to contribute to a joint, long term effort in this direction, making progress both in the analysis of relevant linguistic phenomena and their interaction, and developing resources and approaches that allow more detailed assessment of RTE systems. The authors propose a linguistically-motivated analysis of entailment data, based on a step-wise procedure to resolve entailment decision, by first identifying parts of T that match parts of H, and then identifying connecting structures. Their inherent assumption is that the meanings of T and H could be represented as sets of n-ary relations, where relations could be connected to other relations (i.e. could take other relations as arguments). The authors carried out a feasibility study applying the procedure to 210 examples from RTE-5 (the same that we also included in RTE-5-SAMPLE), marking for each example the entailment phenomena that are required for the inference.[21]

Both our annotation methodology and the ones adopted in these related works attempt to align (or transform) textual snippets of T into H, highlighting all the phenomena that trigger such alignment (or transformation). We all consider levels beyond bags of words, taking syntactic structure into account (depending on the granularity of the phenomena). The direction of the alignment is from H to T, so that H is covered exhaustively while T may contain irrelevant parts that are not aligned. Differently from Sammons et al. (2010), both the annotation we and Garoufi (2007) provide consists in marking the phenomena in the text allowing an easy individuation and their isolation. With respect to the choice of the categories to cluster the phenomena, our work is more similar to Garoufi (2007), since we both rely on more "standard" linguistic categories, even if our classification is more fine-grained (they cluster their categories according to three upper levels, i.e. *Alignment*, *Context* and *Coreference*).

Sammons et al. (2010) propose instead an ontology of phenomena that is iteratively hypothesized and refined while proceeding in the annotation phase, with the goal of identifying: *i)* the roles for background knowledge in terms of domains and general inference steps, *ii)* the linguistic phenomena involved in representing the same information in different ways, or *iii)* detecting the key differences in two similar fragments. The resulting set of labels have less strict definitions with respect to well-established linguistic categories, and are often not very intuitive to understand. More recently, their Entailment Phenomena

---

[21]https://agora.cs.illinois.edu/display/rtedata/Annotation+Resources

Ontology has been revised, and the new proposed annotation adopts more standard labels.[22] Since their categories are not mutually exclusive (and some levels of annotation are transversal with respect to the others, e.g. *domain*), their classification of the phenomena turns out to be more fuzzy, and complex to map on ours for a comparison. Another difference with respect to our approach lies in the fact that we annotate only the differences between T and H (i.e. if two fragments are equal in T and H we do not consider them), while they annotate also the cases of equal Named Entities (NE) in the two sentences.

For instance, given Example 14 (pair 6), we annotate it with one linguistic phenomenon, i.e. *syntax:modifier* (*respected traditional healer* ⇒ *healer*), while Sammons et al. (2010) annotate it as *hyp_has_NE* and *work* (to identify the domain). According to our intuition, in this case their annotation fails to circumscribe the phenomenon that should actually be tackled by a TE system to solve the entailment and provide the correct label to the pair.

(14)   T: *Rain is pelting down on Doña Porcela's treatment room in Puerto Cabezas, the main town on Nicaragua's Northern Caribbean coast. [...] Doña Porcela is a respected traditional healer here and the bottles are filled with her secret medicinal potions. [...]*

   H: *Doña Porcela is a healer.*

Differently from our approach, both Garoufi (2007) and Sammons et al. (2010) add a list of phenomena that are peculiar to negative cases. The former classifies the negative entailment cases into three major categories, according to the most prominent and direct reason why the entailment cannot be established. In particular, they focus on the single phenomenon that they consider as the most obvious "trap" for systems (and humans) judging the entailment. In those negative examples, they do not consider all the other phenomena that are part of the inference process (as we do), omitting some steps that are required while reasoning on such pairs. Also Sammons et al. (2010) define an apriori polarity of the phenomena, adding a set of categories for the negative entailment phenomena, or for missing relations between T and H (e.g. *missing modifier*, or *missing argument*).

In our approach the linguistic categories are neutral (except *semantic opposition*), and we detect the polarity of the phenomena from their occurrences in the data, depending on whether the phenomenon sup-

---

[22]https://wiki.engr.illinois.edu/display/rtedata/Revised+Entailment+Phenomena+Ontology

ports the entailment or the contradiction judgment in a certain pair. For instance, in example 14 the phenomenon *syntax:modifier* supports the entailment relation (*respected traditional healer ⇒ healer*), but if T and H were inverted, it would have triggered a negative judgment (i.e. *healer ⇏ respected traditional healer*).

As in Garoufi (2007), our study confirms that a huge amount of background knowledge and reasoning is required to face the RTE task, given the fact that phenomena belonging to the category *reasoning* are the most frequent. LoBue and Yates (2011) have attempted to characterize them proposing 20 categories of common-sense knowledge that are prevalent in TE. Their categories can be loosely organized into *form-based* categories (e.g. *cause and effect, simultaneous conditions*) and *content-based* categories (e.g. *arithmetic, has parts*). While some of their fine-grained categories can be mapped to ours (e.g. *arithmetic=quantity* and *has parts= meronymy*), we plan to extend our annotation of the *reasoning* phenomena adopting some of the labels they propose, to subcategorize the phenomena we annotated as *reasoning:general_inference*.

5 Analyzing semantic inference by decomposition

Basing ourselves on the classification of the phenomena previously described, in this section we go a step further, and decompose the complexity of TE focusing on single phenomena involved in the inference process. Our goal is to better understand the relations between the entailment judgments supported by each linguistic phenomenon in isolation and the overall judgment of the pair in which it occurs.

5.1 Towards total evidence

The underlying idea is to create *atomic pairs*, i.e. T-H pairs where a phenomenon relevant to the inference task is highlighted and isolated,[23] on the basis of the phenomena which are actually present in the RTE T-H pairs. As claimed before, one of the advantages of testing the proposed methodology on RTE data consists of the fact that the actual distribution of the linguistic phenomena involved in the entailment relation emerges. In Section 4.1 we proposed a classification of the phenomena we detected while analyzing a sample of RTE pairs, and we decided to group them using both fine-grained categories and broader categories. Grouping specific phenomena into macro categories would allow us to create specialized data sets of atomic pairs representing those phenomena, containing enough pairs to train and test

---

[23] In Bentivogli et al. (2010), atomic T-H pairs are referred as *monothematic* pairs. In this work we decided to switch the terminology to be compliant with the theoretical framework we propose.

TE systems. Macro categories are defined referring to widely accepted linguistic categories in the literature (Garoufi 2007), and to the inference types typically addressed in RTE systems: lexical, syntactic, lexical-syntactic, discourse and reasoning.

Moreover, we assume that humans have knowledge about the linguistic phenomena relevant to TE, and that such knowledge can be expressed through *entailment rules* (Szpektor et al. 2007). An entailment rule is either a directional or bidirectional relation between two sides of a pattern, corresponding to text fragments with variables (typically phrases or parse sub-trees, according to the granularity of the phenomenon they formalize). The left-hand side of the pattern (LHS) entails the rights-hand side (RHS) of the same pattern under the same variable instantiation. In addition, a rule may be defined by a set of constraints, representing variable typing (e.g. PoS, NE type) and relations between variables, which have to be satisfied for the rule to be correctly applied. For instance, the entailment rule for demonyms can be expressed as:

Pattern: $XY \Leftarrow / \Rightarrow X(is)$ *from* Y

Constraint: $DEMONYMY(X, Z)$
$TYPE(X) = ADJ\_NATIONALITY; TYPE(Z) = GEO$

meaning that x y entails y *is from* z if there is a *entailment* relation of demonymy between x and y, where x is an adjective expressing a nationality and z is a geographical entity (e.g. *A team of European astronomers* $\Leftarrow / \Rightarrow$ *A team of astronomers from Europe*, pair 205). The entailment rules for a certain phenomenon aim to be as general as possible, but for the cases in which the semantics of the words is essential (e.g. general inference), text snippets extracted from the data are used. Different rules can be needed in order to formalize the variants in which the same phenomenon occurs in the pairs. For example, the following entailment rules both formalize the phenomenon of apposition (syntax):

a) Pattern: $XY \Leftrightarrow YX$
   Constraint: $APPOSITION(Y, X)$

b) Pattern: $X, Y \Leftrightarrow Y$ *is* X
   Constraint: $APPOSITION(Y, X)$

Given such basic concepts, the procedure for the creation of atomic pairs we propose consists of a number of steps carried out manually. We start from a T-H pair taken from the RTE data sets and we decompose T-H in a number of atomic pairs T-H_i, where T is the original Text and H_i are Hypotheses created for each linguistic phenomenon relevant for judging the entailment relation in T-H. The procedure is schematized in the following steps:

1. individuate the linguistic phenomena which contribute to the entailment in T-H

2. For each phenomenon i:
   (a) individuate a general entailment rule r_i for the phenomenon i, and instantiate the rule using the portion of T which expresses i as the LHS of the rule, and information from H on i as the RHS of the rule.
   (b) substitute the portion of T that matches the LHS of r_i with the RHS of r_i.
   (c) consider the result of the previous step as H_i, and compose the atomic pair $T - H_i$. Mark the pair with phenomenon i.

3. Assign an entailment judgment to each atomic pair.

After applying this procedure to the original pairs, all the atomic $T - H_i$ pairs relative to the same phenomenon i should be grouped together in a data set specialized for phenomenon i.

In the following, some examples of the application of the procedure to RTE pairs, namely entailment, contradiction and unknowns pairs are illustrated.

Decomposing entailment pairs.

Table 4 shows the decomposition of an original entailment pair (pair 199) into atomic pairs. In step 1 of the method, the phenomena (i.e. modifier, coreference, transparent head and general inference) are considered relevant to the entailment between T and H. In the following, we apply the procedure step by step to the phenomenon we define as modifier. In step 2a the general rule:

$$
\left[
\begin{array}{ll}
\text{Entailment rule:} & \textbf{modifier} \\
\text{Pattern:} & X\ Y \Leftrightarrow Y \\
\text{Constraint:} & MODIFIER(X,Y) \\
\text{Probability:} & 1
\end{array}
\right.
$$

is instantiated (*The tiny Swiss canton* $\Rightarrow$ *The Swiss canton*), while in step 2b the substitution in T is carried out (*The Swiss canton of Appenzell Innerrhoden has voted to prohibit [. . .]*).

In step 2c the atomic pair $T - H_1$ is composed and marked as *modifier* (macro-category *syntactic*). Finally, in step 3, this pair is judged as *entailment*. Step 2 (a, b, c) is then repeated for all the phenomena individuated in that pair in step 1.

The same token can be an instance of several different phenomena. In such cases, in order to create an atomic H for each phenomenon, the method is applied recursively. It means that after applying it once to the first phenomenon of the chain (thereby creating the pair $T - H_i$), it is applied again to H_i (that becomes T') to solve the second phenomenon of the chain (creating the pair $T' - H_j$).

Decomposing contradiction pairs.

Table 5 shows the decomposition of an original contradiction pair (pair 125) into atomic pairs. In step 1 both the phenomena that preserve the entailment and the phenomena that break the entailment rules causing a contradiction in the pair should be detected. In the example reported in Table 5, the phenomena that should be recognized in order to correctly judge the pair are: argument realization, apposition and semantic opposition. While the atomic pairs created basing on the first two phenomena preserve the entailment, the semantic opposition generates a contradiction. In the following, we apply the procedure step by step to the phenomenon of semantic opposition.

In step 2a the general rule:

$$
\left[
\begin{array}{ll}
\text{Contradiction rule:} & \textbf{semantic\_opposition} \\
\text{Pattern:} & X \not\Leftrightarrow Y \\
\text{Constraint:} & SEMANTIC\_OPPOSITION(Y,X) \\
\text{Probability:} & 1
\end{array}
\right.
$$

is instantiated (*new* $\not\Leftrightarrow$ *outgoing*), and in step 2b the substitution in T is carried out (*Mexico's outgoing president, Felipe Calderon [...]*). In step 2c a negative atomic pair $T - H_1$ is composed and marked as semantic opposition (macro-category *lexical*), and the pair is judged as *contradiction*. We noticed that negative atomic T-H pairs (i.e. both contradiction and unknown) may originate either from the application of contradiction rules (e.g. semantic opposition or negation, as in pair $T - H_1$, in Table 5) or as a wrong instantiation of a positive entailment rule. For instance, the positive rule for active/passive alternation:

$$
\left[
\begin{array}{ll}
\text{Entailment rule:} & \textbf{active/passive\_alternation} \\
\text{Pattern:} & X\ Y\ Z \Leftrightarrow Z\ W\ X \\
\text{Constraint:} & SAME\_STEM(X,W) \\
 & TYPE(X)=V\_ACT;\ TYPE(W)=V\_PASS \\
\text{Probability:} & 1
\end{array}
\right.
$$

when wrongly instantiated, as in *Russell Dunham killed nine German soldiers* $\not\Leftrightarrow$ *Russell Dunham was killed by nine German soldiers* ($x\ y\ z$ $\Leftrightarrow z\ w\ x$), generates a negative atomic pair.

Decomposing unknown pairs.

Table 6 shows the decomposition of an original unknown pair (pair 82) into atomic pairs. As in the previous cases, in step 1 all the relevant phenomena are detected: coreference, general inference, and modifier.

TABLE 4: Decomposition method applied to an *entailment* pair.

	Text (pair 199 RTE-5 test set)	Rule	Phenomena	J.
T	**The tiny Swiss canton of Appenzell Innerrhoden has voted prohibit the phenomenon of naked hiking.** [...]			
H	The Swiss canton of Appenzell has prohibited naked hiking.		**synt:modifier, disc:coref, lsynt:tr_head, reas:gen_infer**	E
H_1	**The Swiss canton** of Appenzell Innerrhoden has voted to prohibit the phenomenon of naked hiking.	**x y ⇒ y modif(x,y)**	**synt:modifier**	E
H_2	The tiny Swiss canton of **Appenzell** has voted to prohibit the phenomenon of naked hiking.	**x⇔y coref(x,y)**	**disc:coref**	E
H_3	The tiny Swiss canton of Appenzell Innerrhoden has **voted to prohibit naked.** **voted to prohibit hiking.**	**x of y ⇒y tr_head(x,y)**	**lsynt:tr_head**	E
H_4	The tiny Swiss canton of Appenzell Innerrhoden **prohibited** the phenomenon of naked hiking.	**vote to prohibit (+ will now be fined) ⇒ prohibit**	**reas:gen_infer**	E

TABLE 5: Decomposition method applied to a *contradiction* pair.

	Text (pair 408 RTE-5 test set)	Rule	Phenomena	J.
T	**Mexico's new president, Felipe Calderon,** seems to be doing all the right things in cracking down on Mexico's drug traffickers. [...]			C
H	Felipe Calderon is the outgoing President of Mexico.		**lex:sem_opp synt:arg_real synt:apposit**	
H_1	Mexico's **outgoing** president, Felipe Calderon, seems to be doing all the right things in cracking down on Mexico's drug traffickers. [...]	$x \not\Leftrightarrow y$	**sem_opp(x,y)**	C
H_2	The new president **of Mexico,** Felipe Calderon, seems to be doing all the right things in cracking down on Mexico's drug traffickers. [...]	**x's y⇒y of x**	**synt:arg_real**	E
H_3	**Felipe Calderon is** Mexico's **new president.**	**x,y ⇒ y is x apposit(y,x)**	**synt:apposit**	E

TABLE 6: Decomposition method applied to an *unknown* pair.

	Text (pair 82 RTE-5 test set)		Rule	Phenomena	J.
T		Currently, there is no specific treatment available against **dengue fever, which is the most widespread tropical disease after malaria.** [...] "Controlling **the mosquitos that transmit dengue** is necessary [...]"			
H		Malaria is the most widespread disease transmitted by mosquitos.		disc:coref, r:gen_infer, synt:modif,	U
	H_1 $\rightarrow T'$	**Dengue fever** is the most widespread tropical disease after malaria.	x⇔y coref(x,y)	disc:coref	E
	H_2	**Malaria is the most widespread** tropical disease.	x is after y⇒ y is the first	r:gen_infer	E
	H_3	Dengue fever is the most widespread disease **transmitted by mosquitos** after malaria.	x =? ⇒ x y (restr. relat. clause)	synt:modif	U

While the first two preserve the entailment relation, the atomic pair resulting from the third phenomenon is judged as unknown. As discussed in Section 3.1, the last atomic pair is an argument with a very low inductive probability (i.e. the fact that a certain disease is the most widespread among the ones transmitted by a certain cause, does not allow us to infer that it is the most widespread ever). If we try to apply the procedure step by step to the phenomenon of modifier, in step 2a the generic rule:

$$\left[\begin{array}{ll} \text{Entailment rule:} & \textbf{modifier} \\ \text{Pattern:} & X \Rightarrow X\ Y \\ \text{Constraint:} & MODIFIER(Y,X) \\ \text{Probability:} & 0.1 \end{array} \right.$$

is instantiated (*disease* ⇒ *disease transmitted by mosquitoes*) (this rule has a very low probability), and in step 2b the substitution in T is carried out. In step 2c the atomic pair T'-H_3 is composed and marked as *modifier* (restrictive relative clause, macro-category *lexical*), and the pair is judged as *unknown*. However, there is no reason to collect such rules for computational purposes, since it would mean to collect almost all the relations among all the words and the expressions of a language. These rules can be obtained in a complementary way with respect to high-probability rules, i.e. if a certain rule is not present among the highly probable ones, it means that it has a low probability, and therefore it is not strong enough to support the related inferential step.

5.2 Applying pair decomposition to RTE-5-SAMPLE

To assess the feasibility of the decomposition strategy, we applied the method described in Section 5.1 to RTE-5-SAMPLE. Table 7 reports both the distribution of the phenomena present in the original RTE-5 pairs (column *RTE pairs*, equal to Table 3), together with their distribution according to the entailment judgment they support (i.e. independently of the overall judgment of the pair, column *Atomic pairs*). Again, the total number of occurrences of each specific phenomenon is given (Column *TOT*), corresponding to the number of atomic pairs created for that phenomenon. The number of atomic pairs is then divided into positive examples, i.e. *entailment* atomic pairs (Column *E*), and negative examples, i.e. *contradiction* and *unknown* atomic pairs (Columns *C* and *U*, respectively).

Comparing the two distributions of the phenomena among E/C/U pairs, we can see that some phenomena appear more frequently or only among the positive examples (e.g. *apposition* or *coreference*) and others among the negative ones (e.g. *quantitative reasoning*). In general, the total number of positive examples is much higher than that of the negative ones and, for some macro-categories no negative examples are found. As can be seen when comparing the two main columns of Table 7, applying our decomposition strategy brings to light the fact that, for instance, all the *lexical-syntactic* phenomena occurring in the RTE pairs we analyzed support the entailment judgment, even if they are present in contradiction or unknown pairs (it means that in those pairs other phenomena trigger the negative judgment). Also from a qualitative standpoint, we notice that compared to the positive pairs the variability of phenomena in negative examples is reduced.

The differences in the distributions of the phenomena when occurring in RTE pairs and with respect to the judgment they independently support, provide also an explanation about the non optimal results obtained by the ablation tests, introduced as a requirement for systems participating in RTE-5 and RTE-6 main tasks. Such ablation tests consist in removing one resource at a time from a TE system, and re-running the system on the test set with the other modules, except the one tested. The results obtained from ablation tests turned out not to be straightforward in determining the actual impact of the resources, since the different uses made by the systems of the same resources, make it difficult to compare the results. Moreover, basing on our observations we can now demonstrate that evaluating for instance the impact of WordNet (Fellbaum 1998) on original RTE pairs would be misleading, since lexical phenomena (as *synonymy*) can be found in

TABLE 7: Distribution of linguistic phenomena in T-H original and atomic pairs (RTE-5-SAMPLE).

Phenomena	TOT	RTE Pairs			Atomic Pairs		
		E	C	U	E	C	U
Lexical:	**60**	**38**	**18**	**4**	**46**	**11**	**3**
Identity/mismatch	8	2	6	0	2	6	0
Format	2	0	2	0	2	0	0
Acronymy	7	6	1	0	7	0	0
Demonymy	4	4	0	0	4	0	0
Synonymy	18	14	3	1	18	0	0
Semantic opposition	4	0	4	0	0	4	0
Hypernymy	13	9	1	3	10	0	3
Geographical knowledge	4	3	1	0	3	1	0
Lexical-syntactic:	**38**	**29**	**5**	**4**	**38**	**0**	**0**
Transparent head	4	2	1	1	4	0	0
Nominalization/verbaliz.	11	7	3	1	11	0	0
Causative	1	0	1	0	1	0	0
Paraphrase	22	20	0	2	22	0	0
Syntactic:	**133**	**98**	**28**	**7**	**116**	**13**	**4**
Negation	1	0	1	0	0	1	0
Modifier	31	24	3	4	26	2	3
Argument Realization	26	21	4	1	26	0	0
Apposition	55	40	15	0	47	8	0
List	1	1	0	0	1	0	0
Coordination	10	7	1	2	9	0	1
Active/Passive alternation	9	5	4	0	7	2	0
Discourse:	**108**	**72**	**26**	**10**	**107**	**1**	**0**
Coreference	64	43	15	6	63	1	0
Apposition	4	4	0	0	4	0	0
Anaphora Zero	26	17	5	4	26	0	0
Ellipsis	9	5	4	0	9	0	0
Statements	5	3	2	0	5	0	0
Reasoning:	**147**	**91**	**43**	**13**	**112**	**29**	**6**
Apposition	4	3	1	0	3	1	0
Modifier	4	4	0	0	4	0	0
Genitive	2	1	1	0	2	0	0
Relative Clause	2	1	1	0	2	0	0
Elliptic Expression	1	1	0	0	1	0	0
Meronymy	6	3	2	1	5	1	0
Metonymy	4	4	0	0	4	0	0
Membership/represent.	2	2	0	0	2	0	0
Quantity	9	3	5	1	3	5	1
Temporal	5	2	1	2	4	0	1
Spatial	1	1	0	0	1	0	0
Common background/ general inferences	107	66	32	9	81	22	4
TOTAL (# atomic pairs)	**486**	**328**	**120**	**38**	**419**	**54**	**13**

both positive and negative pairs, but the phenomenon in itself always supports entailment (even when it is present in a contradiction pair).

To provide a stronger basis for our assumptions, we measured the correlation (linear dependence) between the two observed phenomena distribution. We applied the Pearson product-moment correlation coefficient[24] between the distribution of phenomena on original RTE pairs and in relation to the supported judgment. The Pearson correlation is +1 in the case of a perfect positive (increasing) linear relationship (correlation), -1 in the case of a perfect decreasing (negative) linear relationship (anticorrelation), and some value between -1 and 1 in all other cases, indicating the degree of linear dependence between the variables. As it approaches zero there is less of a relationship (i.e. it is closer to uncorrelated). In our framework, obtaining a low correlation between the two distributions of a certain category of phenomena has to be interpreted as a proof of concept of our decomposition approach, since it would mean that training a TE system only on original pairs is misleading (i.e. the occurrence of a certain phenomenon is not always an indication of the judgment it bears). On the contrary, a high correlation between the two distributions would mean that the mere occurrence of the phenomena in the original pairs is a sufficient condition to learn their judgment (i.e. atomic pairs are not necessary, TE systems would learn the same model when trained on both distributions).

Table 8 shows the correlation indexes we obtained per each macro-category of phenomena and per entailment judgment. The significance (P-value) for the Pearson's correlation is also reported.

TABLE 8: Correlations per macro-categories of phenomena.

Phenomena	Ent		Contr		Unk	
	corr.	$p<0.05$	corr.	$p<0.05$	corr.	$p<0.05$
Lexical	0.62	x	0.66	x	0.97	
Lex-synt	0	-	0	-	0	-
Syntactic	0.96	x	0.97	x	0.47	
Discourse	0.07		-0.06		0	-
Reasoning	0.62	x	0.55	x	0.34	

With the exception of the distributions of the syntactic phenomena that correlate well with the entailment and the contradiction judgment, the correlation values are pretty low, meaning that the linear

---

[24]http://en.wikipedia.org/wiki/Pearson_product-moment_correlation_coefficient. We calculated it on the normalized occurrences of phenomena, and using the open source software Wessa.net (Wessa 2012)

dependence between the two distributions is not very strong. In several cases, it approaches 0 (e.g. for *lexical-syntactic* or for *discourse* phenomena), meaning that training a TE system on the occurrences of the linguistic phenomena in original RTE pairs only is not always reliable. In most of the cases, such correlation is statistically significant (the non-significance for unknown pairs is probably due to the low number of observations). Even for categories of phenomena with a strong correlation between the distributions, for some finer-grained phenomena belonging to those categories the difference between their occurrences in positive and negative pairs is particularly strong. For instance, the correlation index for syntactic phenomena approaches 1, but in Table 7 we can see that for *active passive alternation* the distribution in the two tables is very different, and a TE system trained on the first table would learn that 50% of the times this phenomenon triggers a contradiction, while it is not the case (it supports contradiction only in 20% of the pairs in which it occurs).

Cases of low correlation (e.g. *lexical-syntactic* phenomena) should not be interpreted, however, as absolute evidence that such phenomena are not useful at all as discriminators for textual entailment judgments. Rather, such correlations are always relative to the complexity of the pair: intuitively, the more the phenomena connecting T and H in the pair, the less relevant is a single low-correlated phenomenon. As a consequence, the results presented in Table 8, hold for a data set whose complexity is similar to the RTE data we have analyzed, and could change in case of pairs with a different complexity.

With respect to the approaches proposed by Garoufi (2007) and Sammons et al. (2010), our methodology goes a step further suggesting to decompose the pairs to highlight and isolate the linguistic and knowledge phenomena relevant to semantic inference. Carrying out such decomposition allows for a level of analysis not possible following current methodologies. In particular, the approach of Garoufi (2007) allows for the identification of the phenomena in the text, but, on contradiction and unknown pairs, all the phenomena not triggering these judgments are ignored, so it is not possible to have a clear view of their distributions in the pairs. Sammons et al. (2010) assign an apriori polarity to the phenomena to compensate for the need for a clear distinction between the occurrences of the phenomena in positive or in negative pairs. Instead our approach is grounded in a clearer and standard classification of the phenomena, where their polarity emerges from their occurrences in the data and is not apriori defined. Moreover, beside the annotation of the phenomena on real data, the decomposition method results in the creation of atomic pairs, allowing evaluations of TE sys-

Table 9: Distribution of the atomic pairs wrt original E/C/U pairs.

RTE-5 pairs	Generated atomic pairs			
	E	C	U	Total
E (117)	328	–	–	328/117 (2.8)
C (51)	66	54	–	120/51 (2.35)
U (75)	25	–	13	38/21 (1.8)

tems on specific phenomena both when isolated and when interacting with the others.

As introduced before, due to the natural distribution of phenomena in RTE data, we found that applying the decomposition methodology we generate a higher number of atomic positive pairs (76.7%) than negative ones (23.3%, divided into 17% *contradiction* and 6.3% *unknown*, as shown in Table 7). We analyzed the three subsets composing the RTE-5 sample separately, (i.e. 107 *entailment* pairs, 37 *contradiction* pairs, and 66 *unknown*) in order to verify the productivity of each subset with respect to the atomic pairs created from them. Table 9 shows the absolute distribution of the atomic pairs among the three RTE-5 classes.

When the methodology is applied to RTE-5 *entailment* examples, averagely 2.8 all positive atomic pairs are derived from the original pairs. When the methodology is applied to RTE-5 *contradiction* examples, we create an average of 2.35 atomic pairs, among which 1.29 are entailment pairs and 1.05 are contradiction pairs. This means that the methodology is productive for both positive and negative examples.

As introduced before, in 54 out of 75 *unknown* examples no atomic pairs can be created, due to the lack of specific phenomena relating T and H (typically the H contains information which is neither present in T nor inferable from it). For the 11 pairs that have been decomposed into atomic pairs, we created an average of 1.8 atomic pairs, among which 1.19 are entailment and 0.61 are unknown pairs. This analysis shows that the only source of negative atomic pairs are the *contradiction* pairs, which actually correspond to 20% of RTE-5 data set.

Overall, the study showed that the decomposition methodology we propose can be applied on RTE-5 data. As for the quality of the atomic pairs, the high inter-annotator agreement rate obtained (reported in Section 4.2) shows that the methodology is stable enough to be applied on a large scale.

6 Related work

This section presents a number of studies that analyze RTE data sets from the point of view of linguistic phenomena.

An attempt to isolate the set of T-H pairs whose categorization can be accurately predicted based solely on syntactic cues has been carried out in Vanderwende et al. (2005). The aim of this work is to understand what proportion of the entailment pairs in the RTE-1 test set could be solved using a robust parser. Two human annotators evaluated each T-H pair of the test set, deciding whether the entailment was: *true by syntax*; *false by syntax*; *not syntax*; *can't decide*. Additionally, annotators were allowed to indicate whether the recourse to information in a general purpose thesaurus entry would allow a pair to be judged true or false. Their results show that 37% of the test items can be handled by syntax, broadly defined (including phenomena such as argument assignment, intra-sentential pronoun anaphora resolution); 49% of the test items can be handled by syntax plus a general purpose thesaurus. Even if we carried out our analysis on RTE-5 data, the results we reported in Table 3 are in line with those proposed in Vanderwende et al. (2005). According to their annotators, it is easier to decide when syntax can be expected to return *true*, and it is uncertain when to assign *false*. Basing on their own observations, their system (Vanderwende et al. 2006) predicts entailment using syntactic features and a general purpose thesaurus, in addition to an overall alignment score. The syntactic heuristics used to recognize false entailment rely on the correct alignment of words and multiwords units between T and H logical forms.

Bar-Haim et al. (2005) define two intermediate models of TE, which correspond to lexical and lexical-syntactic levels of representation. Their lexical level captures knowledge about lexical-semantic and morphological relations, as well as lexical world knowledge. The lexical-syntactic level additionally captures syntactic relationships and transformations, lexical-syntactic inference patterns (rules) and co-reference. They manually annotated a sample from the RTE-1 data set according to each model, compared the outcomes for the two models as a whole as well as for their individual components, and explored how well they approximate the notion of entailment. It was shown that the lexical-syntactic model outperforms the lexical one, mainly because of a much lower rate of false-positives, but both models fail to achieve high recall. The analysis also showed that lexical-syntactic inference patterns stand out as a dominant contributor to the entailment task.

Clark et al. (2007) agree that only a few entailments can be recognized using simple syntactic matching, and that the majority rely on a significant amount of "common human understanding" of lexical and world knowledge. We also agree on the same conclusions (see Table 3). The authors present an analysis of 100 (25%) of the RTE-3 positive entailment pairs, to identify where and what kind of world knowledge are needed to fully identify and justify entailment. They discuss several existing resources and their capacity for supplying that knowledge. After showing the frequency of the different entailment phenomena from the sample they analyzed, they state that very few entailments depend purely on syntactic manipulation and a simple lexical knowledge (synonyms, hypernyms), and that the vast majority of entailments require significant world knowledge.

Dagan et al. (2008) present a framework for semantic inference at the lexical-syntactic level. The authors show that the inference module can be also exploited to improve unsupervised acquisition of entailment rules through canonization (i.e. the transformation of lexical-syntactic template variations that occur in a text into their canonical form - this form is chosen to be the active verb form with direct modifier). The canonization rule collection is composed by two kinds of rules: *i)* syntactic-based rules (e.g. passive/active forms, removal of conjunctions, removal of appositions), *ii)* nominalization rules, trying to capture the relations between verbs and their nominalizations. The authors propose to solve the learning problems using this entailment module at learning time as well.

A definition of contradiction for TE task is provided by Marneffe et al. (2008), together with a collection of contradiction corpora. Detecting contradiction appears to be a harder task than detecting entailment, since it requires deeper inferences, assessing event coreference and model building. Contradiction is said to occur when two sentences are extremely unlikely to be true simultaneously; furthermore, they must involve the same event. The first empirical results for contradiction detection are presented in Harabagiu et al. (2006) (they focused only on contradictions involving negation and formed by paraphrases).

Kirk (2009) describes his work of building an inference corpus for spatial inference about motion, while Wang and Zhang (2008) focus on recognizing TE involving temporal expressions. Akhmatova and Dras (2009) experiment current approaches on hypernymy acquisition to improve entailment classification.

Basing on the intuition that frame-semantic information is a useful resource for modeling TE, Burchardt et al. (2009) provide a manual frame-semantic annotation for the test set used in RTE-2 (i.e. the FATE corpus) and discuss experiments conducted on this basis.

Bentivogli et al. (2009a) focus on some problematic issues related to resolving coreferences to entities, space, time and events at the corpus level, as emerged during the annotation of the data set for the RTE Search Pilot. Again at the discourse level, Mirkin et al. (2010b), and Mirkin et al. (2010a) analyze various discourse references in entailment inference (manual analysis on RTE-5 data set) and show that while the majority of them are nominal coreference relations, another substantial part is made up by verbal terms and bridging relations.

7 Conclusion

In this paper we have presented an investigation aiming at highlighting the relations between the logical dimension of textual semantic inferences, i.e. the capacity of the inference to prove the conclusion from its premises, and their linguistic dimension, i.e. the linguistic devices that are used to accomplish the goal of the inference. We think that the relation between the two dimensions has not received enough attention in the current stream of research on textual inferences in Computational Linguistics, and we believe that more empirical data and analysis are actually crucial to the progress of the many supervised systems that have been proposed in recent years in the area.

We have proposed a decomposition approach, where single linguistic phenomena are isolated in what we have called *atomic inference pairs*. It is at this level of granularity that the actual correlation between the linguistic and the logical dimensions of semantic inferences emerges and can be empirically observed. For each of the two dimensions (i.e. logical and linguistic) we have proposed a number of features, mostly derived from previous literature, which help in the analysis. In order to support our thesis we have conducted an empirical analysis over a manually annotated data set of Textual Entailment pairs, derived from the recent RTE-5 evaluation campaign (the data we annotated are available online[25]). The results of the investigation show that the correlation between linguistic phenomena and logical judgments (i.e. entailment, contradiction, unknown) is quite poor, meaning that most of the linguistic phenomena we have observed and that occur in T-H pairs do not have an a priori polarity with respect to the logical relation holding in that pair. A relevant consequence of this fact is that the polarity of most of the phenomena is not predictable from the logical judgments, with an evident impact on the possibility to learn it from the available annotated RTE data sets. On the base of these findings we suggest that future developments should exploit the decomposition

---

[25]http://www-sop.inria.fr/members/Elena.Cabrio/resources.html

approach on specialized data sets, composed of atomic pairs.

In several respects the work we have presented in this paper is incomplete. It opens the way to further research in this direction. Particularly, we think that much more investigation and empirical experiments would be necessary in order to better determine the relations between linguistic phenomena and logical judgments in semantic inferences. Our hope is that these future data oriented studies will support computational approaches by e.g. driving search heuristics in transformation-based approaches, or optimizing feature selection in machine learning systems.

Acknowledgments

The work of the second author has been partially supported by the EX-CITEMENT project (Exploring Customer Interactions through Textual Entailment), under the EU grant FP7 ICT-287923. The authors wish to thank Dr. Sara Tonelli for her help and availability in the annotation phase.

References

Akhmatova, E. and M. Dras. 2009. Using hypernymy acquisition to tackle (part of) textual entailment. In *Proceedings of the 2009 Workshop on Applied Textual Inference (TextInfer 2009)*. Singapore.

Bar-Haim, R., I. Szpektor, and O. Glickman. 2005. Definition and analysis of intermediate entailment levels. In *Proceedings of the ACL 2005 Workshop on Empirical Modeling of Semantic Equivalence and Entailment*. Ann Arbor, MI.

Bentivogli, L., E. Cabrio, I. Dagan, D. Giampiccolo, M. Lo Leggio, and B. Magnini. 2010. Building textual entailment specialized data sets: a methodology for isolating linguistic phenomena relevant to inference. In *Proceedings of the 7th International Conference on Language Resources and Evaluation (LREC)*. Valletta, Malta.

Bentivogli, L., I. Dagan, H.T. Dang, D. Giampiccolo, M. Lo Leggio, and B. Magnini. 2009a. Considering discourse references in textual entailment annotation. In *Proceedings of the 5th International Conference on Generative Approaches to the Lexicon (GL 2009)*. Pisa, Italy.

Bentivogli, L., B. Magnini, I. Dagan, H.T. Dang, and D. Giampiccolo. 2009b. The fifth pascal recognizing textual entailment challenge. In *Proceedings of the TAC 2009 Workshop on Textual Entailment*. Gaithersburg, Maryland.

Bos, J. and K. Markert. 2006. When logical inference helps determining textual entailment (and when it doesn't). In *Proceedings of the second PASCAL Challenge Workshop on Recognizing Textual Entailment*. Venice, Italy.

Burchardt, A., M. Pennacchiotti, S. Thater, and M. Pinkal. 2009. Measures of the amount of ecologic association between species. *Natural Language Engineering (JNLE)* 15(Special Issue 04).

Carletta, Jean. 1996. Assessing agreement on classification tasks: the kappa statistic. *Comput. Linguist.* 22(2):249–254.

Clark, P., P. Harrison, J. Thompson, W. Murray, J. Hobbs, and C. Fellbaum. 2007. On the role of lexical and world knowledge in rte3. In *Proceedings of the ACL-07 Workshop on Textual Entailment and Paraphrasing*. Prague, Czech Republic.

Cooper, R., D. Crouch, J. van Eijck, C. Fox, J. van Genabith, J. Jaspars, H. Kamp, D. Milward, M. Pinkal, M. Poesio, and S. Pulman. 1996. Using the framework. In *Technical Report LRE 62-051 D-16, The FraCaS Consortium*. Prague, Czech Republic.

Dagan, I., R. Bar-Haim, I. Szpektor, I. Greental, and E. Shnarch. 2008. Natural language as the basis for meaning representation and inference. In *Proceedings of the 9th International Conference on Intelligent Text Processing and Computational Linguistics (CICLing08)*. Haifa, Israel.

Dagan, I., B. Dolan, B. Magnini, and D. Roth. 2009. Recognizing textual entailment: Rational, evaluation and approaches. *Natural Language Engineering (JNLE)* 15(Special Issue 04):i–xvii.

Dagan, I., O. Glickman, and B. Magnini. 2005. The pascal recognizing textual entailment challenge. In *Proceedings of the First PASCAL Challenges Workshop on RTE*. Southampton, U.K.

Dagan, I., O. Glickman, and B. Magnini. 2006. The pascal recognizing textual entailment challenge. In *MLCW 2005, LNAI Volume 3944*. Springer-Verlag.

Dice, L. R. 1945. Measures of the amount of ecologic association between species. *Ecology* 26(3):297–302.

Fellbaum, C. 1998. Wordnet: An electronic lexical database. In *Language, Speech and Communication*. MIT Press.

Garoufi, K. 2007. Towards a better understanding of applied textual entailment. In *Master Thesis*. Saarland University. Saarbrücken, Germany.

Harabagiu, S., A. Hickl, and F. Lacatusu. 2006. Negation, contrast, and contradiction in text processing. In *Proceedings of the Twenty-First National Conference on Artificial Intellingence (AAAI-06)*. Boston, Massachusetts.

Hobbs, J. R. 2008. Abduction in natural language understanding. In L. R. Horn and G. Ward, eds., *The Handbook of Pragmatics*. Blackwell Publishing Ltd, Oxford.

Kirk, R. 2009. Building an annotated textual inference corpus for motion and space. In *Proceedings of the 2009 Workshop on Applied Textual Inference (TextInfer 2009)*. Singapore.

LoBue, P. and A. Yates. 2011. Types of common-sense knowledge needed for recognizing textual entailment. In *Proceedings of the 49th annual meeting of the Association for Computational Linguistics*, pages 329–334. Portland, Oregon, USA.

Manning, C.D. 2006. Local textual inference: it's hard to circumscribe, but you know it when you see it - and nlp needs it. In *Proceedings of the Eighth International Conference on Computational Semantics (IWCS-8)*. Unpublished manuscript.

Marneffe, M.C. De, A.N. Rafferty, and C.D. Manning. 2008. Finding contradictions in text. In *Proceedings of the 46th Annual Meeting of the Association of Computational Linguistics (ACL-08)*. Columbus, OH.

Mirkin, S., J. Berant, I. Dagan, and Eyal Shnarch. 2010a. Recognising entailment within discourse. In *Proceedings of the 23rd International Conference on Computational Linguistics (COLING 2010)*. Beijing, China.

Mirkin, S., I. Dagan, and Sebastian Padò. 2010b. Assessing the role of discourse references in entailment inference. In *Proceedings of the 48th Annual Meeting of the Association for Computational Linguistics (ACL-10)*. Uppsala, Sweden.

Nenkova, A., R. Passonneau, and K. McKeown. 2007. The pyramid method: incorporating human content selection variation in summarization evaluation. *ACM Transactions on Computational Logic* V, No. N, February:1–23.

Nolt, J., D. Rohatyn, and A. VArzi. 1998. *Schaum's outline of Theory and Problems of Logic 2nd ed.*. McGraw-Hill.

Peñas, Anselmo, Álvaro Rodrigo, Valentín Sama, and Felisa Verdejo. 2008. Testing the reasoning for question answering validation. *J. Log. and Comput.* 18(3):459–474.

Sammons, M., V.G.V Vydiswaran, and D. Roth. 2010. Ask not what textual entailment can do for you... In *Proceedings of the 48th Annual Meeting of the Association for Computational Linguistics (ACL-10)*. Uppsala, Sweden.

Szpektor, I., E. Shnarch, and I Dagan I. 2007. Instance-based evaluation of entailment rule acquisition. In *Proceedings of the 45th Annual Meeting of the Association of Computational Linguistics (ACL-07)*. Prague, Czech Republic.

Vanderwende, L., D. Coughlin, and B. Dolan. 2005. What syntax can contribute in entailment task. In *Proceedings of the First PASCAL Challenges Workshop on RTE*. Southampton, U.K.

Vanderwende, L., A. Menezes, and R. Snow. 2006. Microsoft research at rte-2: Syntactic contributions in the entailment task: an implementation. In *Proceedings of the Second PASCAL Challenges Workshop on Recognising Textual Entailment*. Venice, Italy.

Wang, R. and Y. Zhang. 2008. Recognizing textual entailment with temporal expressions in natural language texts. In *Proceedings of the IEEE International Workshop on Semantic Computing and Applications (IWSCA-2008)*. Incheon, South Korea.

Wessa, P. 2012. Free statistics software. In *Office for Research Development and Education, version 1.1.23-r7*.

Zaenen, A., L. Karttunen, and R. Crouch. 2005. Local textual inference: can it be defined or circumscribed? In *Proceedings of the Workshop on the Empirical Modeling of Semantic Equivalence and Entailment*. Ann Arbor, MI.

Towards a Semantic Model for Textual Entailment Annotation

Assaf Toledo,[1] Stavroula Alexandropoulou,[1] Sophie Chesney,[2] Sophia Katrenko,[3] Heidi Klockmann,[1] Pepijn Kokke,[4] Benno Kruit,[5] Yoad Winter[1]

We introduce a new formal semantic model for annotating textual entailments that describes restrictive, intersective, and appositive modification. The model contains a formally defined interpreted lexicon, which specifies the inventory of symbols and the supported semantic operators, and an informally defined annotation scheme that instructs annotators in which way to bind words and constructions from a given pair of premise and hypothesis to the interpreted lexicon. We explore the applicability of the proposed model to the Recognizing Textual Entailment (RTE) 1–4 corpora and describe a first-stage annotation scheme on which we based the manual annotation work. The constructions we annotated were found to occur in 80.65% of the entailments in RTE 1–4 and were annotated with cross-annotator agreement of 68% on average. The annotated parts of the RTE corpora are publicly available for further research.

1 Introduction

The *Recognizing Textual Entailment* (RTE) challenges (Dagan et al. 2006) aim to assess a system's ability to automatically determine whether an entailment relation obtains between a naturally occur-

[1] Utrecht University, {a.toledo,s.alexandropoulou,h.e.klockmann,y.winter}@uu.nl
[2] University College London, sophie.chesney.10@ucl.ac.uk
[3] sophia@katrenko.com
[4] Utrecht University, pepijn.kokke@gmail.com
[5] University of Amsterdam, bennokr@gmail.com

LiLT Volume 9
Perspectives on Semantic Representations for Textual Inference.
Copyright © 2014, CSLI Publications.

ring **text** sentence (T) and a **hypothesis** sentence (H). The RTE corpus (Bar Haim et al. 2006; Giampiccolo et al. 2007, 2008; Bentivogli et al. 2009), which is currently the only available resource of textual entailments, marks entailment candidates as valid/invalid.[6] For example:

Example 1

T: The head of the Italian opposition, Romano Prodi, was the last president of the EC.

H: Romano Prodi is a former president of the EC.[7]

Entailment: Valid

This categorization contains no indication of the linguistic and informational processes that underlie entailment. In the lack of a gold standard of inferential phenomena, entailment systems can be compared based on their performance, but not on the basis of the linguistic adequacy of their inferential processes. For further remarks on this problem, see Sammons et al. (2010).

The goal of this work is to elucidate some central inferential processes underlying entailments in the RTE corpus. By doing that, we aim to contribute toward creating a benchmark for modeling entailment recognition. We presume that this goal is to be achieved incrementally by modeling increasingly complex semantic phenomena. To this end, we employ a standard model-theoretic approach to entailment that allows combining gold standard annotations with a computational framework. The model contains a formally defined interpreted lexicon, which specifies the inventory of symbols and semantic operators, and an informally defined annotation scheme that instructs annotators how to bind words and constructions from a given T-H pair to entries in the interpreted lexicon. We choose to focus on the semantic phenomena of restrictive, intersective, and appositive modification. This choice is motivated by the predominance of these phenomena in the RTE datasets, the ability to annotate them with high consistency and the possibility of capturing their various syntactic expressions by a limited set of concepts.

For instance, in Example 1 the inference from *The head of the Italian opposition, Romano Prodi,* to *Romano Prodi* is licensed by the semantics of the appositive construction. Lexical phenomena that are not

---

[6]Pairs of sentences in RTE 1–3 are categorized in two classes: *yes-* or *no-entailment*; pairs in RTE 4–5 are categorized in three classes: *entailment, contradiction* and *unknown*. We label the judgments *yes-entailment* from RTE 1–3 and *entailment* from RTE 4–5 as *valid*, and the other judgments as *invalid*.

[7]Pair 410 from the test set of RTE 2. *EC* stands for European Commission

modeled but intervene in the analysis of these phenomena, such as the inference *last president → former president* in Example 1 are annotated using shallow textual alignment.[8]

In its current stage, this work is only at the beginning of implementing the theoretical semantic model using an annotation platform combined with a theorem prover. In the course of the development of this model, a narrower annotation scheme was adopted. In this scheme, modification phenomena were annotated in all valid entailment pairs from RTE 1–4 without accounting for the way in which the annotated phenomena contributed to the inference being made. This work allowed us to perform data analysis and to further learn about the phenomena of interest as part of the development of the semantic model.

The structure of this paper is as follows. Section 2 reviews some related methods used in Bos et al. (2004) and MacCartney and Manning (2007). In Section 3 we introduce the formal semantic model on which we rely and use it for analyzing some illustrative textual entailments. More RTE data are illustrated in Appendix 1. Section 4 points out a challenge in applying this model to parts of the RTE data and describes our current annotation scheme which aims to address this challenge. We then elaborate on the methods employed in applying this scheme to the datasets of RTE 1–4, and present some quantitative data on the targeted phenomena and inter-annotator agreement. Section 5 concludes.

2 Related Work

Bos and Markert (2005) utilize a CCG parser (Bos et al. 2004) to represent the text and hypothesis in discourse representation structures (DRSs, Kamp and Reyle 1993) that encapsulate information on argument structure, polarity, etc. The DRSs of the text and hypothesis are then translated into formulae in first order logic, and a theorem prover is used in order to search whether there is a logical proof from the text formula to the hypothesis formula. The system reached a relatively high precision score of 76% in recognizing the positive cases in RTE 2 but suffered from a very low recall of 5.8%.

MacCartney and Manning (2007)'s system recognizes monotonic relations (or lack thereof) between aligned lexical items in the text and hypothesis and employs a model of compositional semantics to calculate a sentence-level entailment prediction. The recognition of monotonic relations is done using an adapted version of Sanchez Valencia's Natural Logic (Sánchez Valencia 1991), the alignment between the text and hypothesis is based on a cost function that extends the Levenshtein

---

[8]For more details on this point see Section 3.3.

string-edit algorithm, and the entailment is classified by a decision tree classifier, trained on a small data set of 69 handmade problems. The system was tested on RTE 3 and achieved relatively high precision scores of 76.39% and 68.06% on the positive cases in the development and test sets, respectively. This system also suffers from low recall scores of 26.70% and 31.71%, respectively.

In Bentivogli et al. (2010), a methodology is described for creating specialized entailment data sets by isolating linguistic phenomena relevant for entailment. Pairs of text and hypothesis from the existing corpus were used to generate a set of mono-thematic pairs, each containing one specific phenomenon that takes part in the original entailment. This analysis includes formulation of rules of inferences according to several pre-defined categories, e.g., *argument realization*: "x's y" → "y of x". As part of a feasibility study, this methodology was applied to a sample of 90 pairs randomly extracted from RTE 5 and processed by two annotators. Cross-annotator agreement was reported in two scores: complete agreement in pair analysis was found in 64.4% of the pairs, and partial agreement on the phenomena involved in the inferences was calculated by the Dice (1945) coefficient and reached a value of 0.78. This methodology allows a detailed analysis of the entailments in the corpus, but a full analysis of all entailment patterns in the corpus would necessarily involve complex judgments, and this, in turn, would make high cross-annotator agreement very hard to achieve. Moreover, as discussed in Section 4.7, our experience shows that efficient annotation with high cross-annotator agreement is hard to obtain even in more restricted cases which involve less complex judgments.

The model we propose in this work diverges from these approaches in two respects: (a) its first goal is to develop gold standard semantic annotations based on a general formal semantic model; (b) it does not aim to represent phenomena that are not accounted for in this model. For example, consider the following inference, which is based on causal reasoning: *Khan sold nuclear plans* ⇒ *Khan possessed nuclear plans*.[9] Causal reasoning and lexical relations are not part of the semantic phenomena addressed in this paper, and a pattern in the form of X *sold* Y ⇒ X *possessed* Y should be defined ad-hoc by annotators to align the instances of the verbs *sell* and *possess*. This approach allows us to concentrate on the logical aspects of textual entailment, while phenomena involving lexical semantics and world knowledge are handled by a shallow analysis.[10] Our annotation work is to a large extent in line with

---

[9]This example of causal reasoning is taken from MacCartney and Manning (2007).

[10]Another related work, which approaches inference in natural language as part

the proposal described in Sammons et al. (2010), whose authors appeal to the NLP community to contribute to entailment recognition work by incrementally annotating the phenomena that underlie the inferences in the RTE corpus.

3 Theoretical background and RTE examples

To model entailment in natural language, we assume that entailment describes a *preorder* on natural language sentences. Thus, we assume that any sentence trivially entails itself (reflexivity); and given two entailments $T_1 \Rightarrow H_1$ and $T_2 \Rightarrow H_2$ where H_1 and T_2 are identical sentences, we assume $T_1 \Rightarrow H_2$ (transitivity). A computational theory of entailment should describe an approximation of this preorder on natural language sentences. We use a standard model-theoretic extensional semantics, based on the simple *partial order* on the domain of *truth-values*. Each model M assigns sentences a truth-value in the set $\{0, 1\}$. Such a Tarskian theory of entailment is considered adequate if the intuitive entailment preorder on sentences can be described as the pairs of sentences T and H whose truth-values $[\![T]\!]^M$ and $[\![H]\!]^M$ satisfy $[\![T]\!]^M \leq [\![H]\!]^M$ for all models M. In this section we give the essentials of this model-theoretic approach to entailment that are relevant to the annotated phenomena and illustrate it using a small interpreted lexicon, simplifying the analysis of some representative examples from the RTE.

3.1 Semantic essentials

We adopt a standard semantic framework (Winter 2010) where the types assigned to natural language expressions encode general aspects of their meaning. More specific aspects of an expression's meaning are encoded by its possible denotations within the typed domain assigned to it. Functional types are standardly defined below.

Definition 1. Let B be a finite non-empty set of basic types. The set of functional types over B is the smallest set $\mathcal{T}^B$ that satisfies:

(i) $B \subseteq \mathcal{T}^B$;

(ii) If τ and σ are types in $\mathcal{T}^B$ then $(\tau \rightarrow \sigma)$ is also a type in $\mathcal{T}^B$.

The '$\rightarrow$' symbol is omitted for perspicuity, and parentheses in types are

---

of a semantic paradigm, is the FraCaS test suite (Cooper et al. 1996). This suite concerns examples that mainly rely on generalized quantification, argument monotonicity, plurality, anaphora resolution, ellipsis, etc. Entailments based on these phenomena are not very common in the RTE data that are analyzed here. Further research is needed in order to integrate data like those in FraCaS into a formal annotation scheme like the one suggested in this paper.

TABLE 1: Types commonly used for natural language expressions

t	sentences
e	proper names, referential noun phrases
et	intransitive verbs and common nouns
$e(et)$	transitive verbs
$(et)t$	quantificational noun phrases
$(et)e$	definite article (*the*)
$(et)((et)t)$	determiners (*some, every*)
$\tau\tau$	modifiers (adjectives, adverbs, prepositional phrases, negation, relative clauses)
$\tau(\tau\tau)$	coordinators (conjunction, disjunction, restrictive relative pronouns)

erased whenever this does not lead to ambiguity. Thus, the functional type $(\tau \to \sigma)$ is denoted '$\tau\sigma$'. For our purposes we assume $\mathsf{B} = \{e, t\}$, where e is the type of *entities* and t is the type of *truth-values*. Table 1 gives some examples for types that are commonly used for various natural language expressions, as will be illustrated in the interpreted lexicon in Section 3.2. The type scheme $\tau\tau$ for modifiers and the type scheme $\tau(\tau\tau)$ for coordinators are used for different expressions, with different types instantiating $\tau \in \mathcal{T}^{\{e,t\}}$.

For each type τ in $\mathcal{T}^{\mathsf{B}}$ we inductively define a corresponding *domain* D_τ. For basic types in B the corresponding domains are assigned by assumption. For each non-basic functional type $\tau\sigma \in \mathcal{T}^{\mathsf{B}}$ we define the corresponding domain by:

$$D_{\tau\sigma} \;=\; D_\sigma^{D_\tau} \;=\; \text{the set of functions from } D_\tau \text{ to } D_\sigma$$

The domain D_t of truth-values is assumed to be constant: the set $\{0, 1\}$ with the natural partial order $\leq$. This partial order allows us to semantically capture the preorder relation induced by entailment on natural language sentences. Given a non-empty domain of entities $D_e = E$, we refer to the collection of domains $\mathcal{F}^E = \{D_\tau | \tau \in \mathcal{T}^{\{e,t\}}\}$ as the *frame over E*. Thus, the frame over E contains the respective domain E of entities, the domain of truth-values, and all the one-place functions that are derived from these two sets. For instance, the following sets are all subsets of $\mathcal{F}^E$, where we abbreviate $\mathbf{2} = \{0, 1\}$. The type of members in each set is indicated after each set in brackets:

$$E(e),\ E^E(ee),\ \mathbf{2}(t),\ \mathbf{2}^{\mathbf{2}}(tt),\ E^{\mathbf{2}}(te),\ \mathbf{2}^E(et),\ \mathbf{2}^{(E^E)}((ee)t),$$
$$(\mathbf{2}^E)^E(eet),\ E^{(\mathbf{2}^{\mathbf{2}})}((tt)e),\ (E^{\mathbf{2}})^{\mathbf{2}}(tte)\ldots$$

Let a *lexicon* Σ be a set of terminal symbols (=words). We use a *typing function* TYP for assigning a type to each word in Σ. Using this function and a set of entities E we define a *model M over Σ*. This is done by mapping each word in Σ to a denotation of the appropriate type in the frame $\mathcal{F}^E$. This mapping is called an *interpretation function* and is defined as follows.

Definition 2. An interpretation function I over a lexicon Σ with a typing function TYP and a set E, is a function from the words in Σ to the set $\bigcup \mathcal{F}^E$, which sends every word $w \in \Sigma$ to an element in the corresponding typed domain: $I(w) \in D_{\mathsf{TYP}(w)}$.

For instance: let *see* be a word of type $e(et)$ in a typed lexicon Σ. Then for any non-empty set E, an interpretation function over Σ and E sends the word *see* to a function in $(2^E)^E$: a function f from entities to functions from entities to truth-values. By standard Currying, this function f characterizes a binary relation over E. Informally speaking, this relation describes who sees who in a given model M.

A model is a pair of a set of entities E and an interpretation function I, which is formally defined below.

Definition 3. A model over a lexicon Σ with a typing function TYP is a pair $M = \langle E, I \rangle$ where E is a non-empty set and I is an interpretation function over the typed lexicon Σ and the set E.

Models over a lexicon are used to give denotations to complex expressions over this lexicon. Given a language L over Σ and a model $M = \langle E, I \rangle$ over Σ, we assign every parsed expression *exp* in L a *denotation* $[\![exp]\!]^M$. Every terminal expression w in Σ is assigned the denotation $[\![w]\!]^M = I(w)$. For non-terminal expressions, we assume a binary parse. Thus, any non-terminal expression *exp* in Σ^* is assumed to be parsed into two sub-expressions exp_1 and exp_2 (not necessarily in this order). Such complex expressions are assigned a type and a denotation in M by the following restrictions:

1. If exp_1 (or exp_2) is a word in Σ, the type of exp_1 (or exp_2) is as defined by the typing function TYP.

2. The types of exp_1 and exp_2 are $\tau\sigma$ and τ, respectively.

With these restrictions, we define types and denotations of complex expressions by simple function application. Thus, the type of the expression *exp* is σ, and its denotation $[\![exp]\!]^M$ in M is the following element in D_σ:

$$[\![exp]\!]^M = [\![exp_1]\!]^M ([\![exp_2]\!]^M), \text{ where } [\![exp_1]\!]^M \in D_{\tau\sigma} \text{ and } [\![exp_2]\!]^M \in D_\tau$$

In order to describe lexical denotations of words, interpretation functions within models are restricted by suitable *ad hoc* assumptions. Such assumptions are standardly expressed in higher order lambda-calculus (see Section 3.2). Models that satisfy these *ad hoc* restrictions on lexical denotations are referred to as *intended models*.

A lexicon Σ together with a typing function TYP and a specification of intended models is referred to as an *interpreted lexicon*. Assume now that T and H are parsed text and hypothesis sentences of type t over an interpreted lexicon Σ. *Logical entailment* between T and H is model-theoretically described as the classical Tarskian property below.

The truth-conditionality criterion: *Let T and H be parsed expressions of type t, over an interpreted lexicon Σ. We say that the parsed sentence T logically entails H if and only if the relation $[\![T]\!]^M \leq [\![H]\!]^M$ holds between the truth-value denotations of T and H in all intended models M.*

Example 2

Consider a mini-lexicon $\Sigma = \{Dan, sat, ate, and\}$ with the types e, et, et, $(et)((et)(et))$ respectively. Consider intended models where the interpretation function I assigns the words *Dan, sat* and *ate* arbitrary denotations **dan**, **sit** and **eat**, and where the word *and* is assigned the following denotation in any model:

$$I(and) = \text{AND} = \lambda A_{et}.\lambda B_{et}.\lambda x_e.B(x) \wedge A(x)$$

With the natural binary parses, these intended models explain the entailment *Dan sat and ate* $\Rightarrow$ *Dan ate*, since for each intended model M:

$[\![\,Dan\ [sat\ [and\ ate]]\,]\!]^M$

$=$	$((\text{AND}(\textbf{eat}))(\textbf{sit}))(\textbf{dan})$	analysis
$=$	$(((\lambda A_{et}.\lambda B_{et}.\lambda x_e.B(x) \wedge A(x))(\textbf{eat}))(\textbf{sit}))(\textbf{dan})$	def. of AND
$=$	$\textbf{sit}(\textbf{dan}) \wedge \textbf{eat}(\textbf{dan})$	func. app. to **eat**, **sit** and **dan**
$\leq$	$\textbf{eat}(\textbf{dan})$	def. of $\wedge$
$=$	$[\![\,Dan\ ate\,]\!]^M$	analysis

3.2 An interpreted lexicon

In this section we introduce a small interpreted lexicon that illustrates our treatment of items of some major lexical categories (articles, nouns, (in-)transitive verbs, etc.). Our aim in creating interpreted lexicons like this is to bind words and expressions in annotated RTE sentences to denotations that mark semantic phenomena and allow us to explain inferential processes in the RTE. This approach is illustrated in Section 3.3.

The lexicon is presented in Table 2. For each word we state its literal form, the type assigned to it, and its denotation in intended models. Denotations that are assumed to be arbitrary in intended models are given in boldface. For example, the intransitive use of the verb *eat* is assigned the type *et* and its denotation **eat** is an arbitrary function of this type. By contrast, other lexical items have their denotations restricted by the intended models. For example, the definite article *the* is assigned the type $(et)e$. In each intended model this article denotes the *iota* function – a function from one-place predicates of type *et* to entities of type *e*, which presupposes the uniqueness of the entity that the predicate is true of and returns this entity. This function is denoted 'THE' or 'ι'. The functions that we use for defining denotations are specified in Figure 1.

Several items in the lexicon are assigned more than one type and/or more than one denotation. This is required because of (type) ambiguity in natural language. For example, the adjective *Dutch* has a predicative usage (e.g. *Jan is Dutch*), but it can also serve as a modifier of nouns (*Jan is a Dutch man*). When semantic information on words is described in entailment data, such ambiguities should be resolved.

Below we make some more remarks on the denotations assumed for the lexical entries in Table 2.

- As in Example 2, the coordinator *and* when appearing as a predicate conjunction is analyzed as a function AND mapping any two *et* predicates A and B to the predicate that sends every entity e to the truth-value of the conjunction $A(x) \wedge B(x)$. The resulting predicate characterizes the intersection of the sets characterized by A and B.

- The copula *is* and the article *a* in copular sentences (e.g. *Dan is a man*) denote the identity function on *et* predicates. This $(et)(et)$ function, which is denoted IS or A, maps each *et* predicate to itself. The same analysis of *is* holds for other copular sentences with predicative adjectives (e.g. *Dan is short/Dutch*). The English copula can also express an equality relation between entities (e.g. *Dan is Jan*). In such cases it is analyzed as the equality relation IS_{eq}, of type $e(et)$.

- The word *some* denotes the existential quantifier SOME, as it is used in intransitive sentences such as *some man ate* (transitive sentences like *Jan saw some man* are not treated here). The SOME function gets two predicates of type *et* (e.g. for *man* and *ate*) and

TABLE 2: An Interpreted Lexicon

Word	Type	Denotation	Remarks
Dan	e	**dan**	proper name
Jan	e	**jan**	proper name
Vim	e	**vim**	proper name
Sue	e	**sue**	proper name
man	et	**man**	common noun
boy	et	**boy**	common noun
nun	et	**nun**	common noun
alien	et	**alien**	common noun
girl	et	**girl**	common noun
sat	et	**sit**	intrans. verb
ate	et	**eat**	intrans. verb
saw	$e(et)$	**see**	trans. verb
praised	$e(et)$	**praise**	trans. verb
greeted	$e(et)$	**greet**	trans. verb
and	$(et)((et)(et))$	AND	pred. conj. (coordinator)
is	$(et)(et)$	IS	copula (modifier)
is	$e(et)$	IS$_{eq}$	copula (equality)
a	$(et)(et)$	A	indef. article (modifier)
the	$(et)e$	THE	def. article (iota)
some	$(et)((et)t)$	SOME	indef. determiner
who	$(et)((et)(et))$	WHO$_R$	res. rel. pronoun (coordinator)
who	$(et)(ee)$	WHO$_A$	app. rel. pronoun
Dutch	et	**dutch**$_{et}$	int. adjective (predicate)
Dutch	$(et)(et)$	$I_m(\textbf{dutch}_{et})$	int. adjective (modifier)
black	et	**black**$_{et}$	int. adjective (predicate)
black	$(et)(et)$	$I_m(\textbf{black}_{et})$	int. adjective (modifier)
short	et	$P_r(\textbf{short}_{(et)(et)})$	res. adjective (predicate)
short	$(et)(et)$	$R_m(\textbf{short}_{(et)(et)})$	res. adjective (modifier)
slowly	$(et)(et)$	$R_m(\textbf{slowly}_{(et)(et)})$	res. adverb (modifier)

returns 1 iff an entity that satisfies both predicates exists.

- The relative pronoun *who* is an ambiguous form that allows noun modification either by a restrictive relative clause or by an appositive clause. The former is expressed in sentences such as *[the [alien who is a nun]] sat*. In this case the pronoun *who* creates a complex predicate, *alien who is a nun* from the predicate constituents *alien* and *is a nun*. The function WHO$_R$ that creates this complex predicate for restrictive clauses is the same as the conjunction function AND. The appositive use of the pronoun appears in sentences such as *[[the alien], [who is a nun]], sat*. Here the pronoun adds information on a given entity x by checking whether a given predicate A holds of it. In the example the entity x is denoted by *the alien* and the predicate A by *is a nun*. The resulting entity is x if A holds of x, and undefined otherwise. This appositive usage of the relative pronoun is defined using the function WHO$_A$.

- The adjectives *short* and *Dutch* have both a modifier entry and a predicative entry. When appearing as modifiers, both adjectives restrict the denotation of the noun they attach to: a *short man* is a *man* and a *Dutch man* is also a *man*. Unlike *short*, the adjective *Dutch* is furthermore *intersective*: a *short man* does not necessarily count as *short* but a *Dutch man* is invariably *Dutch*. The denotations of the adjectives are defined accordingly. The predicate denotation of *Dutch* is defined as an arbitrary constant **dutch** of type *et*. The modifier is derived by this arbitrary predicate and a function I_m identical to AND, which requires entities to satisfy both the noun predicate and the predicate denoted by the constant **dutch**. The denotation of *short* is defined based on the function R_m, which only requires entities to satisfy the modified noun, after the denotation of the predicate is modified by the arbitrary $(et)(et)$ function **short**. In the case of *short*, the predicative denotation for *short* is defined using the function P_r as the set of "short things" – the modifier **short** applied to the whole D_e domain. The adverb *slowly* is defined only as a restrictive modifier, similar to the use of the adjective *short* for modification.

For more on the theoretical foundations of this approach, see Pratt-Hartmann (2003), Pratt-Hartmann and Moss (2009), Moss (2010a,b), and the references therein.

These works develop theoretical frameworks that aim at wider coverage than what the interpreted lexicon above treats. Integrating all the phenomena treated by Pratt-Hartmann and Moss into an annotation scheme of the RTE requires further research.

$\textsc{and} = \lambda A_{et}.\lambda B_{et}.\lambda x_e.B(x) \wedge A(x)$

$\textsc{is} = \lambda A_{et}.A$

$\textsc{is}_{eq} = \lambda x_e.\lambda y_e.x = y$

$\textsc{a} = \textsc{is} = \lambda A_{et}.A$

$$\textsc{the} = \iota_{(et)e} = \lambda A_{et}. \begin{cases} a & \text{if } A = (\lambda x_e.x = a) \\ \\ \text{undefined} & \text{otherwise} \end{cases} \quad \text{(iota operator)}$$

$\textsc{some} = \lambda A_{et}.\lambda B_{et}.\exists x_e.A(x) \wedge B(x)$

$\textsc{who}_R = \textsc{and} = \lambda A_{et}.\lambda B_{et}.\lambda x_e.B(x) \wedge A(x)$

$\textsc{who}_A = \lambda A_{et}.\lambda x_e.\iota(\lambda y.y = x \wedge A(x))$

$P_r = \lambda M_{(et)(et)}.\lambda x_e.M(\lambda y_e.1)(x)$ deriving a predicate from a mod.

$I_m = \textsc{and} = \lambda A_{et}.\lambda B_{et}.\lambda x_e.B(x) \wedge A(x)$ deriving an int. mod.

$R_m = \lambda M_{(et)(et)}.\lambda A_{et}.\lambda x_e.M(A)(x) \wedge A(x)$ deriving a res. mod.

FIGURE 1: Functions used in the interpreted lexicon

3.3 Analyzing entailments using the interpreted lexicon

To illustrate our analysis of entailments using the interpreted lexicon, we give some manual analyses of RTE pairs. The analysis is done by binding expressions in the RTE data to structurally equivalent expressions containing items in the interpreted lexicon. This analysis is three-fold:

1. Phenomena Simplification: we simplify the text and hypothesis to exclude inferential phenomena that we do not handle in the scope of this work. For example, the simplification of *Google operates on the web* to *Google is on the web* is based on lexical knowledge, which we do not address here, and therefore it is handled as part of the simplification step in Example 3.[11]

2. Binding to Lexicon: we bind the constructions in the data to parallel constructions in the interpreted lexicon that share the same

---

[11]In the future, we intend to capture lexical relations of this kind by adding non-logical axioms to the assumptions based on which a theorem prover aims to find a proof between the logical representation of T and H. Common sense inferences (LoBue and Yates 2011) will be addressed in a similar vein.

structure and semantic properties. This step produces a text sentence $T_{Lexicon}$ and a hypothesis sentence $H_{Lexicon}$ as new structurally equivalent versions of the simplified text and hypothesis. We assume parse trees which allow the application of the interpreted lexicon.[12]

3. Proof of Entailment: using predicate calculus and lambda calculus reductions, we establish a logical proof between $T_{Lexicon}$ and $H_{Lexicon}$.[13]

Example 3

- Data:
  T: The largest search engine on the web, Google, receives over 200 million queries each day through its various services.
  H: Google operates on the web.[14]

1. Phenomena Simplification:
   In the text: adding an overt appositive WH pronoun, for better match with the interpreted lexicon:
   $T_{Original}$: The largest search engine on the web, Google, receives...
   T_{Simple}: The largest search engine on the web, which is Google, receives...
   In the hypothesis: reducing the meaning of 'X operates on Y' to 'X is on Y':
   $H_{Original}$: Google operates on the web
   H_{Simple}: Google is on the web

2. Binding to Lexicon:
   Text:
   T_{Simple}: [The largest search engine on the web, which is Google], receives...
   $T_{Lexicon}$: [The short Dutch man, who is Jan], saw Dan
   Hypothesis:
   H_{Simple}: Google [is [on the web]]
   $H_{Lexicon}$: Jan [is Dutch]
   Binding Explanation: we bind the restrictive adjective *largest* to *short*, the noun combination *search engine* to *man* and the inter-

---

[12]See Kundu and Roth (2011) for previous work that may facilitate binding unknown entries to an existing lexicon.

[13]The only higher-order constants in the above lexicon are the $(et)(et)$ constants attributed to non-intersective restrictive modifiers. Treating them in predicate calculus theorem provers may require some *ad hoc* assumptions.

[14]Pair 955 from the test set of RTE 4 (Giampiccolo et al. 2008).

sective modifier *on the web* to *Dutch*. The entity *Google* is bound to *Jan* and the VP *receives...* is bound to *saw Dan*.[15,16]

3. Proof of Entailment $T_{Lexicon} \rightarrow H_{Lexicon}$:

Let M be an intended model,
$[\![[\![[The\ [short\ Dutch\ man]\!], [who\ [is\ Jan]\!],]\ saw\ Dan]\!]^M$

$= (\mathbf{see(dan)})((\text{WHO}_A(\text{IS}_{eq}(\mathbf{jan})))(\iota((R_m(\mathbf{short}))$ $((I_m(\mathbf{dutch}))(\mathbf{man})))))$	analysis
$= (\mathbf{see(dan)})((\text{WHO}_A((\lambda x_e.\lambda y_e.x =$ $y)(\mathbf{jan})))(\iota((R_m(\mathbf{short}))\ ((I_m(\mathbf{dutch}))\mathbf{man})))))$	def. of IS_{eq}
$= (\mathbf{see(dan)})((\text{WHO}_A(\lambda y_e.\mathbf{jan} = y))$ $(\iota((R_m(\mathbf{short}))((I_m(\mathbf{dutch}))(\mathbf{man})))))$	func. app. to $\mathbf{jan}$
$= (\mathbf{see(dan)})(((\lambda A_{et}.\lambda x_e.\iota(\lambda y.y =$ $x \wedge A(x)))(\lambda y_e.\mathbf{jan} = y))$ $(\iota((R_m(\mathbf{short}))((I_m(\mathbf{dutch}))(\mathbf{man})))))$	def. of WHO_A
$= (\mathbf{see(dan)})((\lambda x_e.\iota(\lambda y.y = x \wedge (\lambda y_e.\mathbf{jan} = y)(x)))$ $(\iota((R_m(\mathbf{short}))((I_m(\mathbf{dutch}))(\mathbf{man})))))$	func. app. to $\lambda y_e.$ $\mathbf{jan} = y$
$= (\mathbf{see(dan)})((\lambda x_e.\iota(\lambda y.y = x \wedge \mathbf{jan} = x))$ $(\iota((R_m(\mathbf{short}))((I_m(\mathbf{dutch}))(\mathbf{man})))))$	func. app. to x
$= (\mathbf{see(dan)})(\iota(\lambda y.y =$ $(\iota((R_m(\mathbf{short}))((I_m(\mathbf{dutch}))(\mathbf{man})))) \wedge \mathbf{jan} =$ $(\iota((R_m(\mathbf{short}))((I_m(\mathbf{dutch}))(\mathbf{man})))))))$	func. app. to $\iota((R_m($ $\mathbf{short}))((I_m(\mathbf{dutch}))(\mathbf{man})))$

The expression:

$$\iota(\lambda y.y = (\iota((R_m(\mathbf{short}))((I_m(\mathbf{dutch}))(\mathbf{man})))) \wedge$$
$$\mathbf{jan} = (\iota((R_m(\mathbf{short}))((I_m(\mathbf{dutch}))(\mathbf{man})))))$$

---

[15]The post-nominal intersective modifier *on the web* is bound to a pre-nominal modifier *Dutch* in order to match the vocabulary of the interpreted lexicon, in which the only intersective modifier is *Dutch*.

[16]In this example, T_{Simple} (consequently from $T_{Original}$) is structurally ambiguous between *The [largest [search engine on the web]], which is Google, receives...* and *The [[largest search engine] on the web], which is Google, receives....* We here illustrate the former analysis. The latter analysis can be handled in a similar vein.

is defined and returns an entity denoted by z_e only if the following holds:

$$\lambda y.y = (\iota((R_m(\textbf{short}))((I_m(\textbf{dutch}))(\textbf{man})))) \wedge$$
$$\textbf{jan} = (\iota((R_m(\textbf{short}))((I_m(\textbf{dutch}))(\textbf{man})))) = \lambda x_e.x = z_e \quad (1)$$

From (1) it follows that:

$$(\lambda y.y = (\iota((R_m(\textbf{short}))((I_m(\textbf{dutch}))(\textbf{man})))) \wedge$$
$$\textbf{jan} = (\iota((R_m(\textbf{short}))((I_m(\textbf{dutch}))(\textbf{man})))))(z_e)$$

$= z_e = \iota((R_m(\textbf{short}))((I_m(\textbf{dutch}))(\textbf{man}))) \wedge$ $\quad \textbf{jan} = \iota((R_m(\textbf{short}))((I_m(\textbf{dutch}))(\textbf{man})))$	func. app. to z_e
$\leq \textbf{jan} = \iota((R_m(\textbf{short}))((I_m(\textbf{dutch}))(\textbf{man})))$	def. of $\wedge$
$= \textbf{jan} = \iota((R_m(\textbf{short}))(((\lambda A_{et}.\lambda B_{et}.\lambda x_e.B(x) \wedge$ $\quad A(x))\ (\textbf{dutch}))(\textbf{man})))$	def. of I_m
$= \textbf{jan} = \iota((R_m(\textbf{short}))((\lambda B_{et}.\lambda x_e.B(x) \wedge$ $\quad \textbf{dutch}(x))\ (\textbf{man})))$	func. app. to $\textbf{dutch}$
$= \textbf{jan} = \iota((R_m(\textbf{short}))(\lambda x_e.\textbf{man}(x) \wedge \textbf{dutch}(x)))$	func. app. to $\textbf{man}$
$= \textbf{jan} = \iota(((\lambda M_{(et)(et)}.\lambda A_{et}.\lambda x_e.M(A)(x) \wedge A(x))$ $\quad (\textbf{short}))(\lambda x_e.\textbf{man}(x) \wedge \textbf{dutch}(x)))$	def. of R_m
$= \textbf{jan} = \iota(((\lambda A_{et}.\lambda y_e.(\textbf{short}(A))(y) \wedge A(y))$ $\quad (\lambda x_e.\textbf{man}(x) \wedge \textbf{dutch}(x)))$	func. app. to $\textbf{short}$
$= \textbf{jan} = \iota(\lambda y_e.(\textbf{short}\ (\lambda x_e.\textbf{man}(x) \wedge$ $\quad \textbf{dutch}(x)))(y) \wedge (\lambda x_e.\textbf{man}(x) \wedge \textbf{dutch}(x))(y))$	func. app. to $\lambda x_e.$ $\textbf{man}(x) \wedge$ $\textbf{dutch}(x)$
$= \textbf{jan} = \iota(\lambda y_e.(\textbf{short}(\lambda x_e.\textbf{man}(x) \wedge$ $\quad \textbf{dutch}(x)))(y)) \wedge (\textbf{man}(y) \wedge \textbf{dutch}(y)))$	func. app. to y
$= \textbf{jan} = \iota(\lambda y_e.(\textbf{short}(\lambda x_e.\textbf{man}(x) \wedge$ $\quad \textbf{dutch}(x)))(y)) \wedge \textbf{man}(y) \wedge \textbf{dutch}(y) \quad (2)$	from def. of $\wedge$

The expression:

$$\iota(\lambda y_e.(\textbf{short}(\lambda x_e.\textbf{man}(x) \wedge \textbf{dutch}(x)))(y) \wedge \textbf{man}(y) \wedge \textbf{dutch}(y)))$$

is defined and returns an entity denoted by r_e only if the following holds:

(3)
$$\lambda y_e.(\textbf{short}(\lambda x_e.\textbf{man}(x) \wedge \textbf{dutch}(x)))(y) \wedge \textbf{man}(y) \wedge$$
$$\textbf{dutch}(y)) = \lambda x_e.x = r_e$$

From (3) it follows that:

$$(\lambda y_e.(\mathbf{short}(\lambda x_e.\mathbf{man}(x) \wedge \mathbf{dutch}(x)))(y) \wedge \mathbf{man}(y)$$
$$\wedge\, \mathbf{dutch}(y)))r_e$$

$= (\mathbf{short}(\lambda x_e.\mathbf{man}(x) \wedge \mathbf{dutch}(x)))(r_e)\wedge$	func. app.
$\quad \mathbf{man}(r_e) \wedge \mathbf{dutch}(r_e)$	to r_e
$\leq \mathbf{dutch}(r_e)$ $\qquad\qquad\qquad\qquad$ (4)	def. of $\wedge$

From (2) and (3) it follows that:

(5) $\qquad\qquad\qquad\qquad$ $\mathbf{jan} = r_e$

From (4) and (5) it follows that:

$\mathbf{dutch(jan)}$

$= (\textsc{is}(\mathbf{dutch}))(\mathbf{jan})$	def. of \textsc{is}
$= [\![Jan \; [is \; Dutch]]\!]^M$	analysis

A crucial step in this analysis is our assumption that *on the web* is an intersective modifier of *search engine*. This allows the subsumption of *search engine on the web* by *on the web*. In the interpreted lexicon we describe this behavior using the intersective denotation of the modifier *Dutch*. Let us investigate further the implications of this annotation in the following hypothetical example.

Example 4

1. Pair 1
   T_1: Jan is a short Dutch man.
   H_1: Jan is a short man.

   In this example there is no intuitive entailment: a short Dutch man may be tall for an average man.

2. Pair 2
   T_2: Jan is a black Dutch man.
   H_2: Jan is a black man.

   In this example there is intuitively an entailment: a black Dutch man is a man who is both black and Dutch, hence he is a black man.

From a purely textual/syntactic point of view, these two T-H pairs are indistinguishable. The lexical overlap between the text and hypothesis in both pairs is 100%. This does not allow entailment systems to rely on textual measurements for identifying that the pairs need to be classified differently. Such a perfect score of overlap may lead to a false positive classification in Pair 1 or conversely, to a false negative in Pair 2. Also syntactically, both *short* and *black* serve as adjectives attached to a noun phrase *Dutch man*. There is nothing in this syntactic configuration to suggest that omitting *Dutch* in Pair 1 might result in a different entailment classification than omitting it in Pair 2. However, from a semantic point of view, based on annotations of abstract relations between predicates and their modifiers, we can correctly analyze both the non-validity of the entailment in Pair 1 and the validity of the entailment in Pair 2.

- Analysis of Pair 1

  To validate that there is no entailment between a text and a hypothesis requires showing that there is an intended model $M = \langle E, I \rangle$ in which there is no $\leq$ relation between their denotations. Let M be an intended model that satisfies the following:

  - $\mathbf{man}_{et}$ characterizes $\{\mathbf{dan}, \mathbf{jan}, \mathbf{vim}\}$
  - $\mathbf{dutch}_{et}$ characterizes $\{\mathbf{jan}, \mathbf{vim}\}$
  - $\mathbf{short}(\mathbf{man})_{et}$ characterizes $\{\mathbf{dan}\}$
  - $\mathbf{short}(\lambda y_e.\mathbf{man}(y) \wedge \mathbf{dutch}(y))_{et}$ characterizes $\{\mathbf{jan}\}$

  Let us assume parse trees as follows:

  - Text: *Jan* [*is* [*a* [*short* [*Dutch man*]]]]
  - Hypothesis: *Jan* [*is* [*a* [*short man*]]]

  Let M be an intended model that satisfies the restrictions above. Consider the denotations of the text and hypothesis in the model M:

  - Text:

    $[\![\, Jan \, [is \, [a \, [short \, [Dutch \, man]]]] \,]\!]^M$

$= (\text{IS}(\text{A}((R_m(\mathbf{short}))((I_m(\mathbf{dutch}))(\mathbf{man})))))(\mathbf{jan})$ | analysis

$= (\text{A}((R_m(\mathbf{short}))((I_m(\mathbf{dutch}))(\mathbf{man}))))(\mathbf{jan})$ | def. of IS

$= ((R_m(\mathbf{short}))((I_m(\mathbf{dutch}))(\mathbf{man})))(\mathbf{jan})$ | def. of A

$= ((R_m(\mathbf{short}))(((\lambda A_{et}.\lambda B_{et}.\lambda x_e.B(x) \wedge A(x))(\mathbf{dutch}))(\mathbf{man})))(\mathbf{jan})$ | def. of I_m

$= ((R_m(\mathbf{short}))((\lambda B_{et}.\lambda x_e.B(x) \wedge \mathbf{dutch}(x))(\mathbf{man})))(\mathbf{jan})$ | func. app. to **dutch**

$= ((R_m(\mathbf{short}))(\lambda x_e.\mathbf{man}(x) \wedge \mathbf{dutch}(x)))(\mathbf{jan})$ | func. app. to **man**

$= (((\lambda M_{(et)(et)}.\lambda A_{et}.\lambda y_e.M(A)(y) \wedge A(y))(\mathbf{short}))(\lambda x_e.\mathbf{man}(x) \wedge \mathbf{dutch}(x)))(\mathbf{jan})$ | def. of R_m

$= ((\lambda A_{et}.\lambda y_e.(\textbf{short}(A))(y) \wedge A(y))(\lambda x_e.\textbf{man}(x)$ func. app. to
$\wedge \textbf{dutch}(x)))(\textbf{jan})$ **short**

$= ((\lambda y_e.(\textbf{short }(\lambda x_e.\textbf{man}(x) \wedge \textbf{dutch}(x)))(y) \wedge$ func. app. to
$(\lambda x_e.\textbf{man}(x) \wedge \textbf{dutch}(x))(y)))(\textbf{jan})$ $\lambda x_e.\ \textbf{man}(x) \wedge$ **dutch**(x)

$= (\lambda y_e.\textbf{short}(\lambda x_e.\textbf{man}(x) \wedge \textbf{dutch}(x)))(y)$ func. app. to y
$\wedge(\textbf{man}(y) \wedge \textbf{dutch}(y)))(\textbf{jan})$

$= (\textbf{short}(\lambda x_e.\textbf{man}(x) \wedge \textbf{dutch}(x)))(\textbf{jan})$ func. app. to **jan**
$\wedge\textbf{man}(\textbf{jan}) \wedge \textbf{dutch}(\textbf{jan})$

$= 1 \wedge 1 \wedge 1$ denotations in M

$= 1$ def. of $\wedge$

- Hypothesis:
  $[\![\ Jan\ [is\ [a\ [short\ man]]]\ ]\!]^M$

$= (\textsc{is}(\textsc{a}((R_m(\textbf{short}))(\textbf{man}))))(\textbf{jan})$ analysis

$= (\textsc{a}((R_m(\textbf{short}))(\textbf{man})))(\textbf{jan})$ def. of IS

$= ((R_m(\textbf{short}))(\textbf{man}))(\textbf{jan})$ def. of A

$= (((\lambda M_{(et)(et)}.\lambda A_{et}.\lambda y_e.M(A)(y)$ def. of R_m
$\wedge A(y))(\textbf{short}))(\textbf{man}))(\textbf{jan})$

$= ((\lambda A_{et}.\lambda y_e.(\textbf{short}(A))(y) \wedge A(y))(\textbf{man}))(\textbf{jan})$ func. app. to
  short

$= (\lambda y_e.(\textbf{short}(\textbf{man}))(y) \wedge \textbf{man}(y))(\textbf{jan})$ func. app. to
  man

$= (\textbf{short}(\textbf{man}))(\textbf{jan}) \wedge \textbf{man}(\textbf{jan})$ func. app. to **jan**

$= 0 \wedge 1$ denotations in M

$= 0$ def. of $\wedge$

Intuitively, *Jan* can be a man who is considered to be short in the population of Dutch men, hence $(\textbf{short}(\lambda x_e.\textbf{man}(x) \wedge \textbf{dutch}(x)))$ (**jan**) would return 1, but not in the population of all men, hence $(\textbf{short }(\textbf{man}))(\textbf{jan})$ would return 0. This is a direct consequence of having *short* denoting a non-intersective modifier: the set denoted by $\textbf{short}(\lambda x_e.\textbf{man}(x) \wedge \textbf{dutch}(x))$ is not necessarily a subset of $\textbf{short}(\textbf{man})$.

- Analysis of Pair 2
  Let us assume parse trees as follows:
  - Text: *Jan* [*is* [*a* [*black* [*Dutch man*]]]]
  - Hypothesis: *Jan* [*is* [*a* [*black man*]]]
  A proof of entailment:
  Let M be an intended model,
  $[\![\, Jan\ [is\ [a\ [black\ [Dutch\ man]]]]\,]\!]^{M}$

$= (\text{IS}(\text{A}((I_m(\textbf{black}))((I_m(\textbf{dutch}))(\textbf{man})))))(\textbf{jan})$ analysis

$= (\text{A}((I_m(\textbf{black}))((I_m(\textbf{dutch}))(\textbf{man}))))(\textbf{jan})$ def. of IS

$= ((I_m(\textbf{black}))((I_m(\textbf{dutch}))(\textbf{man})))(\textbf{jan})$ def. of A

$= ((I_m(\textbf{black}))(((\lambda A_{et}.\lambda B_{et}.\lambda x_e.B(x) \wedge A(x))$
$(\textbf{dutch}))(\textbf{man})))(\textbf{jan})$ def. of I_m

$= ((I_m(\textbf{black}))((\lambda B_{et}.\lambda x_e.B(x) \wedge \textbf{dutch}(x))$
$(\textbf{man})))(\textbf{jan})$ func. app. to **dutch**

$= ((I_m(\textbf{black}))(\lambda x_e.\textbf{man}(x) \wedge \textbf{dutch}(x)))(\textbf{jan})$ func. app. to **man**

$= (((\lambda A_{et}.\lambda B_{et}.\lambda y_e.B(y) \wedge A(y))(\textbf{black}))$
$(\lambda x_e.\textbf{man}(x) \wedge \textbf{dutch}(x)))(\textbf{jan})$ def. of I_m

$= (((\lambda B_{et}.\lambda y_e.B(x) \wedge \textbf{black}(y)))\ (\lambda x_e.\textbf{man}(x) \wedge$
$\textbf{dutch}(x)))(\textbf{jan})$ func. app. to **black**

$= (((\lambda y_e.(\lambda x_e.\textbf{man}(x) \wedge \textbf{dutch}(x))(y) \wedge$
$\textbf{black}(y))))(\textbf{jan})$ func. app. to $\lambda x_e.$ **man**$(x) \wedge$ **dutch**(x)

$= (\lambda y_e.(\textbf{man}(y) \wedge \textbf{dutch}(y)) \wedge \textbf{black}(y))(\textbf{jan})$ func. app. to y

$= (\textbf{man}(\textbf{jan}) \wedge \textbf{dutch}(\textbf{jan})) \wedge \textbf{black}(\textbf{jan})$ func. app. to **jan**

$= \textbf{dutch}(\textbf{jan}) \wedge (\textbf{man}(\textbf{jan}) \wedge \textbf{black}(\textbf{jan}))$ def. of $\wedge$

$\leq \textbf{man}(\textbf{jan}) \wedge \textbf{black}(\textbf{jan})$ def. of $\wedge$

$= (\lambda y_e.\textbf{man}(y) \wedge \textbf{black}(y))(\textbf{jan})$ beta reduc. (**jan**)

$= (\text{A}(\lambda y_e.\textbf{man}(y) \wedge \textbf{black}(y)))(\textbf{jan})$ def. of A

$= (\text{IS}(\text{A}(\lambda y_e.\textbf{man}(y) \wedge \textbf{black}(y))))(\textbf{jan})$ def. of IS

$= (\text{IS}(\text{A}((\lambda B_{et}.\lambda y_e.B(y) \wedge \textbf{black}(y))(\textbf{man}))))(\textbf{jan})$ beta reduc. (**man**)

$$= (\text{IS}(\text{A}(((\lambda A_{et}.\lambda B_{et}.\lambda y_e.B(y) \wedge A(y))(\textbf{black}))$$
$$(\textbf{man}))))(\textbf{jan}) \qquad\qquad \text{| beta reduc.}$$
$$\text{| (black)}$$

$$= (\text{IS}(\text{A}((I_m(\textbf{black}))(\textbf{man}))))(\textbf{jan}) \qquad \text{| def. of } I_m$$

$$= [\![\, Jan \; [is \; [a \; [black \; man]]] \,]\!]^M \text{W} \qquad\qquad \text{| analysis}$$

In this case we rely on the intersectivity of *black*, which in conjunction with the intersectivity of *Dutch* licenses the inference that the set characterized by the *et* function $[\![\, black \; [Dutch \; man] \,]\!]^M$ equals to the set characterized by $[\![\, Dutch \; [black \; man] \,]\!]^M$, which is a subset of the set characterized by $[\![\, black \; man \,]\!]^M$.

To summarize Example 4, based on semantic information that distinguishes between the restrictive modifier *short* and the intersective modifiers *Dutch* and *black*, we are able to correctly draw a distinction between the non-entailment pair T_1-H_1 and the entailment pair T_2-H_2. Although these simple examples were constructed here for illustrative purposes, the phenomena of intersectivity and restrictiveness that they illustrate are both relevant for analyzing inferential processes in actual RTE examples such as Example 3. See Appendix 1 for more examples from the RTE.

4 Current Annotation Scheme

In the first stages of our attempt to implement the theoretical model described above, we faced a practical problem concerning the binding of expressions in the RTE data to structurally equivalent expressions in the interpreted lexicon: the lack of a user interface that allows annotators to consistently and effectively annotate RTE data. The root of this problem lies in the intricate ways in which the semantic phenomena that we are concerned with are combined with other phenomena or with each other. Simplifying RTE material to an extent that allows binding it to the lexicon as in the above example is often not straightforward. Consider the following example:

Example 5

T: *Comdex – once among the world's largest trade shows, the launching pad for new computer and software products, and a Las Vegas fixture for 20 years – has been canceled for this year.*

H: *Las Vegas hosted the Comdex trade show for 20 years.*[17]

---

[17]Pair 214 from the development set of RTE 1 (Dagan et al. 2006).

Validating the entailment in this pair requires a lexical alignment between an expression in the text and the word *hosted* in the hypothesis. However, there is no expression in the text to establish this alignment. In the text, the noun *Comdex* is in an appositive relation with three conjoined predications: (i) *once among the world's largest trade shows*; (ii) *the launching pad for new computer and software products*; and (iii) *a Las Vegas fixture for 20 years*. The third element contains a locative restrictive modification in which *Las Vegas* modifies *fixture*. The apposition licenses the inference that *Comdex* IS *a Las Vegas fixture* and serves as a prerequisite for the alignment: *Comdex is a Las Vegas fixture* ⇒ *Las Vegas hosted Comdex* that simplifies the lexical inference. This alignment is also required for validating the modification by the temporal prepositional phrase *for 20 years* which in the text modifies a noun, *fixture*, and in the hypothesis modifies a verb, *host* – apparently two unrelated lexical items. This example illustrates the difficulty in separating lexical inferences from the semantic relations that underlie the constructions they appear in. In this sense, the manual annotation process that we exemplified in Section 3, in which the stage of *Phenomena Simplification* takes place before the semantic machinery applies, is challenging and requires further investigation with RTE data in order to see what part of the RTE can be annotated using this paradigm, and what elements are needed in order to extend its coverage.

Due to this challenge, and in order to enhance our understanding of the phenomena in the RTE corpora, we adopted a narrower annotation scheme that was carried out on RTE 1–4, named SemAnTE 1.0 – *Semantic Annotation of Textual Entailment*.[18] In this annotation work we focused on valid entailments involving restrictive, intersective, and appositive modification that contribute to the recognition of the entailment.[19] In this approach, a construction is annotated if its semantics is required for validating the entailment, but no account is made of the compositional method in which the meaning of the full sentence is obtained. Annotations were marked in 80.65% of the entailments in the RTE 1–4 corpora and reached cross-annotator agreement of 67.96% on average in four consistency checks. The internal structure of the annotated XML files and a use-case of the annotations for evaluating

---

[18] The annotated files of SemAnTE are publicly available for download from: http://logiccommonsense.wp.hum.uu.nl/resources/

[19] Annotators were instructed to construct a full inferential process informally and then to recognize the contribution of the phenomena we aimed to annotate. This method could be applied efficiently only to valid entailments. Invalid entailments marked as *unknown* exhibit an unidentified relation between the text and hypothesis, and pairs marked as *contradictory* rarely center upon the phenomena in question.

an entailment component in the BIUTEE recognizer (Stern and Dagan 2011) are presented in Toledo et al. (2012). See Garoufi (2007) for other relevant work on semantic analysis and annotation of textual entailment done on RTE 2.

4.1 Phenomena Annotated

Our annotations mark inferences by aligning strings in the text and the hypothesis. This is done by pairing each annotation in the text with a corresponding annotation in the hypothesis that marks the output of the inferential process of the phenomenon in question. In the rest of this section we illustrate the phenomena and underline the annotated part in the text with its correspondence in the hypothesis.

4.2 Restrictive modification (RMOD)

T: A $\underline{Cuban}_{Modifier}$ $\underline{American}_{Modifiee}$ who is accused of espionage pleads innocent.

H: $\underline{American}$ accused of espionage.

In this case, *Cuban* modifies *American* and restricts the set of Americans to Cuban Americans. This instance of RMOD validates the inference from *Cuban American* to *American* which is required for establishing the entailment. The intersective nature of the process is not exploited in the actual inference, since the hypothesis does not report that the accused person is Cuban. Thus, only the restrictive property of the modifier *Cuban* is here relevant for the validity of the entailment. More syntactic configurations:

- A verb phrase restricted by a prepositional phrase:
  T: The watchdog International Atomic Energy Agency $\underline{meets\ in}$ $\underline{Vienna}_{Modifiee}$ $\underline{on\ September\ 19}_{Modifier}$.
  H: The International Atomic Energy Agency $\underline{holds\ a\ meeting\ in}$ $\underline{Vienna}$.

- A noun phrase restricted by a prepositional phrase:
  T: U.S. officials have been warning for weeks of $\underline{possible\ terror}$ $\underline{attacks}_{Modifiee}$ $\underline{against\ U.S.\ interests}_{Modifier}$.
  H: The United States has warned a number of times of $\underline{possible}$ $\underline{terrorist\ attacks}$.

4.3 Intersective Modification (CONJ)

T: Nixon $\underline{was\ impeached}$ and $\underline{became\ the\ first\ president\ ever\ to\ resign}$ on August 9th 1974.

H: Nixon $\underline{was\ the\ first\ president\ ever\ to\ resign}$.

This conjunction intersects the two verb phrases *was impeached* and *became the first president ever to resign*. The entailment relies on a subsumption of the full construction to the second conjunct. In addition to canonical conjunctive constructions, CONJ appears also in Restrictive Relative Clauses, whereby the relative clause is interpreted intersectively with the noun being modified:

T: *Iran will soon release <u>eight British servicemen detained</u> along with three vessels.*

H: *<u>British servicemen detained</u>.*

4.4 Appositive modification (APP)

- Appositive subsumption (left part):

    T: *<u>Mr. Conway, Iamgold's chief executive officer,</u> said the vote would be close.*

    H: *<u>Mr. Conway</u> said the vote would be close.*

- Appositive subsumption (right part):

    T: *<u>The country's largest private employer, Wal-Mart Stores Inc.,</u> is being sued by a number of its female employees who claim they were kept out of jobs in management because they are women.*

    H: *<u>Wal-Mart</u> sued for sexual discrimination.*

- Identification of the two parts of the apposition as referring to one another:

    T: *The incident in <u>Mogadishu, the Somali capital,</u> came as U.S. forces began the final phase of their promised March 31 pull-out.*

    H: *<u>The capital of Somalia is Mogadishu.</u>*

In addition to appositions, APP is annotated in several more syntactic constructions:

- Non-Restrictive Relative Clauses:

    T: *A senior coalition official in Iraq said <u>the body, which was found by U.S. military police west of Baghdad,</u> appeared to have been thrown from a vehicle.*

    H: *<u>A body has been found by U. S. military police.</u>*

- Title Constructions:

    T: *<u>Prime Minister Silvio Berlusconi</u> was elected March 28 with a mandate to reform Italy's business regulations and pull the economy out of recession.*

    H: *<u>The Prime Minister is Silvio Berlusconi.</u>*

4.5 Marking Annotations

Given a pair from the RTE in which the entailment relation obtains between the text and hypothesis, the task for the annotators is defined as follows:

1. Read the data and verify the entailment.
2. Describe informally why the entailment holds.
3. Annotate all instances of RMOD, APP and CONJ that play a role in the inferential process.

4.6 Statistics

The annotated corpus is based on the scheme described above, applied to the datasets of RTE 1–4 (Dagan et al. 2006; Bar Haim et al. 2006; Giampiccolo et al. 2007, 2008). The statistics in Table 3 are based on analysis of the annotations done on RTE 1–4 (development and test sets).

4.7 Consistency Checks

We performed four cross-annotator consistency checks on the annotations of SemAnTE 1.0. In each check we picked a number of entailments that both annotators worked on independently and compared the phenomena that they annotated. We reached cross-annotator consistency on 67.96% of the annotations on average, as reported in Table 5. In the remaining 32% of nonidentical annotations, 24.94% of the annotations differed due to ambiguity in the understanding of the sentences by the annotators, to several possible analyses of the inference, or to limited specification in the annotation scheme (see Appendix 2 for examples). These annotations reflect different legitimate interpretations of the data by the annotators. An annotator error was found only in 9.4% of the annotations that were checked.

4.8 Annotation Platform

The annotations were performed using GATE Developer (Cunningham et al. 2011) and recorded above the original RTE XML files. The annotators used the GATE annotation schemes that were defined to correspond to RMOD, APP and CONJ, as shown in Table 4.[20]

The work was performed in two steps: (1) marking the relevant string in the text using one of the GATE annotation schemes that had been

---

[20]The scheme *rel_clause* appears twice in this table because it is used for annotating non-restrictive relative clauses, expressing appositive modification (APP), and also restrictive relative clauses, expressing intersective modification (CONJ). The phenomena APP and CONJ are annotated using several annotation schemes in order to capture the different syntactic expressions that they allow.

TABLE 3: Counters of annotations in RTE 1–4 separated into development and test sets.

$A_\#$ indicates the number of annotations, $P_\#$ indicates the number of entailment pairs containing an annotation and $P_\%$ indicates the portion of annotated pairs relative to the total amount of entailment pairs.

(a) RTE 1

Ann.	Dev set			Test set		
	$A_\#$	$P_\#$	$P_\%$	$A_\#$	$P_\#$	$P_\%$
APP	97	87	31	161	134	34
CONJ	90	79	28	126	112	28
RMOD	180	124	44	243	167	42
Any	367	210	74	530	297	74

(b) RTE 2

Ann.	Dev set			Test set		
	$A_\#$	$P_\#$	$P_\%$	$A_\#$	$P_\#$	$P_\%$
APP	179	149	37	155	135	34
CONJ	141	119	30	161	144	36
RMOD	314	205	51	394	236	59
Any	634	318	80	710	350	88

(c) RTE 3   (d) RTE 4

Ann.	Dev set			Test set			Test set		
	$A_\#$	$P_\#$	$P_\%$	$A_\#$	$P_\#$	$P_\%$	$A_\#$	$P_\#$	$P_\%$
APP	188	150	38	166	136	34	259	200	40
CONJ	176	138	35	162	134	34	192	164	33
RMOD	300	201	50	307	193	48	429	271	54
Any	664	329	82	635	328	82	880	413	83

TABLE 4: GATE Annotation Schemes

Phenomenon	Annotation Schemes
RMOD	r_modification
APP	apposition, title, rel_clause
CONJ	conjunction, rel_clause

TABLE 5: Results of Four Consistency Checks.
Each check examined 50-70 annotated pairs from RTE 1–4. In these four checks 66%, 74.11%, 66.67% and 64.66% of the annotations were identical, respectively. On average, 67.96% of the annotations we checked were identical. The rubric *Incorrect Ann.* presents cases of annotations done with an incorrect scheme or with an incorrect scope. *Ambig.-Struct.* are cases of structural or modifier-attachment ambiguity in the text that led to divergent annotations. *Ambig.-Infer.* are cases of divergent annotations stemming from several possible analyses of the inference. *Ambig.-Scheme* refers to instances of divergent annotations due to unclarity or limited specification in the annotation scheme. The last two measures are reported only for the second, third and fourth checks. See Appendix 2 for examples.

Measure	RTE 2	RTE 1+2	RTE 3	RTE 4
Data Source(s)	Dev set	Test sets	Dev+Test sets	Test set
Entailment Pairs	50	70	70	70
Total Ann.	93	112	99	133
Identical Ann.	62	83	66	86
Missing Ann.	2	7	7	10
Incorrect Ann.	10	1	2	2
Ambig.-Struct.	9	16	20	15
Ambig.-Infer.	N/A	8	13	12
Ambig.-Scheme	N/A	0	9	7
Consistency (%)	66.67	74.11	66.67	64.66

defined for the purpose (e.g. *apposition*), and (2) marking a string in the hypothesis that corresponds to the output of the inferential process. The annotation in the hypothesis is done using a dedicated *reference_to* scheme.

4.9 Connection to the interpreted lexicon approach

Consider the following pair from RTE 2:

Example 6

T: *The anti-terrorist court found two men guilty of murdering Shapour Bakhtiar and his secretary Sorush Katibeh, who were found with their throats cut in August 1991.*

H: *Shapour Bakhtiar died in 1991.*

Several entailment patterns in this example can be explained by appealing to the semantics of APP, CONJ and RMOD, as follows:

APP: The appositive modification in *Shapour Bakhtiar and his secretary Sorush Katibeh, who were found with their throats cut in August 1991* licenses the inference that *Shapour Bakhtiar and his secretary Sorush Katibeh were found with their throats cut in August 1991.*

RMOD: The restrictive modification in *August 1991* licenses a subsumption of this expression to *1991.*

CONJ: The conjunction in *Shapour Bakhtiar and his secretary Sorush Katibeh* licenses a subsumption of this expression to *Shapour Bakhtiar.*

By combining these three patterns, we can infer that *Shapour Bakhtiar was found with his throat cut in 1991.* However, additional world knowledge is required to infer that *found with his throat cut* entails *died.* In our current annotation scheme this inference cannot be handled, since lexical alignment of unmodeled phenomena is not supported. This illustrates the limitations of the current annotation scheme and motivates a more robust approach, as proposed in Section 3.

5 Conclusions

We have described an on-going attempt to establish a model for analyzing entailment data as specified in the RTE challenges. The long-term aim of this project is to contribute to a theoretically sound model of entailment recognition. We have presented a model that utilizes standard semantic principles and illustrated the way it accounts for textual entailment from the RTE corpora. The model centers upon an interpreted lexicon that comprises words and operators. These elements are used to represent a fragment of English to which premises and hypotheses may be bound.

We focus on the annotation of semantic phenomena which are predominant in the RTE corpora and can be annotated with high consistency, but which may have several syntactic expressions and therefore allow us to generalize regarding abstract entailment patterns. Nonmodeled phenomena that exist in the data are simplified in a preparatory step but cases in which such phenomena are deeply intertwined with the semantic phenomena that we model pose a challenge for the formalization of an annotation scheme.

At a first stage, we carried out a restricted annotation scheme marking instances of restrictive, intersective, and appositive modification in entailment pairs, with no account for the full inferential process between the premise and the hypothesis. These phenomena were found in 80.65% of the entailments in RTE 1–4 and were marked with cross-annotator agreement of 68% on average.

We are currently developing an annotation platform based on a proof system. This platform allows annotators to immediately receive feedback from the prover on the soundness of their annotation. Preliminary results indicate that the theoretical work reported here is useful as the basis for such a platform. Further research is currently being conducted to check the feasibility of such platforms for large-scale model building and further linguistic annotation.

Appendix 1 – Further examples from the RTE datasets

In this Appendix we illustrate the analysis described in Section 3.3 on several additional examples from RTE 1–4. For each example we specify the steps of *Phenomena Simplification* and *Binding to Lexicon* which enable us to model the entailment.

Example 1

- Source: RTE 2 test set, pair 282
- Data:

  $T_{Original}$: Senator Hill and Foreign Affairs Minister Alexander Downer will host the 20th annual AUSMIN (Australia-United States ministerial consultations) conference at the Adelaide Town Hall.

  $H_{Original}$: Alexander Downer will host a conference.

- Phenomena Simplification:

  T_{Simple}: Hill, who is a Senator, and Alexander Downer, who is the Foreign Affairs Minister, will host the 20th annual conference, AUSMIN, which is Australia-United States ministerial consultations, at the Adelaide Town Hall.

H_{Simple}: Alexander Downer will host a conference.

- Binding to Lexicon:[21]

  $T_{Lexicon}$: Jan, who is a man, and Dan, who is the alien, greeted the tall girl, who is Sue, who is a nun, slowly.

  $H_{Lexicon}$: Dan greeted a boy.

- Binding Explanation: we bind the entities *Hill* and *Alexander Downer* to *Jan* and *Dan* respectively. The nouns *Senator* and *Foreign Affairs Minister* are bound to *man* and *alien* respectively. The expression *will host* is bound to *greeted*, *20th annual* is bound to *tall* and *conference* is bound to *boy*. The appositive *AUSMIN* is bound to *who is Vim* and the relative clause *which is Australia-United States ministerial consultations* is bound to *who is a nun*. The restrictive adverb *at the Adelaide Town Hall* is bound to *slowly*.

Example 2

- Source: RTE 3 development set, pair 118
- Data:

  $T_{Original}$: According to Nelson Beavers, who is a co-owner of the current company, Carolina Analytical Laboratories, LLC., and has ownership/employment history with Woodson-Tenent and Eurofins, the septic system was installed in the early 1990s.

  $H_{Original}$: Nelson Beavers is one of the owners of Carolina Analytical Laboratories.

- Phenomena Simplification:

  T_{Simple}: Nelson Beavers, who is one of the owners of the current company, which is Carolina Analytical Laboratories, LLC. and has ownership/employment history with Woodson-Tenent and Eurofins, said that the septic system was installed in the early 1990s.

  H_{Simple}: Nelson Beavers is one of the owners of Carolina Analytical Laboratories.

---

[21]This entailment cannot be validated using the interpreted lexicon described in Section 3.3 because a conjunction of entities is not modeled. We provide this example to illustrate the general method.

- Binding to Lexicon:

  $T_{Lexicon}$: Jan, who greeted the man, who is Dan, and saw the nun, praised Vim.

  $H_{Lexicon}$: Jan greeted Dan.

- Binding Explanation: we bind the entities *Nelson Beavers* and *Carolina Analytical Laboratories, LLC.* to *Jan* and *Dan* respectively. The noun *current company* is bound to *man*. The predicates *is one of the owners of* and *has ownership/employment history with* are bound to *greeted* and *saw*. The conjunction of entities *Woodson-Tenent and Eurofins* is bound to the entity *the nun*. The verb phrase *said that septic system was installed in the early 1990s* is bound to the verb phrase *praised Vim*.

Example 3

- Source: RTE 4 test set, pair 928
- Data:

  $T_{Original}$: Five prisoners were beheaded and got their heads exhibited by the rioters during a violent riot in the "Zwinglio Ferreira" Prison, located in Presidente Vencesla, Brazil.

  $H_{Original}$: Five people were killed in a Brazilian prison.

- Phenomena Simplification:

  T_{Simple}: Five people were killed in the prison, which is in Presidente Vencesla, which is Brazilian.

  H_{Simple}: Five people were killed in a Brazilian prison.

- Binding to Lexicon:

  $T_{Lexicon}$: Jan saw the nun, who is a man, who is Dutch.

  $H_{Lexicon}$: Jan saw a Dutch nun.

- Binding Explanation: we bind the noun *Five people* to *Jan*, the verb phrase *were killed in* to *saw* and the noun *prison* to *man*. The predicate *in Presidente Vencesla* is bound to *a man* and the adjective *Brazilian* is bound to *Dutch*.

Appendix 2 – Legitimate Nonidentical Annotations in Consistency Checks

In this Appendix we demonstrate the categories *Ambig.-Struct.*, *Ambig.-Infer.* and *Ambig.-Scheme* mentioned in Table 5, respectively. Our goal here is to show how nonidentical annotations stem from different legitimate interpretations of the data by the annotators.

Example 1

- Category: *Ambig.-Struct.* – different annotations due to structural ambiguity.
- Source: RTE 3 test set, pair 750
- Data:

  T: The British government has indicated its readiness to allow Argentine companies to take part in the development of oilfields in the Falkland islands' territorial waters.

  H: The British government is ready to allow Argentine companies to participate in the development of oilfields.

- Annotator 1: Marked *in the Falkland islands' territorial waters* as a modifier of *development of oilfields*, corresponding to the structure: [[development of oilfields][in the Falkland islands' territorial waters]].

- Annotator 2: Marked *in the Falkland islands' territorial waters* as a modifier of *oilfields*, corresponding to the structure: [development of [oilfields [in the Falkland islands' territorial waters]]].

Example 2

- Category: *Ambig.-Infer.* – different annotations due to multiple ways of establishing the inference.
- Source: RTE 2 test set, pair 24
- Data:

  T: Microsoft Corp., on Thursday, posted higher quarterly earnings as revenue rose 12 percent, but its shares fell after the world's largest software market said current quarter sales would fall below Wall Street expectations.

  H: Microsoft showed revenue growth.

- Annotator 1: Inferred *showed revenue growth* from *posted higher quarterly earnings* and therefore marked *as revenue rose 12 percent* as a restrictive modifier of *posted higher quarterly earnings*.

- Annotator 2: Inferred *showed revenue growth* from *posted higher quarterly earnings, as revenue rose 12 percent* and therefore did not mark a restrictive modifier in this construction.

Example 3

- Category: *Ambig.-Scheme.* – different annotations due to limited specification in the annotation scheme.
- Source: RTE 2 development set, pair 154
- Data:

  T: Clonaid said, Sunday, that the cloned baby, allegedly born to an American woman, and her family were going to return to the United States Monday, but where they live and further details were not released.

  H: Clonaid announced that mother and daughter would be returning to the US on Monday.

- Problem Description: The annotation scheme of SemAnTE 1.0 does not specify how to mark modification of a non-continuous modifiee. In this case, *Sunday* modifies the combination of *said* and its complement *that the cloned baby, allegedly born to an American woman* but this annotation cannot be marked because the modifiee is made of two separated constituents in the syntax.
- Annotator 1: Annotated only *said* as the modifiee of an RMOD.
- Annotator 2: Did not mark the modification.

Acknowledgments

The work of Stavroula Alexandropoulou, Sophie Chesney, Sophia Katrenko, Heidi Klockmann, Pepijn Kokke, Assaf Toledo and Yoad Winter was supported by a VICI grant number 277-80-002 by the Netherlands Organisation for Scientific Research (NWO). We thank Ido Dagan, Philippe de Groote, Ian Pratt and Asher Stern for discussions. Part of the work described in Section 4 was also reported in Toledo et al. (2012) and in Toledo et al. (2013).

References

Bar Haim, R., I. Dagan, B. Dolan, L. Ferro, D. Giampiccolo, B. Magnini, and I. Szpektor. 2006. The Second PASCAL Recognising Textual Entailment Challenge. In *Proceedings of the Second PASCAL Challenges Workshop on Recognising Textual Entailment*.

Bentivogli, L., E. Cabrio, I. Dagan, D. Giampiccolo, M. L. Leggio, and B. Magnini. 2010. Building Textual Entailment Specialized Data Sets: A Methodology for Isolating Linguistic Phenomena Relevant to Inference. In *Proceedings of LREC 2010*.

Bentivogli, L., I. Dagan, H. T. Dang, D. Giampiccolo, and B. Magnini. 2009. The Fifth PASCAL Recognizing Textual Entailment Challenge. In *Proceedings of TAC*, vol. 9, pages 14–24.

Bos, J., S. Clark, M. Steedman, J. R. Curran, and J. Hockenmaier. 2004. Wide-Coverage Semantic Representations from a CCG Parser. In *Proceedings of the 20th international conference on Computational Linguistics*, pages 12–40.

Bos, J. and K. Markert. 2005. Recognising Textual Entailment with Logical Inference. In *Proceedings of the conference on Human Language Technology and Empirical Methods in Natural Language Processing*, pages 628–635.

Cooper, Robin, Dick Crouch, Jan Van Eijck, Chris Fox, Josef Van Genabith, Jan Jaspars, Hans Kamp, David Milward, Manfred Pinkal, Massimo Poesio, Steve Pulman, Ted Briscoe, Holger Maier, and Karsten Konrad. 1996. *Using the Framework*. The Fracas Consortium.

Cunningham, Hamish, Diana Maynard, Kalina Bontcheva, Valentin Tablan, Niraj Aswani, Ian Roberts, Genevieve Gorrell, Adam Funk, Angus Roberts, Danica Damljanovic, Thomas Heitz, Mark A. Greenwood, Horacio Saggion, Johann Petrak, Yaoyong Li, and Wim Peters. 2011. *Text Processing with GATE (Version 6)*. GATE.

Dagan, Ido, Oren Glickman, and Bernardo Magnini. 2006. The PASCAL Recognising Textual Entailment Challenge. *Machine Learning Challenges. Evaluating Predictive Uncertainty, Visual Object Classification, and Recognising Textual Entailment* 3944:177–190.

Dice, L. R. 1945. Measures of the Amount of Ecologic Association Between Species. *Ecology* 26(3):297–302.

Garoufi, Konstantina. 2007. *Towards a Better Understanding of Applied Textual Entailment: Annotation and Evaluation of the RTE-2 Ddataset.*. Master's thesis, Saarland University.

Giampiccolo, D., H. T. Dang, B. Magnini, I. Dagan, and E. Cabrio. 2008. The Fourth PASCAL Recognising Textual Entailment Challenge. In *TAC 2008 Proceedings*.

Giampiccolo, Danilo, Bernardo Magnini, Ido Dagan, and Bill Dolan. 2007. The Third PASCAL Recognizing Textual Entailment Challenge. In *Proceedings of the ACL-PASCAL Workshop on Textual Entailment and Paraphrasing*, RTE '07, pages 1–9. Stroudsburg, PA, USA: Association for Computational Linguistics.

Kamp, H. and U. Reyle. 1993. *From Discourse to Logic: Introduction to Model-Theoretic Semantics of Natural Language, Formal Logic and Discourse Representation Theory*, vol. 42. Kluwer Academic Dordrecht,, The Netherlands.

Kundu, G. and D. Roth. 2011. Adapting Text Instead of the Model : An Open Domain Approach. In *CoNLL*.

LoBue, Peter and Alexander Yates. 2011. Types of Common-Sense Knowledge Needed for Recognizing Textual Entailment. In *Proceedings of the 49th Annual Meeting of the Association for Computational Linguistics: Human Language Technologies: short papers - Volume 2*, HLT '11, pages

329–334. Stroudsburg, PA, USA: Association for Computational Linguistics.

MacCartney, B. and C. D. Manning. 2007. Natural Logic for Textual Inference. In *Proceedings of the ACL-PASCAL Workshop on Textual Entailment and Paraphrasing*, pages 193–200.

Moss, Lawrence S. 2010a. Intersecting Adjectives in Syllogistic Logic. In *Proceedings of the 10th and 11th Biennial conference on The mathematics of language*, MOL '07/09, pages 223–237. Berlin, Heidelberg: Springer-Verlag.

Moss, Lawrence S. 2010b. Syllogistic Logics with Verbs. *Journal of Logic and Computation, special issue on papers from Order, Algebra and Logics* 20(4):947–967.

Pratt-Hartmann, Ian. 2003. A Two-Variable Fragment of English. *Journal of Logic, Language and Information* 12(1):13–45.

Pratt-Hartmann, Ian and Lawrence S. Moss. 2009. Logics for the Relational Syllogistic. *The Review of Symbolic Logic* 2:647–683.

Sammons, M., V. G. Vydiswaran, and D. Roth. 2010. Ask Not What Textual Entailment Can Do for You... In *Proceedings of the 48th Annual Meeting of the Association for Computational Linguistics*, pages 1199–1208.

Sánchez Valencia, Victor. 1991. *Studies on Natural Logic and Categorial Grammar*. Ph.D. thesis, University of Amsterdam.

Stern, Asher and Ido Dagan. 2011. A Confidence Model for Syntactically-Motivated Entailment Proofs. In *Proceedings of RANLP 2011*.

Toledo, Assaf, Stavroula Alexandropoulou, Sophia Katrenko, Heidi Klockmann, Pepijn Kokke, and Yoad Winter. 2013. Semantic Annotation of Textual Entailment. In *Proceedings of the 10th International Conference on Computational Semantics (IWCS 2013) – Long Papers*, pages 240–251. Potsdam, Germany: Association for Computational Linguistics.

Toledo, Assaf, Sophia Katrenko, Stavroula Alexandropoulou, Heidi Klockmann, Asher Stern, Ido Dagan, and Yoad Winter. 2012. Semantic Annotation for Textual Entailment Recognition. In *Proceedings of the Eleventh Mexican International Conference on Artificial Intelligence (MICAI)*.

Winter, Y. 2010. *Elements of Formal Semantics*. Unpublished ms., to appear with Edinburgh University Press.

Synthetic logic

ALEX J. DJALALI[1]

The role of inference as it relates to natural language (NL) semantics
has often been neglected. Recently, there has been a move away by
some NL semanticists from the heavy machinery of, say, Montagovian-
style semantics to a more proof-based approach.

Although researchers tend to study each type of system independently,
MacCartney (2009) and MacCartney and Manning (2009) (henceforth
M&M) recently developed an algorithmic approach to natural logic
that attempts to combine insights from both monotonicity calculi and
various syllogistic fragments to derive compositionally the relation between two NL sentences from the relations of their parts.

At the heart of their system, M&M begin with seven intuitive lexical-
semantic relations that NL expressions can stand in, e.g., synonymy
and antonymy, and then ask the question: if φ stands in some lexical-
semantic relation to ψ; and ψ stands in (a possibly different) lexical-
semantic relation to θ; what lexical-semantic relation (if any) can be
concluded about the relation between φ and θ? This type of reasoning
has the familiar shape of a logical inference rule.

However, the logical properties of their join table have not been explored in any real detail. The purpose of this paper is to give M&M's
table a proper logical treatment. As I will show, the table has the
underlying form of a syllogistic fragment and relies on a sort of generalized transitive reasoning.

1 Introduction

The role of inference as it relates to natural language (NL) semantics
has oft been neglected. Recently, there has been a move away by some
NL semanticists from the heavy machinery of, say, Montagovian-style
semantics to a more proof-based approach. This represents a belief
that the notion of *derivability* plays as central a role in NL semantics

---

[1]Stanford University

LiLT Volume 9
Perspectives on Semantic Representations for Textual Inference.
Copyright © 2014, CSLI Publications.

as that of *entailment*. Beginning with van Benthem (1986), and continuing on with Valencia (1991), Dowty (1994), Gilad and Francez (2005), Moss (2008), Moss (2010), van Benthem (2008), Moss (2009) and Moss (2012) among others, the study of various *natural logics* has become commonplace.

Natural logicians place an emphasis on the development and study of proof theories that capture the sort of inferences speakers of a particular NL like English make *in practice*. It should be said, though, that 'natural logic' is a catchall term that refers to either the study of various monotonicity calculi à la van Benthem or Aristotelean-style syllogistic fragments à la Moss. Although researchers tend to study each type of system independently, MacCartney (2009) and MacCartney and Manning (2009) (henceforth M&M) recently developed an algorithmic approach to natural logic that attempts to combine insights from both monotonicity calculi and various syllogistic fragments to derive compositionally the relation between two NL sentences from the relations of their parts.

At the heart of their system, M&M begin with seven intuitive lexical-semantic relations that NL expressions can stand in, e.g., *synonymy* and *antonymy*, and then ask the question: if φ stands in some lexical-semantic relation to ψ; and ψ stands in (a possibly different) lexical-semantic relation to ϑ; what lexical-semantic relation (if any) can be concluded about the relation between φ and ϑ? This type of reasoning has the familiar shape of a logical inference rule, a schema of which is given in (1):

$$(1) \qquad \frac{\varphi R \psi \qquad \psi S \vartheta}{\varphi T \vartheta}$$

Drawing from their stock of lexical-semantic relations, for every instance of R and S, M&M reason semantically to calculate T, and present their results in what they call a *join table*. However, to my knowledge at least, the logical properties of their join table have not been explored in any real detail. The purpose of this paper is to give M&M's table a proper logical treatment. As I will show, the table has the underlying form of a syllogistic fragment and relies on a sort of *generalized transitive reasoning*. Here, I define a basic set-theoretic semantics and proof calculus for M&M's join table and prove a completeness theorem for it.

2 Synthetic Logic

I begin first by defining the syntax of a *synthetic language* $\mathcal{SYN}$.

Definition 2.1 (Syntax of $\mathcal{SYN}$). Let $p_1, \ldots p_n$ be *atoms* for $n < \omega$, which themselves are all elements of Φ the set of *proper terms*. Then

1. If φ is a proper term, then so is $\overline{\varphi}$. Nothing else is a proper term.
2. If φ and ψ are proper terms, then

$$\varphi \equiv \psi, \quad \varphi \sqsubset \psi, \quad \varphi \sqsupset \psi,$$
$$\varphi \wedge \psi, \quad \varphi \between \psi, \quad \varphi \smile \psi$$

are *synthetic terms*.

I let $\mathcal{SYN}$ be the smallest set containing both sets of proper and synthetic terms given by definition 2.1. I say $\overline{\varphi}$ is the *complement* of φ and refer to the set $\mathcal{M} = \{\equiv, \sqsubset, \sqsupset, \wedge, \between, \smile\}$ as the set of *MaCcartney relations*, as they are taken from MacCartney (2009) and MacCartney and Manning (2009). The relations themselves can be read as *equality, strict forward* and *reverse entailment, negation, alternation* and *cover* respectively. I use R, S and T as meta-logical variables ranging over elements of $\mathcal{M}$; and I will use φ, ψ and ϑ as meta-logical variables ranging over proper terms. Finally, I assume that $\varphi \equiv \overline{\overline{\varphi}}$ for all φ.

In definition 2.1, I use the term 'atoms' as opposed to, say, 'proposition letters'. This is purposeful. Intuitively, there is nothing that prevents the atoms of a synthetic language $\mathcal{SYN}$ from being NL expressions of any type, assuming some sort of syntactic typing. From a formal perspective, this would simply amount to considering a family of synthetic languages $\{\mathcal{SYN}_\alpha \mid \alpha \in \text{Types}\}$, where *Types* is the set of, say, Montagovian types. To better understand this, suppose

(2)   run $\sqsubset$ move

is a member of some intransitive verb synthetic language $\mathcal{SYN}_{\text{IV}}$. Intuitively, (2) makes the meta-semantic statement, "The intransitive verb *run* strictly forward entails the intransitive verb *move*". In this way, synthetic languages are quite general – they just are languages of the lexicon.

No doubt synthetic languages are impoverished, as they lack the classical boolean connectives. This is not to say that a synthetic language could not be extended. I refer the reader to Moss (2010) for a natural logic with boolean connectives both *inside* and *out*. In our setting, the addition of 'inside' boolean connectives would be to augment the class of proper terms by, say, the elements of the set $\{\neg, \wedge\}$. This would result in terms like the following:

(3) $\varphi \wedge \psi$

where φ and ψ are proper terms.

To have 'outside' boolean connectives would be to augment the class of synthetic terms by a functionally complete set of connectives like the one above. Examples of such terms would be

(4) $\qquad (\varphi \sqsubset \psi) \wedge (\vartheta \sqsupset \chi)$

where φ, ψ, ϑ and χ are proper terms. Given both outside and inside boolean connectives, the following would be a valid expression exhibiting both types of coordination:

(5) $\qquad ((\varphi \wedge \psi) \sqsubset \varphi) \vee ((\varphi \wedge \psi) \sqsupset \varphi)$

Without relying on semantic intuitions, it may be difficult to intuit the difference between inside and outside Boolean connectives. From a syntactic perspective, the analogy, here, is between entity level, or more generally, non-sentential level, coordination in a NL language like English, e.g., *John and Mary*, versus sentential level coordination, e.g., *John went to the store and Mary went to the store*. The former would be an instance of inside Boolean coordination, and the latter would be an instance of outside Booelean coordination. As it turns out, augmenting definition 2.1 in this way would be productive for reasons which will become clearer. However, I leave this extension for future work.

Turning now to the semantics of $\mathcal{SYN}$, I begin first by defining the sorts of models I will be working with.

Definition 2.2 (Synthetic Models). Let a *synthetic model* $\mathbb{M}$ be the pair $\langle D, AAA \cdot BBB \rangle$, where D is a non-empty set and $AAA \cdot BBB$ is an interpretation function such that $AAA\varphi BBB \subseteq D$ and

1. $AAA\overline{\varphi}BBB = D - AAA\varphi BBB$;

2. $AAA\overline{\overline{\varphi}}BBB = AAA\varphi BBB$;

3. $AAA\varphi BBB \neq AAA\overline{\varphi}BBB$; and

4. $AAA\varphi BBB \neq \begin{cases} \varnothing \\ D \end{cases}$ or

for all proper terms φ

The first three conditions on the interpretation function $AAA \cdot BBB$ force the standard semantics of set-theoretic complementation. The fourth condition restricts the possible model space to just those models which interpret each proper term *non-vacuously*, where a 'non-vacuous' term is a term which denotes neither the domain in its entirety nor the empty-set. In fact, I call the logic 'synthetic' after Popper (1968) who argues that "synthetic statements in general are placed, by the entailment relation, in the open interval between self-contradiction and tautology".[2]

---

[2]Instead of reanalyzing non-vacuous terms, such as *the square circle* as a pred-

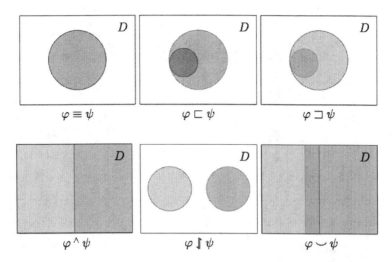

FIGURE 1: A graphical representation of the $\mathcal{M}$-relations

The semantics of the various synthetic terms can be naturally defined set-theoretically, as in definition 2.3. A pictorial representation of the semantics of each relation is shown in figure 1.

Definition 2.3 (Tarski-Style Truth-Conditions). Let φ and ψ be proper terms and R a $\mathcal{M}$-relation. Define the denotation of the synthetic term $\varphi R \psi$, written $AAA\varphi R\psi BBB$, as follows:

$\mathbb{M} \models \varphi \equiv \psi \Leftrightarrow AAA\varphi BBB = AAA\psi BBB$

$\mathbb{M} \models \varphi \sqsubset \psi \Leftrightarrow AAA\varphi BBB \subset AAA\psi BBB$

$\mathbb{M} \models \varphi \sqsupset \psi \Leftrightarrow AAA\varphi BBB \supset AAA\psi BBB$

$\mathbb{M} \models \varphi \wedge \psi \Leftrightarrow (AAA\varphi BBB \cap AAA\psi BBB = \varnothing) \wedge (AAA\varphi BBB \cup AAA\psi BBB = D)$

$\mathbb{M} \models \varphi \int \psi \Leftrightarrow (AAA\varphi BBB \cap AAA\psi BBB = \varnothing) \wedge (AAA\varphi BBB \cup AAA\psi BBB \neq D)$

$\mathbb{M} \models \varphi \smile \psi \Leftarrow (AAA\varphi BBB \cap AAA\psi BBB \neq \varnothing) \wedge (AAA\varphi BBB \cup AAA\psi BBB = D)$

---

icate having an empty-extension à la Russell (1905), M&M bar them from their logic altogether, claiming that such terms fail to divide the world into meaningful conceptual categories. This might seem odd to logicians or philosophers, however, as M&M's formal system is the basis for this work, I see no harm in assuming it here.

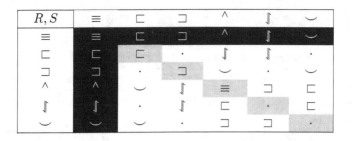

FIGURE 2: $\mathcal{M}$-Rules

No doubt the logic could be simplified drastically by giving the semantics of forward entailment in terms of (set-theoretic) sloppy forward containment ($\subseteq$) and negation ($\neg$) and defining the other $\mathcal{M}$-relations in terms of these connectives. However, M&M make the purposeful decision to effectively tease apart the $\subseteq$ relation into two different ones. I follow suit and sacrifice formal elegance in attempt to capture a finite, primitive stock of semantic relations that humans, at least intuitively, seem to reason in terms of. Having said that, the meta-logical relation of *entailment* will be defined in the usual way.

Definition 2.4 (Entailment). Let Γ be a set of synthetic terms. Γ *entails* $\varphi R\psi$ written, $\Gamma \models \varphi R\psi$ just in case

$$\mathbb{M} \models \varphi'S\psi' \Rightarrow \mathbb{M} \models \varphi R\psi$$

for all $\varphi'S\psi' \in \Gamma$.

To conclude this section, the members of $\mathcal{M}$ can be shown to be mutually exclusive.

Theorem 2.1 (Mutual Exclusivity of the $\mathcal{M}$-relations). If $\mathbb{M}$ is a synthetic model then

$$\mathbb{M} \models \varphi R\psi \Rightarrow \mathbb{M} \not\models \varphi S\psi$$

for $R \neq S$.

The proof is trivial but tedious and relies on basic set theory and the fact that all proper terms are interpreted non-vacuously.

2.1 The Proof Calculus

The proof system of this logic effectively takes the form of a *natural deduction* system. There will be two types of rules: M-rules and D-rules, the former named after MacCartney because they are effectively the rules he works with in his dissertation; and the latter so-named to distinguish the fact that I have added them in this paper to ultimately create a complete proof-calculus.

I begin with the former, a schema of which is given in definition 2.5.

Definition 2.5 (M-Rules). Let Γ be a set of synthetic formulas. Then,

$$\frac{\Gamma \vdash \varphi R \psi \qquad \Gamma \vdash \psi S \vartheta}{\Gamma \vdash \varphi T \vartheta} \ R, S$$

are rules of the calculus.

This schema is instantiated by taking T to be the M-relation gotten by intersecting the M-relations in the R-row and S-column in Figure (2). So, for example, (6) is a valid rule in the synthetic proof calculus:

(6)
$$\frac{\Gamma \vdash \varphi \equiv \psi \qquad \Gamma \vdash \psi \sqsubset \vartheta}{\Gamma \vdash \varphi \sqsubset \vartheta} \ \equiv, \sqsubset$$

It reads, 'If there are derivations from a set of premises Γ of $\varphi \equiv \psi$ and $\psi \sqsubset \vartheta$, then there is a derivation of $\varphi \sqsubset \vartheta$ from the same set of premises'.

Figure 2 is a modified version of M&M's join table. In their table, the value of the cells marked here with the dot '·' correspond to a disjunction of synthetic terms. Translating these cells of their table in terms of the calculus presented here, the pseudo-rule $\sqsubset, \sqsupset$ would be given as follows:

(7)
$$\frac{\Gamma \vdash \varphi \sqsubset \psi \qquad \Gamma \vdash \psi \sqsupset \vartheta}{\Gamma \vdash (\varphi \equiv \vartheta) \vee (\varphi \sqsubset \vartheta) \vee (\varphi \sqsupset \vartheta) \vee (\varphi \,\| \, \vartheta)} \ \sqsubset, \sqsupset$$

Although M&M do not define a proper proof a calculus, in this instance, their semantic reasoning reasoning would be as follows:

- Given that (i) the set denoted by φ is strictly contained in the set denoted by ψ, and (ii) the set denoted by ϑ is strictly contained in the set denoted by ψ, what can one say about the set-theoretic relation that holds between the sets denoted by φ and χ?

- One can certainly construct a model in which the set denoted by φ is equal to the set denoted by ϑ; but one can construct a model in which the set denoted by φ is strictly contained in the set denoted by ϑ; but one can also construct ... and so on and so forth for all the disjuncts in (7).

- Given (i) and (ii), at best, one can say that φ is equivalent to ϑ or φ strictly forward entails ϑ or ... and so on and so forth.[3]

---

[3]M&M observe that, given the assumptions in (i) and (ii), it is not possible to construct a model in which φ and ϑ denote complementary sets, lest a contradiction ensue. So, they do not include the synthetic statement $\varphi \wedge \vartheta$ in the disjunctive statement. (Similarly, for $\varphi \smile \vartheta$).

The logic, as I have laid it out here, is not expressive enough to capture the above disjunctive reasoning. This is because it lacks 'outside' boolean connectives in the sense made explicit above. This being the case, I omit the values in figure 2 marked with a '·' from being possible instantiations of the above schema.

Although not in M&M's original system, I include the following proof rules in the calculus:

Definition 2.6 (*D-rules*). Again, let Γ be a set of synthetic terms. Then,

$$\frac{}{\Gamma \vdash \varphi \equiv \varphi} \equiv_1 \qquad \frac{\Gamma \vdash \varphi \equiv \psi}{\Gamma \vdash \psi \equiv \varphi} \equiv_2 \qquad \frac{}{\Gamma \vdash \varphi \wedge \overline{\varphi}} \wedge_1 \qquad \frac{\Gamma \vdash \varphi \wedge \psi}{\Gamma \vdash \psi \wedge \varphi} \wedge_2$$

$$\frac{\Gamma \vdash \varphi \sqsubset \psi}{\Gamma \vdash \psi \sqsupset \varphi} \sqsubset_1 \qquad \frac{\Gamma \vdash \varphi \sqsupset \psi}{\Gamma \vdash \psi \sqsubset \varphi} \sqsupset_1 \qquad \frac{\Gamma \vdash \varphi \, \talloblong \, \psi}{\Gamma \vdash \psi \, \talloblong \, \varphi} \talloblong_1 \qquad \frac{\Gamma \vdash \varphi \smile \psi}{\Gamma \vdash \psi \smile \varphi} \smile_1$$

$$\frac{\varphi \in \Gamma}{\Gamma \vdash \varphi} \text{ Refl}$$

are rules of the calculus.

The *D*-rules syntactically encode for the basic relational properties of the $\mathcal{M}$-relations. $\equiv_2$, for example, allows us to prove the fact that set-theoretic equality is *symmetric*.

From a logical perspective, Γ is nothing more than a set of premises. However, in natural logic, it is understood as being a *lexicon* that encodes for the basic lexical semantic relations expressions of a language stand in. A sample lexicon might look something like the following:

(8) $\Gamma = \{$ Dutchman $\talloblong$ Frenchman,   Dutchman $\sqsubset$ man $\}$

In (8), Γ encodes for the fact that the noun *Dutchman* alternates with the noun *Frenchman* and the fact that the noun *Dutchman* strictly forward entails the noun *man*. (In this case, I am working with a synthetic language of common nouns).

More generally, from a lexicon, various other relations that natural language statements stand in can be proven. To see how the synthetic proof calculus works in practice, consider the following derivations shown in theorem 2.2:

Theorem 2.2. Let Γ be a set of premises. The following theorems are all derivable in the proof calculus:[4]

---

[4]I also provide natural language instances of each theorem to demonstrate that given certain intuitive assumptions about the relations natural language expressions stand in, other intuitive statements about those relations can be inferred.

1. $\Gamma', \varphi \equiv \psi \vdash \varphi \wedge \overline{\psi}$

   Proof.

$$\cfrac{\cfrac{\varphi \equiv \psi \in \Gamma}{\Gamma \vdash \varphi \equiv \psi}\;\text{Refl} \qquad \cfrac{}{\Gamma \vdash \psi \wedge \overline{\psi}}\;{}^{\wedge}{}_1}{\Gamma \vdash \varphi \wedge \overline{\psi}}\;{}_{\equiv,\,\wedge}$$

   □

(9) $\Gamma', \mathsf{Superman} \equiv \mathsf{Clark\ Kent} \vdash \mathsf{Superman} \wedge \overline{\mathsf{Clark\ Kent}}$

2. $\Gamma', \varphi \wedge \psi \vdash \varphi \equiv \overline{\psi}$

   Proof.

$$\cfrac{\cfrac{\varphi \wedge \psi \in \Gamma}{\Gamma \vdash \varphi \wedge \psi}\;\text{Refl} \qquad \cfrac{}{\Gamma \vdash \psi \wedge \overline{\psi}}\;{}^{\wedge}{}_1}{\Gamma \vdash \varphi \equiv \overline{\psi}}\;{}_{\wedge,\,\wedge}$$

   □

(10) $\Gamma', \mathsf{hate} \wedge \overline{\mathsf{hate}} \vdash \mathsf{hates} \equiv \overline{\mathsf{hate}}$

3. $\Gamma \vdash \varphi \equiv \overline{\overline{\varphi}}$

   Proof.

$$\cfrac{\cfrac{}{\Gamma \vdash \varphi \wedge \overline{\varphi}}\;{}^{\wedge}{}_1 \qquad \cfrac{}{\Gamma \vdash \overline{\varphi} \wedge \overline{\overline{\varphi}}}\;{}^{\wedge}{}_1}{\Gamma \vdash \varphi \equiv \overline{\overline{\varphi}}}$$

   □

(11) $\Gamma \vdash \mathsf{human} \equiv \overline{\overline{\mathsf{human}}}$

4. $\Gamma', \varphi \sqsubset \psi \vdash \overline{\psi} \sqsubset \overline{\varphi}$

   Proof.

$$\cfrac{\cfrac{\cfrac{}{\Gamma \vdash \varphi \wedge \overline{\varphi}}\;{}^{\wedge}{}_1}{\Gamma \vdash \overline{\varphi} \wedge \varphi}\;{}^{\wedge}{}_2 \qquad \cfrac{\cfrac{\varphi \sqsubset \psi \in \Gamma}{\Gamma \vdash \varphi \sqsubset \psi}\;\text{Refl} \qquad \cfrac{}{\Gamma \vdash \psi \wedge \overline{\psi}}\;{}^{\wedge}{}_1}{\Gamma \vdash \varphi \int \overline{\psi}}\;{}_{\sqsubset,\,\wedge}}{\cfrac{\cfrac{\Gamma \vdash \overline{\varphi} \sqsupset \overline{\psi}}{}\;{}_{\wedge,\,\int}}{\Gamma \vdash \overline{\psi} \sqsubset \overline{\varphi}}\;{}_{\sqsupset_1}}$$

   □

(12) $\Gamma', \mathsf{dane} \sqsubset \mathsf{dog} \vdash \overline{\mathsf{dog}} \sqsubset \overline{\mathsf{dane}}$

5. $\Gamma', \varphi \sqsupset \psi \vdash \overline{\psi} \sqsupset \overline{\varphi}$

   Proof.

$$\cfrac{\cfrac{\cfrac{\Gamma \vdash \varphi \wedge \overline{\varphi}}{\Gamma \vdash \overline{\varphi} \wedge \varphi} {}_{\wedge_1} }{}_{\wedge_2} \qquad \cfrac{\cfrac{\varphi \sqsupset \psi \in \Gamma}{\Gamma \vdash \varphi \sqsupset \psi} \text{ Refl} \qquad \cfrac{\Gamma \vdash \psi \wedge \overline{\psi}}{} {}_{\wedge_1}}{\Gamma \vdash \varphi \smile \overline{\psi}} {}_{\sqsupset, \wedge}}{\cfrac{\cfrac{\Gamma \vdash \overline{\varphi} \sqsubset \overline{\psi}}{}{}_{\wedge, \smile}}{\Gamma \vdash \overline{\psi} \sqsupset \overline{\varphi}} {}_{\sqsubset_1}}$$

$\square$

(13) $\qquad\qquad \Gamma', \text{dog} \sqsupset \text{dane} \vdash \overline{\text{dane}} \sqsupset \overline{\text{dog}}$

6. $\Gamma', \varphi \wr \psi \vdash \varphi \sqsubset \overline{\psi}$

   Proof.

$$\cfrac{\cfrac{\varphi \wr \psi \in \Gamma}{\Gamma \vdash \varphi \wr \psi} \text{ Refl} \qquad \cfrac{\Gamma \vdash \psi \wedge \overline{\psi}}{}{}_{\wedge_1}}{\Gamma \vdash \varphi \sqsubset \overline{\psi}} {}_{\wedge, \wedge}$$

$\square$

(14) $\quad \Gamma', \text{Dutchman} \wr \text{Frenchman} \vdash \text{Dutchman} \sqsubset \overline{\text{Frenchman}}$

7. $\Gamma', \varphi \smile \psi \vdash \varphi \sqsupset \overline{\psi}$

   Proof.

$$\cfrac{\cfrac{\varphi \smile \psi \in \Gamma}{\Gamma \vdash \varphi \smile \psi} \text{ Refl} \qquad \cfrac{\Gamma \vdash \psi \wedge \overline{\psi}}{}\text{ Neg}}{\Gamma \vdash \varphi \sqsupset \overline{\psi}} {}_{\smile, \wedge}$$

$\square$

(15) $\qquad\qquad \Gamma', \text{animal} \smile \overline{\text{human}} \vdash \text{animal} \sqsupset \overline{\overline{\text{human}}}$

Importantly, all of the above proofs are *invertible*. That is to say, $\Gamma', \varphi R \psi \vdash \varphi' S \psi'$ just in case $\Gamma', \varphi' S \psi' \vdash \varphi R \psi$.

Finally, in order to capture the notion of an inconsistent premise set, I instead add the inference rule given in definition 2.7 to the proof calculus:

Definition 2.7 (Explosion). Let Γ be a set of synthetic terms. Then,

$$\frac{\Gamma \vdash \varphi R \psi \qquad \Gamma \vdash \varphi S \psi \qquad \text{for } R \neq S}{\Gamma \vdash \varphi' T \psi' \text{ for all } \varphi' T \psi'} \text{ Exp}$$

is a rule of the calculus.

This rule states that if, from an arbitrary premise set Γ, two synthetic statements that claim the proper term φ stands in a $\mathcal{M}$-relation with the proper term ψ different from the other, then every synthetic term is derivable from that premise set. The principle of explosion has its roots in the latin term *ex falso quodlibet*, which means 'from a contradiction anything follows'. In this setting, Exp is the proof-theoretic realization of theorem 2.1. Now I can define what it is for a premise set to be consistent:

Definition 2.8 (Consistency). Γ is consistent if, and only if $\Gamma \nvdash \varphi R\psi$ for some synthetic term $\varphi R\psi$.

In classical propositional logic, for example, a consistent set of premises is a set that does not prove falsum. From this definition, for any arbitrary premise set Γ to prove every formula of a language is for that premise set to be *inconsistent*. So, I take what is a theorem in classical logic as my definition for inconsistency here. Theorem 2.3 gives an example of an inconsistent set:

Theorem 2.3. $\Gamma = \{\varphi \sqsubset \psi, \psi \sqsupset \vartheta, \varphi \smile \vartheta\}$ is *inconsistent*.

Proof.

$$
\cfrac{\cfrac{\cfrac{\cfrac{\varphi \sqsubset \psi \in \Gamma}{\Gamma \vdash \varphi \sqsubset \psi}\text{ Refl}}{\Gamma \vdash \psi \sqsupset \varphi}\sqsubset_1 \quad \cfrac{\cfrac{\varphi \smile \vartheta \in \Gamma}{\Gamma \vdash \varphi \smile \vartheta}\text{ Refl}}{\Gamma \vdash \psi \smile \vartheta}\sqsupset,\smile}{\Gamma \vdash \psi \smile \vartheta} \quad \cfrac{\cfrac{\psi \sqsupset \vartheta \in \Gamma}{\Gamma \vdash \psi \sqsupset \vartheta}\text{ Refl}}{}}{\Gamma \vdash \varphi'T\psi' \text{ for all } \varphi'T\psi'}\text{ Exp}
$$

$\square$

2.2 Completeness

Finally, the logic laid out here can be shown to be complete.

Theorem 2.4 (Completeness). Let Γ be a set of synthetic terms. Then

$$\Gamma \vdash \varphi R\psi \Leftrightarrow \Gamma \models \varphi R\psi$$

As usual, *soundness* is trivial, but tedious, as it involves proving the statement of the theorem for all the inference rules of the calculus. I leave it as an exercise to the reader; and the remainder of this section proving the *adequacy of the calculus*, reasoning via the contraposition.

(16) $\qquad\qquad \Gamma \nvdash \varphi R\psi \Rightarrow \Gamma \nvDash \varphi R\psi$

The proof will proceed as normal via a model existence lemma, and essentially follows Moss (2010). The model we construct will be a *term model*.

Lemma 2.1 (Model Existence). Let Γ be a set of synthetic terms. If Γ is consistent, then Γ has a model.

Model existence will be proved via a *representation theorem*.

I begin first by defining the necessary algebraic machinery.

Definition 2.9 (Orthoposets). An *orthoposet* is a tuple $(P, \leq, 0, -)$ such that

1. $(P, \leq)$ is a partial order;
2. 0 is a minimal element, i.e., $0 \leq x$ for all $x \in P$;
3. $x \leq y$ if, and only if $\bar{y} \leq \bar{x}$;
4. $\bar{\bar{x}} = x$
5. If $x \leq y$ and $x \leq \bar{y}$, then $x = 0$.

An orthoposet is a partial order with a minimal element. The third clause guarantees that the contraposition holds; clause four is the law of double negation; and the final clause guarantees that any inconsistent element just is the minimal element. Importantly for me, every consistent set of premises Γ induces an orthoposet on the domain of proper terms Φ.

Lemma 2.2. If Γ is consistent, then Γ induces an orthoposet on Φ.

Proof. For $\varphi, \psi \in \Phi$, define the relation $\leq_\Gamma$ as follows:

$$(17) \qquad \varphi \leq_\Gamma \psi \Leftrightarrow \Gamma \vdash \varphi \equiv \psi \text{ or } \Gamma \vdash \varphi \sqsubset \psi$$

$\leq_\Gamma$ induces an equivalence relation on Φ:

$$(18) \qquad [\varphi]_{=_\Gamma} = \{\psi \mid \varphi \leq_\Gamma \psi \text{ and } \psi \leq_\Gamma \varphi\}$$

To prove that $=_\Gamma$ is an equivalence relation, observe that $\varphi \leq_\Gamma \psi$ and $\psi \leq_\Gamma \varphi$ if, and only if $\Gamma \vdash \varphi \equiv \psi$ and $\Gamma \vdash \psi \equiv \varphi$, lest Γ be inconsistent. So, the only interesting case is transitivity, which is guaranteed by the M-rule $\equiv, \equiv$.

Now, let Φ^* be the quotient $\Phi/=_\Gamma$ and define the relation $\leq$ as follows:

$$(19) \qquad [\varphi]_{=_\Gamma} \leq [\psi]_{=_\Gamma} \Leftrightarrow \forall x \in [\varphi]_{=_\Gamma} \forall y \in \leq [\psi]_{=_\Gamma} (x \leq_\Gamma y)$$

Observe that $[\varphi]_{=_\Gamma} \leq [\psi]_{=_\Gamma}$ if, and only if $\forall x, y$ such that $x \in [\varphi]_{=_\Gamma}, y \in [\psi]_{=_\Gamma}, \Gamma \vdash x \equiv y$ or $\forall x, y$ such that $x \in [\varphi]_{=_\Gamma}, y \in [\psi]_{=_\Gamma}, \Gamma \vdash x \sqsubset y$. Clearly, $\leq$ is a partial order. Reflexivity and anti-symmetry are trivial. Transitivity can be gotten from either $\equiv, \equiv$ or $\sqsubset, \sqsubset$.

As Γ is assumed to be consistent, there is no $\varphi \leq \bar{\varphi}$. Therefore, add fresh elements $0, 1$ to Φ^*, setting $\bar{0} = 1$ and $0 < x < 1$ for all $x \in \Phi^*$. Finally, set $[\bar{\varphi}]_{=_\Gamma} = \overline{[\varphi]}_{=_\Gamma}$. I claim $(\Phi^*, \leq, 0, -)$ is an orthposet. Condition 3 of definition 2.9 can be gotten by theorem 2.2.4, and condition 4 is obtained by theorem 2.2.3. The final condition holds vacuously, as Γ is assumed to be consistent. □

Before continuing with the proof proper, I will need a few more algebraic notions.

Definition 2.10 (Points). A *point* of an orthoposet is a subset $S \subseteq P$ with the following properties:

1. If $x \in S$ and $x \leq y$, then $y \in S$ (S is *upward-closed*);
2. For all x, either $x \in S$ or $\overline{x} \in S$ (S is *complete*), but not both (S is *consistent*).

A point is similar to an *ultrafilter*. It is closed under upward entailment and makes a decision for every element in the domain whether that element or its complement, but not both, is a member of that point.

The following lemma, due to Moss (2010), will prove useful in the construction of the necessary model.

Lemma 2.3. For a subset, T, of an orthoposet $P = (P, \leq, 0, -)$, the following are equivalent:

1. T is a subset of a point S in P;
2. For all $x, y \in T, x \not\leq \overline{y}$.

As is common in algebra, the notion of a *morphism* will play an essential role in proof by representation.

Definition 2.11 (Morphism). A *morphism* of orthoposets is a map f such that

1. if $x \leq y$ then $f(x) \leq f(y)$;
2. $f(\overline{x}) = \overline{f(x)}$;
3. $f(0) = 0$.

We say that f is *strictly* order-preserving if $x \leq y$ if, and only if $f(x) \leq f(y)$. That is to say a strict morphism is a bi-directional order and complementation preserving map.

At the outset, we stated our proof of completeness will proceed via representation. The most well-known representation theorem is Stone's, which states that every boolean algebra can be represented as a system of sets ordered by the inclusion relation. As Moss (2010) observes, it has long been established in quantum logic that every orthoposet can be represented as a system of sets also ordered by the inclusion relation (Zierler and Schlessinger 1965; Calude et al. 1999).

Theorem 2.5 (Representation). Let $P = (P, \leq, 0, -)$ be an orthoposet. There is a set, points(P), and a strict morphism f such that

$$f : P \rightarrow \mathcal{P}(\text{points}(P))$$

The proof is gotten by defining $f(x) = \{S \in \text{point}(P) \mid x \in S\}$. I refer the reader to Moss (2010) for the remainder of the proof.

We are now equipped with all the algebraic machinery we need to prove lemma 2.1.

Proof. As Γ is consistent, I invoke lemma 2.2 and theorem 2.5 to conclude Φ can be represented as a system of sets. In particular, define $g : \Phi \to \Phi_{=_\Gamma}$ such that $\varphi \mapsto [\varphi]_{=_\Gamma}$ and let f be the strict morphism defined in theorem 2.5.

Now, let $\mathbb{M} = (\text{points}(\Phi^*), AAA \cdot BBB)$, such that $AAA \cdot BBB = g \circ f$, the composition of g with f. I claim that $\mathbb{M}$ a synthetic model. I must check that it has the properties stipulated in definition 2.2. The first condition on the valuation function can be shown to hold as follows:

$$AAA\overline{\varphi}BBB = f(g(\overline{\varphi})) \qquad\qquad \text{by construction of}$$
$$AAA \cdot BBB$$
$$= f(\overline{g(\varphi)}) \qquad\qquad \overline{[\varphi]} = [\overline{\varphi}]$$
$$= \overline{f(g(\varphi))} \qquad\qquad f \text{ is a morphism}$$
$$= \text{points}(\Phi^*) - f(g(\varphi)) \qquad\qquad \text{by set theory}$$
$$= \text{points}(\Phi^*) - AAA\varphi BBB \qquad\qquad \text{by construction of}$$
$$AAA \cdot BBB$$

To show that no proper term is interpreted vacuously two conditions must be shown to hold. I begin by proving no proper term is interpreted as $\varnothing$. Consider the set $T = \{[\varphi]_{=_\Gamma}\}$. $[\varphi]_{=_\Gamma} \not\sqsubseteq [\overline{\varphi}]_{=_\Gamma}$, else Γ would be inconsistent, contradicting the initial assumption. So, $[\varphi]_{=_\Gamma} \not\sqsubseteq \overline{[\varphi]}_{=_\Gamma}$, and applying lemma 2.3, I conclude T to be a subset of some point $S \in \text{points}(\Phi_\Gamma^*)$. By the construction of $AAA \cdot BBB$, $T \in AAA\varphi BBB = f(g(\varphi))$, a non-empty set.

To show that no proper term is interpreted as $\text{points}(\Phi^*)$, observe that, by the above, $AAA\overline{\varphi}BBB$ is non-empty. Let S be such a witness. Suppose that $S \in AAA\varphi BBB$. So, $g(\varphi) \in S$, but so is $g(\overline{\varphi}) = \overline{g(\varphi)}$ by the construction of the function. This contradicts the fact that S is consistent. So, $S \notin AAA\varphi BBB$ and we have found the necessary point. $\qquad\square$

Lemma 2.4. Let $\mathbb{M}$ be the model constructed above. Then

$$\mathbb{M} \models \varphi R\psi \Leftrightarrow \Gamma \vdash \varphi R\psi$$

Proof. This proof relies on the fact that both g and f are monotone functions. The most important cases, here, are where $R =\equiv$ and $R =\sqsubset$, as every other case can be derived from these two, as theorem 2.2 indicates. Technically, one need consider the various possibilities where $\varphi = \psi$ or $\psi = \overline{\varphi}$, etc. However, most of these cases contradict the fact that Γ was assumed to be consistent, and the remainder are analagous to the following.

1. $R = \equiv$

$$\Gamma \vdash \varphi \equiv \psi \Leftrightarrow \varphi \leq_\Gamma \psi \text{ and } \psi \leq_\Gamma \varphi$$
$$\Leftrightarrow g(\varphi) = g(\psi)$$
$$\Leftrightarrow f(g(\varphi)) = f(g(\psi))$$
$$\Leftrightarrow AAA\varphi BBB = AAA\psi BBB$$
$$\Leftrightarrow \Gamma \models \varphi \equiv \psi$$

2. $R = \sqsubset$

$$\Gamma \vdash \varphi \sqsubset \psi \Leftrightarrow \varphi \leq_\Gamma \psi \text{ and } \psi \not\leq_\Gamma \varphi$$
$$\Leftrightarrow g(\varphi) \leq g(\psi) \text{ and } g(\psi) \not\leq g(\varphi)$$
$$\Leftrightarrow f(g(\varphi)) \subset f(g(\psi))$$
$$\Leftrightarrow AAA\varphi BBB \subset AAA\psi BBB$$
$$\Leftrightarrow \Gamma \models \varphi \sqsubset \psi$$

$\square$

The remainder of the proof of theorem 2.4 is gotten in the standard way.

3 Conclusion

When I first began work in this area, my intention was to understand the underlying logic of M&M's join table. I did so by giving it a natural set-theoretic semantics and a simple proof calculus. Having done so, I was able to prove completeness via representation. I think, though, that there are broader implications in this line of research.

First and foremost, the logic I have presented here can be understood as a logic underlying a NL lexicon like that of English, if the MacCartney relations are interpreted as lexical semantic relations. More specifically, a synthetic logic can be understood as being the logic of a lexical network like that of, say, WordNet, as it allows us to (begin to) answer the question: If an expression α stands in a lexical semantic relation with β, and β stands in a (possibly different) lexical semantic relation with γ, what lexical semantic relation does α stand in with γ?

Second, I conjecture that the logic here can be embedded in Moss's (2010) syllogistic fragment that contains complements, suggesting that there is much work left to be done with synthetic logic itself. Third, I have not begun to explore the complexity of a synthetic language. If we are interested in logics that have (viable) computational reflexes, to determine complexity results of a synthetic logic would be an obvious next step in this line of research.

References

Calude, Cristian, Peter Hertling, and Karl Svozil. 1999. Embedding quantum universes in classical ones. *Foundations of Physics* 29:349–379. 10.1023/A:1018862730956.

Dowty, David. 1994. The role of negative polarity and concord marking in natural language reasoning. In M. Harvey and L. Santelmann, eds., *Proceedings of Semantics and Linguistic Theory 4*, pages 114–144. CLC Publications.

Gilad, Ben Avi and Nissim Francez. 2005. Proof-theoretic semantics for a syllogistic fragment. In *Proceedings of the Fifteenth Amsterdam Colloquium*, pages 9–15. ILLC/Department of Philosophy, University of Amsterdam.

MacCartney, Bill. 2009. *Natural Language Inference*. Ph.D. thesis, Stanford University.

MacCartney, Bill and Christopher Manning. 2009. An extended model of natural logic. In *The Eighth International Conference on Computational Semantics (IWCS-8)*. Tilburg, The Netherlands.

Moss, Larry. 2008. Completeness theorems for syllogistic fragments. In F. Hamm and S. Kepser, eds., *Logics for Linguistic Structures*, pages 143–173. Mouton de Gruyter. Draft.

Moss, Larry. 2010. Syllogistic logic with complements. In J. van Benthem, A. Gupta, and E. Pacuit, eds., *Games, Norms and Reasons: Logic at the Crossroads*, pages 185–203. Springer Synthese Library Series.

Moss, Larry. 2012. The soundness of internalized polarity marking. *Studia Logica* 100:683–704.

Moss, Lawrence S. 2009. Natural logic and semantics. In M. Aloni, H. Bastiaanse, T. de Jager, P. van Ormondt, and K. Schulz, eds., *Preproceedings of the 17th Amsterdam Colloquium*, pages 71–80. University of Amsterdam.

Popper, Karl. 1968. *The Logic of Scientific Discovery*. Harper Torchebooks.

Russell, Bertrand. 1905. On denoting. *Mind* 14(56):479–493. ArticleType: research-article / Full publication date: Oct., 1905 / Copyright © 1905 Oxford University Press.

Valencia, Sanchez. 1991. *Studies on Natural Logic and Categorial Grammar*. Ph.D. thesis, Universiteit van Amsterdam.

van Benthem, Johan. 1986. *Essays in Logical Semantics*. Dodrecht: D. Reidel.

van Benthem, Johan. 2008. A brief history of natural logic. In M. Chakraborty, B. Löwe, M. Nath Mitra, and S. Sarukki, eds., *Logic, Navya-Nyaya and Applications: Homage to Bimal Matilal*.

Zierler, Neal and Michael Schlessinger. 1965. Boolean embeddings of orthomodular sets and quantum and logic. *Duke Math Journal* 32(2).

Recent Progress on Monotonicity

Thomas F. Icard, III[1] and Lawrence S. Moss[2]

This paper serves two purposes. It is a summary of much work concerning formal treatments of monotonicity and polarity in natural language, and it also discusses connections to related work on exclusion relations, and connections to psycholinguistics and computational linguistics. The second part of the paper presents a summary of some new work on a formal Monotonicity Calculus.

1 Introduction

It has been known since Aristotle that many entailment patterns between linguistic expressions can be derived by simple predicate replacement. *Monotonicity reasoning*, involving a particular sort of predicate replacement, has played an especially important role in the development of logic and semantics, and continues to do so today.

Monotonicity is a pervasive feature of natural language, and it has been linked to many fundamental aspects of linguistic processing, reasoning, and even grammar. In the late 1980s van Benthem (1986, 1991) and Sánchez-Valencia (1991) defined proof systems for reasoning about entailment using monotonicity in higher-order languages. Working in a simply-typed language and building on the long line of work in categorial grammars, the idea behind the so-called Monotonicity Calculus was to mark expressions of functional type with monotonicity information, and use this in a proof system. Work on this topic has recently been revived by computational linguists, and it has found its way into

---

[1]Department of Philosophy, Stanford University.

[2]Department of Mathematics, Indiana University, Bloomington. This work was partially supported by a grant from the Simons Foundation (#245591 to Lawrence Moss).

important applications (see Section 4).

This paper offers an overview of recent developments in the study of monotonicity in natural language. Strictly speaking, monotonicity (and its opposite *antonicity*) is a property of functions, and is therefore a semantic notion. However, we will also be concerned with what is usually called *polarity*, a syntactic notion. In fact, the Monotonicity Calculus and related logical systems can be thought of as exploiting the close connection between polarity and monotonicity. We use syntactic markings to define proof systems whose soundness is guaranteed by the correspondences between positive polarity and monotonicity on the one hand, and negative polarity and antitonicity on the other. One of the main contributions of this paper is to make these notions fully precise, and to present a completeness result for the Monotonicity Calculus.

The outline of the paper is as follows. Section 2 is a less technical introduction to the fundamental concepts involved. In Sections 2.1-2.3, we introduce the notions of *monotonicity, antitonicity,* and *polarity.* Using examples from natural language semantics and basic algebra, we illustrate the use of marked types, and explain how expressions of these types are interpreted model-theoretically. We also outline the fundamental algorithms used for marking parsed expressions with polarity information. In Section 2.5, we discuss a variation on this approach, called *internalized polarity marking.* Section 3 contains a short summary of recent work on extending monotonicity calculi to reasoning about exclusion relations in addition to inclusion relations.

In Section 4 we offer a brief summary of recent work in psychology and computational linguistics that has made critical use of earlier theoretical work on monotonicity. Finally Section 5 presents formal details underpinning the Monotonicity Calculus, including explicit development of a suitable type system (Section 5.1), a precise statement of the proof rules (Section 5.4), and a discussion of soundness and completeness (Section 5.5). We omit some technical details and proofs, which appear in a companion manuscript in progress (Icard and Moss 2013).

2 Reasoning about Monotonicity

2.1 Basic Definitions and Examples

Monotonicity is a pervasive feature in natural language inference, and it is not only interesting in its own right but is tied up with other features of language. However, it is not always so easy to get a handle on what monotonicity actually *is*, to say what it comes to semantically. Perhaps the clearest explanation takes monotonicity to be a property of functions defined on pre-orders. A *pre-order* is a pair $(D, \leq)$ consisting of a set D and a relation $\leq$ on D which is reflexive ($d \leq d$ for all $d \in D$) and transitive (if $c \leq d$ and $d \leq e$, then also $c \leq e$). If we have two (pre-)ordered domains $(D_1, \leq_1)$ and $(D_2, \leq_2)$, a function $f : D_1 \to D_2$ is *monotonic* if, whenever $a \leq_1 b$ we have $f(a) \leq_2 f(b)$. We say f is *antitonic* if, whenever $a \leq_1 b$ it follows that $f(b) \leq_2 f(a)$.

This paper is concerned with two general examples: the first, pertaining to language, is close to what we see in areas of formal semantics, and is related to work in Montague grammar and the theory of generalized quantifiers. The second is a mathematical example that in some ways is a variation on the first.

Example 1. Consider a word like every. If we think of every as taking two arguments, then intuitively it is a function antitonic in its first argument and monotonic in its second argument. For a sentence such as, Every aardvark sees a hyena, if we replace aardvark with the more specific brave aardvark, the resulting sentence is entailed by the first: Every brave aardvark sees a hyena. Likewise, if we replace hyena by the less specific carnivore, then this sentence is also entailed: Every aardvark sees a carnivore. Both of these facts can easily be seen to follow from the standard interpretation of every as the subset relation on predicates.

Indeed, each quantifier in English has its own *monotonicity profile*, where $+$ means monotonic, $-$ antitonic, and $\cdot$ neither monotonic nor antitonic in general:

$-$ every $+$	$+$ not every $-$	$\cdot$ exactly n $\cdot$
$+$ some $+$	$\cdot$ most $+$	$+$ at least n $+$
$-$ no $-$	$\cdot$ few $-$	$-$ at most n $-$

Here is how to read this notation, starting with the first example of every. The idea is that in a sentence of the form every A B, if we replace A by $C \subseteq A$, then every A B entails every C B (Example 1). Similarly if we replace B by $D \supseteq B$, then every A B entails every A D. The $-$ indicates that the sentence as a whole is antitonic in A; similarly, the $+$ indicates that the sentence is monotonic in B. The monotonicity profiles above are the strongest possible statements. That is, we could have put $\cdot$ in all the profiles. But then this would mean that we failed to recognize important information. To put things differently, we can read $\cdot$ as saying neither monotonic nor antitonic in general.

Expressions other than determiners also have interesting monotonicity profiles. For instance, a preposition like 'without' is clearly antitonic: without a doubt entails without a reasonable doubt. Moreover, we can reason about expressions with embedded operators:

(1)   No aardvark without a keen sense of smell can find food
     implies   No aardvark without a sense of smell can find food

Here sense of smell is embedded under three operators: a, without, and no. Since keen sense of smell "implies" sense of smell, it follows that without a sense of smell "implies" without a keen sense of smell. Applying no reverses this once more.

So far we are treating the "implies" relation between English expressions informally. Between predicates this is assumed to be the "more specific than" relation; between sentences it is the "entails" relation. This can be made more precise by assigning semantic *types* to English expressions and interpreting typed expressions in appropriately ordered domains. A precise type system will be defined later in Section 5.1. The following is a mathematical example, illustrating domains for interpreting a simple mathematical language.

Example 2. Let $D_1 = D_2 = \mathbb{R}$ be the real numbers, and $\leq_1 = \leq_2 = \leq$ the ordinary "less than or equal to" relation on $\mathbb{R}$. Then it is easy to check that, e.g., as functions of a variable x, the functions 2^x and $7 + x$ are monotonic, while $-x$ is antitonic. As an example of monotonicty reasoning, consider how one might determine which of the following two expressions is larger: $-(7 + 2^{-3})$ or $-(7 + 2^{-4})$? One way to do it would simply be to evaluate both sides and then compare. This is *not* of interest to us, because it avoids the general principles that are our main topic. Instead, we can argue as follows:

$$\cfrac{\cfrac{\cfrac{\cfrac{3 < 4}{-4 < -3} \quad -x \text{ is antitone}}{2^{-4} < 2^{-3}} \quad 2^x \text{ is monotone}}{7 + 2^{-4} < 7 + 2^{-3}} \quad 7 + x \text{ is monotone}}{-(7 + 2^{-3}) < -(7 + 2^{-4})} \quad -x \text{ is antitone}$$

Naturally, linguistic examples are more relevant for our purposes than mathematical examples. However, it will often simplify the presentation to see the mathematical examples.

2.2 Monotonicity in algebra *via* grammatical inference

Consider the function

$$f(v, w, x, y, z) \;=\; \frac{x - y}{2^{z-(v+w)}}.$$

We intend this to be a function from five real numbers back to the reals. Suppose we fix numerical values for the variables v, w, x, y, z, and then we take each variable in turn, and (while keeping the others fixed) increase its value. For v, w, and x, the overall value goes up. For y and z, it goes down. We would summarize all of the observations by:

$$f(v^+, w^+, x^+, y^-, z^-).$$

The notations $^+$ and $^-$ are what we mean by *polarities*. Note that these really are properties of *occurrences* of variables: a given variable might have both positive and negative occurrences in a given function. For example, consider x in $(x+1)/(x+2)$.

Here is how we can think about this in terms close to the way formal semantics works with the simply typed lambda calculus. We take a single type r, and then we have function symbols

(2)
$$\begin{aligned}
&\mathsf{plus} : r \to (r \to r) \qquad \mathsf{minus} : r \to (r \to r) \\
&\mathsf{times} : r \to (r \to r) \qquad \mathsf{div2} : r \to (r \to r)
\end{aligned}$$

The variables v, w, ..., z may be taken as constants of type r.

We should mention that the natural semantics of these symbols are going to be *higher-order one-place* functions, rather than the more usual binary functions. For example, $[\![\mathsf{plus}]\!]$ is the function from $\mathbb{R}$ to functions from $\mathbb{R}$ to itself which takes a real number a to the function $\lambda b.a + b$. So we would write $(\mathsf{plus}(x))(y)$ to indicate $x + y$. Dropping the parentheses and writing $\mathsf{plus}\, x\, y$ allows one to read through the higher-order functions, but officially they are still going to be there. See Example 10 for more on the semantics of our syntax for algebraic expressions. We also must mention that $\mathsf{div2}$ is *not* supposed to be one-place version of the usual division operation. The idea is that $\mathsf{div2}(x)(y)$ should be $x \div 2^y$, not x/y. This complication is to make everything monotone. We obtain terms in Polish notation:

$$\frac{\dfrac{\dfrac{\mathsf{minus} : r \to (r \to r) \quad x : r}{\mathsf{minus}\, x : r \to r} \quad y : r}{\mathsf{minus}\, x\, y : r \to r}}{\cdots}$$

(3)
$$\frac{\dfrac{\mathsf{div2} : r \to (r \to r) \qquad \dfrac{\mathsf{minus}\, x\, y : r}{}}{\mathsf{div2}\,\mathsf{minus}\, x\, y : r \to r} \qquad \dfrac{\dfrac{\mathsf{minus} : r \to (r \to r) \quad z : r}{\mathsf{minus}\, z : r \to r} \quad t}{\mathsf{minus}\, z\, \mathsf{plus}\, v\, w : r}}{\mathsf{div2}\,\mathsf{minus}\, x\, y\, \mathsf{minus}\, z\, \mathsf{plus}\, v\, w : r}$$

where t above is $\mathsf{minus}\, z\, \mathsf{plus}\, v\, w$ with the derivation

(4)
$$\frac{\dfrac{\mathsf{minus} : r \to (r \to r) \quad z : r}{\mathsf{minus}\, z : r \to r} \qquad \dfrac{\dfrac{\mathsf{plus} : r \to (r \to r) \quad v : r}{\mathsf{plus}\, v : r \to r} \quad w : r}{\mathsf{plus}\, v\, w : r}}{\mathsf{minus}\, z\, \mathsf{plus}\, v\, w : r}$$

The term in (3) corresponds to the term at the beginning of this section, $(x-y)/2^{z-(v+w)}$, and the term in (4) corresponds to the subterm $z - (v+w)$. We are presenting a derivation of the term in the style familiar from categorial grammar (CG), and we assume that the reader has some familiarity with these ideas. In fact, we will only appeal to the *elimination* rules (the application of functions to arguments) in this paper, which will mostly be suppressed.

We are interested in a term corresponding to f from above. For reasons of space, we leave the type information implicit:

$$
(5) \quad
\begin{array}{c}
\dfrac{
\dfrac{
\dfrac{\text{minus} \quad x}{\text{minus } x \quad y}
}{
\begin{array}{cc} \text{div2} & \text{minus } x \ y \end{array}
} \\[2pt]
\text{div2 minus } x \ y
}{}
\end{array}
$$

Polarity determination The central question is whether we can determine the polarities of the variables from the tree representation. Here is one presentation of the algorithm proposed by van Benthem (1986).

1. Label the root with +.

2. Propagate notations up the tree. The right branches of nodes for div2 and minus of type r flip notations. Otherwise, we maintain the notations as we go up the tree.

For example, here is how this works with the term in (5):

$$(6)$$

Notice that the polarity markings on the variables agree with what we saw before: $f(v^+, w^+, x^+, y^-, z^-)$.

The algorithm was first proposed in categorial grammar in van Benthem (1986) to formalize the $+$ and $-$ notation (he used $\uparrow$ for $+$ and $\downarrow$ for $-$). His proposal was then worked out by Sánchez-Valencia (1991).

2.3 New types

We have seen the function symbols plus, ..., div2 in (2) along with their types as higher order functions. In the polarity determination algorithm described above, we started with the type declarations in (2) and then used the extra monotonicity features of the lexical items.

However, we could also proceed in a different manner. We could record additional monotonicity/antitonicity information concerning our symbols *into the types*. For example, minus is monotone in its first argument and antitone in its second. We therefore elaborate on (2) with a different set of type declarations:

$$(7) \qquad \begin{aligned} &\text{plus} : r \xrightarrow{+} (r \xrightarrow{+} r) \qquad \text{minus} : r \xrightarrow{+} (r \xrightarrow{-} r) \\ &\text{times} : r \xrightarrow{+} (r \xrightarrow{+} r) \quad \text{div2} : r \xrightarrow{+} (r \xrightarrow{-} r) \end{aligned}$$

We can be more general by using the types in (7) directly. We are therefore reconsidering the *syntax* of the algebraic expressions. For example, we revisit (4) in this new regime:

$$\frac{\dfrac{\text{plus} : r \xrightarrow{+} (r \xrightarrow{+} r) \quad v : r}{\text{plus } v : r \xrightarrow{+} r} \quad w : r}{\dfrac{\text{minus} : r \xrightarrow{+} (r \xrightarrow{-} r) \quad z : r}{\text{minus } z : r \xrightarrow{-} r} \qquad \dfrac{}{\text{plus } v\, w : r}}{\text{minus } z \text{ plus } v\, w : r}$$

We wish to understand the connection of the new syntactic types to something in the semantics, and so we introduce new *type domains*. These will be preorders, not simply unstructured sets.

$$\begin{aligned} \mathbb{D}_r &= \mathbb{R}, \text{ the real numbers with the usual order } \le \\ \mathbb{D}_{r \xrightarrow{+} r} &= \text{the monotone functions from } \mathbb{D}_r \text{ to } \mathbb{D}_r \\ \mathbb{D}_{r \xrightarrow{-} r} &= \text{the antitone functions from } \mathbb{D}_r \text{ to } \mathbb{D}_r \\ \mathbb{D}_{r \xrightarrow{+} (r \xrightarrow{+} r)} &= \text{the monotone functions from } \mathbb{D}_r \text{ to } \mathbb{D}_{r \xrightarrow{+} r} \\ \mathbb{D}_{r \xrightarrow{+} (r \xrightarrow{-} r)} &= \text{the monotone functions from } \mathbb{D}_r \text{ to } \mathbb{D}_{r \xrightarrow{-} r} \end{aligned}$$

The natural interpretations of the functions plus, minus, etc., belong to the appropriate domains. However, we will not be concerned with the precise functions these terms denote, only with whether they are monotone or antitone. Notice all of our functions in this example are either monotone or antitone.

The issue once again is how to determine the polarities of the individual occurrences. We re-state the bottom-up (root-to-leaves) algorithm that we saw before, this time in a more general form. (In our statement, the root is at the "bottom" of the tree, and the parents are "above" their child.)

1. Label the root with $+$.
2. Propagate notations up the tree.

    (a) If a node is labeled ℓ and its parents are of type $\sigma \xrightarrow{+} \tau$ and σ, then both parents are labeled ℓ.

    (b) If a node is labeled ℓ and its parents are of type $\sigma \xrightarrow{-} \tau$ and σ, then the former parent is to be labeled ℓ and the latter parent is to be labeled $-\ell$, that is, the flipped version of ℓ.

The point is to present the algorithm using only the $+$ and $-$ signs on the arrows, rather than the particular lexical items used. That is, the

+ and − signs on the type arrows encode all the information that the polarity algorithm would use. We simply ignore anything else we might know about these functions. All inference is driven by monotonicty information alone.

A variation on the polarity determination presented here was proposed by van Eijck (2007), who observed that the same result can be achieved by marking nodes in the syntax tree based on whether they *respect* or *flip* the markings.

2.4 Operations which are neither monotone nor antitone

Not every operation of interest is monotone or antitone. We have already seen that the semantics of most would be neither monotone nor antitone in its first argument. For an easy mathematical example, consider the absolute value function $|x| : \mathbb{R} \to \mathbb{R}$. To continue our treatment, we take a function symbol abs : $r \xrightarrow{\cdot} r$. We write $\xrightarrow{\cdot}$ because, while the interpretation is a function, we cannot classify this interpretation as monotone or antitone. More formally, we can say that the interpretation of abs belongs to the set $\mathbb{D}_r$ given as follows:

$$\mathbb{D}_{r \xrightarrow{\cdot} r} = \text{the set of all functions from } \mathbb{D}_r \text{ to } \mathbb{D}_r$$

That is, all we know about abs is that it is some function from $\mathbb{R}$ to $\mathbb{R}$.

We can extend the algorithm above in a straightforward way. Perhaps the most elegant extension involves considering the set $\mathcal{M} = \{+, -, \cdot\}$ of *markings* on the arrows to be an algebraic structure, using the operation ∘ defined in the table below:

∘	+	−	·
+	+	−	·
−	−	+	·
·	·	·	·

This tiny algebra is the basis of much work on natural logic (van Benthem 2008; Sánchez-Valencia 1991; van Eijck 2007; Zamansky et al. 2006). We can generalize the bottom-up algorithm in point 2(b):

2(b) If a node is labeled ℓ and its parents are of type $\sigma \xrightarrow{m} \tau$ and σ, then the former parent is to be labeled ℓ and the latter parent is to be labeled $m \circ \ell$.

2.5 Internalized types

At this point, we have seen several ways to determine polarities in a parse tree given by a categorial grammar. Either way, the determination of polarities is an *external* feature of the syntax tree, something determined by an algorithm. Instead of complicating the architecture of grammar, we could complicate the particular grammar that we use and achieve the same thing. We introduce *negative signs on types*, to denote *opposite preorders*. And we allow a lexical item to have more than one type. (This is standard in categorial grammar.) We use the following lexicon:

$$v, w, x, y, z : r \qquad\qquad v, w, x, y, z : -r$$
$$\mathsf{plus} : r \to (r \to r) \qquad \mathsf{plus} : -r \to (-r \to -r)$$
$$\mathsf{minus} : r \to (-r \to r) \qquad \mathsf{minus} : -r \to (r \to -r)$$
$$\mathsf{times} : r \to (r \to r) \qquad \mathsf{times} : -r \to (-r \to -r)$$
$$\mathsf{div2} : r \to (-r \to r) \qquad \mathsf{div2} : -r \to (r \to -r)$$

Here is an explanation of what the types refer to, along the lines of what we did above.

$$\mathbb{D}_r \qquad = \quad \mathbb{R}, \text{ the real numbers with the usual order } \leq$$
$$\mathbb{D}_{-r} \qquad = \quad \mathbb{R}, \text{ the real numbers with the opposite order } \geq$$
$$\mathbb{D}_{r \to r} \qquad = \quad \text{the monotone functions from } \mathbb{D}_r \text{ to } \mathbb{D}_r$$
$$\mathbb{D}_{r \to -r} \qquad = \quad \text{the monotone functions from } \mathbb{D}_r \text{ to } \mathbb{D}_{-r}$$
$$\qquad = \quad \text{the antitone functions from } \mathbb{D}_r \text{ to } \mathbb{D}_r$$
$$\mathbb{D}_{-r \to (r \to -r)} \quad = \quad \text{the monotone functions from } \mathbb{D}_{-r} \text{ to } \mathbb{D}_{r \to -r}$$

A term corresponding to $z/2^{x-y}$ parses as

$$\cfrac{\cfrac{}{\mathsf{div2} : r \to (-r \to r) \quad z : r}\quad \mathsf{div2}\ z : -r \to r \qquad \cfrac{\cfrac{\mathsf{minus} : -r \to (r \to -r) \quad x : -r}{\mathsf{minus}\ x : r \to -r} \quad y : r}{\mathsf{minus}\ x\ y : -r}}{\mathsf{div2}\ z\ \mathsf{minus}\ x\ y : r}$$

The parse tree automatically indicates the polarities. For example, the term as a whole is antitone in x, since its type is $-r$; there is no parse of the term which has $x : r$ as a leaf, even though this typing is available in the grammar. Similarly, the term is monotone in y and z. The point here is that there is no need to have a separate algorithm for polarity determination.

For linguistic reasons for this *internalized* line of work, see Dowty (1994). For more on this flavor of monotonicity in categorial grammar, see Moss (2012).

In the rest of this paper, we are not going to discuss the internalized approach. One reason for this is that we are interested in presenting an account that also allows functions to be labeled as neither monotone nor antitone, as explained above in Section 2.4.

2.6 Monotonicity reasoning

Up until now, we have mainly been concerned with developing tools which allow one to look at a syntactic representation and see which positions are monotone, which antitone, and which neither. But this is only the beginning. As we mentioned at the outset of this paper, much of the interest in monotonicity is connected with *inference*.

Here is an example of what we are after in this regard; the formal details will appear in Section 5 below. Suppose that we have acquired some lexical monotonicity information, for example that

$$\text{run} \leq \text{move}$$
$$\text{cat} \leq \text{animal}$$

We also assume we have the monotonicity information that we codify in the typing for the determiner every and for a transitive verb like see. Independent of how an agent would learn any of this information, we explain how these facts could be exploited in simple reasoning. For instance, how is it that

(8) Everything which sees every cat runs
 implies Everything which sees every animal moves

Indeed, we would like the inference to be formalized in the same kind of proof-theoretic manner that we saw with derivation trees in categorial grammar in the first place; these are derivations in *natural deduction*. The difference is that in addition to inference between sentences, we want a general notion of $\leq$ between items of any syntactic category. What we have written here is on the level of noun phrases, and on the VP level it would be

$$\text{see every animal} \leq \text{see every cat}$$

This is the first step in our semi-formal derivation below, going from the assumption (the leaf of the tree) to the line below it.

$$\frac{\dfrac{\text{cat} \leq \text{animal}}{\text{see every animal} \leq \text{see every cat}}}{\text{Everything which sees every cat runs} \leq \text{Everything which sees every animal runs}}$$

Notice that both steps are a kind of antitonicity: the positions of animal and cat have switched. Going further, we might like to combine the derivation above with one involving runs and moves to give an account of the inference in (8). By the monotonicity of the second argument of every, we have:

$$\frac{\text{runs} \leq \text{moves}}{\text{Everything which sees ev. animal runs} \leq \text{Everything which sees ev. animal moves}}$$

Finally, if we let

$t = $ Everything which sees every cat runs

$u = $ Everything which sees every animal runs

v = Everything which sees every animal moves

then from $t \le u$ (first derivation) and $u \le v$ (second derivation), we derive $t \le v$, i.e., the entailment in (8).

All of these steps can be formalized in a Monotonicity Calculus that we shall see in Section 5. Here is a preview of the rules:

$$(\text{Refl}) \ \frac{}{t \le t} \qquad\qquad (\text{Trans}) \ \frac{t \le u \qquad u \le v}{t \le v}$$

$$(\text{Mono}) \ \frac{u \le v}{t[u^{+}] \le t^{v \leftarrow u}} \qquad (\text{Anti}) \ \frac{u \le v}{t^{v \leftarrow u} \le t[u^{-}]}$$

$$(\text{Point}) \ \frac{s \le t}{s(u) \le t(u)}$$

See Section 5 for details. The names are for the evident abbreviations: Refl for *reflexive*, Trans for *transitive*, Mono for *monotone*, Anti for *antitone*, and Point for *pointwise*.

Finally, note that in natural language this kind of reasoning is not limited to *predicate* restriction and expansion. It also includes reasoning about events, locations, times, sums, and more general mereological domains. All of these have natural associated pre-orders (often with more structure), and we can consider monotone and antitone functions over such domains. For instance, lives in is monotonic with respect to the "part-of" relation on locations, whereas lasts more than is antitonic with respect to the "subinterval" relation on times. Moreover, these interact with the quantifiers in the expected ways. For instance:

$$\frac{\dfrac{\dfrac{\text{2 hours} \le \text{6 hours}}{\text{more than 6 hours} \le \text{more than 2 hours}}}{\text{play that lasts more than 6 hours} \le \text{play that lasts more than 2 hours}}}{\text{Every play\ldots more than 2 hrs is too long} \le \text{Every play\ldots more than 6 hrs is too long}}$$

For simplicity, our natural language examples will be based on the simple model of individuals, predicates and properties (sets of individuals), quantifiers, and so on. But it is important to point out that the sort of reasoning we are describing is quite general.

3 Reasoning about Exclusion

Monotonicity reasoning certainly does not exhaust the inferential patterns that follow from the standard logical interpretations of natural language expressions. An obvious question is whether we can go further with the "surface reasoning" approach of marking types with useful inferential information. Recent work by MacCartney (2009) and MacCartney and Manning (2009) has shown that many new inferential patterns can be derived by tracking how functional expressions project *exclusion* relations, in addition to the *inclusion* relations on which monotonicity reasoning is based. It was then shown in Icard (2012) that the resulting system can be understood formally as an extension of the Monotonicity Calculus, with more type markings and correspondingly more classes of functions refining the classes of monotonic and antitonic functions.

A simple example of an inference that depends on exclusion is:

Every porcupine is nocturnal $\Rightarrow$ Not every porcupine is diurnal.

Notice that nocturnal and diurnal do not stand in an inclusion relation, nor do every and not every. Thus, we cannot perform replacements as in the examples above. For that we need to know how the exclusion relations between such expressions are projected in different contexts.

The important observation, essentially made first in Keenan and Faltz (1984), is that type domains have more structure than an arbitrary pre-order. The relevant structure here is that of a *bounded distributive lattice*. This is a tuple $\mathbb{X} = (X, \vee, \wedge, \bot, \top)$, where X is a set, $\vee$ and $\wedge$ are commutative, associative, and idempotent operations which distribute over each other, and $\bot$ and $\top$ satisfy the identities $\bot \wedge x = \bot$, $\bot \vee x = x$, $\top \wedge x = x$, $\top \vee x = \top$. For instance, $\mathbb{D}_t$ is the smallest nontrivial bounded distributive lattice $\mathbf{2} = (\{0,1\}, +, \cdot, 0, 1)$; and the bounded distributive structure for predicates is the "powerset algebra" $(\wp(E), \cup, \cap, \emptyset, E)$. In fact, whenever $\mathbb{D}_\tau$ is a bounded distributive lattice, so is $\mathbb{D}_{\sigma \to \tau}$. All of this holds for the smaller class of "Boolean" lattices as well, but we do not need to make use of complements here.

Following MacCartney (2009) (as presented in Icard (2012)), we introduce the following set of relations, which are well-defined on elements of any bounded distributive lattice $\mathbb{X} = (X, \vee, \wedge, \bot, \top)$:

$$
\begin{aligned}
x \leq y & \quad : \quad x \wedge y = x \\
x \geq y & \quad : \quad x \vee y = x \\
x \,|\, y & \quad : \quad x \wedge y = \bot \\
x \smile y & \quad : \quad x \vee y = \top
\end{aligned}
$$

We write $x \equiv y$ if both $x \leq y$ and $x \geq y$; write $x \curlywedge y$ if both $x \,|\, y$ and $x \smile y$ (and we say that x and y are *mutually exclusive*); and write $x \# y$ for the universal (uninformative) relation on X. Thus we define the set $\mathcal{R}$ of relations to be: $\{\equiv, \leq, \geq, \curlywedge, |, \smile, \#\}$.

Example 3. The predicates square and circular stand in the '|' relation since the set of square things and the set of circular things are disjoint. In the space of quantifier meanings, we have more than five $\smile$ fewer than eight, since at least one of these holds of every two sets. Finally, animate stands in the '$\curlywedge$' relation to inanimate, since these are mutually exclusive and exhaustive.

Monotone functions preserve the basic inequalities $\leq$ and $\geq$, while antitone functions reverse them. Now that we have introduced several new relations, what classes of functions do we need to predict the relation between two complex expressions that differ only with respect to some subexpressions whose relation is known? That is, supposing uRv, what do we need to know about t in order to determine for which $R' \in \mathcal{R}$ we have $t[u]R't[v]$? It turns out, some familiar refinements of the classes of monotonic and antitonic functions are sufficient:

Definition 1. Suppose $f : \mathbb{X} \to \mathbb{Z}$ is a function on lattices.

f is *additive* if $f(x \vee y) = f(x) \vee f(y)$.
f is *multiplicative* if $f(x \wedge y) = f(x) \wedge f(y)$.
f is *anti-additive* if $f(x \vee y) = f(x) \wedge f(y)$.
f is *anti-multiplicative* if $f(x \wedge y) = f(x) \vee f(y)$.

That additivity and multiplicativity refine monotonicity follows from the easy observation that the following three conditions are equivalent: (a) f is monotonic; (b) $f(x) \vee f(y) \leq f(x \vee y)$; (c) $f(x \wedge y) \leq f(x) \wedge f(y)$. Similarly, anti-additivity and anti-multiplicativity refine antitonicity since the following three are equivalent: (a) f is antitonic; (b) $f(x \vee y) \leq f(x) \wedge f(y)$; (c) $f(x) \vee f(y) \leq f(x \wedge y)$.

It has been observed, at least since Zwarts (1981), that, for instance, no is anti-additive in both of its arguments, while every is anti-additive in its first argument and multiplicative in its second argument:

No aardvark eats kelp or carrots $\equiv$
No aardvark eats kelp and no aardvark eats carrots
Every animal is a child and a grandchild $\equiv$
Every animal is a child and every animal is a grandchild

In fact, all of these function classes are exemplified by expressions in English. We introduce a new set of type markings Σ extending $\mathcal{M}$:

$$\Sigma = \{\cdot, +, -, \oplus, \ominus, \boxplus, \boxminus, \oplus, \ominus\}.$$

Terms labeled with $\oplus$ will be additive; those with $\ominus$ anti-additive; $\boxplus$ corresponds to multiplicative; $\boxminus$ to anti-multiplicative; $\oplus$ corresponds to additive and multiplicative (for an expressions like *is*); finally, $\ominus$ is reserved for expressions that are anti-additive and anti-multiplicative, nearly amounting to outright negation.

The important observation for understanding exclusion-based inferences like those above is that these function classes "project" the relations in $\mathcal{R}$ in predictable ways. For instance, from the fact that nocturnal λ diurnal and the fact that every is multiplicative, we can conclude:

> Every porcupine is nocturnal | Every porcupine is diurnal

If every were merely monotone in its second argument, this relation would not necessarily hold. Indeed, we can say explicitly what the "projectivity" behavior for each type of function is (MacCartney 2009). With $R \in \mathcal{R}$ and $\varphi \in \Sigma$, the *projection of R under φ*, written $[R]^{\varphi}$, is the strongest $R^* \in \mathcal{R}$ such that, whenever xRy and f is a φ-function, we must have $f(x)R^*f(y)$. The projectivity behavior of these function classes is summarized below.

[ ]	⊑	⊒	⋏	∣	⌣
+	⊑	⊒	#	#	#
⟠	⊑	⊒	⌣	#	⌣
⊞	⊑	⊒	∣	∣	#
⊕	⊑	⊒	⋏	∣	⌣

[ ]	⊑	⊒	⋏	∣	⌣
−	⊒	⊑	#	#	#
⟠	⊒	⊑	∣	#	∣
⊟	⊒	⊑	⌣	⌣	#
⊖	⊒	⊑	⋏	⌣	∣

The final ingredient of exclusion reasoning is a *join* operation ⋈, where $R \bowtie R'$ is understood to be the strongest relation $R^* \in \mathcal{R}$ such that whenever xRy and $yR'z$, it follows that xR^*z:

⋈	⊑	⊒	⋏	∣	⌣
⊑	⊑	#	∣	∣	#
⊒	#	⊒	⌣	#	⌣
⋏	⌣	∣	≡	⊒	⊑
∣	#	∣	⊑	#	⊒
⌣	⌣	#	⊒	⊒	#

We now have enough to finish deriving the example above, that No porcupine is diurnal follows from Every porcupine is nocturnal. We first observed that Every porcupine is nocturnal | Every porcupine is diurnal. Moreover, we have every ⋏ not every, and in particular Every porcupine is diurnal ⋏ Not every porcupine is diurnal. Since the join | ⋈ ⋏ = ≤, we can conclude Every porcupine is nocturnal ≤ Not every porcupine is diurnal. Summarizing in a natural-deduction-style proof, where $t =$ Every porcupine is diurnal, $s =$ Every porcupine is nocturnal, and $r =$ Not every porcupine is nocturnal:

$$\frac{\dfrac{\text{nocturnal} \barwedge \text{diurnal}}{t \mid s} \qquad \dfrac{\text{every} \barwedge \text{not every}}{s \barwedge r}}{t \leq r} \quad (\mid \bowtie \barwedge \; = \; \leq)$$

To treat more complex cases that involve embeddings under multiple functional expressions, as in

> No porcupine that misses a warning sign is safe ≤
> Some porcupine that misses an important warning sign is in danger

we must understand the extension of the composition (∘) operator from

$\mathcal{M}$ to Σ which we saw in Section 2.4. The structure $(\Sigma, \circ)$ forms a monoid, with identity element $\oplus$ (Icard 2012). For example, from the fact that a is additive, misses is antitonic, and no is anti-additive and anti-multiplicative, we can conclude that No porcupine who misses a [ ] is safe is monotonic in [ ], since in fact $\ominus \circ -\circ \Phi = +$.

4 Applications

The systems and algorithms sketched above have found applications in psychology of language and computational linguistics. Before turning to formal foundations of the Monotonicity Calculus, we first offer an overview of some of the areas where these systems have proven useful.

4.1 Psychological

Monotonicty has been implicated in a number of psychological phenomena in language processing and language-based reasoning tasks. To take a simple example, consider the following sentence (inspired by an example in Geurts and van der Slik (2005)):

(a) Most Americans who know a foreign language speak it at home.

A typical speaker may not be able to judge under what conditions such a sentence will be true. Does it hold in a situation where most Americans who know two foreign languages speak only one of them at home? Or is it sufficient that most Americans know at least one of the languages they speak at home? Or need they speak most of the languages they know at home? Contrast this apparent underdeterminacy with the patent fact that the sentence in (a) entails that in (b).

(b) Most who know a foreign language speak it at home or at work.

In some sense, it does not matter which of the readings above is correct. This entailment holds on all of them. Relatedly, while there are significant logical differences between the quantifiers most and every, Oaksford and Chater (2001) have shown that inference patterns like

$$\frac{\text{most } X \, Y \qquad Y \leq Z}{\text{most } X \, Z} \quad \text{and} \quad \frac{\text{every } X \, Y \qquad Y \leq Z}{\text{every } X \, Z},$$

of which the inference from (a) to (b) is an instance, seem to be equally easy for subjects, despite the difference in logical complexity. One might take such evidence to suggest people sometimes are able to recognize entailments on the basis of these general monotonicity patterns.

Geurts (2003) has taken this idea further, demonstrating how a simple processing model based on a calculus closely related to what we outline here can explain many aspects of Oaksford and Chater's (1999) meta-analysis of syllogistic reasoning. For instance, among valid syllogisms those that require two applications of the monotonicity rule (our (Mono) below in Section 5.4) turn out to be more difficult for subjects than those that require only one, all other things equal. Generally, the results of this work are suggestive, if also preliminary.

One of the most intriguing aspects of monotonicty from a psycholinguistic point of view is the robust correspondence between antitone contexts and the syntactic distribution of a class of expressions called *negative polarity items* (NPIs). Perhaps the simplest generalization about these expressions—which include as examples in English at all, yet, any, a wink, . . . —is that they seem to appear almost solely in (locally) antitone contexts. For instance, while Everyone found any evidence is ungrammatical, No one found any evidence is perfectly grammatical. In fact, one of the intended uses of the internalized schema (Dowty 1994; Moss 2012) sketched above in Section 2.5 is to define categorial grammars that properly govern the syntactic distribution of NPIs. Thus, the monotonicity markings play a double role of licensing monotonicity inferences, as well as restricting which expressions will typically be recognized or generated by a grammar.

Within the class of NPIs, Zwarts (1981) and others have distinguished several subclasses of NPIs based on the strength of their preferred syntactic environments. Weak NPIs like any appear in arbitrary antitone contexts; strong NPIs, e.g., in years, require anti-additive contexts; while super-strong NPIs such as one bit require anti-additive and anti-multiplicative contexts. Thus, curiously, the correspondence between logical features and grammaticality extends to exclusion-based reasoning as well, in light of Section 3. Extending the internalized schema from monotonicity and antitonicity to internalized markings for exclusion relations, so as to govern the syntactic distribution of weak, strong, and super strong NPIs, is an interesting avenue for future work.

The exact nature of the generalizations about NPIs has been a matter of some controversy, as they also appear in questions and other contexts that are not antitone in any straightforward sense, e.g. Do you have any evidence?. Giannakidou (2011) contains an up-to-date summary of the data and theoretical proposals, as well as references to the literature on NPIs. There is some preliminary experimental work on this topic. Chemla et al. (2011), for example, suggest that speakers' perceived judgments of monotonicity may be better predictors of their grammaticality judgments than, say, the "true" logical facts about monotonicity in a given formalization. See also Szabolcsi et al. (2008) for experimental work on the link between antitonicity and negative polarity. It is an intriguing question why there should be such a close, if not perfect, correspondence at all between these logical features licensing monotonicity inferences and issues of which sentences are judged as well-formed. To our knowledge, this is still somewhat mysterious.

4.2 Computational

The computational problem of recognizing textual entailment (RTE)—that is, automatically determining which strings of text intuitively follow from which other strings of text—is an integral part of natural language processing. RTE is implicated in other critical natural language understanding tasks, including question answering, search, summarization, translation, and many others. The general RTE task is quite a difficult problem. Determining whether one claim follows from another can depend on just about any aspect of human knowledge, experience, and understanding. Just consider what might be required to recognize that The floor is very slippery follows from The floor is made of teflon and coated with motor oil. Other plausible entailments may be controversial to begin with: does it follow from Freedonia possesses enriched uranium that Freedonia is developing nuclear weapons? Many examples of this sort do show up in RTE contests and test suites, and certainly one would like to have an approach that works in open-ended domains. However, one of the intriguing observations from a logician's point of view is that a wide range of entailments follow distinct patterns—monotonicity being one of the most notable—and the basic world knowledge necessary may not go beyond simple lexical relations available from WordNet or some other lexical database. It seems reasonable to take advantage of these general "logical" patterns, that is, patterns validated on the basis of form alone, whenever possible.

MacCartney and Manning (2009) have developed an RTE system that includes monotonicity reasoning as the central component. Their "NatLog" system begins with some basic linguistic preprocessing: tokenization, parsing, named entity recognition, and so on. The system also runs a monotonicty marking algorithm like those outlined in Section 2, and builds on related work by Nairn et al. (2006) on so-called implicativity. In the end, NatLog makes a guess about the relation between the premise text and the hypothesis text using a sequence of edits bridging the two texts. Testing the system on the PASCAL RTE Challenge data (Dagan et al. 2005), NatLog outperformed the state-of-the-art Stanford RTE System on precision, though it fell far short on recall. The Stanford System is based on a maximum entropy classifier, which learns to make predictions from labeled text pairs using hand-coded features. Interestingly, a hybrid of the two systems outperformed both NatLog and the Stanford System on overall accuracy, suggesting that an integrated approach incorporating both statistical learning and logical reasoning may be desirable. The most detailed explanation of NatLog can be found in MacCartney (2009).

Given the importance and prevalence of monotonicity in ordinary reasoning, maintaining a list of expressions together with their monotonicity information promises to be useful. However, doing this manually may become quite cumbersome, particularly if we want to use the same basic algorithms and tools across multiple languages. Danescu et al. (2009) have taken a first step in addressing this by showing how antitone contexts in particular can be learned automatically. The trick is to capitalize on the close correspondence between antitone contexts and the distribution of NPIs, sketched above in Section 4.1. Intuitively, the more often an expression co-occurs with NPIs, the more likely it is to create antitone contexts. Using a list of well-established NPIs, Danescu et al. (2009) collect candidate expressions w by determining whether the following inequality holds, where $c_{NPI}(w)$ is the number of times w co-occurs with an NPI, $c(w)$ is the count of w in the corpus, and W is the lexicon:

$$\frac{c_{NPI}(w)}{\sum_{w' \in W} c_{NPI}(w')} > \frac{c(w)}{\sum_{w' \in W} c(w')}.$$

That is, the frequency of occurrences of w with NPIs should be greater than what we would expect from the frequency of w occurrences in the overall corpus. Their algorithm has good precision (80%), and most importantly, they discover a long list of antitone expressions that had not appeared on previous inventories. The algorithm has even been extended to achieve co-learning of antitone contexts and NPIs, e.g. for languages where extensive lists of NPIs are not already established (Danescu and Lee 2010). See also Cheung and Penn (2012) for related work. Note finally that in view of the connection between the inference patterns based on exclusion relations (Section 3) and subclasses of NPIs (Section 4.1), these methods could also be used to discover subclasses of antitone operators—anti-additive and anti-multiplicative—based on co-occurrence with weak, strong, and superstrong NPIs.

Generally, we believe that the formal investigation of logical and mathematical aspects of these systems for natural reasoning should be developed alongside these applied projects. Each stands to gain from insights the other can provide.

5 Formal Treatment

The centerpiece of this paper is a formal development of what we have seen. The material here is based on Icard and Moss (2013).

5.1 Types and Domains

Definition 2. As above, let $\mathcal{M} = \{+, -, \cdot\}$. We call $\mathcal{M}$ the set of *markings*, and we use m to denote an element of $\mathcal{M}$.

Definition 3. Let $\mathcal{B}$ be a set of *base types*. Working over some fixed set $\mathcal{B}$ and therefore suppressing mention of it, the full set of types $\mathcal{T}$ is defined as the smallest superset of $\mathcal{B}$, such that whenever $\sigma, \tau \in \mathcal{T}$, so is $\sigma \xrightarrow{m} \tau$, for each $m \in \mathcal{M}$.

Expressions of type $\sigma \xrightarrow{+} \tau$ will denote monotone functions, those of type $\sigma \xrightarrow{-} \tau$ antitone functions, and those of type $\sigma \xrightarrow{\cdot} \tau$ arbitrary functions. We therefore have a natural preorder on $\mathcal{M}$, whereby $m \sqsubseteq m'$ iff $m = m'$ or $m' = \cdot$. This ordering can be used to define a natural preorder on $\mathcal{T}$. Intuitively $\sigma \preceq \tau$ will mean that anything of type σ could also be considered as of type τ. So for function spaces, we take $\preceq$ to be "antitone in the domain argument and monotone in the codomain."

Example 4. In standard Montague semantics, we take $\mathcal{B}$ to be $\{e, t\}$. (However, recall from Section 2.6 that the work here extends to types for locations, times, sums, and other natural language categories with ordered domains.) In our example from algebra, we took it to be $\{r\}$.

Definition 4 ($\preceq$ on types). Define $\preceq \in \mathcal{T} \times \mathcal{T}$ to be least such that $\tau \preceq \tau$, and whenever $\sigma' \preceq \sigma$ and $\tau \preceq \tau'$, and $m \sqsubseteq m'$, we have $\sigma \xrightarrow{m} \tau \preceq \sigma' \xrightarrow{m'} \tau'$.

Example 5. We return to the linguistic example, using base types e and t. We abbreviate $e \xrightarrow{\cdot} t$ by p (for "property"). A determiner (quantifier) such as every might be interpreted as an element of a marked type $p \xrightarrow{-} (p \xrightarrow{+} t)$. In some sense, this is the most specific type we could assign to every. But it could also be considered of type $p \xrightarrow{-} (p \xrightarrow{\cdot} t)$, for example, or even $p \xrightarrow{\cdot} (p \xrightarrow{\cdot} t)$. Note that according to Def. 4,

$$p \xrightarrow{-} (p \xrightarrow{+} t) \preceq p \xrightarrow{\cdot} (p \xrightarrow{\cdot} t).$$

The same holds for the type of some: $p \xrightarrow{+} (p \xrightarrow{+} t) \preceq p \xrightarrow{\cdot} (p \xrightarrow{\cdot} t)$, and no: $p \xrightarrow{-} (p \xrightarrow{-} t) \preceq p \xrightarrow{\cdot} (p \xrightarrow{\cdot} t)$.

Definition 5 ($\uparrow$ and $\vee$ on types). We endow $\mathcal{M}$ with the obvious upper semilattice structure, writing $m_1 \vee m_2$ for m_1 if $m_1 = m_2$, and $\cdot$ otherwise. (Again, the dot $\cdot$ is one of the markings, hence an element of $\mathcal{M}$.) $\uparrow$ is the smallest relation on types, and $\vee$ is the smallest function on types, with the properties that for all σ, τ_1, and τ_2:

    1. $\sigma \uparrow \sigma$, and $\sigma \vee \sigma = \sigma$.

2. If $\tau_1 \uparrow \tau_2$, then $(\sigma \overset{m_1}{\to} \tau_1) \uparrow (\sigma \overset{m_2}{\to} \tau_2)$ for all $m_1, m_2 \in \mathcal{M}$, and

$$(\sigma \overset{m_1}{\to} \tau_1) \vee (\sigma \overset{m_2}{\to} \tau_2) \;=\; \sigma \overset{m_1 \vee m_2}{\longrightarrow} (\tau_1 \vee \tau_2).$$

We define $\sigma \mapsto \hat{\sigma}$ on $\mathcal{T}$ by $\hat{\sigma} = \sigma$ for σ basic, and $(\sigma \overset{m}{\to} \tau)\hat{} = \sigma \overset{\cdot}{\to} \hat{\tau}$.

Lemma 1. $\uparrow$ is an equivalence, and $\hat{\sigma}$ is the least upper bound in $\preceq$ of the (finite) $\uparrow$-equivalence class of σ.

As an ordered set, $(\mathcal{T}, \preceq)$ has some undesirable properties. For example, there are pairs of types that have incomparable upper bounds. These pathologies are largely "tamed" by Definition 5.

Example 6. Returning to Ex. 5, we have

$$p \overset{-}{\to} (p \overset{+}{\to} t) \;\uparrow\; p \overset{+}{\to} (p \overset{+}{\to} t) \;\uparrow\; p \overset{-}{\to} (p \overset{-}{\to} t).$$

The least upper bound for this $\uparrow$-equivalence class is $p \overset{\cdot}{\to} (p \overset{\cdot}{\to} t)$. Intuitively, any expression of any of these types can just as well be considered an expression of type $p \overset{\cdot}{\to} (p \overset{\cdot}{\to} t)$, the type of an arbitrary generalized quantifier.

Up until now, we have been dealing with the basics of the type system. We have yet to go into details on the syntax of higher-order terms. But before we do this, it will be informative to give the intended models for our languages. We call these *standard structures*.

Definition 6 (Structures). A *standard structure* is a system $\mathcal{S} = \{\mathbb{D}_\tau\}_{\tau \in \mathcal{T}}$ of preorders (called *type domains*), one for each type $\tau \in \mathcal{T}$. We write $\mathbb{D}_\tau = (D_\tau, \leq_\tau)$ for the domain of type τ. For the base types $\beta \in \mathcal{B}$ there is no requirement on $\mathbb{D}_\beta$. For complex types $\sigma \overset{m}{\to} \tau$, we have some requirements:

1. $D_{\sigma \overset{+}{\to} \tau}$ is the set of all monotone functions from $\mathbb{D}_\sigma$ to $\mathbb{D}_\tau$.
2. $D_{\sigma \overset{-}{\to} \tau}$ is the set of all antitone functions from $\mathbb{D}_\sigma$ to $\mathbb{D}_\tau$.
3. $D_{\sigma \overset{\cdot}{\to} \tau}$ is the set of all functions from $\mathbb{D}_\sigma$ to $\mathbb{D}_\tau$.
4. For all markings $m \in \mathcal{M}$, all types $\sigma, \tau \in \mathcal{T}$, and all $f, g \in D_{\sigma \overset{m}{\to} \tau}$, we have $f \leq_{\sigma \overset{m}{\to} \tau} g$ if and only if $f(a) \leq_\tau g(a)$ for all $a \in D_\sigma$. This is called the *pointwise* order.

Example 7. With $\mathcal{B} = \{e, t\}$, usually one takes $\mathbb{D}_e$ to be an arbitrary set, made into a *discrete preorder*: $x \leq y$ iff $x = y$. $\mathbb{D}_t$ is usually taken to be the two-element order $0 \leq 1$. Then we get a standard structure by defining $\mathbb{D}_\sigma$ by recursion on complex types. For example, $\mathbb{D}_{(e \overset{\cdot}{\to} t) \overset{\cdot}{\to} t}$ will be the set of *all* functions from $\mathbb{D}_{e \overset{\cdot}{\to} t}$ to $\mathbb{D}_t$, $\mathbb{D}_{(e \overset{\cdot}{\to} t) \overset{+}{\to} t}$ will be the set of monotone functions, and $\mathbb{D}_{(e \overset{\cdot}{\to} t) \overset{-}{\to} t}$ will be the set of antitone functions. In all cases, these are taken to be preorders using the pointwise order.

Continuing the algebra example, we take $\mathbb{D}_r$ to be $\mathbb{R} = (R, \leq)$, the real numbers with the usual order.

Incidentally, we speak of *standard structures* because one could instead interpret the language that we shall soon define on a more general class of structures (e.g., so called "Henkin models"). This is sometimes useful, but for our purposes in this paper the standard structures are sufficient, and the general definition is rather complicated.

We clearly have a natural embedding from $\mathbb{D}_\sigma$ to $\mathbb{D}_\tau$ whenever $\sigma \preceq \tau$. This captures the sense in which anything of type σ could also be considered of type τ. When two types are related by $\uparrow$, their respective domains can both be embedded in a single domain. Since objects in this domain will be ordered, it will make sense to define ordering statements between expressions of $\uparrow$-related types in the formal language.

5.2 Language and Interpretation

Definition 7 (Unlabeled Typed Terms). We begin the syntax with a set Con of *constants* together with a function type : Con $\to \mathcal{T}$. The set T of typed terms $t : \tau$ is defined recursively, as follows:

1. If $c \in$ Con, then $c :$ type(c) is a typed term.

2. If $t : \sigma \overset{m}{\to} \tau$ and $u : \rho$ are typed terms and $\rho \preceq \sigma$, then $t(u) : \tau$ is a typed term.

Example 8. For an example pertaining to algebra, we take Con and type to be as given in (7), and with several more symbols

$$\text{abs} : r \overset{+}{\to} r$$
$$0, 1, 2 : r$$

Example 9. Here is a set of typed constants pertinent to natural language. We take plural nouns like cat, person, ... : p. Also, we take determiners (dets)

$$\text{every} : p \overset{-}{\to} (p \overset{+}{\to} t)$$
$$\text{not every} : p \overset{+}{\to} (p \overset{-}{\to} t)$$
$$\text{some} : p \overset{+}{\to} (p \overset{+}{\to} t)$$
$$\text{no} : p \overset{-}{\to} (p \overset{-}{\to} t)$$
$$\text{most} : p \overset{\cdot}{\to} (p \overset{+}{\to} t)$$
$$\text{exactly } n : p \overset{\cdot}{\to} (p \overset{\cdot}{\to} t)$$

Transitive verbs like see could have type $(p \overset{+}{\to} t) \overset{+}{\to} t$. Then sentences of the form det+noun+verb+det+noun would correspond to terms of type t. (See Example 14.)

The typings of the determiners illustrate the use of this schema most clearly. They are reflections of the monotonicity phenomena that we have already seen. The observation that **every** is antitonic in its first argument and monotone in its second argument is exactly what the typing $p \xrightarrow{-} (p \xrightarrow{+} t)$ expresses.

A *term* is an object t such that there is a type τ with $t : \tau$. We assume that our notations arrange that every term has exactly one type. We interpret this language in a type domain as expected.

Definition 8 (Denotation). For each term $t : \tau$, and for each $\tau' \succeq \tau$, we define $[\![t]\!]_{\tau'}^{\mathcal{S}}$ by induction on t.

1. The semantics begins with values $[\![c]\!]_{\tau}^{\mathcal{S}}$. We require that $[\![c]\!]_{\tau}^{\mathcal{S}}$ belong to $\mathbb{D}_{\tau}$.

2. If $t : \sigma \xrightarrow{m} \tau$ and $u : \sigma'$ with $\sigma' \preceq \sigma$, then $[\![t(u)]\!]_{\tau}^{\mathcal{S}} = [\![t]\!]_{\sigma \xrightarrow{m} \tau}^{\mathcal{S}} ([\![u]\!]_{\sigma'}^{\mathcal{S}})$.

In all cases, where $t : \tau \preceq \tau'$, we let $[\![t]\!]_{\tau'}^{\mathcal{S}} = [\![t]\!]_{\tau}^{\mathcal{S}}$.

Frequently we omit the superscript $\mathcal{S}$.

Example 10. Let $\mathcal{B} = \{r\}$, and $\mathcal{S}$ be the standard structure defined as follows. We take $\mathbb{D}_r$ to be $(\mathbb{R}, \leq)$. We take $[\![\mathsf{plus}]\!]$ to be the function from $\mathbb{R}$ to functions from $\mathbb{R}$ to itself which takes a real number a to the function $\lambda b.a + b$. For example, $[\![\mathsf{plus}]\!](67)(-3) = 64$. We have to check that $[\![\mathsf{plus}]\!]$ really belongs to $\mathbb{D}_{r \xrightarrow{+} (r \xrightarrow{+} r)}$. This means: For each a, $[\![\mathsf{plus}]\!](a)$ is a monotone function: If $b \leq b'$, then $a+b \leq a+b'$. Moreover, the function from $\mathbb{R}$ to $(\mathbb{R} \xrightarrow{+} \mathbb{R})$ taking a to $[\![\mathsf{plus}]\!](a)$ is itself monotone. This means that if $a \leq a'$, then for all b, $a + b \leq a' + b$. We similarly use

$$
\begin{aligned}
[\![\mathsf{minus}]\!](a)(b) &= a - b & [\![0]\!] &= 0 \\
[\![\mathsf{times}]\!](a)(b) &= a \times b & [\![1]\!] &= 1 \\
[\![\mathsf{div2}]\!](a)(b) &= a \div 2^b & [\![2]\!] &= 2 \\
[\![\mathsf{abs}]\!](a) &= |a|
\end{aligned}
$$

It is now a fact of arithmetic that our semantics is appropriate in the sense that $[\![c]\!] \in \mathbb{D}_{\sigma}$ whenever $c : \sigma$ is part of the lexicon. That is, we have a *bona fide* semantics of all constants.

We then may work out the semantics of all terms. For example,

$$
\begin{aligned}
[\![\mathsf{plus}\ 1\ 1]\!] &= [\![\mathsf{plus}]\!]([\![1]\!])([\![1]\!]) \\
&= [\![\mathsf{plus}]\!](1)(1) \\
&= 2.
\end{aligned}
$$

5.3 Labeled terms

Because our typed terms may involve subterms within the scope of multiple functions, it is useful to *label* subterm occurrences to make clear what position that term is in. In fact, we make crucial use of this labeling in our proof system. For instance, if $t : \sigma \xrightarrow{} \tau$ and $u : \rho \xrightarrow{}$ σ, then in $t(u(v)) : \tau$, subterm $v : \rho$ is in a monotone position. We have seen the simple algebra of markings $(\mathcal{M}, \circ)$ in Section 2.4, and the definition below captures the result of the monotonicity marking algorithms we outlined in Section 2.

Definition 9 (Labeled Terms). Suppose u is a subterm occurrence in t. We shall find some $l \in \mathcal{M}$ which indicates the polarity of u inside t, and call it the *label* of the occurrence of u in t. We shall write this as $t[u^l]$. The definition is by recursion on terms:

1. If $u = t$, then $u[u^+]$; that is, the label of u is $+$ in u ;

2. If $s[u^l]$, then $s(v)[u^l]$; that is, subterms of a functor inherit their labels from the functor itself.

3. If $v[u^l]$ and $s : \tau \xrightarrow{m} \sigma$, then $s(v)[u^{m \circ l}]$; that is, an occurrence of u in an argument v of an application $s(v)$ has label $m \circ l$ in the overall term $s(v)$, where m is the label on the arrow in $\xrightarrow{m}$, and l is the label of the occurrence inside v.

Example 11. Let us compute the polarity of cat inside see every cat. The occurrence of cat inside itself is positive: $\text{cat}[\text{cat}^+]$. Recall that the type of every is of the form $\sigma \xrightarrow{} \tau$. (Its type is $p \xrightarrow{} (p \xrightarrow{+} t)$.) So the polarity of cat inside every cat is $- \circ + = -$. That is, every $\text{cat}[\text{cat}^-]$. Finally, a look at the type of verbs shows that see every $\text{cat}[\text{cat}^-]$.

It is also sensible to shorten the notation a bit and write every $[\text{cat}^-]$ and see every $[\text{cat}^-]$. In the same way, we would have see some $[\text{cat}^+]$ and see most $[\text{cat}^.]$.

Example 12. We have already seen several different definitions of the polarity operation. In particular, Example 6 shows that

$$\text{div2 minus } [x^+] \, [y^-] \text{ minus } [z^-] \text{ plus } [v^+] \, [w^+].$$

Lemma 2 (Soundness of Labeling Scheme). Suppose $t : \tau$ and $u : \rho$ is a subterm occurrence of t such that $t[u^l]$ with subterm u labeled by $l \in \{+, -\}$. Then for any structure $\mathcal{S}$, supposing $[\![u]\!]_{\hat\rho} \leq_{\hat\rho} [\![v]\!]_{\hat\rho}$:

1. If $l = +$, then $[\![t]\!]_\tau \leq_\tau [\![t^{v \leftarrow u}]\!]_\tau$;

2. If $l = -$, then $[\![t^{v \leftarrow u}]\!]_\tau \leq_\tau [\![t]\!]_\tau$.

Here $t^{v \leftarrow u}$ is the term that results from substituting v for the occurrence of u in t. In other words, if a subterm occurrence is labeled by $+$ $(-)$, it is indeed in a monotone (antitone) position. This is the crucial point about the correspondence between polarity and monotonicity.

5.4 Monotonicity Calculus

We are interested in proof relations between sets of inequalities Γ and individual inequality statements $s \leq t$. As discussed above, we allow inequality statements between terms whose types are $\uparrow$-related, since these are exactly the terms that should be $\leq$-comparable semantically.

Definition 10 (Satisfaction). Where $s : \sigma$ and $t : \tau$, and if $\sigma \uparrow \tau$, we write $\mathcal{S} \models s \leq t$ if $[\![s]\!]_{\hat{\sigma}} \leq_{\hat{\sigma}} [\![t]\!]_{\hat{\sigma}}$. We shall always use Γ to denote a set of statements of the form $u \leq v$. We write $\Gamma \models s \leq t$ if, whenever $\mathcal{S} \models u \leq v$ for all statements $u \leq v \in \Gamma$, also $\mathcal{S} \models s \leq t$.

Definition 11 (Monotonicity Calculus). The Monotonicity Calculus is given by the following rules:

$$(\text{Refl}) \ \frac{}{t \leq t} \qquad\qquad (\text{Trans}) \ \frac{t \leq u \qquad u \leq v}{t \leq v}$$

$$(\text{Mono}) \ \frac{u \leq v}{t[u^+] \leq t^{v \leftarrow u}} \qquad (\text{Anti}) \ \frac{u \leq v}{t^{v \leftarrow u} \leq t[u^-]}$$

$$(\text{Point}) \ \frac{s \leq t}{s(u) \leq t(u)}$$

If Γ is a set of statements of the form $u \leq v$, we say $\Gamma \vdash s \leq t$ if $s \leq t \in \Gamma$, or there is a proof of $s \leq t$ from inequalities in Γ using the rules above.

Example 13. It might be amusing to see that some facts of arithmetic can now be derived from assumptions. For example,

$$\{0 \leq 1, 1 \leq 2\} \vdash \mathsf{minus}\ 1\ 1 \leq \mathsf{minus}\ 2\ 0.$$

That is, if we assume (the facts about numbers) that $0 \leq 1$ and $1 \leq 2$, and if we work in our logic, and in particular if we assume the typing of minus that we have seen, then we can prove that $1 - 1 \leq 2 - 0$:

$$\frac{\dfrac{\dfrac{1 \leq 2}{\mathsf{minus}\ [1^+] \leq \mathsf{minus}\ 2}\ (\text{Mono})}{\mathsf{minus}\ 1\ 1 \leq \mathsf{minus}\ 2\ 1}\ (\text{Point}) \qquad \dfrac{0 \leq 1}{\mathsf{minus}\ 2\ [1^-] \leq \mathsf{minus}\ 2\ 0}\ (\text{Anti})}{\mathsf{minus}\ 1\ 1 \leq \mathsf{minus}\ 2\ 0}\ (\text{Trans})$$

We need our set of assumptions $\Gamma = \{0 \leq 1, 1 \leq 2\}$ because the assertions in it are not true in all structures that we could conceivably use to interpret the language. The point of the calculus is not to tell us specific facts about numbers but rather to allow us to infer generalities, assertions which hold in all models of some set of assumptions. This is the standard account of model-theoretic consequence used in semantics.

Example 14. Let Γ contain $\mathsf{every} : p \xrightarrow{-} (p \xrightarrow{+} t) \leq \mathsf{most} : p \to (p \xrightarrow{+} t)$, $\mathsf{cat} : p \leq \mathsf{animal} : p$, and $\mathsf{child} : p \leq \mathsf{person} : p$. Below is a small derivation in the calculus:

$$\dfrac{\dfrac{\text{cat} \le \text{animal}}{\text{every } [\text{animal}^-] \le \text{every cat}} \ (\text{ANTI}) \qquad \dfrac{\text{every} \le \text{most}}{\text{every cat} \le \text{most cat}} \ (\text{POINT})}{\dfrac{\text{every animal} \le \text{most cat}}{\text{every animal runs} \le \text{most cat runs}} \ (\text{POINT})} \ (\text{TRANS})$$

Example 15. We can also fruitfully combine the numerical example with the linguistic one. We take the set $\mathcal{B}$ of base types to be $\{e, t, r\}$. We use all the syntax which we have already seen, and also

$$\text{at least} : r \xrightarrow{-} (p \xrightarrow{+} (p \xrightarrow{+} t))$$
$$\text{at most} : r \xrightarrow{+} (p \xrightarrow{-} (p \xrightarrow{-} t))$$
$$\text{more than} : r \xrightarrow{-} (p \xrightarrow{+} (p \xrightarrow{+} t))$$
$$\text{less than} : r \xrightarrow{+} (p \xrightarrow{-} (p \xrightarrow{-} t)).$$

Then the natural set Γ of assumptions would include

$$0 \le 1, 1 \le 2, \ldots, \quad \text{more than} \le \text{at least}, \quad \text{less than} \le \text{at most},$$
$$\text{some} \le \text{at least 1}, \quad \text{at least 1} \le \text{some}$$

For example, we could prove

$$\text{more than three people walk} \le \text{at least two people walk}.$$

All three of the above examples use only unembedded versions of the (MONO) and (ANTI) rules. That is, we could have stated these rules as follows, where $t : \sigma \xrightarrow{+} \tau$, $s : \sigma \xrightarrow{-} \tau$, and $u, v : \sigma' \preceq \sigma$.

$$(\text{MONO}^*) \ \dfrac{u \le v}{t(u) \le t(v)} \qquad (\text{ANTI}^*) \ \dfrac{u \le v}{s(v) \le s(u)}$$

It is then easily shown that the more common presentations of the rules, viz. (MONO) and (ANTI), can be derived from the system with (MONO*) and (ANTI*) instead. It is an interesting question, which of these is more psychologically natural or computationally sensible: deriving labelings for terms as in Section 5.3 above, or restricting application of the monotonicity and antitonicity rules to only atomic function symbols? We leave this as an open question for future work.

5.5 Soundness and Completeness

A natural question about any axiomatic system is whether it is *sound* and *complete* with respect to an intended class of interpretations. Soundness means that every inequality which is proved in the calculus holds in all of the interpretations we are considering, no matter what the meanings of the individual lexical items. Completeness is the converse; it says that the calculus is strong enough to derive (from a set Γ of assumptions) all of the inequalities true in all models of Γ.

Theorem 1 (Soundness of the Monotonicity Calculus). *If* $\Gamma \vdash s \leq t$, *then* $\Gamma \models s \leq t$. (For the proof see Icard and Moss (2013).)

Completeness—the statement that $\Gamma \models s \leq t$ implies $\Gamma \vdash s \leq t$—we have proven in some special cases (Icard and Moss 2013). For instance, when we consider a wider class of structures than those defined above in Def. 6, the result holds. We also conjecture that it holds for this smaller class of standard structures based on hierarchies of functions, as defined here.

We also should point out that in many applications, one is not interested in *truth in all possible models* but rather in truth in all "reasonable" models. For instance, in the linguistic example, when we think of the inferential patterns of determiners, many important patterns go beyond monotonicity (and even the extension to reasoning about exclusion relations). We did not incorporate de Morgan's laws, so we will not be able to infer someone does not cry from not everyone cries. To mention another source of incompleteness, from Pat is a clarinetist, it follows that everyone who likes every clarinetist likes Pat, and even everyone who likes everyone who likes Pat likes everyone who likes every clarinetist. Our calculus as it stands is not strong enough to derive these. Furthermore, we have no way to use variables. For example, in the algebra example, we might like to include a numerical variable $x : r$ and take Γ to contain $x \leq \mathsf{abs}(x)$. Then we could deduce things like

$$\mathsf{minus}\ 0\ 1 \quad \leq \quad \mathsf{abs}\ \mathsf{minus}\ 0\ 1.$$

Indeed, there are some linguistic applications involving introduction rules and "hypothetical reasoning" in extended categorial grammars, which make crucial use of variables and lambda abstraction.[3] We leave such extensions of the formalism developed here for future work.

6 Conclusion

Monotonicity is an important concept in the study of logic and language. We hope to have shown some of the reasons for this, both from a linguistic point of view and from a logical point of view. There are certainly many extensions to pursue beyond what we have discussed, both regarding psycholinguistic aspects of monotonicty and polarity, and regarding more expressive logical systems.

From the point of view of language technology, in Section 4 we described some of the exciting recent work applying ideas and algorithms from logic, viz. Monotonicity Calculus, to practical tasks in natural

---

[3]See Zamansky et al. (2006) for a natural logic system similar to what we present here, but based on Lambek Calculus.

language processing, particularly for the problem of recognizing textual entailment. In turn, some of the logical work we described, e.g. in Section 3, was inspired by practical work in computational linguistics. It is our hope, and our prediction, that this trend of mutual influence will continue well into the future.

References

Chater, Nick and Mike Oaksford. 1999. The probability heuristics model of syllogistic reasoning. *Cognitive Psychology* 38:191–258.

Chemla, Emmanuel, Vincent Homer, and Daniel Rothschild. 2011. Modularity and intuitions in formal semantics: the case of polarity items. *Linguistics and Philosophy* 34(6):537–570.

Cheung, Jackie and Gerald Penn. 2012. Unsupervised detection of downward-entailing operators by maximizing classification certainty. In *13th Conference of the European Chapter of the Association for Computational Linguistics*.

Dagan, Ido, Oren Glickman, and Bernardo Magnini. 2005. The PASCAL Recognizing Textual Entailment Challenge. In *Proceedings of the PASCAL Challenges Workshop on Recognizing Textual Entailment*.

Danescu, Cristian and Lillian Lee. 2010. Don't 'have a clue'? Unsupervised co-learning of downward-entailing operators. In *Proceedings of ACL*.

Danescu, Cristian, Lillian Lee, and Richard Ducott. 2009. Without a 'doubt'? Unsupervised discovery of downward-entailing operators. In *Proceedings of NAACL HLT*.

Dowty, David. 1994. The role of negative polarity and concord marking in natural language reasoning. In *Proceedings of Semantics and Linguistic Theory (SALT) IV*.

Geurts, Bart. 2003. Reasoning with quantifiers. *Cognition* 86(3):223–251.

Geurts, Bart and Frans van der Slik. 2005. Monotonicity and processing load. *Journal of Semantics* 22.

Giannakidou, Anastasia. 2011. Negative and positive polarity items. In C. Maienborn, K. von Heusinger, and P. Portner, eds., *Semantics: An International Handbook of Natural Language Meaning*. Wouter de Gruyter.

Icard, Thomas F. 2012. Inclusion and exclusion in natural language. *Studia Logica* 100(4):705–725.

Icard, Thomas F. and Lawrence S. Moss. 2013. A complete calculus of monotone and antitone higher-order functions. Unpublished ms.

Keenan, Edward L. and Leonard M. Faltz. 1984. *Boolean Semantics for Natural Language*. Springer.

MacCartney, Bill. 2009. *Natural Language Inference*. Ph.D. thesis, Stanford University.

MacCartney, Bill and Christopher D. Manning. 2009. An extended model of natural logic. In *Proceedings of the Eighth International Conference on Computational Semantics (IWCS-8)*.

Moss, Lawrence S. 2012. The soundness of internalized polarity marking. *Studia Logica* 100(4):683–704.

Nairn, Rowan, Cleo Condoravdi, and Lauri Karttunen. 2006. Computing relative polarity for textual inference. In *Proceedings of ICoS-5 (Inference in Computational Semantics)*. Buxton, UK.

Oaksford, Mike and Nick Chater. 2001. The probabilistic approach to human reasoning. *Trends in Cognitive Sciences* 5:349–357.

Sánchez-Valencia, Victor. 1991. *Studies on Natural Logic and Categorial Grammar*. Ph.D. thesis, Universiteit van Amsterdam.

Szabolcsi, Anna, Lewis Bott, and Brian McElree. 2008. The effect of negative polarity items on inference verification. *Journal of Semantics* 25(4):411–450.

van Benthem, Johan. 1986. *Essays in Logical Semantics*. Reidel, Dordrecht.

van Benthem, Johan. 1991. *Language in Action: Categories, Lambdas, and Dynamic Logic*, vol. 130 of *Studies in Logic*. Elsevier, Amsterdam.

van Benthem, Johan. 2008. A brief history of natural logic. In M. N. M. M. Chakraborty, B. Löwe and S. Sarukkai, eds., *Logic, Navya-Nyaya and Applications, Homage to Bimal Krishna Matilal*. London: College Publications.

van Eijck, Jan. 2007. Natural logic for natural language. In B. ten Cate and H. Zeevat, eds., *6th International Tbilisi Symposium on Logic, Language, and Computation*. Springer.

Zamansky, A., N. Francez, and Y. Winter. 2006. A 'natural logic' inference system using the Lambek calculus. *Journal of Logic, Language, and Information* 15(3):273–295.

Zwarts, Frans. 1981. Negatief polaire uitdrukkingen I. In *GLOT*, vol. 4, pages 35–132.

The Relational Syllogistic Revisited

IAN PRATT-HARTMANN[1]

The relational syllogistic is an extension of the language of Classical syllogisms in which predicates are allowed to feature transitive verbs with quantified objects. It is known that the relational syllogistic does not admit a finite set of syllogism-like rules whose associated (direct) derivation relation is sound and complete. We present a modest extension of this language which does.

1 Introduction

By the *Classical syllogistic*, we mean the language featuring the four sentence-forms of standard Aristotelian syllogisms: "Every p is a q", "Some p is a q", "No p is a q" and "Some p is not a q", where p and q are substituted by common (count) nouns. By the *relational syllogistic*, we mean the extension of the Classical syllogistic in which predicates are additionally allowed to feature transitive verbs with quantified objects. For example, the following is a valid argument in this language.

> Some artist admires no beekeeper
> Every beekeeper admires some artist
> ―――――――――――――――――――――――――
> Some artist is not a beekeeper

Indeed, consider any artist, a, who admires no beekeeper. If he is not a beekeeper himself, the conclusion is certainly true. On the other hand, if he is a beekeeper, the second premise guarantees the existence of an artist b, whom he admires, and who cannot therefore be a beekeeper (since otherwise a would not admire b), whence the conclusion is again true. Thus, the relational syllogistic allows us to formulate arguments that—subjectively at least—are more difficult than those we encounter

---

[1] University of Manchester

LiLT Volume 9
Perspectives on Semantic Representations for Textual Inference.
Copyright © 2014, CSLI Publications.

in the Classical syllogistic.

For the Classical syllogistic, the familiar collection of syllogisms constitutes, together with one or two ancillary rules, a (sound and) complete inference system: if an argument in this language is valid, in the sense that there is no possible world making its premises true and its conclusion false, then that validity can be demonstrated using syllogistic inference steps alone. This was first shown, in a slightly weakened form, by Corcoran Corcoran (1972) and Smiley Smiley (1973). Specifically, these authors proved certain systems of syllogism-like rules to be (sound and) *refutation-complete*: if an argument is valid, then an absurdity can be derived from its premises together with the negation of its conclusion. Subsequently, Pratt-Hartmann and Moss Pratt-Hartmann and Moss (2009) obtained the following results: (i) there is a finite set of syllogism-like rules in the Classical syllogistic which is sound and complete (not just refutation-complete); (ii) there is a finite set of syllogism-like rules in the relational syllogistic which is sound and refutation complete; (iii) there is *no* finite set of syllogism-like rules in the relational syllogistic which is sound and complete. In other words, for the relational syllogistic, indirect reasoning is essential.

This paper presents a modest extension of the relational syllogistic, which additionally features sentences of the form: "If there are p's, there are q's." The following is a valid argument in this language.

> If there are artists, there are carpenters
> If there are beekeepers, there are dentists
> Every carpenter admires every electrician
> No carpenter admires any flautist
> Every dentist is an electrician
> Every dentist is a flautist
> _____
> No artist is a beekeeper

Indeed, suppose some artist were a beekeeper. By the first two premises, some carpenter would exist, and so would some dentist. But the remaining four premises evidently rule out the possibility that both carpenters and dentists exist, since the latter would be electricians and flautists, and hence both admired and not admired by the former.

In the sequel, we provide a finite set of syllogism-like rules for this extended relational syllogistic, and show that the resulting proof system is sound and complete. That is: the impossibility of providing a such ruleset for the relational syllogistic can be overcome by a modest increase in expressive power. Thus, the existence of a proof-system defined by a finite set of syllogism-like rules does not represent a 'boundary' with respect to the expressiveness of fragments of natural language.

2   The languages $\mathcal{S}$, $\mathcal{R}$ and $\mathcal{RE}$

2.1   Syntax and semantics

In this section, we define the formal languages: $\mathcal{S}$, $\mathcal{R}$ and $\mathcal{RE}$, corresponding to the Classical syllogistic, the relational syllogistic and the extended relational syllogistic, respectively. We review known results concerning $\mathcal{S}$ and $\mathcal{R}$ and, in particular, give a sketch of the proof that $\mathcal{R}$ does not admit a finite set of syllogistic rules defining a sound and complete proof system. The motivation for defining the language $\mathcal{RE}$ as we have should at that point be obvious.

Let $\mathbf{P}$ and $\mathbf{R}$ be countably infinite sets. We call the elements of $\mathbf{P}$ *unary atoms* and the elements of $\mathbf{R}$ *binary atoms*; we use the (possibly decorated) letters o, p, q to range over unary atoms, and r to range over binary atoms. A *unary literal* is an expression of the form p or $\bar{p}$, and a *binary literal* is an expression of the form r or $\bar{r}$; we use ℓ, m to range over unary literals, and t to range over binary literals. A unary literal is called *positive* if it is a unary atom, otherwise *negative*; similarly for binary literals. The set of *c-terms* is defined by

$$c := \ell \quad | \quad \forall(p, t) \quad | \quad \exists(p, t);$$

we use c, d to range over c-terms. The set of $\mathcal{S}$-*formulas* is defined by

$$\varphi := \forall(p, \ell) \quad | \quad \exists(p, \ell);$$

the set of $\mathcal{R}$-*formulas* is defined by

$$\varphi := \forall(p, c) \quad | \quad \exists(p, c);$$

and the set of $\mathcal{RE}$-*formulas* is defined by

$$\varphi := \forall(p, c) \quad | \quad \exists(p, c) \quad | \quad \not\forall(p, q).$$

We refer to formulas of the form $\exists(p, c)$ as *existential formulas*, and to formulas of the forms $\forall(p, c)$ and $\not\forall(p, q)$ as *universal formulas*,

Intuitively, the elements of $\mathbf{P}$ stand for common count-nouns— "artist", "beekeeper", "carpenter", etc.—and those of $\mathbf{R}$ for transitive verbs—"despises", "envies", etc. We then read the c-terms $\forall(p, r)$ and $\exists(p, r)$ as "thing which r's every p" and "thing which r's some p", respectively; and we read the sentence forms $\forall(p, c)$ and $\exists(p, c)$ as "Every p is a c" and "Some p is a c", respectively. Thus we have the following informal glosses for $\mathcal{R}$-formulas.

$\exists(\text{artist}, \text{beekeeper})$	Some artist is a beekeeper
$\forall(\text{artist}, \forall(\text{beekeeper}, \text{admire}))$	Every artist (is a thing which) admires every beekeeper.

A negative unary literal $\bar{p}$ is then read as "is not a p", and a negative binary literal $\bar{r}$ as "does not r", but with negation having narrow scope with respect to the quantification of the predicate. In idiomatic English:

$\exists$(artist, $\overline{\text{beekeeper}}$)   Some artist is not a beekeeper

$\forall$(artist, $\forall$(beekeeper, $\overline{\text{admire}}$))   No artist admires *any* beekeeper.

Finally, the additional forms $\exists\!\!\!/(p, q)$ in $\mathcal{RE}$ are read "If there are p's, then there are q's," thus:

$\exists\!\!\!/$(artist, beekeeper)   If there are artists, then there are beekeepers.

We use the symbol $\mathcal{S}$ to denote the set of all $\mathcal{S}$-formulas, and similarly for $\mathcal{R}$ and $\mathcal{RE}$. When the language in question ($\mathcal{S}$, $\mathcal{R}$ or $\mathcal{RE}$) is clear from context, we speak simply of *formulas*, and we use φ, ψ to range over formulas of that language. Notice that none of these languages includes formulas such as $\forall(\bar{p}, q)$ or $\exists(p, \forall(\bar{q}, r))$. Thus, we cannot say "Every *non*-artist is a beekeeper" or "Some artist admires every *non*-beekeeper" etc. We comment on the significance of this restriction below.

The semantics of these languages is given in the standard way. A *structure* is a triple $\mathfrak{A} = \langle A, \{p^{\mathfrak{A}}\}_{p \in \mathbf{P}}, \{r^{\mathfrak{A}}\}_{r \in \mathbf{R}}\rangle$, where A is a non-empty set, $p^{\mathfrak{A}} \subseteq A$, for every $p \in \mathbf{P}$, and $r^{\mathfrak{A}} \subseteq A \times A$, for every $r \in \mathbf{R}$. The set A is called the *domain* of $\mathfrak{A}$. We extend the maps $p \mapsto p^{\mathfrak{A}}$ and $r \mapsto r^{\mathfrak{A}}$ to all unary and binary literals by setting, for any p, r:

$$\bar{p}^{\mathfrak{A}} = A \setminus p^{\mathfrak{A}}$$
$$\bar{r}^{\mathfrak{A}} = (A \times A) \setminus r^{\mathfrak{A}}$$

and thence to all c-terms by setting, for any p, t:

$$\forall(p, t)^{\mathfrak{A}} = \{a \in A \mid \text{for all } b \in p^{\mathfrak{A}}, \langle a, b\rangle \in t^{\mathfrak{A}}\}$$
$$\exists(p, t)^{\mathfrak{A}} = \{a \in A \mid \text{there exists } b \in p^{\mathfrak{A}} \text{ such that } \langle a, b\rangle \in t^{\mathfrak{A}}\}.$$

If $a \in c^{\mathfrak{A}}$, we say that a *satisfies* c (*in* $\mathfrak{A}$), and think of a as having the property denoted by c, according to the structure $\mathfrak{A}$. If $\ell = \bar{p}$ is a negative unary literal, we write $\bar{\ell} = p$; similarly for binary literals. We write $\bar{\forall} = \exists$ and $\bar{\exists} = \forall$. For any c-term of the form $Q(p, t)$ with $Q \in \{\forall, \exists\}$, we write $\bar{c} = \bar{Q}(p, \bar{t})$. Thus, for any c-term c, $(\bar{c})^{\mathfrak{A}} = A \setminus c^{\mathfrak{A}}$.

Having defined the notion of satisfaction for c-terms relative to a structure, we define the truth-relation $\models$ between structures and formulas as follows:

$$\mathfrak{A} \models \forall(p, c) \text{ iff } p^{\mathfrak{A}} \subseteq c^{\mathfrak{A}}$$
$$\mathfrak{A} \models \exists(p, c) \text{ iff } p^{\mathfrak{A}} \cap c^{\mathfrak{A}} \neq \emptyset$$
$$\mathfrak{A} \models \exists\!\!\!/(p, q) \text{ iff } p^{\mathfrak{A}} \neq \emptyset \text{ implies } q^{\mathfrak{A}} \neq \emptyset.$$

If $\mathfrak{A} \models \theta$, we say that θ is *true* in $\mathfrak{A}$. We take *false* to mean *not true*. As usual, when Θ is a set of formulas, we write $\mathfrak{A} \models \Theta$ if $\mathfrak{A} \models \theta$ for all $\theta \in \Theta$; in this case, we say that $\mathfrak{A}$ is a *model* of Θ, and that Θ is *satisfiable*. If, for every structure $\mathfrak{A}$, $\mathfrak{A} \models \Theta$ implies $\mathfrak{A} \models \theta$, then we write $\Theta \models \theta$, and we say the argument from *premises* Θ to *conclusion* θ is *valid*, or simply Θ *entails* θ. A formula of the form $\exists(p, \bar{p})$ is evidently true in no structure; indeed, no other $\mathcal{RE}$-formulas have this property. We consequently refer to any formula of this form as an *absurdity*, and use $\bot$ to stand, indifferently, for any absurdity.

It is easy to see that the formulas $\exists(p, q)$ and $\exists(q, p)$ are true in exactly the same structures, as indeed are the formulas $\forall(p, \bar{q})$ and $\forall(q, \bar{p})$. For this reason, we henceforth regard these pairs as identical, silently transforming one into the other as required. Indeed, we allow ourselves to write *any* $\mathcal{RE}$-formula $\exists(p, c)$ as $\exists(c, p)$, and *any* $\mathcal{RE}$-formula $\forall(p, c)$ as $\forall(\bar{c}, \bar{p})$, again performing these transformations silently, as required. This (inessential) notational shortcut will allow inference rules to be stated more succinctly. It is likewise easy to see that the formula $\exists(p, c)$ is true in exactly those structures in which $\forall(p, \bar{c})$ is false (and vice versa); moreover, $\not\forall(p, q)$ is true in exactly those structures in which $\exists(p, p)$ and $\forall(q, \bar{q})$ are not both true. Thus, the language $\mathcal{RE}$ in effect allows negation of formulas. We remark that $\not\forall(p, \bar{q})$ is not an $\mathcal{RE}$-formula.

2.2 Proof-theory

Let $\mathcal{L}$ be any of the languages $\mathcal{S}$, $\mathcal{R}$ or $\mathcal{RE}$. A *syllogistic rule* (or simply: *rule*) in $\mathcal{L}$ is a pair Θ/θ, where Θ is a finite set (possibly empty) of $\mathcal{L}$-formulas, and θ an $\mathcal{L}$-formula. We generally display rules with premises and conclusion separated by a horizontal line. Thus, the rules

$$\frac{\forall(p, q) \quad \forall(o, p)}{\forall(o, q)} \qquad \frac{\forall(p, \bar{q}) \quad \forall(o, p)}{\forall(o, \bar{q})}$$

correspond to the familiar syllogisms *Barbara* and *Celarent*:

$$\frac{\text{Every } p \text{ is a } q \quad \text{Every } o \text{ is a } p}{\text{Every } o \text{ is a } q} \qquad \frac{\text{No } p \text{ is a } q \quad \text{Every } o \text{ is a } p}{\text{No } o \text{ is a } q}.$$

To save space, and using the convention that ℓ ranges over literals, we can merge these rules as follows:

$$\frac{\forall(p, \ell) \quad \forall(o, p)}{\forall(o, \ell)} \quad (\text{A1}').$$

We employ this convention heavily in the sequel, with ℓ ranging over unary literals, t over binary literals, c, d over c-terms, and ψ over formulas. We remark that the label $(\text{A1}')$ is simply there to identify uses of this rule in derivations, and has no formal significance.

We are invited to think of a set of rules X as specifying the allowed steps in a *derivation* involving a set of formulas, Θ, (the *premises*), and a formula, θ (the *conclusion*). Any derivation has the shape of a tree whose leaves are labelled with elements of Θ (repeats allowed), and whose root is labelled with θ. We write $\Theta \vdash_X \theta$ to indicate the existence of such a derivation. Thus, for example, if X contains the rule (A1′), the derivation

$$\cfrac{\forall(\text{carpenter}, \overline{\text{dentist}}) \qquad \cfrac{\forall(\text{beekeeper}, \text{carpenter}) \quad \forall(\text{artist}, \text{beekeeper})}{\forall(\text{artist}, \text{carpenter})} \;(\text{A1}')}{\forall(\text{artist}, \overline{\text{dentist}})} \;(\text{A1}')$$

shows that

$$\{\forall(\text{artist}, \text{beekeeper}), \forall(\text{beekeeper}, \text{carpenter}),$$
$$\forall(\text{carpenter}, \overline{\text{dentist}})\} \vdash_X \forall(\text{artist}, \overline{\text{dentist}}).$$

It is important to realize in this regard that all proof systems considered here are *direct*, proceeding step-by-step from premises to conclusion. In particular, they incorporate no mechanism of *indirect* proof, in which a conclusion is derived by first supposing its negation and then deriving an absurdity. (We hasten to add that there is nothing *wrong* with indirect proofs: we are simply interested in the circumstances under which they are dispensable.)

The rule-sets X of most interest to us are those whose associated derivation relation, $\vdash_X$, constitutes necessary and sufficient conditions for entailment. Formally, we say that $\vdash_X$ is *sound* if $\Theta \vdash_X \theta$ implies $\Theta \models \theta$, and *complete* if $\Theta \models \theta$ implies $\Theta \vdash_X \theta$. In this paper, we shall be concerned exclusively with *finite* rule-sets X, since there trivially exist infinite (computable) rule-sets for $\mathcal{S}$, $\mathcal{R}$ and $\mathcal{RE}$ whose associated derivation relation is sound and complete. A set of formulas Θ is said to be *inconsistent* (with respect to a derivation relation $\vdash$) if there is a derivation of some absurdity from Θ. We say that $\vdash_X$ is *refutation-complete* if any unsatisfiable set of formulas is inconsistent. It is easy to see that completeness implies refutation-completeness, but not, it transpires, vice versa. Indeed, the following results were shown in Pratt-Hartmann and Moss Pratt-Hartmann and Moss (2009).

Theorem 2.1. There exists a finite set X of syllogistic rules in $\mathcal{S}$ such that $\vdash_X$ is sound and complete.

Theorem 2.2. There exists a finite set X of syllogistic rules in $\mathcal{R}$ such that $\vdash_X$ is sound and refutation-complete.

Theorem 2.3. There exists no finite set X of syllogistic rules in $\mathcal{R}$ such that $\vdash_X$ is sound and complete.

The sole result of this paper is

Theorem 2.4. There exists a finite set X of syllogistic rules in $\mathcal{RE}$ such that $\vdash_{\mathsf{X}}$ is sound and complete.

We are now in a position to understand the motivation for the particular language, $\mathcal{RE}$, that we are concerned with in this paper. To do so, we need to consider the proof Theorem 2.3, which we sketch here informally; for full details, see Pratt-Hartmann and Moss Pratt-Hartmann and Moss (2009), pp. 661 ff.

Sketch proof of Theorem 2.3. For n positive, let $p_1, \ldots, p_n$ be distinct unary atoms, r a binary atom, γ_n the $\mathcal{R}$-formula $\forall(p_1, \exists(p_n, r))$ and Γ_n the set of $\mathcal{R}$-formulas:

$$\forall(p_i, \exists(p_{i+1}, r)) \qquad\qquad (1 \leq i < n)$$
$$\forall(p_1, \forall(p_n, r)).$$

We claim that $\Gamma_n \models \gamma_n$. Indeed, suppose $\mathfrak{A} \models \Gamma_n$. If $p_1^{\mathfrak{A}} = \emptyset$, then trivially $\mathfrak{A} \models \gamma_n$; on the other hand, if $p_1^{\mathfrak{A}} \neq \emptyset$, a simple induction using the formulas $\forall(p_i, \exists(p_{i+1}, r))$ shows that $p_n^{\mathfrak{A}} \neq \emptyset$, whence, from $\forall(p_1, \forall(p_n, r))$, $\mathfrak{A} \models \gamma_n$. Call any formula of the form $\forall(p, p)$ *trivial*. For any i ($1 \leq i \leq n$), let $\Gamma_{n,i}$ be the result from removing from Γ_n the formula $\forall(p_i, \exists(p_{i+1}, r))$. It can be shown, by a detailed examination of cases, that $\Gamma_{n,i}$ entails *no* non-trivial $\mathcal{R}$-formulas that are not already in Γ_n. Now consider any finite, non-empty set X of rules in $\mathcal{R}$, and let n be greater than the maximum number of premises in any of these rules. For any instance, Θ/θ, of one of these rules, if $\Theta \subseteq \Gamma_n$, then $\Theta \subseteq \Gamma_{n,i}$ for some i ($1 \leq i \leq n$). Hence, if the rules of X are valid, θ must be trivial or contained in Γ_n. In other words, the rules of X never yield non-trivial conclusions outside Γ_n, and in particular never yield γ_n. Therefore $\vdash_{\mathsf{X}}$ is not complete. $\qquad\qquad\square$

It is easy to see what is going wrong here: $\Gamma_{n,i}$ does indeed entail $\exists(p_1, p_j)$ for $1 \leq j < i$; however, these formulas are not in $\mathcal{R}$, and so cannot feature in $\mathcal{R}$-derivations. But now suppose we work within the language $\mathcal{RE}$, where we can write rules

$$\frac{\forall(p, \exists(q, r))}{\exists(p, q)} \text{ (C4)} \qquad \frac{\exists(o, p) \quad \exists(p, q)}{\exists(o, q)} \text{ (C2)} \qquad \frac{\forall(p, \forall(q, t)) \quad \exists(p, q)}{\forall(p, \exists(q, t))} \text{ (D1)}.$$

We may derive $\not\exists(p_1, p_2)$, $\not\exists(p_1, p_3)$ and $\not\exists(p_1, p_4)$ as follows:

$$
\cfrac{\cfrac{\forall(p_1, \exists(p_2, r))}{\not\exists(p_1, p_2)} \text{ (C4)} \quad \cfrac{\cfrac{\forall(p_2, \exists(p_3, r))}{\not\exists(p_2, p_3)} \text{ (C4)}}{\not\exists(p_1, p_3)} \text{ (C2)}}{\not\exists(p_1, p_4)} \quad \cfrac{\cfrac{\forall(p_3, \exists(p_4, r))}{\not\exists(p_3, p_4)} \text{ (C4)}}{} \text{ (C2)}.
$$

$$\therefore$$

Continuing in this way, we can derive $\not\exists(p_1, p_i)$ for all i ($2 \leq i \leq n$), and hence derive γ_n, thus:

$$
\vdots
$$

$$
\cfrac{\not\exists(p_1, p_n) \quad \forall(p_1, \forall(p_n, r))}{\forall(p_1, \exists(p_n, r))} \text{ (D1)}
$$

The existence of such a derivation is no accident: formulas of the form $\not\exists(p, q)$ are precisely what we need to add to $\mathcal{R}$ in order to secure the existence of a sound and complete (finite) set of rules.

We mentioned above that the languages $\mathcal{S}$ and $\mathcal{R}$ do not include the formulas $\forall(\bar{p}, q)$ or $\exists(\bar{p}, \bar{q})$, and indeed that $\mathcal{R}$ does not feature the c-terms $\forall(\bar{p}, t)$ or $\exists(\bar{p}, t)$. That is, we cannot say in these languages "Every non-artist is a beekeeper", or "Every artist admires some non-beekeeper". Extensions of $\mathcal{S}$ and $\mathcal{R}$ featuring such 'noun-level' negation were investigated in detail in Pratt-Hartmann and Moss Pratt-Hartmann and Moss (2009), where they are denoted by $\mathcal{S}^{\dagger}$ and $\mathcal{R}^{\dagger}$, respectively. It was shown there that $\mathcal{S}^{\dagger}$ has a finite system of syllogistic rules which is sound and complete; however, there can be no such system for $\mathcal{R}^{\dagger}$, even with un-restricted use of *reductio ad absurdum*. It was further shown that the satisfiability problem for $\mathcal{R}^{\dagger}$ is ExpTime-complete. It then follows from the fact that PTime$\neq$ ExpTime that no extension of $\mathcal{R}^{\dagger}$ can have a sound and complete (or indeed sound and refutation-complete) finite set of syllogistic rules. Therefore, noun-level negation will not be further discussed in this paper.

2.3 A sound and complete rule-set for $\mathcal{RE}$

We now proceed to define a rule-set, RE, which we later show to be sound and complete for $\mathcal{RE}$, under application of the proof-theoretic machinery outlined above, thus proving Theorem 2.4. Recall that we are to regard $\exists(c, p)$ as an alternative way of writing the formula $\exists(p, c)$, and similarly for the pair $\forall(\bar{c}, \bar{p})$, $\forall(p, c)$. These alternations will be performed silently in derivations, whenever required. Since RE is very complicated, we divide the rules into groups, with brief remarks concerning their validity.

The first group consists of simple generalizations of familiar syllogistic rules:

$$\frac{\forall(p,q) \quad \forall(q,c)}{\forall(p,c)} \text{ (A1)} \qquad \frac{\forall(p,c) \quad \forall(q,\bar{c})}{\forall(p,\bar{q})} \text{ (A2)} \qquad \frac{\exists(p,c)}{\exists(p,p)} \text{ (A3)}$$

$$\frac{\exists(p,c) \quad \forall(p,q)}{\exists(q,c)} \text{ (A4)} \qquad \frac{\exists(p,c) \quad \forall(q,\bar{c})}{\exists(p,\bar{q})} \text{ (A5)} \qquad \frac{\exists(p,q) \quad \forall(q,c)}{\exists(p,c)} \text{ (A6)}$$

$$\frac{\exists(p,\bar{p})}{\psi} \text{ (A7)} \qquad \frac{\forall(p,\bar{p})}{\forall(p,c)} \text{ (A8)} \qquad \frac{}{\forall(p,p)} \text{ (A9).}$$

Most of these rules should be self-explanatory: indeed, we have already met the rule (A1), though in the slightly restricted form (A1′), where c was limited to literals. The rule (A7) is the rule of *ex falso quodlibet*, and allows us to infer anything from an absurdity. Do not confuse this rule with the strategy of *reductio ad absurdum*, which allows us to retract a premise and infer its negation having derived an absurdity: *reductio ad absurdum* cannot be understood—in the technical sense employed in this paper—as a syllogistic rule. The rule (A9) allows us to infer $\forall(p,p)$ from no premises.

The second group consists of rules governing quantified predicates. In these rules, the subject-quantifier, Q, stands for either $\forall$ or $\exists$.

$$\frac{Q(o,\forall(p,t)) \quad \exists(p,q)}{Q(o,\exists(q,t))} \text{ (B1)} \qquad \frac{Q(o,\forall(q,t)) \quad \forall(p,q)}{Q(o,\forall(p,t))} \text{ (B2)}$$

$$\frac{Q(o,\exists(p,t)) \quad \forall(p,q)}{Q(o,\exists(q,t))} \text{ (B3)} \qquad \frac{\forall(q,\bar{q})}{\forall(p,\forall(q,t))} \text{ (B4)}$$

$$\frac{\exists(p,\exists(q,t))}{\exists(q,q)} \text{ (B5).}$$

These rules are almost trivially valid, and require no comment.

The third group consists of rules governing the quantifier $\not\exists$

$$\frac{}{\not\exists(p,p)} \text{ (C1)} \qquad \frac{\not\exists(o,p) \quad \not\exists(p,q)}{\not\exists(o,q)} \text{ (C2)} \qquad \frac{\forall(p,q)}{\not\exists(p,q)} \text{ (C3)}$$

$$\frac{\forall(p,\exists(q,r))}{\not\exists(p,q)} \text{ (C4)} \qquad \frac{\exists(q,q)}{\not\exists(p,q)} \text{ (C5)} \qquad \frac{\exists(p,p) \quad \not\exists(p,q)}{\exists(q,q)} \text{ (C6)}$$

$$\frac{\forall(q,\bar{q}) \quad \not\exists(p,q)}{\forall(p,c)} \text{ (C7).}$$

Notice that (C2) expresses the transitivity of the relation $\not\exists(p,q)$. The rule (C7) may be surprising at first sight. The premises assert that there are no qs, and that if there are ps, then there are qs; it follows, of course, that there are no ps, and hence that every p is a c, for any c-term c.

The fourth group concerns interactions between formulas with quantified predicates and formulas involving the quantifier $\not\exists$

$$\frac{\forall(p,\forall(q,t)) \quad \not\exists(p,q)}{\forall(p,\exists(q,t))} \text{ (D1)}$$

$$\frac{\exists(q,q) \quad \not\exists(p,o) \quad \forall(o,q) \quad \forall(o,\forall(p,r))}{\exists(q,\forall(p,r))} \text{ (D2)}$$

$$\frac{\exists(p,p) \quad \not\exists(q,o) \quad \forall(o,\bar{q}) \quad \forall(o,p)}{\exists(p,\bar{q})} \text{ (D3)}$$

$$\frac{\forall(p,\forall(q',r)) \quad \forall(o,q) \quad \forall(o,q') \quad \not\exists(p,o)}{\forall(p,\exists(q,r))} \text{ (D4)}$$

$$\frac{\forall(o,\forall(o',t')) \quad \forall(o,\forall(o',\bar{t}')) \quad \not\exists(p,o) \quad \not\exists(q,o')}{\forall(p,\forall(q,t))} \text{ (D5)}$$

$$\frac{\forall(o,\forall(o',t')) \quad \forall(o,\forall(o',\bar{t}')) \quad \not\exists(p,o) \quad \not\exists(q,o')}{\forall(p,\bar{q})} \text{ (D6).}$$

Consider (D1). The premises assert that every p is related by t to every q, and that, if ps exist then q's exist. If no ps exist, the conclusion is vacuously true; otherwise, we may choose some q to which every p is related, and the conclusion is certainly true.

The fifth group allows slightly less obvious inferences involving formulas with quantified predicates. Rule (E2) has the form of the argument displayed on the first page of this article, and we have already demonstrated its validity; the other rules in this group may be treated similarly.

$$\frac{\forall(o, \forall(p, t)) \quad \exists(o, \forall(q, \bar{t}))}{\forall(p, \bar{q})} \text{ (E1)} \qquad \frac{\forall(q, \exists(p, t)) \quad \exists(p, \forall(q, \bar{t}))}{\exists(p, \bar{q})} \text{ (E2)}$$

$$\frac{\exists(p, \exists(p, t)) \quad \forall(q, \forall(q, \bar{t}))}{\exists(p, \bar{q})} \text{ (E3).}$$

The sixth group allows us to conclude, from premises with quantified predicates, a conclusion of the form $\exists(p, \bar{q})$:

$$\frac{\exists(p, \forall(o, t)) \quad \forall(q, \forall(q, \bar{t})) \quad \forall(o, p) \quad \forall\!\!\!/(q, o)}{\exists(p, \bar{q})} \text{ (F1)}$$

$$\frac{\exists(p, \forall(q, t)) \quad \forall(q, \forall(o, \bar{t})) \quad \forall(o, p) \quad \forall\!\!\!/(q, o)}{\exists(p, \bar{q})} \text{ (F2)}$$

$$\frac{\forall(o, \exists(p, t)) \quad \forall(o, \forall(q, \bar{t})) \quad \forall\!\!\!/(q, o) \quad \exists(p, p)}{\exists(p, \bar{q})} \text{ (F3)}$$

$$\frac{\forall(o, \forall(o', t)) \quad \forall(o, \forall(q, \bar{t})) \quad \forall\!\!\!/(q, o) \quad \forall\!\!\!/(q, o') \quad \forall(o', p) \quad \exists(p, p)}{\exists(p, \bar{q})} \text{ (F4)}$$

$$\frac{\forall(o, \exists(p, t)) \quad \forall(q, \forall(q, \bar{t})) \quad \forall\!\!\!/(q, o) \quad \forall(o, p) \quad \exists(p, p)}{\exists(p, \bar{q})} \text{ (F5)}$$

$$\frac{\forall(o, \forall(q, t)) \quad \forall(q, \exists(p, \bar{t})) \quad \forall\!\!\!/(q, o) \quad \forall(o, p) \quad \exists(p, p)}{\exists(p, \bar{q})} \text{ (F6)}$$

$$\frac{\forall(o', \forall(o, t)) \quad \forall(q, \forall(o, \bar{t})) \quad \forall\!\!\!/(q, o') \quad \forall(o', p) \quad \forall\!\!\!/(q, o) \quad \exists(p, p)}{\exists(p, \bar{q})} \text{ (F7)}$$

$$\frac{\forall(o', \forall(o, t)) \quad \forall(q, \forall(q, \bar{t})) \quad \forall\!\!\!/(q, o') \quad \forall(o', p) \quad \forall\!\!\!/(q, o) \quad \forall(o, p) \quad \exists(p, p)}{\exists(p, \bar{q})} \text{ (F8)}$$

$$\frac{\forall(o', \forall(q, t)) \quad \forall(q, \forall(o, \bar{t})) \quad \forall\!\!\!/(q, o') \quad \forall(o', p) \quad \forall\!\!\!/(q, o) \quad \forall(o, p) \quad \exists(p, p)}{\exists(p, \bar{q})} \text{ (F9)}$$

We demonstrate the validity of the most complicated of these rules, (F9). From the last premise, $\exists(p,p)$, let a be some p. If a is not a q, the conclusion is true. Otherwise, from the premises $\exists\!\!\!/\,(q,o')$ and $\exists\!\!\!/\,(q,o)$, let b, b' satisfy o, o', respectively. From $\forall(o,p)$, and $\forall(o',p)$, b and b' are both ps. If either of these is not a q, the conclusion is true. Otherwise, from $\forall(q,\forall(o,\bar{t}))$, and $\forall(o',\forall(q,t))$, b' both is and is not related to b by t—contradiction. The validity of rules (F1)–(F8) may be demonstrated by similar arguments.

The seventh group allows us to conclude, from premises with quantified predicates, a conclusion of the form $\forall(p,\bar{q})$.

For any $o_1, o_2, o_3, o_4 \in \{p,q\}$:

$$\frac{\forall(o_1,\forall(p',t)) \quad \forall(o_2,\forall(q',\bar{t})) \quad \forall(o_3,p') \quad \forall(o_4,q')}{\forall(p,\bar{q})} \quad \text{(G1)}$$

$$\frac{\forall(o_1,\forall(q',t)) \quad \forall(o_2,\forall(q',\bar{t})) \quad \exists\!\!\!/\,(o_3,o) \quad \forall(o,p') \quad \forall(o,q')}{\forall(p,\bar{q})} \quad \text{(G2)}$$

$$\frac{\exists\!\!\!/\,(o_1,o) \quad \forall(o,\forall(p',t)) \quad \forall(o,\forall(q',\bar{t})) \quad \forall(o_2,p') \quad \forall(o_3,q')}{\forall(p,\bar{q})} \quad \text{(G3)}$$

$$\frac{\exists\!\!\!/\,(p,o) \quad \exists\!\!\!/\,(q,o') \quad \forall(o,\forall(p',t)) \quad \forall(o,\forall(q',\bar{t})) \quad \forall(o',p') \quad \forall(o',q')}{\forall(p,\bar{q})} \quad \text{(G4)}$$

To demonstrate the validity of (G1), suppose, to the contrary, that some p is a q. Choose any such element, a. Then, no matter how $o_1,\ldots,o_4$ are chosen from p and q, the premises guarantee that a is a p' and a q', and hence both is and is not related to itself by t—contradiction. The validity of rules (G2)–(G4) may be demonstrated by similar arguments.

We make no claim regarding the non-redundancy of the rule-set RE.

3 Proof of main result

This section is devoted entirely to the proof of Theorem 2.4. Soundness of $\vdash_{\mathsf{RE}}$ is straightforward, since, as may readily be verified, every rule in RE is valid. It therefore remains to show that, if Φ is a set of $\mathcal{RE}$-formulas, and ψ is an $\mathcal{RE}$-formula such that $\Phi \models \psi$, then $\Phi \vdash_{\mathsf{RE}} \psi$. As RE is the only rule-set we shall be concerned with in the sequel, we henceforth write $\vdash$ in place of $\vdash_{\mathsf{RE}}$. In addition, we continue to take the letters o, p, q to range over unary atoms, ℓ, m over unary literals, r over binary atoms, t over binary literals, c, d over c-terms, and φ, ψ

over formulas, without further comment.

We provide the reader with some help in navigating the proof. We must show that, for any set of formulas Φ and any formula ψ, $\Phi \models \psi$ implies $\Phi \vdash \psi$. The proof is divided into a series of cases, corresponding to the possible forms of ψ, with each case covered by a specific lemma as follows.

Form of ψ	Lemma	Form of ψ	Lemma
$\exists(p,q)$	3.12	$\exists(p,\bar{q})$	3.21
$\exists(p,\exists(q,t))$	3.12	$\exists(p,\forall(q,t))$	3.15
$\forall(p,q)$	3.15	$\forall(p,\bar{q})$	3.16
$\forall(p,\exists(q,t))$	3.15	$\forall(p,\forall(q,t))$	3.18
$\bar{\forall}(p,q)$	3.15		

We consider these cases roughly in order of difficulty—by far the most complicated being that of $\exists(p,\bar{q})$. For each case, we assume that $\Phi \models \psi$, and attempt to build a structure $\mathfrak{A}$ satisfying Φ, possibly together with additional formulas. Two conditions then arise: either these formulas are jointly unsatisfiable, and the structure $\mathfrak{A}$ is shown to contain a *defect* (as we shall call it); or $\mathfrak{A}$ yields a model of Φ, and hence of ψ. We then show that, on either condition, $\Phi \vdash \psi$.

3.1 Two transitive closures

Let Π be a set of universal formulas. Define the binary relation $\xrightarrow{\Pi}$ to be the smallest reflexive, transitive relation on unary atoms satisfying

$$p \xrightarrow{\Pi} q \qquad \text{if } \Pi \text{ contains } \forall(p,q), \forall(p,\exists(q,t)) \text{ or } \bar{\forall}(p,q).$$

The key lemma regarding $\xrightarrow{\Pi}$ is:

Lemma 3.1. If $p \xrightarrow{\Pi} q$, then $\Phi \vdash \bar{\forall}(p,q)$.

Proof. Immediate given the rules

$$\frac{}{\bar{\forall}(p,p)} \text{ (C1)} \qquad \frac{\bar{\forall}(o,p) \quad \bar{\forall}(p,q)}{\bar{\forall}(o,q)} \text{ (C2)}$$

$$\frac{\forall(p,q)}{\bar{\forall}(p,q)} \text{ (C3)} \qquad \frac{\forall(p,\exists(q,r))}{\bar{\forall}(p,q)} \text{ (C4).}$$

$\square$

Let Π be a set of universal formulas. Define the binary relation $\xRightarrow{\Pi}$

to be the smallest reflexive, transitive relation on c-terms satisfying

$$p \overset{\Pi}{\Rightarrow} c \qquad\qquad \text{if } \forall(p,c) \in \Pi$$

$$\forall(q,t) \overset{\Pi}{\Rightarrow} \forall(p,t) \qquad\qquad \text{if } \forall(p,q) \in \Pi$$

$$\exists(p,t) \overset{\Pi}{\Rightarrow} \exists(q,t) \qquad\qquad \text{if } \forall(p,q) \in \Pi.$$

The key lemma regarding $\overset{\Pi}{\Rightarrow}$ is:

Lemma 3.2. If $p \overset{\Pi}{\Rightarrow} d$, then $\Pi \vdash \forall(p,d)$.

Proof. Immediate given the rules

$$\frac{}{\forall(p,p)} \text{ (A9)} \qquad\qquad \frac{\forall(p,q) \quad \forall(q,c)}{\forall(p,c)} \text{ (A1)}$$

$$\frac{\forall(o,\exists(p,t)) \quad \forall(p,q)}{\forall(o,\exists(q,t))} \text{ (B3)} \qquad \frac{\forall(o,\forall(q,t)) \quad \forall(p,q)}{\forall(o,\forall(p,t))} \text{ (B2)}.$$

$\square$

The following lemma will be used implicitly at various points in the sequel.

Lemma 3.3. If $c \overset{\Pi}{\Rightarrow} q$, then c is a unary atom. Indeed, if $p \overset{\Pi}{\Rightarrow} q$, then: (i) $p \overset{\Pi}{\rightarrow} q$; (ii) $\forall(q,t) \overset{\Pi}{\Rightarrow} \forall(p,t)$; and (iii) $\exists(p,t) \overset{\Pi}{\Rightarrow} \exists(q,t)$.

Proof. Obvious. $\square$

Similarly, we have:

Lemma 3.4. If $o \overset{\Pi}{\Rightarrow} \exists(p,t)$ then $o \overset{\Pi}{\rightarrow} p$. If $c \overset{\Pi}{\Rightarrow} \exists(p,t)$ and c is not a unary atom, then $c = \exists(o,t)$ for some o such that $o \overset{\Pi}{\Rightarrow} p$, whence $o \overset{\Pi}{\rightarrow} p$.

3.2 Some technical machinery

Let s be any set of c-terms. We think of s as a description of an individual: that individual satisfies all the c-terms in s. For any set Σ of existential formulas, define

$$U_\Sigma = \{\{p,c\} \mid \exists(p,c) \in \Sigma\}$$

We think of U_Σ as a collection of (descriptions of) individuals that obviously exist on the assumption that the formulas in Σ are true. In addition, for any set Σ of existential formulas and any set Π of universal formulas, define

$$O_{\Sigma,\Pi} = \left\{ o \mid p \xrightarrow{\Pi} o \text{ for some } p \in \bigcup U_\Sigma \right\}$$

$$\bigcup \left\{ o \mid p \xrightarrow{\Pi} o \text{ for some } \exists(p,t) \in \bigcup U_\Sigma \right\}$$

$$V_{\Sigma,\Pi} = U_\Sigma \cup \left\{ \{o\} \mid o \in O_{\Sigma,\Pi} \right\}.$$

Think of $O_{\Sigma,\Pi}$ as the set of unary predicates that must be instantiated on the assumption that the formulas in $\Sigma \cup \Pi$ are true; and think of $V_{\Sigma,\Pi}$ as a set of (descriptions of) individuals that exist on the assumption that the formulas in $\Sigma \cup \Pi$ are true.

For any set s of c-terms and any set Π of universal formulas, define

$$s^\Pi = \left\{ d \mid c \xRightarrow{\Pi} d \text{ for some } c \in s \right\}.$$

We think of s^Π as an elaboration of the description s: any individual described by s is in fact described by s^Π, provided the formulas in Π are all true. We remark in passing that it is useful to imagine s^Π as the union of a sequence $s_0, s_1, \ldots$ of sets of c-terms, defined inductively as follows

$$s_0 = s$$
$$s_{3k+1} = s_{3k} \cup \{c \mid p \in s_{3k} \text{ and } \forall(p,c) \in \Pi\}$$
$$s_{3k+2} = s_{3k+1} \cup \{\forall(p,t) \mid \forall(q,t) \in s_{3k+1} \text{ and } \forall(p,q) \in \Pi\}$$
$$s_{3(k+1)} = s_{3k+2} \cup \{\exists(q,t) \mid \exists(p,t) \in s_{3k+2} \text{ and } \forall(p,q) \in \Pi\}.$$

We refer to the sequence $s_0, s_1, \ldots$ as the *staged construction of s^Π*.

Finally, define

$$W_{\Sigma,\Pi} = \left\{ s^\Pi \mid s \in V_{\Sigma,\Pi} \right\}.$$

We think of $W_{\Sigma,\Pi}$ as a collection of elaborated descriptions of the individuals that must exist on the assumption that the formulas in $\Sigma \cup \Pi$ are true. Sometimes, things can go wrong with $W_{\Sigma,\Pi}$. Suppose $w \in W_{\Sigma,\Pi}$ and, for some c-term c, both c and $\bar{c}$ are elements of w: in that case, the description w cannot be satisfied, and we say that $W_{\Sigma,\Pi}$ contains a *local defect* at w. Or suppose that $u, v \in W_{\Sigma,\Pi}$ and, for some unary atoms p, q and binary atom r, u contains both $\forall(p,r)$ and $\forall(q,\bar{r})$, while v contains both p and q: in that case, the descriptions u and v cannot be simultaneously satisfied, and we say that $W_{\Sigma,\Pi}$ contains a *global defect* involving u and v. A *defect* is a local or global defect.

Lemma 3.5. If $\exists(p,t) \in u \in W_{\Sigma,\Pi}$, then $\{p\}^\Pi \in W_{\Sigma,\Pi}$.

Proof. Lemma 3.4. $\qquad\qquad\qquad\qquad\qquad\qquad\qquad\qquad\qquad\qquad\qquad\qquad$ □

Given a set $W_{\Sigma,\Pi}$, let $A = W_{\Sigma,\Pi} \times \{0,1\}$, and define structures $\mathfrak{A}$ and $\bar{\mathfrak{A}}$ over A by setting, for all $p \in \mathbf{P}$ and $r \in \mathbf{R}$:

$$p^{\mathfrak{A}} = p^{\bar{\mathfrak{A}}} = \{(u,i) \in A \mid p \in u\}$$

$$r^{\mathfrak{A}} = \left\{ \langle (u,i), (\{p\}^{\Pi}, 1) \rangle \in A \times A \mid \exists (p,r) \in u \right\} \cup$$

$$\{ \langle (u,i), (v,j) \rangle \in A \times A \mid \text{ there exists } p \in v \text{ s.t. } \forall (p,r) \in u \}$$

$$r^{\bar{\mathfrak{A}}} = (A \times A) \setminus$$

$$\left(\left\{ \langle (u,i), (\{p\}^{\Pi}, 1) \rangle \in A \times A \mid \exists (p,\bar{r}) \in u \right\} \cup \right.$$

$$\left. \{ \langle (u,i), (v,j) \rangle \in A \times A \mid \text{ there exists } p \in v \text{ s.t.} \forall (p,\bar{r}) \in u \} \right)$$

In the definitions of $r^{\mathfrak{A}}$ and $r^{\bar{\mathfrak{A}}}$, Lemma 3.5 ensures that we never have to worry that $(\{p\}^{\Pi}, 1)$ might not be an element of A. We write $\mathfrak{A}_{\Sigma,\Pi} = \mathfrak{A}$ and $\bar{\mathfrak{A}}_{\Sigma,\Pi} = \bar{\mathfrak{A}}$ when we need to make the parameters Σ and Π explicit.

A word of motivation is in order here. For any description $w \in W_{\Sigma,\Pi}$, the domain A contains a pair of objects: $(w,0)$ and $(w,1)$. It helps to think of these objects as individuals which 'want' to satisfy the description w; the construction of $\mathfrak{A}$ and $\bar{\mathfrak{A}}$ will ensure that, in the absence of defects, these desires are satisfied. The doubling of individuals is motivated by the need to provide witnesses for certain c-terms: in $\mathfrak{A}$, the individual $(\{q\}^{\Pi}, 1)$ serves as witnesses for c-terms of the form $\exists(q,r)$, while the individual $(\{q\}^{\Pi}, 0)$ serves as a witness for c-terms of the form $\exists(q,\bar{r})$; in $\bar{\mathfrak{A}}$, these roles are reversed. Both structures interpret unary atoms in the natural way: (w,i) is taken to satisfy p just in case $p \in w$. For binary atoms, $\mathfrak{A}$ and $\bar{\mathfrak{A}}$ employ opposite strategies, with $\mathfrak{A}$, roughly speaking, making extensions as small as possible, and $\bar{\mathfrak{A}}$ making them as large as possible. In particular, for elements $a = (u,i)$ and $b = (v,j)$, the structure $\mathfrak{A}$ takes a to stand in relation r to b if and only if, for some unary atom q, *either* $\exists(q,r) \in u$ and $b = (\{q\}^{\Pi}, 1)$ *or* $\forall(q,r) \in u$ and $q \in v$. By contrast, the structure $\bar{\mathfrak{A}}$ takes a always to stand in relation r to b unless, for some unary atom q, *either* $\exists(q,\bar{r}) \in u$ and $b = (\{q\}^{\Pi}, 1)$ *or* $\forall(q,\bar{r}) \in u$ and $q \in v$. Equivalently, $\bar{\mathfrak{A}}$ takes a to stand in relation r to b if and only if, for every unary atom q, $\exists(q,\bar{r}) \in u$ implies $b \neq (\{q\}^{\Pi}, 1)$ *and* $\forall(q,\bar{r}) \in u$ implies $q \notin v$.

Lemma 3.6. Let Σ be any set of existential formulas and Π any set of universal formulas. Let $c \in u \in W_{\Sigma,\Pi}$ and $i \in \{0,1\}$. If $W_{\Sigma,\Pi}$ contains no defects, then $a = (u,i)$ satisfies c in both $\mathfrak{A}_{\Sigma,\Pi}$ and $\bar{\mathfrak{A}}_{\Sigma,\Pi}$.

Proof. Write $\mathfrak{A} = \mathfrak{A}_{\Sigma,\Pi}$ and $\bar{\mathfrak{A}} = \bar{\mathfrak{A}}_{\Sigma,\Pi}$. We show that $a \in c^{\mathfrak{A}}$. If c is of any of the forms p, $\exists(p,r)$, $\forall(p,r)$, this is immediate by the construction of $\mathfrak{A}$. If $c = \bar{p}$, then $p \notin u$, since W contains no local defects, whence $a \in c^{\mathfrak{A}}$. If $c = \exists(p,\bar{r})$, then, $c \in u \in W_{\Sigma,\Pi}$ implies $\{p\}^{\Pi} \in W_{\Sigma,\Pi}$, and hence $b = (\{p\}^{\Pi}, 0) \in p^{\mathfrak{A}}$. To establish $a \in c^{\mathfrak{A}}$, it suffices to show that $\langle a,b \rangle \notin r^{\mathfrak{A}}$. By definition of $\mathfrak{A}$, $\langle a,b \rangle \in r^{\mathfrak{A}}$ only if there exists $q \in \{p\}^{\Pi}$ such that $\forall(q,r) \in u$. But then, since u is closed under $\overset{\Pi}{\Longrightarrow}$, we have $\forall(p,r) \in u$, contrary to the hypothesis that $W_{\Sigma,\Pi}$ contains no local defect. If $c = \forall(p,\bar{r})$, suppose $b = (v,j) \in p^{\mathfrak{A}}$, so that $p \in v$. To establish $a \in c^{\mathfrak{A}}$, it suffices to show that $\langle a,b \rangle \notin r^{\mathfrak{A}}$. By definition of $\mathfrak{A}$, $\langle a,b \rangle \in r^{\mathfrak{A}}$ only if, for some q, either (i) $v = \{q\}^{\Pi}$, $j = 1$ and $\exists(q,r) \in u$, or (ii) $q \in v$ and $\forall(q,r) \in u$. In case (i), since u is closed under $\overset{\Pi}{\Longrightarrow}$, we have $\exists(p,r) \in u$, contrary to the hypothesis that $W_{\Sigma,\Pi}$ contains no local defect. Case (ii) is instantly contrary to the hypothesis that $W_{\Sigma,\Pi}$ contains no global defect.

To show that $a \in c^{\bar{\mathfrak{A}}}$, we proceed in exactly the same way, except that references to r and $\bar{r}$ are exchanged. $\qquad\square$

Lemma 3.7. Let Σ be any set of existential formulas and Π any set of universal formulas. If $W_{\Sigma,\Pi}$ contains no defects, then both $\mathfrak{A}_{\Sigma,\Pi}$ and $\bar{\mathfrak{A}}_{\Sigma,\Pi}$ are models of $\Sigma \cup \Pi$.

Proof. Write $\mathfrak{A}$ ambiguously for $\mathfrak{A}_{\Sigma,\Pi}$ or $\bar{\mathfrak{A}}_{\Sigma,\Pi}$, and A for the domain of $\mathfrak{A}$. Consider first any $\varphi = \exists(p,c) \in \Sigma$. Then $a = (\{p,c\}^{\Pi}, 1) \in A$. By Lemma 3.6, $a \in p^{\mathfrak{A}} \cap c^{\mathfrak{A}}$; therefore, $\mathfrak{A} \models \varphi$. Consider next any $\varphi = \forall(p,c) \in \Pi$, and suppose $a = (u,i) \in p^{\mathfrak{A}}$. By definition of $\mathfrak{A}$, $p \in u$. Taking account of the fact that u is closed under the relation $\overset{\Pi}{\Longrightarrow}$, we have $c \in u$, whence, by Lemma 3.6, $a \in c^{\mathfrak{A}}$; therefore, $\mathfrak{A} \models \varphi$. Consider finally any $\varphi = \exists\!\!\!/(p,q) \in \Pi$, and suppose $a = (u,i) \in p^{\mathfrak{A}}$. By definition of $\mathfrak{A}$, $p \in u$, whence $q \in O_{\Sigma,\Pi}$, whence $b = (\{q\}^{\Pi}, 1) \in A$. By definition of $\mathfrak{A}$, $b \in q^{\mathfrak{A}}$; therefore, $\mathfrak{A} \models \varphi$. $\qquad\square$

3.3 Completeness proof

Fix a set of formulas Φ and a formula ψ. Our task is to demonstrate that, if $\Phi \models \psi$, then $\Phi \vdash \psi$. We consider the various forms of ψ separately. Write $\Phi = \Lambda \cup \Gamma$, where Λ is the set of universal formulas in Φ, and Γ, the set of existential formulas in Φ. (Recall that formulas of the form $\exists\!\!\!/(p,q)$ count as universal.)

Lemma 3.8. If $p \in w \in W_{\Lambda,\Gamma}$, then $\Phi \vdash \exists(p,p)$.

Proof. We first prove the result for $p \in s \in V_{\Lambda,\Gamma}$. If $s = \{p,c\} \in U_{\Lambda}$, the result is immediate from the definition of U_{Λ} and the rule (A3). So we may assume $s = \{p\}$, and either there exists $\{p', c'\} \in U_\Lambda$ such that $p' \xrightarrow{\Pi} p$, or there exists $\{p', \exists(q', t)\} \in U_\Lambda$ such that $q' \xrightarrow{\Pi} p$. Noting Lemma 3.1, we have either of the derivations

$$\dfrac{\dfrac{\exists(p', c')}{\exists(p', p')}\,(A3) \qquad \vdots \atop \exists'(p', p)}{\exists(p, p)}\,(C6) \qquad\qquad \dfrac{\dfrac{\exists(p', \exists(q', t))}{\exists(q', q')}\,(B5) \qquad \vdots \atop \exists'(q', p)}{\exists(p, p)}\,(C6).$$

Finally, suppose $p' \xRightarrow{\Pi} p$ for some $p' \in s \in V_{\Lambda, \Gamma}$. By Lemma 3.2, $\Phi \vdash \forall(p', p)$, whence we have the derivation

$$\dfrac{\dfrac{\vdots \qquad\qquad \vdots \atop \exists(p', p') \quad \forall(p', p)}{\exists(p, p')}\,(A4) \qquad \vdots \atop \forall(p', p)}{\exists(p, p)}\,(A6).$$

$\square$

Let us say that c-terms c and d are *sisters* if they are identical, or if there exist $Q \in \{\forall, \exists\}$, unary literals p and q, and binary literal t, such that $c = Q(p, t)$ and $d = Q(q, t)$. Notice in particular that no pair of c-terms of the form c, $\bar{c}$ can be sisters.

Lemma 3.9. Let u be an element of $W_{\Lambda, \Gamma}$.

(i) If $c, d \in u$ with c and d not sisters, then there exist $o \in u$ and $Q \in \{\forall, \exists\}$ such that $\Phi \vdash Q(o, c)$ and $\Phi \vdash \bar{Q}(o, d)$.

(ii) If $q, d \in u$, then $\Phi \vdash \exists(q, d)$.

Proof. Any element of $W_{\Lambda, \Gamma}$ has the form s^Γ, with $s = \{p, c\} \in V_{\Lambda, \Gamma}$; recall that we earlier described the staged construction of s^Γ. Suppose c is introduced at stage i and d at stage j: we proceed by induction on $i + j$.

If $i = j = 0$ then $c, d \in s \in V_{\Lambda, \Gamma}$. Since c and d are not identical, we have $\{c, d\} \in U_\Lambda$, and indeed, by exchanging c and d if necessary $c = p$ with $\exists(p, d) \in \Phi$. From rule (A9), we have $\Phi \vdash \forall(p, p)$, so that putting $o = p$ secures the lemma. Suppose, then $i + j > 0$, and assume, by exchanging c and d if necessary, that $i > 0$. If $i = 3k + 1$, let $p \in s_{3k}$ such that $\forall(p, c) \in \Gamma$. If $p = d$, then, by Lemma 3.8, $\Phi \vdash \exists(d, d)$, so that putting $o = p$ again secures the lemma. On the other hand, if $p \neq d$, then, since p is not the sister anything but itself, we have by inductive hypothesis o and Q such that $\Phi \vdash Q(o, p)$ and $\Phi \vdash \bar{Q}(o, d)$. But then we have either of the derivations

$$\frac{\forall(o,p) \quad \forall(p,c)}{\forall(o,c)} \text{ (A1)} \qquad \frac{\exists(o,p) \quad \forall(p,c)}{\exists(o,c)} \text{ (A6)},$$

so that $\Phi \vdash Q(o,c)$, as required.

If $i = 3k+2$, let $c = \forall(p,t)$ and suppose $\forall(q,t) \in s_{3k+1}$ with $\forall(p,q) \in \Gamma$. If c is not d's sister, then neither is $\forall(q,t)$, so, by inductive hypothesis, let o and Q be such that $\Phi \vdash Q(o,\forall(q,t))$ and $\Phi \vdash \bar{Q}(o,d)$. But then we have the derivation

$$\frac{Q(o,\forall(q,t)) \quad \forall(p,q)}{Q(o,\forall(p,t))} \text{ (B2)}.$$

If $i = 3(k+1)$, we proceed similarly, but using rule (B3) instead of (B2).

The second statement of the lemma follows from the first by a single application of either (A4) or (A6). □

Lemma 3.10. If $W_{\Lambda,\Gamma}$ contains a local defect, then Φ is inconsistent.

Proof. Let $u \in W_{\Lambda,\Gamma}$ contain $c, \bar{c}$. By Lemma 3.9 (i), there exists $o \in u$ and $Q \in \{\forall, \exists\}$ such that $\Phi \vdash Q(o,c)$ and $\Phi \vdash \bar{Q}(o,\bar{c})$. Thus, we have the derivation

$$\frac{Q(o,c) \quad \bar{Q}(o,\bar{c})}{\exists(o,\bar{o})} \text{ (A5)}.$$

□

Lemma 3.11. If $W_{\Lambda,\Gamma}$ contains a global defect, then Φ is inconsistent.

Proof. Suppose $\forall(p,r), \forall(q,\bar{r}) \in u \in W_{\Lambda,\Gamma}$ and $p, q \in v \in W_{\Lambda,\Gamma}$. By Lemma 3.9 (i), there exists $o \in u$ and $Q \in \{\forall, \exists\}$ such that $\Phi \vdash Q(o,\forall(p,r))$ and $\Phi \vdash \bar{Q}(o,\forall(q,\bar{t}))$. And by Lemma 3.9 (ii), $\Phi \vdash \exists(p,q)$. Thus, we have the derivation

$$\frac{\dfrac{Q(o,\forall(p,r)) \quad \exists(p,q)}{Q(o,\exists(q,r))} \text{ (B1)} \quad \bar{Q}(o,\forall(q,\bar{r}))}{\exists(o,\bar{o})} \text{ (A5)}.$$

□

Lemma 3.12. Suppose $\Phi \models \psi$, where ψ is of either of the forms $\exists(p,q)$ or $\exists(p, \exists(q,t))$. Then $\Phi \vdash \psi$.

Proof. If $W_{\Lambda,\Gamma}$ contains any local or global defects, then Φ is inconsistent, whence $\Phi \vdash \psi$ by rule (A7). Otherwise, let $\mathfrak{A} = \mathfrak{A}_{\Lambda,\Gamma}$, so that by Lemma 3.7, $\mathfrak{A} \models \Phi$, whence $\mathfrak{A} \models \psi$. If $\psi = \exists(p,q)$, then, by definition of $\mathfrak{A}$, there exists $u \in W_{\Lambda,\Gamma}$ such that $p, q, \in u$. By Lemma 3.9 (ii), $\Phi \vdash \exists(p,q)$. If $\psi = \exists(p, \exists(q,t))$, let us assume first of all that t is positive, and write $t = r$. Then there exists $a = (u,i)$ and $b = (v,j)$ in $W_{\Lambda,\Gamma}$ such that $a \in p^{\mathfrak{A}}$, $b \in q^{\mathfrak{A}}$ and $\langle a, b \rangle \in r^{\mathfrak{A}}$. By definition of $\mathfrak{A}$, $p \in u$ and $q \in v$. Furthermore, either (a) $\exists(o,r) \in u$ and $v = \{o\}^*$, or (b) $\forall(o,r) \in u$ and $o \in v$. In case (a), $\Phi \vdash \forall(o,q)$ by Lemma 3.2, and $\Phi \vdash \exists(p, \exists(o,r))$ by Lemma 3.9 (ii), whence we have the derivation

$$\frac{\exists(p, \exists(o,r)) \quad \forall(o,q)}{\exists(p, \exists(q,r))} \text{ (B3)}.$$

In case (b), by Lemma 3.9 (ii), $\Phi \vdash \exists(o,q)$, and $\Phi \vdash \exists(p, \forall(o,r))$, whence we have the derivation

$$\frac{\exists(p, \forall(o,r)) \quad \exists(o,q)}{\exists(p, \exists(q,r))} \text{ (B1)}.$$

Finally, if $t = \bar{r}$ is negative, we proceed in exactly the same way, but use $\bar{\mathfrak{A}}$ in place of $\mathfrak{A}$. $\square$

We next deal with conclusions of the forms $\forall(p,q)$, $\forall(p, \exists(q,t))$, $\exists(q, \forall(p,t))$ $\exists\!\!\!/(p,q)$, $\forall(p, \bar{q})$, and $\forall(p, \forall(q,t))$. We note in connection with the machinery introduced in Sec. 3.2 that, if Σ and Σ' are sets of existential formulas and Γ a set of universal formulas, then $W_{\Sigma \cup \Sigma', \Gamma} = W_{\Sigma,\Gamma} \cup W_{\Sigma',\Gamma}$.

Lemma 3.13. If $W_{\Lambda \cup \{\exists(p,q)\},\Gamma}$ contains a local defect, then $\Phi \vdash \forall(p, \bar{q})$.

Proof. Observe that the statement of the lemma would be unaffected by exchanging p and q. Suppose $u \in W_{\Lambda \cup \{\exists(p,q)\},\Gamma}$ contains both c and $\bar{c}$. If $u \in W_{\Lambda,\Gamma}$, then the result is secured by Lemma 3.10 and rule (A7). So we may assume $u \in W_{\{\exists(p,q)\},\Gamma}$. By Lemmas 3.1 and 3.2, and exchanging p and q if necessary, either (a) $\Gamma \vdash \forall(p,c)$ and $\Gamma \vdash \forall(q, \bar{c})$, or (b) there exists o (possibly, $o = p$) such that $\Gamma \vdash \exists\!\!\!/(p,o)$, $\Gamma \vdash \forall(o,c)$

and $\Gamma \vdash \forall(o, \bar{c})$. Hence, we have either of the derivations

$$\cfrac{\forall(p, c) \quad \forall(q, \bar{c})}{\forall(p, \bar{q})}\ (\text{A2}) \qquad\qquad \cfrac{\cfrac{\forall(o, c) \quad \forall(o, \bar{c})}{\forall(o, \bar{o})}\ (\text{A2}) \qquad \not\exists(p, o)}{\forall(p, \bar{q})}\ (\text{C7}).$$

$\square$

Lemma 3.14. If $W_{\Lambda \cup \{\exists(p, q)\}, \Gamma}$ contains a global defect, then $\Phi \vdash \forall(p, \bar{q})$.

Proof. Observe that the statement of the lemma would be unaffected by exchanging p and q. Suppose $u \in W_{\Lambda \cup \{\exists(p, q)\}, \Gamma}$ contains both $\forall(p', t)$ and $\forall(q', \bar{t})$, and $v \in W_{\Lambda \cup \{\exists(p, q)\}, \Gamma}$ contains both p' and q'. If $u, v \in W_{\Lambda, \Gamma}$, the result is secured by Lemma 3.11 and rule (A7). So we may assume that either u or v is in $W_{\{\exists(p, q)\}, \Gamma}$. We have three cases.

(i) Suppose first that $u \in W_{\{\exists(p, q)\}, \Gamma}$ and $v \in W_{\Lambda, \Gamma}$. By Lemmas 3.1 and 3.2, and exchanging p and q if necessary, either (a) $\Gamma \vdash \forall(p, \forall(p', t))$ and $\Gamma \vdash \forall(q, \forall(q', \bar{t}))$, or (b) there exists o (possibly, $o = p$) such that $\Gamma \vdash \not\exists(p, o)$, $\Gamma \vdash \forall(o, \forall(p', t))$ and $\Gamma \vdash \forall(o, \forall(q', \bar{t}))$. Furthermore, by Lemma 3.9 (ii), $\Phi \vdash \exists(p', q')$. In case (a), we have the derivation

$$\cfrac{\forall(p, \forall(p', t)) \qquad \cfrac{\forall(q, \forall(q', \bar{t})) \quad \exists(p', q')}{\forall(q, \exists(p', \bar{t}))}\ (\text{B1})}{\forall(p, \bar{q})}\ (\text{A2}).$$

In case (b), we have the derivation

$$\cfrac{\cfrac{\forall(o, \forall(p', t)) \qquad \cfrac{\forall(o, \forall(q', \bar{t})) \quad \exists(p', q')}{\forall(o, \exists(p', \bar{t}))}\ (\text{B1})}{\forall(o, \bar{o})}\ (\text{A2}) \qquad \not\exists(p, o)}{\forall(p, \bar{q})}\ (\text{C7}).$$

(ii) Suppose next that $u \in W_{\Lambda, \Gamma}$ and $v \in W_{\{\exists(p, q)\}, \Gamma}$. Since $\forall(p', t)$ and $\forall(q', \bar{t})$ are not sisters, by Lemma 3.9 (i), there exist o, Q such that $\Phi \vdash Q(o, \forall(p', t))$ and $\Phi \vdash \bar{Q}(o, \forall(q', \bar{t}))$. By Lemmas 3.1 and 3.2, and exchanging p and q if necessary, either (a) $\Gamma \vdash \forall(p, p')$ and $\Gamma \vdash \forall(q, q')$, or (b) there exists o' (possibly, that $o' = p$) such that $\Gamma \vdash \not\exists(p, o')$,

$\Gamma \vdash \forall(o', p')$ and $\Gamma \vdash \forall(o', q')$. In case (a), we have the derivation

$$
\cfrac{
  \vdots \qquad \cfrac{
    \cfrac{Q(o, \forall(p', t)) \quad \bar{Q}(o, \forall(q', \bar{t}))}{\forall(p', \bar{q}')} \text{(E1)} \qquad \vdots}{
    \cfrac{\forall(p', \bar{q}') \qquad\qquad\qquad \forall(p, p')}{\forall(p, \bar{q}')} \text{(A1)}
  }
}{\forall(p, \bar{q})} \text{(A2).}
$$

with $\forall(q, q')$ on the left.

In case (b), we have the derivation

$$
\cfrac{
  \cfrac{
    \cfrac{\cfrac{Q(o, \forall(p', t)) \quad \bar{Q}(o, \forall(q', \bar{t}))}{\forall(p', \bar{q}')}\text{(E1)} \quad \forall(o', p')}{\forall(o', \bar{q}')}\text{(A1)} \quad \forall(o', q')}{\forall(o', \bar{o}')}\text{(A2)} \quad \exists'(p, o')
}{\forall(p, \bar{q})} \text{(C7)}
$$

(iii) Suppose, finally, that $u, v \in W_{\{\exists(p,q)\}, \Gamma}$. Here we have four subcases to consider.

(a) If $u = v = \{p, q\}^\Gamma$, then by Lemma 3.2, there exist $o_1, o_2, o_3, o_4 \in \{p, q\}$ such that $\Gamma \vdash \forall(o_1, \forall(p', t))$, $\Gamma \vdash \forall(o_2, \forall(q', \bar{t}))$, $\Gamma \vdash \forall(o_3, p')$, and $\Gamma \vdash \forall(o_4, q')$. Thus we have the derivation

$$
\cfrac{\forall(o_1, \forall(p', t)) \quad \forall(o_2, \forall(q', \bar{t})) \quad \forall(o_3, p') \quad \forall(o_4, q')}{\forall(p, \bar{q})} \text{(G1).}
$$

(b) If $u = \{p, q\}^\Gamma$ and $v = \{o'\}^\Gamma$, where $o' \in O_{\{\exists(p,q)\}, \Gamma}$, then, by Lemmas 3.1 and 3.2, there exist $o_1, o_2, o_3 \in \{p, q\}$ such that $\Gamma \vdash \forall(o_1, \forall(p', t))$, $\Gamma \vdash \forall(o_2, \forall(q', \bar{t}))$, $\Gamma \vdash \exists'(o_3, o')$, $\Gamma \vdash \forall(o', p')$ and $\Gamma \vdash \forall(o', q')$ Thus we have the derivation

$$
\cfrac{\forall(o_1, \forall(p', t)) \quad \forall(o_2, \forall(q', \bar{t})) \quad \exists'(o_3, o') \quad \forall(o', p') \quad \forall(o', q')}{\forall(p, \bar{q})} \text{(G2).}
$$

(c) If $v = \{p, q\}^\Gamma$ and $u = \{o\}^\Gamma$, where $o \in O_{\{\exists(p,q)\}, \Gamma}$, then, by Lemmas 3.1 and 3.2, there exist $o_1, o_2, o_3 \in \{p, q\}$ such that $\Gamma \vdash \forall(o_1, o)$, $\Gamma \vdash \forall(o, \forall(p', t))$, $\Gamma \vdash \forall(o, \forall(q', \bar{t}))$, $\Gamma \vdash \forall(o_2, p')$ and $\Gamma \vdash \forall(o_3, q')$. Thus we have the derivation

$$
\cfrac{\exists'(o_1, o) \quad \forall(o, \forall(p', t)) \quad \forall(o, \forall(q', \bar{t})) \quad \forall(o_2, p') \quad \forall(o_3, q')}{\forall(p, \bar{q})} \text{(G3).}
$$

(d) If $u = \{o\}^{\Gamma}$ and $v = \{o'\}^{\Gamma}$, where $o, o' \in O_{\{\exists(p,q)\},\Gamma}$, then by Lemma 3.1, we have $\Gamma \vdash \forall(o, \forall(p', r))$, $\Gamma \vdash \forall(o, \forall(q', \bar{r}))$, $\Gamma \vdash \forall(o', p')$, and $\Gamma \vdash \forall(o', q')$; and by Lemma 3.1, exchanging p and q if necessary, we have $\Gamma \vdash \not\exists(p, o)$, and either $\Gamma \vdash \not\exists(p, o')$ or $\Gamma \vdash \not\exists(q, o')$. Thus we have either the derivation

$$\frac{\not\exists(p,o) \quad \not\exists(q,o') \quad \forall(o,\forall(p',t)) \quad \forall(o,\forall(q',\bar{t})) \quad \forall(o',p') \quad \forall(o',q')}{\forall(p,\bar{q})} \text{ (G4)}$$

or the derivation

$$\frac{\dfrac{\not\exists(p,o) \quad \not\exists(p,o') \quad \forall(o,\forall(p',t)) \quad \forall(o,\forall(q',\bar{t})) \quad \forall(o',p') \quad \forall(o',q')}{\forall(p,\bar{p})} \text{ (G4)}}{\forall(p,\bar{q})} \text{ (A8).}$$

$\square$

Lemma 3.15. Suppose $\Phi \models \psi$, where ψ is of any of the forms $\forall(p,q)$, $\forall(p,\exists(q,t))$, $\exists(q,\forall(p,t))$ or $\not\exists(p,q)$. Then $\Phi \vdash \psi$.

Proof. Consider the set $W = W_{\Lambda \cup \{\exists(p,p)\},\Gamma}$. If this set contains a defect, then $\Phi \vdash \forall(p,\bar{p})$ by Lemmas 3.13 and 3.14. Further, if $\psi = \exists(q,\forall(p,t))$, then since $\Phi \models \exists(q,q)$, Lemma 3.12 guarantees $\Phi \vdash \exists(q,q)$. Hence we have one of the derivations:

$$\frac{\forall(p,\bar{p})}{\forall(p,q)} \text{ (A8)} \qquad \frac{\forall(p,\bar{p})}{\forall(p,\exists(q,t))} \text{ (A8)} \qquad \frac{\exists(q,q) \quad \dfrac{\forall(p,\bar{p})}{\forall(q,\forall(p,t))} \text{ (B4)}}{\exists(q,\forall(p,t))} \text{ (A6)} \qquad \frac{\dfrac{\forall(p,\bar{p})}{\dfrac{\forall(p,q)}{\not\exists(p,q)} \text{ (C3)}} \text{ (A8)}}{} $$

as required. Therefore, we may assume that W contains no defect. Let $\mathfrak{A} = \mathfrak{A}_{\Lambda \cup \{\exists(p,p)\},\Gamma}$ and $\bar{\mathfrak{A}} = \bar{\mathfrak{A}}_{\Lambda \cup \{\exists(p,p)\},\Gamma}$. By Lemma 3.6, both $\mathfrak{A}$ and $\bar{\mathfrak{A}}$ are models of Φ, and hence of ψ. We consider the various forms of ψ in turn.

$\psi = \forall(p,q)$: By construction of $\mathfrak{A}$, $a = (\{p\}^{\Gamma}, 1) \in p^{\mathfrak{A}}$. Since $\mathfrak{A} \models \psi$, $a \in q^{\mathfrak{A}}$, whence $q \in \{p\}^{\Gamma}$, whence $\Phi \vdash \forall(p,q)$, by Lemma 3.2.

$\psi = \forall(p,\exists(q,t))$: We assume first that t is positive, and write $t = r$. By construction of $\mathfrak{A}$, $a = (\{p\}^{\Gamma}, 1) \in p^{\mathfrak{A}}$. Since $\mathfrak{A} \models \psi$, there exists $b \in q^{\mathfrak{A}}$ such that $\langle a, b \rangle \in r^{\mathfrak{A}}$. Thus, there exists q' such that either (i) $b = (\{q'\}^{\Gamma}, 1)$ with $\exists(q', r) \in \{p\}^{\Gamma}$ and $q \in \{q'\}^{\Gamma}$, or (ii) $b = (v, j)$ with $\forall(q', r) \in \{p\}^{\Gamma}$ and $q, q' \in v$. In case (i), by Lemma 3.2, $\Phi \vdash \forall(p, \exists(q', r))$

and $\Phi \vdash \forall(q', q)$, whence we have the derivation

$$\frac{\forall(p, \exists(q', r)) \quad \forall(q', q)}{\forall(p, \exists(q, r))} \text{ (B3)}.$$

In case (ii), by Lemma 3.2, $\Phi \vdash \forall(p, \forall(q', r))$; moreover, either (a) $v \in W_{\Lambda, \Gamma}$, in which case $\Phi \vdash \exists(q', q)$, by Lemma 3.9 (ii), or (b) $v = \{o\}^\Gamma$, where $o \in O_{\{\exists(p,p)\}, \Gamma}$, in which case, by Lemmas 3.1 and 3.2, $\Phi \vdash \exists\!\!\!/(p, o)$, $\Phi \vdash \forall(o, q)$, and $\Phi \vdash \forall(o, q')$. Hence, we have either of the derivations

$$\frac{\forall(p, \forall(q', r)) \quad \exists(q, q')}{\forall(p, \exists(q, r))} \text{ (B1)} \qquad \frac{\forall(p, \forall(q', r)) \quad \forall(o, q) \quad \forall(o, q') \quad \exists\!\!\!/(p, o)}{\forall(p, \exists(q, r))} \text{ (D4)}.$$

If $t = \bar{r}$ is negative, then we proceed as before, but replacing $\mathfrak{A}$ by $\bar{\mathfrak{A}}$.

$\psi = \exists(q, \forall(p, t))$: Assume first that $t = r$ is positive, and recall our earlier observation that $\Phi \vdash \exists(q, q)$. By construction, $b = (\{p\}^\Gamma, 0) \in p^{\mathfrak{A}}$. Since $\mathfrak{A} \models \psi$, let $a = (u, i)$ be such that $a \in q^{\mathfrak{A}}$ and $\langle a, b \rangle \in r^{\mathfrak{A}}$. Thus there exists p' such that $\forall(p', r) \in u$ and $p' \in \{p\}^\Gamma$. Now, either: (a) $u \in W_{\Lambda, \Gamma}$; or (b) $u = \{o\}^\Gamma$, where $\{o\} \in V_{\{\exists(p,p)\}, \Gamma}$. In case (a), $\Phi \vdash \exists(q, \forall(p', r))$ by Lemma 3.9 (ii), and $\Phi \vdash \forall(p, p')$ by Lemma 3.2, whence we have the derivation

$$\frac{\exists(q, \forall(p', r)) \quad \forall(p, p')}{\exists(q, \forall(p, r))} \text{ (B2)}.$$

In case (b), by Lemmas 3.1 and 3.2, $\Phi \vdash \exists\!\!\!/(p, o)$, $\Phi \vdash \forall(o, q)$, $\Phi \vdash \forall(o, \forall(p', r))$ and $\Phi \vdash \forall(p, p')$, whence we have the derivation

$$\frac{\exists(q, q) \quad \exists\!\!\!/(p, o) \quad \dfrac{\forall(o, \forall(p', r)) \quad \forall(p, p')}{\forall(o, \forall(p, r))} \text{ (B2)} \quad \forall(o, q)}{\exists(q, \forall(p, r))} \text{ (D2)}.$$

If $t = \bar{r}$ is negative, then we proceed as before, but replacing $\mathfrak{A}$ by $\bar{\mathfrak{A}}$.

$\psi = \exists\!\!\!/(p, q)$: By construction, $a = (\{p\}^\Gamma, 1) \in p^{\mathfrak{A}}$. Since $\mathfrak{A} \models \psi$, let $b = (v, j)$ be such that $b \in q^{\mathfrak{A}}$. Thus, $q \in v$. Either (a) $v \in W_{\Lambda, \Gamma}$ or (b) $v = \{o\}^\Gamma$ where $o \in O_{\{\exists(p,p)\}, \Gamma}$. In case (a), $\Phi \vdash \exists(q, q)$, by Lemma 3.9

(ii), and we have the derivation

$$\frac{\vdots}{\dfrac{\exists(q,q)}{\not\forall(p,q)}} \text{ (C5)}.$$

In case (b), $\Phi \vdash \not\forall(p,q)$ by Lemma 3.1, and we are done. $\qquad\square$

Lemma 3.16. Suppose $\Phi \models \forall(p,\bar{q})$. Then $\Phi \vdash \forall(p,\bar{q})$.

Proof. Let $\mathfrak{A} = \mathfrak{A}_{\Lambda \cup \{\exists(p,q)\},\Gamma}$. By construction, $\mathfrak{A} \not\models \forall(p,\bar{q})$, and hence $\mathfrak{A} \not\models \Phi$. By Lemma 3.6, $W_{\Lambda \cup \{\exists(p,q)\},\Gamma}$ contains a defect. By Lemmas 3.13 and 3.14, $\Phi \vdash \forall(p,\bar{q})$. $\qquad\square$

Lemma 3.17. If $W_{\Lambda \cup \{\exists(p,p),\exists(q,q)\},\Gamma}$ contains a defect, then, for any binary literal t, $\Phi \vdash \forall(p,\forall(q,t))$.

Proof. If $W_{\Lambda \cup \{\exists(p,p)\},\Gamma}$ contains a defect, then, by Lemmas 3.13 and 3.14 (setting $q = p$), $\Phi \vdash \forall(p,\bar{p})$. Similarly, if $W_{\Lambda \cup \{\exists(q,q)\},\Gamma}$ contains a defect, then $\Phi \vdash \forall(q,\bar{q})$. Hence we have either of the derivations

$$\frac{\vdots}{\dfrac{\forall(p,\bar{p})}{\forall(p,\forall(q,t))}} \text{ (A8)} \qquad\qquad \frac{\vdots}{\dfrac{\forall(q,\bar{q})}{\forall(p,\forall(q,t))}} \text{ (B4)}.$$

The only other possibility is a global defect involving one element of $W_{\{\exists(p,p)\},\Gamma}$ and another of $W_{\{\exists(q,q)\},\Gamma}$. Suppose, then, $\forall(p',t'),\forall(q',\bar{t}') \in u \in W_{\{\exists(p,p)\},\Gamma}$, and $p',q' \in v \in W_{\{\exists(q,q)\},\Gamma}$. By Lemmas 3.1 and 3.2, there exist o, o' (possibly, $o = p$, $o' = q$) such that $\Phi \vdash \not\forall(p,o)$, $\Phi \vdash \forall(o,\forall(p',t'))$, $\Phi \vdash \forall(o,\forall(q',\bar{t}'))$, $\Phi \vdash \not\forall(q,o')$, $\Phi \vdash \forall(o',p')$ and $\Phi \vdash \forall(o',q')$. Thus, we have the derivation

$$\frac{\dfrac{\vdots \quad \vdots}{\dfrac{\forall(o,\forall(p',t')) \quad \forall(o',p')}{\forall(o,\forall(o',t'))} \text{ (B2)} \quad \dfrac{\forall(o,\forall(q',\bar{t}')) \quad \forall(o',q')}{\forall(o,\forall(o',\bar{t}'))} \text{ (B2)} \quad \vdots \quad \vdots}{\not\forall(p,o) \quad \not\forall(q,o')}}{\forall(p,\forall(q,t))} \text{ (D5)}$$

$\qquad\square$

Lemma 3.18. Suppose $\Phi \models \forall(p,\forall(q,t))$. Then $\Phi \vdash \forall(p,\forall(q,t))$.

Proof. Assume for the moment t is positive and write $t = r$. Let $\mathfrak{A} = \mathfrak{A}_{\Lambda \cup \{\exists(p,p),\exists(q,q)\},\Gamma}$. If $W_{\Lambda \cup \{\exists(p,p),\exists(q,q)\},\Gamma}$ contains a defect, then the conclusion follows by Lemma 3.17. Otherwise, by Lemma 3.6, $\mathfrak{A} \models \Phi$, whence $\mathfrak{A} \models \forall(p,\forall(q,t))$, and, by construction, the domain of $\mathfrak{A}$ contains $a = (\{p\}^{\Gamma},1)$ and $b = (\{q\}^{\Gamma},0)$. Since $a \in p^{\mathfrak{A}}$ and $b \in q^{\mathfrak{A}}$, we have $\langle a,b \rangle \in r^{\mathfrak{A}}$, whence $\forall(q',r) \in \{p\}^{\Gamma}$ for some $q' \in \{q\}^{\Gamma}$. By

Lemma 3.2, $\Gamma \vdash \forall(p, \forall(q', r))$ and $\Gamma \vdash \forall(q, q')$, whence we have the derivation:

$$
\frac{\forall(p, \forall(q', r)) \quad \forall(q, q')}{\forall(p, \forall(q, r))} \text{ (B2)}.
$$

If t is negative, we write $t = \bar{r}$ and proceed as above, but replacing $\mathfrak{A}$ by $\bar{\mathfrak{A}} = \bar{\mathfrak{A}}_{\Lambda \cup \{\exists(p,p), \exists(q,q)\}, \Gamma}$. $\qquad\square$

We turn finally to conclusions of the form $\exists(p, \bar{q})$. Fixing the unary atoms p and q, consider the set $W_{\Lambda, \Gamma \cup \{\forall(p,q)\}}$, together with the structures $\mathfrak{A}_{\Lambda, \Gamma \cup \{\forall(p,q)\}}$ and $\bar{\mathfrak{A}}_{\Lambda, \Gamma \cup \{\forall(p,q)\}}$, as defined in Sec. 3.2. By way of preparing the ground, let us examine $W_{\Lambda, \Gamma \cup \{\forall(p,q)\}}$ and its relation to $W_{\Lambda, \Gamma}$. Evidently, if $p \notin \bigcup W_{\Lambda, \Gamma}$, then $W_{\Lambda, \Gamma \cup \{\forall(p,q)\}} = W_{\Lambda, \Gamma}$. So let us assume $p \in \bigcup W_{\Lambda, \Gamma}$, and consider $w \in W_{\Lambda, \Gamma \cup \{\forall(p,q)\}}$. Let us write $w = s^{(\Gamma \cup \{\forall(p,q)\})}$, where $s \in V_{\Lambda, \Gamma \cup \{\forall(p,q)\}}$. Observe that, since $p \in \bigcup W_{\Lambda, \Gamma}$, we in fact have $V_{\Lambda, \Gamma \cup \{\forall(p,q)\}} = V_{\Lambda, \Gamma} \cup V_{\{\exists(q,q)\}, \Gamma}$. We may therefore distinguish two cases: either $s \in V_{\Lambda, \Gamma}$ or $V_{\{\exists(q,q)\}, \Gamma}$. But note that, in either case, if $p \notin s^\Gamma$, then $s^{(\Gamma \cup \{\forall(p,q)\})} = s^\Gamma$; otherwise $s^{(\Gamma \cup \{\forall(p,q)\})} = s^\Gamma \cup \{q\}^\Gamma$. Fig. 1 illustrates the four possible kinds of elements of $W_{\Lambda, \Gamma \cup \{\forall(p,q)\}}$ that result: elements of the form s^Γ, where $s \in V_{\Lambda, \Gamma}$, but $p \notin s^\Gamma$; elements of the form $s^\Gamma \cup \{q\}^\Gamma$, where $s \in V_{\Lambda, \Gamma}$, and $p \in s^\Gamma$; elements of the form $\{o\}^\Gamma$, where $\{o\} \in V_{\{\exists(q,q)\}, \Gamma}$, but $p \notin \{o\}^\Gamma$; elements of the form $\{o\}^\Gamma \cup \{q\}^\Gamma$, where $\{o\} \in V_{\{\exists(q,q)\}, \Gamma}$, and $p \in \{o\}^\Gamma$. Indeed, if c, d are c-terms realized in the same element w of $W_{\Lambda, \Gamma \cup \{\forall(p,q)\}}$, one of the following six cases obtains. To aid readability, we write $[q]^\Gamma$ for the set of unary atoms $\left\{ o \mid q \xrightarrow{\Pi} o \right\} = O_{\{\exists(q,q)\}, \Gamma}$.

(i) there exists $w' \in W_{\Lambda, \Gamma}$ such that $c, d \in w'$;

(ii) there exists $w' \in W_{\Lambda, \Gamma}$ such that $c, p \in w'$, and $d \in \{q\}^\Gamma$;

(iii) there exists $w' \in W_{\Lambda, \Gamma}$ such that $d, p \in w'$, and $c \in \{q\}^\Gamma$;

(iv) $p \in \bigcup W_{\Lambda, \Gamma}$, and there exists $o \in [q]^\Gamma$ such that $c, d \in \{o\}^\Gamma$;

(v) $p \in \bigcup W_{\Lambda, \Gamma}$, and there exists $o \in [q]^\Gamma$ such that $c, p \in \{o\}^\Gamma$ and $d \in \{q\}^\Gamma$;

(vi) $p \in \bigcup W_{\Lambda, \Gamma}$, and there exists $o \in [q]^\Gamma$ such that $d, p \in \{o\}^\Gamma$ and $c \in \{q\}^\Gamma$.

This six-fold division of cases will be used extensively in the next two lemmas.

Lemma 3.19. If $W_{\Lambda, \Gamma \cup \{\forall(p,q)\}}$ contains a local defect, then $\Phi \vdash \exists(p, \bar{q})$.

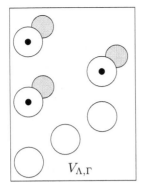
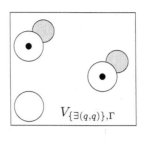

FIGURE 1: Schematic illustration of $W_{\Lambda,\Gamma\cup\{\forall(p,q)\}}$ when $p \in \bigcup W_{\Lambda,\Gamma}$: white circles illustrate the elements s^Γ, where s is in either $V_{\Lambda,\Gamma}$ or $V_{\{\exists(q,q)\},\Gamma}$, as indicated by the labels in the rectangles; black dots indicate the presence of the unary atom p in these sets; grey blobs indicate the sets of added elements $\{q\}^\Gamma$.

Proof. We have six cases to consider. (i) If $c, \bar{c} \in w \in W_{\Lambda,\Gamma}$, Φ is inconsistent, by Lemma 3.10, and the result follows by rule (A7). (ii) If $c, p \in w \in W_{\Lambda,\Gamma}$, and $\bar{c} \in \{q\}^\Gamma$, then by Lemma 3.9 (ii), $\Phi \vdash \exists(p, c)$ and by Lemma 3.2, $\Phi \vdash \forall(q, \bar{c})$; hence we have the derivation

$$\frac{\vdots \qquad \vdots}{\dfrac{\exists(p, c) \quad \forall(q, \bar{c})}{\exists(p, \bar{q})}} \text{ (A5).}$$

(iii) If $\bar{c}, p \in w \in W_{\Lambda,\Gamma}$, and $c \in \{q\}^\Gamma$, we replace c by $\bar{c}$ and proceed as in case (ii). (iv) If $p \in \bigcup W_{\Lambda,\Gamma}$, $o \in [q]^\Gamma$ and $c, \bar{c} \in \{o\}^\Gamma$, then, by Lemma 3.9 (ii), $\Phi \vdash \exists(p, p)$, and by Lemmas 3.1 and 3.2, $\Gamma \vdash \not\forall(q, o)$, $\Gamma \vdash \forall(o, c)$ and $\Gamma \vdash \forall(o, \bar{c})$; hence we have the derivation

$$\dfrac{\dfrac{\dfrac{\vdots \qquad \vdots}{\dfrac{\forall(o, c) \quad \forall(o, \bar{c})}{\forall(o, \bar{o})} \text{ (A2)}} \quad \dfrac{\vdots}{\not\forall(q, o)}}{\forall(q, \bar{p})} \text{ (C7)} \quad \dfrac{\vdots}{\exists(p, p)}}{\exists(p, \bar{q})} \text{ (A5).}$$

(v) If $p \in \bigcup W_{\Lambda,\Gamma}$, $o \in [q]^\Gamma$ $c, p \in \{o\}^\Gamma$ and $\bar{c} \in \{q\}^\Gamma$, then, by Lemma 3.9 (ii), $\Phi \vdash \exists(p, p)$, and by Lemmas 3.1 and 3.2, $\Gamma \vdash \not\forall(q, o)$,

$\Gamma \vdash \forall(o, c)$, $\Gamma \vdash \forall(o, p)$ and $\Gamma \vdash \forall(q, \bar{c})$; hence we have the derivation

$$\cfrac{\exists(p,p) \quad \not\exists(q,o) \quad \forall(o,p) \quad \cfrac{\forall(o,c) \quad \forall(q,\bar{c})}{\forall(o,\bar{q})}\text{ (A2)}}{\exists(p,\bar{q})}\text{ (D3)}$$

(vi) If $p \in \bigcup W_{\Lambda,\Gamma}$, $o \in [q]^{\Gamma}$ $\bar{c}, p \in \{o\}^{\Gamma}$ and $c \in \{q\}^{\Gamma}$, we replace c by $\bar{c}$ and proceed as in case (v). $\qquad\qquad\qquad\qquad\qquad\qquad\square$

Lemma 3.20. If $W_{\Lambda,\Gamma\cup\{\forall(p,q)\}}$ contains a global defect, then $\Phi \vdash \exists(p, \bar{q})$.

Proof. Let u, v be elements of $W_{\Lambda,\Gamma\cup\{\forall(p,q)\}}$ and t a binary literal such that $\forall(p', t), \forall(q', \bar{t}) \in u$, and $p', q' \in v$. We apply the six-fold distinction noted above to both u and v, yielding thirty-six cases in total.

(i) Suppose $\forall(p', t), \forall(q', \bar{t}) \in u' \in W_{\Lambda,\Gamma}$. By Lemma 3.9 (i), there exist o, Q such that $\Phi \vdash Q(o, \forall(p', t))$ and $\Phi \vdash \bar{Q}(o, \forall(q', \bar{t}))$. Hence we have the derivation

$$\cfrac{Q(o, \forall(p', t)) \quad \bar{Q}(o, \forall(q', \bar{t}))}{\forall(p', \bar{q}')}\text{ (E1)}$$

Recall that $\forall(p', \bar{q}')$ is symmetric in p' and q'. We consider the sub-cases: (a) $p', q', \in v' \in W_{\Lambda,\Gamma}$; (b) $p', p \in v' \in W_{\Lambda,\Gamma}$, and $q' \in \{q\}^{\Gamma}$; (c) $q', p \in v' \in W_{\Lambda,\Gamma}$, and $p' \in \{q\}^{\Gamma}$; (d) $p', q' \in \{o\}^{\Gamma}$, where $o \in [q]^{\Gamma}$, and $p \in \bigcup W_{\Lambda,\Gamma}$; (e) $p', p \in \{o\}^{\Gamma}$, where $o \in [q]^{\Gamma}$, $q' \in \{q\}^{\Gamma}$, and $p \in \bigcup W_{\Lambda,\Gamma}$; (f) $q', p \in \{o\}^{\Gamma}$, where $o \in [q]^{\Gamma}$, $p' \in \{q\}^{\Gamma}$, and $p \in \bigcup W_{\Lambda,\Gamma}$. If (a), by Lemma 3.9 (ii), $\Phi \vdash \exists(p', q')$, and we have the derivation

$$\cfrac{\cfrac{\forall(p', \bar{q}') \quad \exists(p', q')}{\exists(p', \bar{p}')}\text{ (A5)}}{\exists(p, \bar{q})}\text{ (A7)}.$$

If (b), by Lemma 3.9 (ii), $\Phi \vdash \exists(p', p)$, and by Lemma 3.2, $\Phi \vdash \forall(q, q')$. Hence, we have the derivation

$$\cfrac{\cfrac{\forall(p', \bar{q}') \quad \exists(p, p')}{\exists(p, \bar{q}')}\text{ (A6)} \quad \forall(q, q')}{\exists(p, \bar{q})}\text{ (A5)}.$$

Sub-case (c) is identical to (b) by transposing p' and q'. If (d), by Lemmas 3.1 and 3.2, $\Gamma \vdash \not\forall(q,o)$, $\Gamma \vdash \forall(o,p')$, and $\Gamma \vdash \forall(o,q')$, and by Lemma 3.9 (ii), $\Phi \vdash \exists(p,p)$. Hence, we have the derivation:

$$
\cfrac{
  \cfrac{
    \cfrac{\forall(p',\bar{q}') \quad \forall(o,p')}{\forall(o,\bar{q}')} \text{ (A1)} \quad \vdots \; \forall(o,q')
  }{\forall(o,\bar{o})} \text{ (A2)} \quad \not\forall(q,o)
}{
  \cfrac{\forall(p,\bar{q})}{} \text{ (C7)} \quad \vdots \; \exists(p,p)
} \quad \cfrac{}{\exists(p,\bar{q})} \text{ (A6)}.
$$

If (e), then by Lemmas 3.1 and 3.2, $\Gamma \vdash \not\forall(q,o)$, $\Gamma \vdash \forall(o,p')$, $\Gamma \vdash \forall(o,p)$ and $\Gamma \vdash \forall(q,q')$, and by Lemma 3.9 (ii), $\Phi \vdash \exists(p,p)$. Hence, we have the derivation:

$$
\cfrac{
  \vdots \; \exists(p,p) \quad \vdots \; \not\forall(q,o) \quad
  \cfrac{
    \cfrac{\forall(p',\bar{q}') \quad \forall(o,p')}{\forall(o,\bar{q}')} \text{ (A1)} \quad \vdots \; \forall(q,q')
  }{\forall(o,\bar{q})} \text{ (A2)} \quad \vdots \; \forall(o,p)
}{\exists(p,\bar{q})} \text{ (D3)}.
$$

Sub-case (f) is identical to (e) by transposing p' and q'.

(ii) Suppose $\forall(p',t), p \in u' \in W_{\Lambda,\Gamma}$, and $\forall(q',\bar{t}) \in \{q\}^{\Gamma}$. By Lemma 3.9 (ii), $\Phi \vdash \exists(p,\forall(p',t))$, and by Lemma 3.2, $\Phi \vdash \forall(q,\forall(q',\bar{t}))$. We consider the sub-cases (a)–(f) regarding v, exactly as in Case (i). If (a), by Lemma 3.9 (ii), $\Phi \vdash \exists(p',q')$, whence we have the derivation

$$
\cfrac{
  \cfrac{\exists(p,\forall(p',t)) \quad \exists(p',q')}{\exists(p,\exists(q',t))} \text{ (B1)} \quad \vdots \; \forall(q,\forall(q',\bar{t}))
}{\exists(p,\bar{q})} \text{ (A5)}.
$$

If (b), by Lemma 3.9 (ii), $\Phi \vdash \exists(p,p')$, and by Lemma 3.2, $\Phi \vdash \forall(q,q')$, whence we have the derivation

$$
\cfrac{
  \cfrac{\exists(p,\forall(p',t)) \quad \exists(p,p')}{\exists(p,\exists(p,t))} \text{ (B1)} \quad
  \cfrac{\forall(q,\forall(q',\bar{t})) \quad \forall(q,q')}{\forall(q,\forall(q,\bar{t}))} \text{ (B2)}
}{\exists(p,\bar{q})} \text{ (E3)}.
$$

If (c), by Lemma 3.9 (ii), $\Phi \vdash \exists(p,q')$, and by Lemma 3.2, $\Phi \vdash \forall(q,p')$, whence we have the derivation

$$\dfrac{\dfrac{\exists(p,\forall(p',t)) \quad \forall(q,p')}{\exists(p,\forall(q,t))}\ (\text{B2}) \quad \dfrac{\forall(q,\forall(q',\bar{t})) \quad \exists(p,q')}{\forall(q,\exists(p,\bar{t}))}\ (\text{B1})}{\exists(p,\bar{q})}\ (\text{E2}).$$

If (d), by Lemmas 3.1 and 3.2, $\Phi \vdash \exists\!\!\!/(q,o)$, $\Phi \vdash \forall(o,p')$, and $\Phi \vdash \forall(o,q')$, whence we have the derivation

$$\dfrac{\dfrac{\exists(p,\forall(p',t)) \quad \forall(o,p')}{\exists(p,\forall(o,t))}\ (\text{B2}) \quad \dfrac{\dfrac{\forall(q,\forall(q',\bar{t})) \quad \forall(o,q')}{\forall(q,\forall(o,\bar{t}))}\ (\text{B2}) \quad \exists\!\!\!/(q,o)}{\forall(q,\exists(o,\bar{t}))}\ (\text{D1})}{\exists(p,\bar{q})}\ (\text{A5}).$$

If (e), then by Lemmas 3.1 and 3.2, $\Gamma \vdash \exists\!\!\!/(q,o)$, $\Gamma \vdash \forall(o,p')$, $\Gamma \vdash \forall(o,p)$ and $\Gamma \vdash \forall(q,q')$. Hence, we have the derivation:

$$\dfrac{\dfrac{\exists(p,\forall(p',t)) \quad \forall(o,p')}{\exists(p,\forall(o,t))}\ (\text{B2}) \quad \dfrac{\forall(q,\forall(q',\bar{t})) \quad \forall(q,q')}{\forall(q,\forall(q,\bar{t}))}\ (\text{B2}) \quad \forall(o,p) \quad \exists\!\!\!/(q,o)}{\exists(p,\bar{q})}\ (\text{F1}).$$

If (f), then by Lemmas 3.1 and 3.2, $\Gamma \vdash \exists\!\!\!/(q,o)$, $\Gamma \vdash \forall(o,q')$, $\Gamma \vdash \forall(o,p)$ and $\Gamma \vdash \forall(q,p')$. Hence, we have

$$\dfrac{\dfrac{\exists(p,\forall(p',t)) \quad \forall(q,p')}{\exists(p,\forall(q,t))}\ (\text{B2}) \quad \dfrac{\forall(q,\forall(q',\bar{t})) \quad \forall(o,q')}{\forall(q,\forall(o,\bar{t}))}\ (\text{B2}) \quad \forall(o,p) \quad \exists\!\!\!/(q,o)}{\exists(p,\bar{q})}\ (\text{F2}).$$

(iii) Suppose $\forall(q',\bar{t}), p \in u' \in W_{\Lambda,\Gamma}$, and $\forall(p',t) \in \{q\}^{\Gamma}$. We argue exactly as for case (ii), with p' and q' exchanged, and t replaced by $\bar{t}$.

(iv) Suppose $\forall(p',t), \forall(q',\bar{t}) \in \{o'\}^{\Gamma}$, where $o' \in [q]^{\Gamma}$; and suppose $p \in \bigcup W_{\Lambda,\Gamma}$. By Lemmas 3.1 and 3.2, $\Phi \vdash \exists\!\!\!/(q,o')$, $\Phi \vdash \forall(o',\forall(p',t))$, and $\Phi \vdash \forall(o',\forall(q',\bar{t}))$; and by Lemma 3.9 (ii), $\Phi \vdash \exists(p,p)$. We consider the sub-cases (a)–(f) regarding v exactly as in Case (i). If (a), by Lemma 3.9

(ii), $\Phi \vdash \exists(p', q')$, whence we have the derivation

$$\cfrac{\cfrac{\forall(o', \forall(p', t)) \quad \exists(p', q')}{\forall(o', \exists(q', t))} \text{ (B1)} \quad \cfrac{\vdots}{\forall(o', \forall(q', \bar{t}))}}{\cfrac{\forall(o', \bar{o}')}{\cfrac{\forall(q, \bar{p})}{\exists(p, \bar{q})}} \text{ (A2)} \quad \cfrac{\vdots}{\not\forall(q, o')} \text{ (C7)} \quad \cfrac{\vdots}{\exists(p, p)}} \text{ (A5)}.$$

If (b), by Lemma 3.9 (ii), $\Phi \vdash \exists(p, p')$, and by Lemma 3.2, $\Phi \vdash \forall(q, q')$, whence we have the derivation

$$\cfrac{\cfrac{\forall(o', \forall(p', t)) \quad \exists(p, p')}{\forall(o', \exists(p, t))} \text{ (B1)} \quad \cfrac{\forall(o', \forall(q', \bar{t})) \quad \forall(q, q')}{\forall(o', \forall(q, \bar{t}))} \text{ (B2)} \quad \cfrac{\vdots}{\not\forall(q, o')} \quad \cfrac{\vdots}{\exists(p, p)}}{\exists(p, \bar{q})} \text{ (F3)}.$$

Sub-case (c) is identical to (b) by transposing p' and q' and replacing t by $\bar{t}$. If (d), by Lemmas 3.1 and 3.2, $\Phi \vdash \not\forall(q, o) \quad \Phi \vdash \forall(o, p')$ and $\Phi \vdash \forall(o, q')$, whence we have the derivations

$$\cfrac{\forall(o', \forall(p', t)) \quad \forall(o, p')}{\forall(o', \forall(o, t))} \text{ (B2)} \qquad \cfrac{\forall(o', \forall(q', \bar{t})) \quad \forall(o, q')}{\forall(o', \forall(o, \bar{t}))} \text{ (B2)},$$

and hence the derivation

$$\cfrac{\cfrac{\cfrac{\forall(o', \forall(o, t)) \quad \forall(o', \forall(o, \bar{t})) \quad \not\forall(q, o) \quad \not\forall(q, o')}{\forall(q, \bar{q})} \text{ (D6)}}{\forall(q, \bar{p})} \text{ (A8)} \quad \cfrac{\vdots}{\exists(p, p)}}{\exists(p, \bar{q})} \text{ (A5)}.$$

If (e), then by Lemmas 3.1 and 3.2, $\Gamma \vdash \not\forall(q, o)$, $\Gamma \vdash \forall(o, p')$, $\Gamma \vdash \forall(o, p)$ and $\Gamma \vdash \forall(q, q')$, and by Lemma 3.9 (ii), $\Phi \vdash \exists(p, p)$. Hence, we have the derivations:

$$\cfrac{\forall(o, \forall(p', t)) \quad \forall(o', p')}{\forall(o, \forall(o', t))} \text{ (B2)} \qquad \cfrac{\forall(o, \forall(q', \bar{t})) \quad \forall(q, q')}{\forall(o, \forall(q, \bar{t}))} \text{ (B2)},$$

and hence the derivation

$$\cfrac{\forall(o, \forall(o', t)) \quad \forall(o, \forall(q, \bar{t})) \quad \not\forall(q, o) \quad \not\forall(q, o') \quad \forall(o', p) \quad \exists(p, p)}{\exists(p, \bar{q})} \text{ (F4)}.$$

Case (f) is identical to (e) by transposing p' and q' and replacing t by $\bar{t}$.

(v) Suppose $\forall(p',t), p \in \{o'\}^\Gamma$, where $o' \in [q]^\Gamma$, $\forall(q',\bar{t}) \in \{q\}^\Gamma$; and suppose $p \in \bigcup W_{\Lambda,\Gamma}$. By Lemmas 3.1 and 3.2, $\Phi \vdash \not\forall(q,o')$, $\Phi \vdash \forall(o',\forall(p',t))$, $\Phi \vdash \forall(o',p)$, $\forall(q,\forall(q',\bar{t}))$; and by Lemma 3.9 (ii), $\Phi \vdash \exists(p,p)$. We consider the cases (a)–(f) regarding v exactly as for (i). If (a), by Lemma 3.9 (ii), $\Phi \vdash \exists(p',q')$, whence we have the derivation

$$\cfrac{\forall(o',p) \quad \cfrac{\forall(o',\forall(p',t)) \quad \cfrac{\forall(q,\forall(q',\bar{t})) \quad \exists(p',q')}{\forall(q,\exists(p',\bar{t}))}\,(B1)}{\forall(o',\bar{q})}\,(A2) \quad \not\forall(q,o') \quad \exists(p,p)}{\exists(p,\bar{q})}\,(D3).$$

If (b), by Lemma 3.9 (ii), $\Phi \vdash \exists(p,p')$, and by Lemma 3.2, $\Phi \vdash \forall(q,q')$, whence we have the derivation

$$\cfrac{\cfrac{\forall(o',\forall(p',t)) \quad \exists(p,p)}{\forall(o',\exists(p,t))}\,(B1) \quad \cfrac{\forall(q,\forall(q',\bar{t})) \quad \forall(q,q')}{\forall(q,\forall(q,\bar{t}))}\,(B2) \quad \not\forall(q,o') \quad \forall(o',p) \quad \exists(p,p')}{\exists(p,\bar{q})}\,(F5)$$

If (c), by Lemma 3.9 (ii), $\Phi \vdash \exists(p,q')$, and by Lemma 3.2, $\Phi \vdash \forall(q,p')$, whence we have the derivation

$$\cfrac{\cfrac{\forall(o',\forall(p',t)) \quad \forall(q,p')}{\forall(o',\forall(q,t))}\,(B2) \quad \cfrac{\forall(q,\forall(q',\bar{t})) \quad \exists(p,q')}{\forall(q,\exists(p,\bar{t}))}\,(B1) \quad \not\forall(q,o') \quad \forall(o',p) \quad \exists(p,p)}{\exists(p,\bar{q})}\,(F6)$$

If (d), by Lemmas 3.1 and 3.2, $\Phi \vdash \not\forall(q,o)$ $\Phi \vdash \forall(o,p')$ and $\Phi \vdash \forall(o,q')$, whence we have the derivations

$$\cfrac{\forall(o',\forall(p',t)) \quad \forall(o,p')}{\forall(o',\forall(o,t))}\,(B2) \qquad \cfrac{\forall(q,\forall(q',\bar{t})) \quad \forall(o,q')}{\forall(q,\forall(o,\bar{t}))}\,(B2),$$

and hence the derivation

$$\cfrac{\forall(o',\forall(o,t)) \quad \forall(q,\forall(o,\bar{t})) \quad \not\forall(q,o') \quad \forall(o',p) \quad \not\forall(q,o) \quad \exists(p,p)}{\exists(p,\bar{q})}\,(F7).$$

If (e), then by Lemmas 3.1 and 3.2, $\Gamma \vdash \not\forall(q,o)$, $\Gamma \vdash \forall(o,p')$, $\Gamma \vdash \forall(o,p)$ and $\Gamma \vdash \forall(q,q')$, and by Lemma 3.9 (ii), $\Phi \vdash \exists(p,p)$. Hence, we have the derivations:

$$\cfrac{\forall(o',\forall(p',t)) \quad \forall(o,p')}{\forall(o',\forall(o,t))}\,(B2) \qquad \cfrac{\forall(q,\forall(q',\bar{t})) \quad \forall(q,q')}{\forall(q,\forall(q,\bar{t}))}\,(B2),$$

and hence the derivation

$$\frac{\forall(o',\forall(o,t)) \quad \forall(q,\forall(q,\bar{t})) \quad \exists\!\!\!/(q,o') \quad \forall(o',p) \quad \exists\!\!\!/(q,o) \quad \forall(o,p) \quad \exists(p,p)}{\exists(p,\bar{q})} \quad \text{(F8)}$$

If (f), then by Lemmas 3.1 and 3.2, $\Gamma \vdash \exists\!\!\!/(q,o)$, $\Gamma \vdash \forall(o,q')$, $\Gamma \vdash \forall(o,p)$ and $\Gamma \vdash \forall(q,p')$, and by Lemma 3.9 (ii), $\Phi \vdash \exists(p,p)$. Hence, we have the derivations:

$$\frac{\forall(o',\forall(p',t)) \quad \forall(q,p')}{\forall(o',\forall(q,t))} \quad \text{(B2)} \qquad \frac{\forall(q,\forall(q',\bar{t})) \quad \forall(o,q')}{\forall(q,\forall(o,\bar{t}))} \quad \text{(B2)},$$

and hence the derivation

$$\frac{\forall(o',\forall(q,t)) \quad \forall(q,\forall(o,\bar{t})) \quad \exists\!\!\!/(q,o') \quad \forall(o',p) \quad \exists\!\!\!/(q,o) \quad \forall(o,p) \quad \exists(p,p)}{\exists(p,\bar{q})} \quad \text{(F9)}$$

(vi) Suppose $\forall(q',\bar{t}), p \in \{o'\}^{\Gamma}$, where $o' \in [q]^{\Gamma}$, $\forall(p',t) \in \{q\}^{\Gamma}$; and suppose $p \in \bigcup W_{\Lambda,\Gamma}$. We argue exactly as for case (v), with p' and q' exchanged, and t replaced by $\bar{t}$. □

Lemma 3.21. Suppose $\Phi \models \exists(p,\bar{q})$. Then $\Phi \vdash \exists(p,\bar{q})$.

Proof. Let $\mathfrak{A} = \mathfrak{A}_{\Lambda,\Gamma\cup\{\forall(p,q)\}}$. By construction, $\mathfrak{A} \models \forall(p,q)$, and hence $\mathfrak{A} \not\models \Phi$. By Lemma 3.6, $W_{\Lambda,\Gamma\cup\{\forall(p,q)\}}$ contains a defect. By Lemmas 3.19 and 3.20, $\Phi \vdash \exists(p,\bar{q})$. □

Proof of Theorem 2.4. Lemmas 3.12, 3.15, 3.16, 3.18 and 3.21. □

References

Corcoran, John. 1972. Completeness of an ancient logic. *Journal of Symbolic Logic* 37(4):696–702.

Pratt-Hartmann, Ian and Lawrence S. Moss. 2009. Logics for the relational syllogistic. *Review of Symbolic Logic* 2(4):647–683.

Smiley, T.J. 1973. What is a syllogism? *Journal of Philosophical Logic* 2:135–154.

Intensions as Computable Functions

SHALOM LAPPIN[1]

Classical intensional semantic frameworks, like Montague's Intensional Logic (IL), identify intensional identity with logical equivalence. This criterion of co-intensionality is excessively coarse-grained, and it gives rise to several well known difficulties. Theories of fine-grained intensionality have been been proposed to avoid this problem. Several of these provide a formal solution to the problem, but they do not ground this solution in a substantive account of intensional difference. Applying the distinction between operational and denotational meaning, developed for the semantics of programming languages, to the interpretation of natural language expressions, offers the basis for such an account. It permits us to escape some of the complications generated by the traditional modal characterization of intensions.

1 Introduction

Classical intensional semantic representation languages, like Montague (1974)'s Intensional Logic (IL) do not accommodate fine-grained intensionality. Montague, following Carnap (1947), characterizes intensions as functions from worlds (indices of worlds and times) to denotations, and so reduces intensional identity to equivalence of denotation across possible worlds. Logically equivalent expressions are semantically indistinguishable. This is too course a criterion for semantic identity. Logical equivalence is not a sufficient condition for intersubstitutability in all contexts.

(1) a. Every prime number is divisible only by itself and 1. <=>

b. If $A \subseteq B$ and $B \subseteq A$, then $A = B$.

---

[1] King's College London

LiLT Volume 9
Perspectives on Semantic Representations for Textual Inference.
Copyright © 2014, CSLI Publications.

(2) a. John believes that every prime number is divisible only by
itself and 1. <$\neq$>

   b. John believes that if $A \subseteq B$ and $B \subseteq A$, then $A = B$.

To avoid this difficulty a fine-grained theory of intensionality must
be able to distinguish between provable equivalence and intensional
identity.

2   Intensional Identity

Fox and Lappin (2005, 2010) propose Property Theory with Curry
Typing (PTCT) as an alternative intensional semantic representation
framework. It is a first-order system that consists of three components:
(i) an untyped λ-calculus, which generates the language of terms, (ii)
a rich Curry typing system for assigning types to terms, (iii) and a
first-order language of well-formed formulas for reasoning about the
truth of propositional terms, where these are term representations of
propositions. A tableaux proof theory constrains the interpretation of
each component of this federative representation language, and it relates the expressions of the different components. Restrictions on each
component prevent semantic paradoxes. A model theory allows us to
prove the soundness and completeness of the proof theory.

The terms of the untyped λ-calculus encode computable functions.
These correspond to the intensions of the representation language. Iden-
tity in the λ-calculus is defined in terms of the α, β, and η conditions
for substitution.

PTCT uses two notions of equality: intensional identity and extensional equivalence. $t \cong_T s$ states that the terms t, s are extensionally
equivalent in type T. In the case where two terms t, s are propositions
($t, s \in$ Prop), then $t \cong_{\text{Prop}} s$ corresponds to $t \leftrightarrow s$. If two predicates
of T are extensionally equivalent ($t \cong_{(T \Longrightarrow \text{Prop})} s$), then t, s each hold
of the same elements of T. Therefore $\forall x(x \in T \rightarrow (^\mathsf{T} t(x) \leftrightarrow {}^\mathsf{T} s(x)))$,
where $^\mathsf{T} t(x)$ asserts that the proposition represented by the term $t(x)$
is true.

$t =_T s$ states that two terms are intensionally identical in type T.
As noted, the rules for intensional identity are essentially those of the
$\lambda\alpha\beta\eta$-calculus. We are able to derive $t =_T s \rightarrow t \cong_T s$ for all types
inhabited by t, s, but not $t \cong_T s \rightarrow t =_T s$. Therefore PTCT avoids
the reduction of provable equivalence to intensional identity. Two terms
can be provably equivalent by the proof theory, but not identical. In
this case, they remain intensionally distinct.

PTCT allows us to sustain both the logical equivalence of (1)a and
(1)b, and the non-equivalence of (2)a and (2)b. The former are provably

equivalent, but they correspond to non-identical propositional terms in PTCT.

The proof theory of PTCT induces a prelattice on the terms in Prop. In this prelattice the members of an equivalence class of mutually entailing propositional terms (terms that encode mutually entailing propositions) are non-identical and so correspond to distinct propositions.[2] While this result achieves the formal property of fine-grained intensionality, it does not, in itself, explain what intensional non-identity consists in, beyond the fact that two distinct expressions in the language of terms are identified with different intensions. This leaves us with what we can describe as a problem of ineffability. Intensional difference is posited as (a certain kind of) inscriptional distinctness in the λ-calculus of terms, but this reduction does not offer a substantive explanation of the semantic properties that ground the distinction. Intensional difference remains ineffable.

This is an instance of a general problem with inscriptional treatments of fine-grained intensionality.[3] They identify differences of meaning with distinctions among terms in a semantic representation language. But without an account of how difference in terms generates intensional distinction, the inscriptional view leaves intensional non-identity unexplained. Inscriptionalist theories avoid problems created by the characterisation of intensions as functions on possible worlds at the risk of rendering intensions primitive to the point of inscrutability.

3 Expressing Intensional Difference Operationally

We can characterize the distinction between intensional identity and provable equivalence computationally by invoking the contrast between operational and denotational semantics in programming language. Two simple examples illustrate this contrast.

For the first example take the function $predecessorSet(x)$, which maps an object in an ordered set into the set of its predecessors. So, for example, if $x \in \{0,1,2,3,4,5\}$, $predecessorSet(x) = PredSet_x \subset \{0,1,2,3,4,5\}$ such that $\forall y \in PredSet_x (y < x)$. It follows that $predecessorSet(0) = \emptyset$.

It is possible to define (at least) two variants of this function, $predecessorSet_a$ and $predecessorSet_b$, that are denotationally equivalent but operationally distinct. $predecessorSet_a$ is specified directly

---

[2]Fox et al. (2002); Fox and Lappin (2005); Pollard (2008) construct higher-order hyperintensional semantic systems using an extended version of Church's SST and a prelattice of propositions in which the entailment relation is a preorder.

[3]See Fox and Lappin (2005) for a discussion of inscriptionalist theories of intentionality.

in terms of an immediate predecessor relation, while $predecessorSet_b$ depends upon a successor relation.

(3) a. $predecessorSet_a(x) = PredSet_x$, if
$\forall y(y \in PredSet_x \rightarrow predecessor(y, x))$.

    b. $predecessor(y, x)$ if
$predecessor_{immediate}(y, x)$; else
      (i) $predecessor(y, x)$ if
$predecessor_{immediate}(y, z)$, and
$predecessor(z, x)$.

(4) a. $predecessorSet_b(x) = PredSet_x$, if
$\forall y(y \in PredSet_x \rightarrow successor(x, y))$.

    b. $successor(x, y)$ if
$successor_{immediate}(x, y)$; else
      (i) $successor(x, y)$ if
$successor_{immediate}(x, z)$, and
$successor(z, y)$.

The second example involves functions $g : \Sigma^* \rightarrow \{1, 0\}$ from Σ^*, the set of strings formed from the alphabet of a language, to the Boolean values 1 and 0, where $g(s) = 1$ if $s \in L$, and 0 otherwise. Let g_{csg1} be defined by the Definite Clause Grammar (DCG) in (5), and g_{csg2} by the DCG in (6).[4]

(5) $S \rightarrow [a],\ S(i)$.
$S(I) \rightarrow [a],\ S(i(I))$.
$S(I) \rightarrow Bn(I),\ Cn(I)$.
$Bn(i(I)) \rightarrow [b],\ Bn(I)$.
$Bn(i) \rightarrow [b]$.
$Cn(i(I)) \rightarrow [c],\ Cn(I)$.
$Cn(i) \rightarrow [c]$.

(6) $S \rightarrow A(I),\ B(I),\ C(I)$.
$A(i) \rightarrow [a]$.
$A(i(I)) \rightarrow [a],\ A(I)$.
$B(i) \rightarrow [b]$.
$B(i(I)) \rightarrow [b],\ B(I)$.
$C(i) \rightarrow [c]$.
$C(i(I)) \rightarrow [c],\ C(I)$.

---

[4]See Pereira and Shieber (1987) for an explanation of Definite Clause Grammars. The DCG in (5) is from Gazdar and Mellish (1989). Matthew Purver and I constructed the DCG in (6) as a Prolog programming exercise for a computational linguistics course that I gave in the Computer Science Department at King's College London in 2002.

Both these DCGs define the same context-sensitive language

$$\{a^n b^n c^n \mid 1 \leq n\},$$

the language whose strings consist of n occurrences of a, followed by n bs, and then n cs. The number of as, bs, and cs match in all strings. Each DCG uses a counting argument I for a non-terminal symbol to build up a stack of indices i that gives the successive number of occurrences of as, bs, and cs in a string. But the grammar in (5) counts from the bottom up, adding an i for each non-terminal that the recognizer encounters. By contrast the grammar in (6) imposes the requirement that the three stacks for the non-terminals A, B, and C be identical, and then it computes the indices top down. The two grammars are computationally distinct, and using each of them to recognize a string can produce different sequences of operations, of different lengths and relative efficiency. Therefore, g_{csg1} and g_{csg2} are operationally distinct, but denotationally equivalent. They compute the same string set through different sets of procedures.

4 Computable Functions and Natural Language Expressions

Recall that the terms of PTCT are λ-expressions that encode computable functions. We have identified these with the intensions of words and phrases in a natural language. Given the distinction between denotational and operational meaning we can now interpret the non-identity of terms in the representation language as an operational difference in the functions that these terms express. But a class of such terms can still be provably equivalent in the sense that they yield the same values for the same arguments by virtue of the specifications of the functions that they correspond to. This provides a straightforward account of fine-grained intensionality in PTCT which avoids taking intensional difference as ineffable.

It is reasonable to ask what it could mean to characterise the interpretation of a natural language expression as a computable function. Rich type theories, like PTCT and Type Theory with Records (TTR, Cooper (2012)), are based on the type systems used in programming languages. In some of these systems propositions are identified with proofs, where the proof of a proposition is the procedure applied to establish that it is assertable.[5] This can be a formal procedure, like the application of the rules of a proof theory, but it need not be. It could also be the sequence of operations involved in making the observations

---

[5] See Martin-Löf (1984) for a type theory in which propositions are characterised as proofs in a formal system.

that support the application of a classifier predicate to an object or an event.

On the view proposed here we are taking the semantic content of terms in a natural language to be the functions that we use to compute the denotations of these expressions. If such a term is a predicate, then the function that corresponds to its meaning encodes the procedure through which we determine the values that it returns for its domain of arguments (n-tuples of arguments for relational predicates).

Two predicates may correspond to distinct functions which happen to yield the same values for each argument in a given domain, but they would diverge if defined for an alternative domain. This would be the situation for predicates that are contingently co-extensive. However, as we have seen in Section 3, it is possible for two (or more) distinct computable functions to be provably equivalent. In this case they will generate the same range of values for all domains for which they are defined, through different sequences of operations, by virtue of the way in which these sequences are specified.

5 Two Alternative Operational Approaches

Muskens (2005) suggests a similar approach to hyperintensionality. He identifies the intension of an expression with an algorithm for determining its extension.[6] There are two major points of difference between Musken's theory and the one proposed here. First, he embeds his account in a logic programming approach, which he seems to take as integral to his explanation of hyperintensionality, while I have developed my analysis in a functional programming framework. This is, in fact, not an issue of principle. The same algorithm can be formulated in any programming language. So, for example, the definitions of $predecessorSet_a$ and $predecessorSet_b$ correspond to two Horn clause definitions in Prolog for variant predecessor predicates, $predecessorA(Y, X)$ and $predecessorB(Y, X)$.

(7) $predecessorA(Y, X) :- predecessorImmediate(Y, X)$.
$predecessorA(Z, X) :-$
$predecessorImmediate(Y, X)$,
$predecessorA(Y, Z)$.

(8) $predecessorB(Y, X) :- successor(X, Y)$.

---

[6] Duží et al. (2010) also adopt an operational view of hyperintensionality within Tichý (1988)'s Transparent Intensional Logic. However, the computational details of their account are left largely unspecified. Both Muskens (2005) and Duží et al. (2010) regard their respective proposals as working out Frege (1892)'s idea that a sense is a rule for identifying the denotation of an expression.

$successor(X, Y) :- successorImmediate(X, Y).$
$successor(X, Z) :-$
$successorImmediate(X, Y),$
$successor(Y, Z).$

Similarly, the DCGs in (5) and (6) that we used to define g_{csg1} and g_{csg2}, respectively, are (close to) Prolog executable code.

However, the functional programming formulation of the operational view of fine-grained intensionality follows straightforwardly from PTCT, where the untyped λ-calculus generates the intensional terms of the semantic representation language, and these encode computable functions. PTCT also offers rich Curry typing with weak polymorphism, and a logic of wffs for reasoning about truth and entailment, within a first-order system. The fact that it implies the operational account of intensional difference without further stipulation renders it attractive as a framework for developing computational treatments of natural language semantic properties.

The second, more substantive point of difference concerns the role of possible worlds in characterizing intensions. Muskens develops his hyperintensional semantics on the basis of Thomason (1980)'s Intentional Logic. In this logic Thomason proposes a domain of propositions as intensional objects, where the set of propositions is recursively defined with intensional connectives and quantifiers. He posits a homomorphism that maps propositions (and their constituents) to their extensions, and he constrains this homomorphism with several meaning postulates that restrict this mapping.[7] Muskens modifies and extends Thomason's logic by specifying a homomorphism between the intensional expressions of the logic and their extensions across the set of possible worlds. Propositions are mapped to the set of worlds in which they are true. As the homomorphism can be many-to-one, distinct propositions can receive the same truth-value across worlds.[8]

By contrast, PTCT adopts Thomason's possible worlds-free strategy of mapping propositions to truth-values. It does this by using a truth

---

[7]Fox and Lappin (2005) point out that Thomason's logic is problematic because it does not characterize the algebraic structure of the domain of propositions. It does not offer a proof theory that defines entailment for propositions, and so it leaves the relation between intentional identity and extensional equivalence crucially under-determined.

[8]Fox et al. (2002); Fox and Lappin (2005); Pollard (2008) adopt a similar view for the fine-grained higher-order logics that they construct. They define worlds as untrafilters in the prelattice of propositions, and they take the truth of a proposition, relative to a world, to be its membership in such an ultrafilter. As entailment in the prelattice is defined by a preorder, distinct propositions can belong to the same set of ultrafilters.

predicate to form a wff $^\top(\phi)$ to assert the truth of the proposition that the term $\phi \in$ Prop represents. Therefore, like Intentional Logic, PTCT de-modalizes intensions. This is a positive result. It is not clear why, on the fine-grained view, possible worlds must be essentially connected with the specification of intensions.

On both Musken's account and the one proposed here, the content of an intension is the set of computational operations through which it determines its denotational value, where these do not make essential reference to possible worlds. In the case of a proposition, the denotation that it determines is a truth-value, rather than a truth-value relative to a world. There may be independent epistemic, or even semantic reasons for incorporating possible worlds into one's general theory of interpretation, but worlds are not required for an adequate explanation of fine-grained intensionality. On the contrary, such an account must dispense with the original characterization of intensions as functions from worlds to extensions in order to explain the persistence of intensional difference beyond provable equivalence. Therefore, a radically possible worlds-free view of fine-grained intensionality offers the cleaner approach.

Moschovakis (2006) proposes an operational treatment of meaning within the framework of the typed λ-calculus. He constructs a language L^λ_{ar} as an extension of Gallin (1975)'s Ty_2. He specifies acyclic recursive procedures for reducing the terms of L^λ_{ar} to unique cannonical forms, and he identifies the meaning ("referential intension") of a term in this language with the "abstract algorithm" for computing its denotation.

There are two major points of difference between Moschovakis' algorithmic theory of intensions and the account proposed here. First, while in PTCT α, β, and η reduction sustain intensional identity, in L^λ_{ar} β reduction does not. His primary motivation for this move seems to be his concern to maintain the non-synonymy of sentences like *John loves himself* on one hand, and those like *John loves John* on the other. In L^λ_{ar} the canonical form of the former is $(\lambda(x)loves(x,x))(j)$ *where* $j := john$, while that of the latter is $loves(j_1, j_2)$ *where* $j_1 := John, j_2 := John$.

But this issue would appear to be an artifact of the way that Moschovakis has chosen to formalize proper names and reflexive pronouns. If one represented them as distinct sorts of generalized quantifiers, or constants, then this problem would not arise. In any case, it is not a deep question of principle. We take α, β, and η reduction to support intensional identity because they are normalizing operations on λ-terms in the semantic representation language, and so they do not correspond, in any obvious way, to processes or relations of natural languages. However, it is perfectly possible to narrow the specification of intensional identity in PTCT to exclude β (as well as η, and even α) reduction, without altering the proposed account of intensions as computable functions. This would simply involve imposing a particularly fine-grained notion of intensional identity.

The second point of difference is more significant. Moschovakis specifies a Kripke frame semantics for L_{ar}^{λ} which is a variant of Montague's possible worlds models (he refers to them as "Carnap states"). These are n-tuples of indices corresponding to worlds, times, speakers, and other parameters of context. Intensions are characterized as algorithmic procedures for determining the denotation of a term relative to a world and the other elements of such an n-tuple. Therefore, like Muskens Moschovakis' operational view of intensions treats them as inextricably bound up with possible worlds. The arguments that I brought against this view in Muskens' case apply with equal force here. An important advantage of the proposed account is that it factors modality and possible worlds out of the specification of intensions.

6 Conclusion

While theories of fine-grained intensionality may avoid the reduction of intensional identity to provable equivalence, many of them do not go beyond a bare inscriptionalist treatment of intensional difference. Therefore they leave this notion ineffable. On the proposal developed here intensional difference is the operational distinctions among computable functions, and extensional identity is the denotational equivalence of the values that functions compute. This account grounds fine-grained intensionality in a way that naturally accommodates cases of intensional difference combined with provable denotational equivalence.

Given that PTCT uses the untyped λ-calculus to generate the Curry typed term representations for the intensions of the language, and these terms encode computable functions, the proposed operational characterization of intensional difference is already implicit in this semantic framework.

This account yields a radically non-modal view of intensions in which possible worlds play no role in their specification or their interpretation. An intension is identified directly with the sequence of operations performed in computing the value of the function that expresses it. Fine-grained intensionality becomes the operational contents of computable functions.

Acknowledgements

An earlier version of this paper appeared as "An Operational Approach to Fine-Grained Intensionality" in Thomas Graf, Denis Paperno, Anna Szabolcsi, and Jos Tellings (eds.), *Theories of Everything: In Honor of Ed Keenan, UCLA Working Papers in Linguistics 17*, 2012, under the terms of a Creative Commons Non-Commercial License (http://creativecommons.org/licenses/by-nc/3.0/).

The main ideas in this paper developed out of my NASSLLI 2012 course Alternative Paradigms of Computational Semantics, and from talks that I gave at the University of Gothenburg in April 2012, and in December 2012. I am grateful to the participants in the course and to the audiences of the talks for stimulating feedback. I would also like to thank Robin Cooper, Chris Fox, and Dag Westerståhl for very helpful discussion of some of the issues addressed here. A more detailed presentation of the approach proposed here is given in Lappin (forthcoming).

References

Carnap, R. 1947. *Meaning and Necessity*. Chicago: University of Chicago Press.

Cooper, Robin. 2012. Type theory and semantics in flux. In R. Kempson, T. Fernando, and N. Asher, eds., *Philosophy of Linguistics*, pages 271–323. Amsterdam: Elsevier.

Duží, M., B. Jespersen, and P. Materna. 2010. *Procedural Semantics for Hyperintensional Logic*. Dordrecht, New York: Springer.

Fox, C. and S. Lappin. 2005. *Foundations of Intensional Semantics*. Oxford: Blackwell.

Fox, C. and S. Lappin. 2010. Expressiveness and complexity in underspecified semantics. *Linguistic Analysis, Festschrift for Joachim Lambek* 36:385–417.

Fox, C., S. Lappin, and C. Pollard. 2002. A higher-order, fine-grained logic for intensional semantics. In G. Alberti, K. Balough, and P. Dekker, eds., *Proceedings of the Seventh Symposium for Logic and Language*, pages 37–46. Pecs, Hungary.

Frege, Gottlob. 1892. On sense and reference. In P. Geach and M. Black, eds., *Translations from the Philosophical Writings of Gottlob Frege, 3rd Edition, 1980*, pages 56–78. Oxford: Basil Blackwell.

Gallin, D. 1975. *Intensional and Higher-Order Modal Logic*. Amsterdam: North-Holland.

Gazdar, G. and C. Mellish. 1989. *Natural Language Processing in Prolog*. Waltham, MA: Addison-Wesley.

Lappin, Shalom. forthcoming. Curry typing, polymorphism, and fine-grained intensionality. In S. Lappin and C. Fox, eds., *The Handbook of Contempo-*

rary Semantic Theory, Second Edition. Malden, MA and Oxford: Wiley-Blackwell.

Martin-Löf, Per. 1984. *Intuitionistic Type Theory.* Napoli: Bibliopolis.

Montague, R. 1974. *Formal Philosophy: Selected Papers of Richard Montague.* New Haven, CT/London, UK: Yale University Press. Edited with an introduction by R. H. Thomason.

Moschovakis, Y. 2006. A logical calculus of meaning and synonymy. *Linguistics and Philosophy* 29:27–89.

Muskens, R. A. 2005. Sense and the computation of reference. *Linguistics and Philosophy* 28:473–504.

Pereira, F. and S. Shieber. 1987. *Prolog and Natural-Language Analysis.* Stanford, CA: CSLI.

Pollard, Carl. 2008. Hyperintensions. *Journal of Logic and Computation* 18:257–282.

Thomason, R. 1980. A model theory for propositional attitudes. *Linguistics and Philosophy* 4:47–70.

Tichý, P. 1988. *The Foundations of Frege's Logic.* Berlin: De Gruyter.

Frege in Space: A Program for Compositional Distributional Semantics

MARCO BARONI,[1] RAFFAELLA BERNARDI[1] AND
ROBERTO ZAMPARELLI[1]

To Emanuele Pianta,
in memoriam

The lexicon of any natural language encodes a huge number of distinct word meanings. Just to understand this article, you will need to know what thousands of words mean. The space of possible sentential meanings is infinite: In this article alone, you will encounter many sentences that express ideas you have never heard before, we hope. Statistical semantics has addressed the issue of the vastness of word meaning by proposing methods to harvest meaning automatically from large collections of text (corpora). Formal semantics in the Fregean tradition has developed methods to account for the infinity of sentential meaning based on the crucial insight of *compositionality*, the idea that meaning of sentences is built incrementally by combining the meanings of their constituents. This article sketches a new approach to semantics that brings together ideas from statistical and formal semantics to account, in parallel, for the richness of lexical meaning and the combinatorial power of sentential semantics. We adopt, in particular, the idea that word meaning can be approximated by the patterns of co-occurrence of words in corpora from statistical semantics, and the idea that compositionality can be captured in terms of a syntax-driven calculus of function application from formal semantics.

---

[1] Center for Mind/Brain Sciences and Department of Information Engineering and Computer Science, University of Trento (IT)

LiLT Volume 9
Perspectives on Semantic Representations for Textual Inference.
Copyright © 2014, CSLI Publications.

1 Introduction

Semantic compositionality is the crucial property of natural language according to which the meaning of a complex expression is a function of the meaning of its constituent parts and of the mode of their combination. Compositionality makes the meaning of a sentence such as *"carnivorous plants digest slowly"*, in (1), a function of the meaning of the noun phrase *"carnivorous plants"* combined as a subject with the meaning of the verb phrase *"digest slowly"*, which is in turn derived by the combination of the meaning of the verb *digest* and a modifier, the adverb *slowly*.

(1)

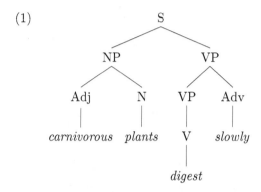

Together with the property of syntactic recursivity, which grants humans the possibility of constructing indefinitely long grammatical sentences, semantic compositionality allows us to compose arbitrarily complex meanings into sentences, and extract meanings from arbitrarily long and complex sentences, starting from a finite lexicon.

While the compositional nature of human language has been in some sense acknowledged since Aristotle's subject-predicate distinction, it has been brought to the foreground only in modern times, mainly with the work of the German logician Gottlob Frege (hence the alternative name *Frege's Principle*, see especially Frege 1892).[2] Compositionality was later operationalized by Richard Montague (see in particular Montague 1970b, 1973). Together with the assumption that meaning can be accounted for *denotationally* (that is in terms of whether a linguistic utterance is truthful with respect to a *model* of the world) compositionality has since informed the whole area of theoretical linguistics

---

[2]As Emilano Guevara and Dominic Widdows (p.c.) point out, surprisingly, the principle was never explicitly stated by Frege (Pelletier 2001), and it was arguably already assumed by Boole (1854) decades before Frege's work. We will stick to the traditional name despite its historical inaccuracy.

known as *natural language semantics* or *formal semantics* (see Partee 2004, and Werning et al. 2012 for a broad overview of compositionality covering the application of the principle also in general cognition and computer science).[3]

Compositionality is well-known not to apply in expressions such as *"red herring"* or *"kick the bucket"*, whose dominant, idiomatic meanings have nothing to do with fish or pail-hitting. However, even in these cases a 'literal', compositional route cannot be blocked (i.e., these expressions could be used, and understood, as descriptions of a real herring dyed red, the kicking of a real bucket, etc.). This suggests that the compositional mode of meaning construction is a primitive in human language, and a crucial ingredient in any theory that tries to model the way humans use language.

Consider again the schematic binary tree structure in (1). Most (though not all) theories of sentential semantics implement compositionality by building meanings bottom-up. Moving from the lexicon, (here *digest, carnivorous, plants* and *slowly*), which can be retrieved from memory, they follow the syntactic tree up to the main clause (S), combining pairs of sister nodes (both lexical, like [*carnivorous plants*] and non-lexical, like [NP VP]) by means of a small set of primitive operations, possibly just one, *function application*. In function application, one of two sister nodes is treated as a function and applied to the other to return the meaning of their mother node, which can in turn be an argument or a function in further combinations (see Heim and Kratzer 1998; for a thorough introduction to the function application approach to composition).

This general line of research, split into many different strands and flavours which will not concern us here, has enjoyed a great success in terms of constructions covered and depth of the explanation, generating thorough descriptions of the behaviour of quantifiers and articles, long-distance dependencies, coordination and comparatives, and many other individual phenomena most often linked to the lexicon of *grammatical* elements, such as determiners and conjunctions. However, the success of a scientific enterprise can and ultimately must be measured outside of a lab. For a semantic theory, which has few products to send out to the market, this means the ability to give understandable descriptions of the whole semantic behavior of an arbitrary sentence, which can easily contain dozens of intertwined semantic phenomena. In contrast, most semantic studies have dealt with individual constructions, and

---

[3]Following standard practice, in this article we sometimes use the term *denotational semantics* synonymously with *formal semantics*, especially when we want to emphasize the denotational side of the latter.

have been carried out under highly simplifying assumptions, in true lab conditions. If these idealizations are removed it is not clear at all that modern semantics can give a full account of all but the simplest sentences.

Consider for instance the problem of lexical ambiguity: Nearly all papers in formal semantics start from the assumption that all the words in the examples under study have been neatly disambiguated before being combined. But this is not an innocent or easy assumption. To evaluate the truth or falsity of (2)in a model, one would have to assume that *paper* is not the material, but the text in a certain page format (and not in a purely abstract sense, as in *"his paper has been reprinted in ebook format"*); that *runs* means something like *extends*, and not the *running* of horses, the *running* of cars or what Obama did as he *"ran for presidency"* (despite the presence of *for*). In turn, *for* does not indicate a goal (*"I ran for the exit"*), nor a benefactive (one could say: *"in the Olympics, the British team ran for their Queen"*, but nobody would run for a simple *page*, not even for 105 of them).

(2)   This paper runs for 105 pages.

Often, choosing to combine the 'wrong' meanings does not lead to falsity, but to non-sensicality. It is not easy, however, to figure out which possibilities are odd without trying the semantic combinations, and many will remain uncertain. With more complex sentences, such as (3), a wealth of additional complexities emerge: You have to understand that in this context *analysts* are technology analysts, that *every* actually ranges over a subpart of them, that *paid* has a special meaning due to the presence of *attention* before it, that *attention* here means 'amount of attention', that *unbelievable* actually means 'hard to believe', etc.

(3)   Every analyst knows that the attention Jobs paid to details was simply unbelievable.

Even in the limited domain of modification, the variability of meaning that emerges has long been recognized, but its consequences not always fully appreciated. As Lahav remarks:

> In order for a cow to be brown most of its body's surface should be brown, though not its udders, eyes, or internal organs. A brown crystal, on the other hand, needs to be brown both inside and outside. A book is brown if its cover, but not necessarily its inner pages, are mostly brown, while a newspaper is brown only if all its pages are brown. For a potato to be brown it needs to be brown only outside... Furthermore, in order for a cow or a bird to be brown the brown color should be the animal's natural color, since it is regarded as being 'really' brown even if it is painted white all over. A table,

on the other hand, is brown even if it is only painted brown and its 'natural' color underneath the paint is, say, yellow. But while a table or a bird are not brown if covered with brown sugar, a cookie is. In short, what is to be brown is different for different types of objects. To be sure, brown objects do have something in common: a salient part that is wholly brownish. But this hardly suffices for an object to count as brown. A significant component of the applicability condition of the predicate 'brown' varies from one linguistic context to another.   (Lahav 1993:76)

What happens with *brown* is replicated in the large majority of adjective-noun combinations. Treating them all like 'idioms' would turn the exception into the rule. After all, there must be many regularities in their combinatorial behaviour, or children would not be able to learn modification correctly, and indeed semanticists have long recognized that many cases of context-driven polysemy are systematic (on the notion of *regular polysemy* see, e.g., Apresjan 1974; Pustejovsky 1995).

Add to this that the meaning of abstract terms has only begun to be investigated by formal semantics (what is the denotational meaning of *numerosity* or *bravery*?), and the outlook for a semantic analysis that can span real-life sentences and not just sterilized constructions starts to look not particularly promising.

As is easy to see, many of the problems come from the lexicon of *content words*, such as nouns, verbs and adjectives, and not from grammatical terms. Content words constitute the area of the lexicon with the greatest amount of items (by the end of high-school, an average Western person might know the meaning of as many as 60,000 content words, see Aitchison 1993), characterized by a lot of idiosyncratic meaning combinations. Of course, there have been important attempts to tackle the lexicon problem from the point of view of formal semantics, like Pustejovsky's (1995) theory of the generative lexicon. More recently, Asher (2011) has approached lexical semantics with a theory of predication that uses a sophisticated system of semantic types, plus a mechanism of type coercion. This gives an interesting account of difficult phenomena that relate to the ambiguity and context-dependent nature of content words, such as *co-predication*, exemplified in (4), (where *lunch* is interpreted as referring to the food in one conjunct and to the event of eating in the other) or *predicate coercion*, where a predicate is provided to 'fix' a type mismatch, as in (5).

(4)   Lunch was delicious but took forever.

(5)   John enjoyed a beer.   *he enjoyed DRINKING it*

However, the problem of lexical semantics is primarily a problem of *size*: even considering the many subregularities found in the content lexicon, a hand-by-hand analysis is simply not feasible for the thousands of elements that populate the content word lexicon. For many of these elements, we would have to manually specify how they are affected by the context-dependent process of polysemy resolution: from regular polysemy to non-systematic meaning shifts, down to the *co-composition* phenomena illustrated by the citation above (see Section 2.3).Without such an analysis, the goal of a semantic treatment for actual *sentences* rather than abstract *constructions* remains out of reach.

Similar problems are familiar elsewhere in linguistics. The problem of assigning reasonable (if not exhaustive) syntactic structures to arbitrary, real-life sentences is perhaps equally hard. Here, however, technology has provided an important part of the answer: Natural language parsers, which automatically assign a syntactic structure to sentences, have made great advances in recent years by exploiting probabilistic information about parts of speech (POS tags) and syntactic attachment preferences. This in turn has been made possible by the availability of medium-sized corpora annotated for POS and syntactic information, such as the Penn Treebank (Marcus et al. 1993), that serve as the basis for extracting probabilistic information from. Today's state-of-the-art parsers can process dozens of unannotated, possibly noisy real-life sentences per second (Clark and Curran 2007; Nivre 2003).[4]

Learning from pre-annotated data has been less directly applicable to the goal of providing a semantic representation for sentences because there are few learning samples marked for meaning (but see Basile et al. 2012). Moreover, the range, variety and often 'fuzzy' nature of semantic phenomena makes the prospect of manual semantic markup of text data a lot less appealing than for syntax. As a consequence, data-driven semantics—which would in principle be a way to address the vastness of lexical meanings—has not advanced as rapidly as data-driven syntax.

What sort of data-driven methods could truly help semantics? If the main problem for the semantics of sentences is the content lexicon, we should try to find methods that use vast corpora to extract the meaning of content words and represent them in appropriate ways.[5] But these

---

[4]The error margin remains high. Its bounds are given by the accuracy of the structures the parser has learned from. Better structures in the learning sample should lead to better parsing across the whole corpus to be parsed, and it is possible that in the future incorporating DS measures in parsing preferences might lead to better results, perhaps to the point of modeling human garden-path effects. See Manning (2011) for similar considerations with respect to part-of-speech tagging.

[5]An alternative approach is to rely on *lexical resources* that contain rich semantic information about content words (e.g., Baker et al. 1998; Fellbaum 1998; Kipper et al. 2008). We find the corpus route more appealing because it is not *a priori*

meaning representations should be objects that compose together to form more complex meanings, while accounting for how composition causes more or less sytematic shifts in word meaning, as in the co-composition, co-predication and coercion examples above. Moreover, the meaning of content words as we can extract them from a corpus should be able to combine with the meaning of *grammatical* words, formal semantics' special focus, in ways that account for the importance of structure in sentence meaning, and which can shed light also on the linguistic phenomena that interest the theoretical linguist. This is what this paper is about. We propose it as a research program for linguistics, both theoretical and computational, but also as a description of the thriving subfield of *compositional distributional semantics.*

As we shall see in the next sections, this field takes a stand which might be counterintuitive for the formal linguist—that the meaning of content words lies in their distribution over large spans of text. We believe that this aspect of meaning is very real and concrete, and that it complements a denotational approach in which words 'mean' the objects they stand for.

In the remainder of this article, we make our case as follows. Section 2 is a concise introduction to distributional semantics, focusing on its implications for linguistics and cognitive science. Section 3 presents *compositional* distributional semantics, and in particular the Fregean approach to the challenge of composing distributional representations we endorse. Section 4 contains a brief review of empirical evidence in favour of our specific proposal, while Section 5 offers more general motivations for the need of a theory of compositional distributional semantics. The emphasis is not on applications, but on what this approach can bring to a theory of linguistic meaning. Section 6 briefly reviews some related work that has not been discussed in the previous sections, or to which we felt the need to return given how closely connected it is to our. The heroic reader who made it to the end of this unusually long paper will discover, in our valedictory in Section 7, that we left so many important issues unaddressed that we are already working on Part 2.

---

limited by the amount of manually coded data entered in a resource. Many fuzzy aspects of word meaning are arguably better captured by the distributional representations we are about to introduce than by the hand-coded symbolic formalisms encoded in lexical resources. Moreover, we hope that the very process of *inducing* meaning from naturally occurring data will be very instructive about what meaning really is, and possibly about how we humans come to possess it.

TABLE 1: Distributional vectors representing the words *dog*, *hyena* and *cat*.

	dog	hyena	cat
runs	1	1	4
barks	5	2	0

2 Distributional Semantics

The *distributional hypothesis* states that words occurring in similar (linguistic) contexts are semantically similar. This idea has its theoretical roots in various traditions, including American structuralist linguistics, British lexicology and certain schools of psychology and philosophy (Firth 1957; Harris 1954; Miller and Charles 1991; Wittgenstein 1953). It had a huge impact on computational linguistics mainly because it suggests a practical way to automatically harvest word "meanings" on a large scale: If we can equate meaning with context, we can simply record the contexts in which a word occurs in a collection of texts (a *corpus*) to create a summary of the distributional history of the word that can then be used as a surrogate of its semantic representation.

While nearly all corpus-based approaches to computational semantics exploit distributional information in one way or another, we focus here on *Distributional Semantic Models* (DSMs), that are the most direct realization of the distributional hypothesis in computational linguistics (Clark 2013b; Erk 2012; Landauer and Dumais 1997; Lund and Burgess 1996; Sahlgren 2006; Schütze 1997; Turney and Pantel 2010). In a DSM, each word is represented by a mathematical *vector*, that is, an ordered list of numbers. The values in the vector *components* are a function of the number of times that the words occur in the proximity of various linguistic contexts in a corpus. As a toy example, suppose that our target vocabulary contains the nouns *dogs*, *hyena* and *cat* and our contexts are the words *barks* and *runs*. We traverse the corpus and find out that *dog* occurs in proximity of *runs* 1 time and near *barks* 5 times. We can thus represent *dog* with the *distributional vector* that constitutes the first column of Table 1. Similarly, *hyena* and *cat* are represented by the next two columns in the table, reflecting how many times they co-occur with *runs* and *barks* in the corpus.

Intuitively, based on this evidence we can deduce that *dog* is more similar to *hyena* than to *cat* because they both occur one time with *runs* and multiple times with *barks*, whereas *cat* occurs more frequently with *runs* and never with *barks*. Distributional vectors allow a precise quantification of similarity deriving from their representation as ge-

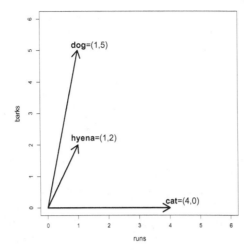

FIGURE 1: Geometric representation of the vectors in Table 1.

ometric objects. In Figure 1, the vectors are represented as oriented segments ("arrows") running from the origin of a Cartesian plane to x and y coordinates corresponding to the values in their first and second components (e.g., the endpoint of the **dog** vector has coordinates $x = 1$ and $y = 5$).[6]

In this geometric view, the similarity of the contexts in which words occur (and thus, according to the distributional hypothesis, their semantic similarity) is measured by the distance of the corresponding vectors on the Cartesian plane. In particular, DSMs typically use the *cosine* of the angle formed by two vectors as a measure of semantic similarity. The cosine is a function of the width of the angle, and ranges from 1 for parallel vectors to 0 for perpendicular (or orthogonal) vectors.[7] In the running example, **dog** has a cosine of 0.96 with **hyena** (the angle between the corresponding vectors is very narrow), and a

---

[6] Following common practice, we use boldface lowercase letters, e.g., **a**, to represent vectors, boldface capital letters, e.g., **A**, to represent matrices and Euler script letters, e.g., $\mathcal{X}$, to represent higher-order tensors (matrices and tensors are introduced in Section 3.3 below). However, when we want to emphasize the linguistic interpretation of a mathematical structure, we might denote it by its linguistic label in italics: Depending on the context we might refer to the vector representing the word *dog* either as **dog** or as *dog*.

[7] If the vectors contain components with negative values, the cosine can also be negative, with the minimum value of -1 for parallel vectors pointing in opposite directions. In distributional semantics, negative values may arise when counts are transformed into other kinds of scores; see Section 2.1 below.

much lower cosine of 0.2 with **cat** (wider angle).

We refer to the number of components of a vector as the *size* of the vector. The vectors in our toy example have size 2. Of course, real DSMs encode many more contexts, and consequently work with vectors of much larger sizes (ranging from hundreds to millions of components). The same geometric properties we can easily visualize on the Cartesian plane for the size-2 case (such as angular width) generalize to vectors of arbitrary size.

Mathematicians refer to the set of all possible vectors of size N as the *N-dimensional vector space*. Hence, sets of distributional vectors are often said to inhabit a "semantic" or "distributional" space. However, when we interpret the values in the components of a distributional vector as (function of) co-occurrences with contexts, the same N-dimensional vector space will have different interpretations depending on the labels (linguistic contents) attached to the components. For example, in the running example we associated the first component to *runs* and the second to *barks*. If we associated the two components to *red* and *banana*, respectively, mathematically we would still be operating in the same mathematical vector space (the 2-dimensional vector space), but the vectors we would be obtaining would represent different linguistic meanings. Thus, in what follows, whenever we talk of a vector space, we implicitly refer to the set of all possible vectors of a fixed size *whose components are associated, in the same order, to the same set of linguistic contents*. Under this definition, there are many (possibly infinite) distinct vector spaces of dimensionality N.

In the next subsections, we briefly survey the main steps necessary to build a DSM (Section 2.1), we review how DSMs have been used in practice (Section 2.2), and then turn to some theoretical issues pertaining to them (Sections from 2.3 to 2.6). More thorough recent introductions to DSMs are provided by Clark (2013b), Erk (2012) and Turney and Pantel (2010).

2.1   Parameters of DSMs

Most research on DSMs focuses on the many parameters of the pipeline to extract distributional vectors from corpora.[8] Surprisingly, there is relatively little research on how the nature of the source corpus affects the quality of the resulting vectors, but, as in many other areas of computational linguistics, the general consensus is that "more data is better data" (Curran and Moens 2002b). The most popular data source

---

[8] Bullinaria and Levy (2007, 2012) provide a sysstematic evaluation of how some of the pipeline parameters affect DSM quality.

is the British National Corpus,[9] a 100 million word corpus attempting to provide a "balanced" sample of various registers and genres of both written and spoken English. More recently, larger corpora (in the order of a few billion words), often made up of Web documents (including Wikipedia pages), are also widely used.[10]

Probably the most important decision when developing a DSM pertains to defining what is a *context* for purposes of counting co-occurrences. Definitions of context range from simple ones (such as documents or the occurrence of another word inside a fixed window from the target word) to more linguistically sophisticated ones (such as the occurrence of words of certain syntactic categories connected to the target by special syntactic relations) (Curran and Moens 2002a; Grefenstette 1994; Padó and Lapata 2007; Sahlgren 2006; Turney and Pantel 2010). Different contexts capture different kinds of semantic similarity or "relatedness" (Budanitsky and Hirst 2006). At the two extremes, counting documents as contexts captures "topical" relations (the words *war* and *Afghanistan* will have a high cosine, because they often co-occur in documents), whereas DSMs based on word co-occurrence within narrow windows or constrained by syntactic relations tend to capture tighter "taxonomic" relations (such as the one between *dog* and *hyena*). Unsurprisingly, no single definition of context is appropriate for all tasks, and the jury on the "best" context model is still out (Sahlgren 2008).

Next, raw target-context counts are typically transformed into *association scores* that discount the weights of components associated to contexts with high probability of chance occurrence (Evert 2005). For example, co-occurring with a relatively rare word such as *barks* is enormously more informative about the meaning of *dog* than co-occurring with *the*, despite the fact that, in any corpus, *dog* will occur many more times with the latter than with the former. An association measure such as Pointwise Mutual Information or Log-Likelihood Ratio will increase the value in the *barks* component, dampening the one in the *the* component.

Optionally, the collection of vectors of association scores produced in the previous step globally undergoes *dimensionality reduction*, after which the same target words are represented in a lower-dimensionality space whose components (deriving from the original ones via a statis-

---

[9] http://www.natcorp.ox.ac.uk/

[10] See for example http://wacky.sslmit.unibo.it/. A potential problem with Web corpora is their systematic skewness, as in the probable overassociation of *page* with *home*. This can presumably be addressed with better sampling and filtering techniques (see Fletcher 2004, 2012).

tical process that considers their correlation patterns) should capture more robust "latent" aspects of meaning (Blei et al. 2003; Dinu and Lapata 2010; Griffiths et al. 2007; Landauer and Dumais 1997; Sahlgren 2005; Schütze 1997).

Although it is not strictly a parameter in the construction of DSMs, researchers measure distributional (and thus semantic) similarity of pairs of target words with different *similarity functions*. The already introduced cosine of the angle formed by vectors is the most natural, geometrically justified and widely used of these functions.[11]

We conclude this short survey of DSM engineering by observing that, while in our discussion below we assume that the components of a semantic space can be interpreted as a distribution over contexts in which words tend to occur, in real DSMs, after the transformation into association scores and dimensionality reduction, the relationship between target words and contexts is often rather indirect.

2.2 Applications and cognitive simulations

The large-scale semantic representations provided by DSMs can profitably be embedded in applications that require a representation of word meaning, and in particular an objective measure of meaning similarity. Such applications range from document retrieval and classification to question answering, automated thesaurus construction and machine translation (Dumais 2003; Turney and Pantel 2010). DSMs are also very effective in simulating psychological and linguistic phenomena related to word meaning, such as predicting similarity judgments and semantic priming, categorizing nominal concepts into hypernyms, generating salient properties of concepts (and qualia of nouns), capturing

---

[11] A natural alternative to cosines is the Euclidean distance between vectors, that is, the length of the segment that connects their endpoints. An important property of Euclidean distance is that it is sensitive to vector length. *Hyena* is a less frequent word than *dog*. Consequently, it occurs less often in the contexts of interest and its distributional vector is geometrically shorter. Thus, in Figure 1 the endpoints of the **dog** and **hyena** vectors are relatively distant, while the width of the angle between the vectors is not affected by length. If we kept collecting *dog* data without finding any further *hyena* occurrences in the corpus, as long as *dog* maintained the same rate of occurrence with *runs* and *barks*, the angle (and consequently the cosine) between the two vectors would not be affected, while Euclidean distance would keep growing. The cosine can thus be seen as a more robust similarity measure than Euclidean distance. This is not to say that vector *length* by itself is not an informative quantity. For example, since it is a function of how frequently the word represented by the vector was encountered in the corpus (modulo possible statistical transformations of the input values), it is a measure of the reliability of the distributional evidence encoded in the vector. Finally, note that Euclidean distance and cosine are in a bijective functional relation if Euclidean distance is computed on vectors that have been normalized to length 1.

intuitions about the thematic fit of verb arguments and even spotting the alternation classes of verbs (Baroni and Lenci 2010; Baroni et al. 2010; Landauer and Dumais 1997; Lenci 2011; Lund and Burgess 1996; McDonald and Brew 2004; Padó and Lapata 2007; Padó et al. 2007; and references there).

For example, starting with the classic work of Landauer and Dumais (1997), researchers have shown that cosines in distributional space predict which word, among a set of candidates, is the synonym of a target item (e.g., DSMs pick *pinnacle* as synonym of *zenith* over the foils *completion, outset* and *decline*). DSM performance on this task approximates that of native English speakers with a college education (Rapp 2004). Padó and Lapata (2007) and others have shown how the cosines between vectors of word pairs can predict whether the corresponding words will "prime" each other or not (that is, whether a subject will recognize the second word faster when the first one has just been presented). Kotlerman et al. (2010) and others use DSMs to predict lexical entailment (discovering whether the concept denoted by one word implies the one denoted by another; for example, *dog* entails *animal*). Padó et al. (2007) show that (simplifying somewhat) the cosine between a vector representing the typical subject or object of a verb and a vector representing an arbitrary noun correlates with human intuitions about the plausibility of the noun as subject or object of the verb. For example, the *monster* vector is closer to the average "subject-of-*frighten*" vector than to the corresponding object vector, reflecting subject intuitions that monsters are more likely to be frighteners than frightees.

2.3 Polysemy and word meaning in context

We have suggested in the introduction that traditional formal semantics might not be the right approach to capture the rich polysemous patterns of (mainly) content words. On the face of it, standard DSMs do not address the issue of polysemy, since they represent each word with a single distributional vector. In the common case in which a word has more than one facet of meaning (ranging from full-fledged instances of homonymy such as *river bank* vs. *central bank* to subtler alternations such as *chicken in the farm* vs. *chicken in the oven* or the cases of co-predication and coercion discussed in the introduction), the distributional vector will be a summary of these facets. There has however been a lot of work on handling polysemy in DSMs (e.g., Boleda et al. 2012a; Erk 2010; Pantel and Lin 2002; Schütze 1998) showing that these models are actually very well-suited to capture various kinds of polysemy on a large scale. Note that polysemy is naturally modeled in terms of the contexts in which a word appears: In a sentence containing words such as *farm*, *free-range* and *outdoors*, the word *chicken* is more likely to mean the animal than its meat (albeit an animal with a clear culinary destiny). Consequently, a large subset of work on polysemy in DSMs (e.g., Dinu and Lapata 2010; Erk and Padó 2008, 2010; Kintsch 2001; Mitchell and Lapata 2008; Reisinger and Mooney 2010; Thater et al. 2009) has focused on the goal of modeling word meaning in context.

There is a clear connection between distributional models of word meaning in context and distributional models of compositionality, which is the main topic of this article. For example, Mitchell and Lapata (2008) discriminate between the senses of *running* in *water runs* vs. *horse runs* by composing vectors representing the two phrases, whereas Erk and Padó (2008) and others approach the same task in terms of how the *runs* vector changes due to contextual effects triggered by the presence of *water* vs. *horse*. Mitchell and Lapata construct a vector for *water runs*, Erk and Padó for *runs-in-the-context-of-water*, so to speak (both the task and the latter approach are reminiscent of Pustejovsky's 1995 notion of co-composition, whereby the meaning of a verb is affected by the arguments it composes with). In our research, we follow Mitchell and Lapata and focus on more general compositional methods, hoping to develop composition operations that are flexible enough to also capture word-meaning-in-context effects, and consequently handle polysemy correctly. In Section 3.4, we will see why the specific framework for composition we are proposing might be well-suited to handle context-driven meaning changes, and in Section 4.2 we will present evidence that we can successfully capture the sort of co-compositional effects briefly sketched above.

There are cases where immediate (co-)composition does not suffice for disambiguation, and only the wider context makes the difference. However, disambiguation based on direct syntactic composition takes precedence; in a sentence such as *"The fisherman saw from his boat that the bank near the river docks was being robbed"*, the verb *robbed* overrides all the contextual features pointing to the *river* sense of bank. But in cases like *"The heavy rains made the river grow wild. The bridge fell and the banks collapsed"*, no current model of syntax-driven composition could disambiguate *banks*, since financial institutions are prone to collapsing just as easily as river sides. In the long term, discourse composition models will probably have their say on these cases. Note, finally, that the problem of representing homonymy in terms of DSMs will ultimately require a way to handle *disjunctive* meanings. We will return to this issue in Section 7.

2.4 DSMs as linguistically and psychologically viable feature-based theories of word meaning

The process to build DSMs relies on the standard toolbox of computational linguists (corpus parsing, statistical measures of association, etc.), but the resulting set of distributional vectors is not a tool in and of itself. It is not immediately obvious, for instance, how to use it to improve the performance of syntactic parsers, semantic role labelers or sentiment polarity detectors. A DSM should rather be viewed as a portion of the lexicon containing semantic representations for (a considerable proportion of) the words in a language. Unlike definitions or subject-derived labels, these representations are intrinsically graded, thus ameanable to be processed by a range of mathematical techniques, depending on the specific task we want to use them for. Baroni and Lenci (2010), in particular, have shown how the very same set of distributional vectors can be exploited for a large variety of different lexical semantic tasks. A DSM, in this sense of a set of distributional vectors for the words of a language, is rather more like a concrete implementation of a feature-based theory of semantic representation, akin to the Generative Lexicon (Pustejovsky 1995) or Lexical Conceptual Structures (Jackendoff 1990). Unlike these theories, however, DSMs can be induced on a large scale from corpus data, which makes them both attractive from the acquisitional point of view and amenable to systematic evaluation on realistically sized data sets. DSMs, moreover, use hundreds of features (that is, vector components), and assign them (automatically induced) real-valued scores.[12]

A cautious view of DSMs is that they are a handy engineering surrogate of a semantic lexicon. Various considerations support, however, the bolder stance that DSMs *are* models of a significant part of meaning as it is encoded in human linguistic competence (see Lenci 2008, for related conjectures on the status of DSMs).[13]

First, these models are successful at simulating many aspects of human semantic performance, as briefly reviewed in Section 2.2 above.

Second, they achieve this performance using only large amounts of naturally occurring linguistic data as learning input, a kind of input

---

[12]This latter property makes them particularly well-suited to capture prototypicality effects (*penguins* are less "birdy" than *robins*) and more in general all the fuzzy, continuous aspects of lexical meaning that are intensively investigated by psychologists (Murphy 2002) but problematic for formal semantics approaches to the lexicon (Kamp and Partee 1995).

[13]We do not claim that distributional vectors are the *only* kind of semantic representations that people store in their heads, just one of possibly many aspects of meaning that might be stored in the semantic lexicon.

that human learners also receive in generous doses (although, admittedly, text corpora are very different sorts of linguistic data from those that children are exposed to when acquiring their native tongue, in terms of amount of data, order and presence of an associated external context).

Third, even those language acquisition theorists who stress the role of extra-linguistic cues (e.g., Bloom 2000) recognize that the vocabulary size that teenagers command by end of high-school (in the order of tens of thousands of words) can only be acquired by bootstrapping from linguistic data.[14] This bootstrapping is likely to take the form of distributional learning: We all have the experience of inferring the meaning of an unknown term encountered in a novel just from the context in which it occurs,[15] and there is psycholinguistic evidence that statistical patterns of co-occurrence influence subjects' intuitions about the meaning of nonce words just as they do in DSMs (McDonald and Ramscar 2001).[16]

Fourth and last, in neuroscience there is strong support for the view that concepts are represented in the brain as patterns of neural activation over broad areas (Haxby et al. 2001), and vectors are a natural way to encode such patterns (Huth et al. 2012); this suggests intriguing similarities between neural and distributional representations of meaning. Indeed, recent work in brain-computer interaction (Mitchell et al. 2008; Murphy et al. 2012) has shown that corpus-based distributional vectors are good predictors of the patterns of brain activation recorded in subjects thinking of a concept. This suggests, albeit in a very speculative way, that there might be a direct link between the distributional information encoded in DSMs and the way in which concepts are evoked in the brain.

Of course, we do not want to suggest that DSMs are models of

---

[14]Bloom and others emphasize the role of interaction and attention in language acquisition. Rather than providing extra cues to meaning, however, these cognitive functions help learners to focus on the most informative portions of the input stream. As such, they are compatible with distributional (as well as other forms of) learning.

[15]Humans often only require a single exposure to a word in context to learn its meaning, a phenomenon known as "fast mapping" (Carey and Bartlett 1978). We are not aware of studies systematically evaluating the quality of distributional vectors extracted from single occurrences of words (although there is no doubt that the distributional representation of words generally improves with more contexts).

[16]Chung-chieh Shan (personal communication) remarks that demonstrating that humans rely on contexts to learn meaning is not the same as demonstrating that meaning *is* given by a summary of these contexts, as they are embedded in distributional vectors. However, as Shan suggested to us, Occam's razor favors a semantic representation that is close to the distributional cues it derives from, until the latter is proven wrong empirically.

meaning *acquisition*. To name just one crucial difference, the sequence of texts used to form a context vector for a certain word is essentially random (corpora are not internally ordered), whereas the linguistic input that a child receives follows a fairly predictable progression both in form (cf. the "motherese" hypothesis; see for example Newport et al. 1977) and domains of conversation, which are also likely to affect the statistical properties of word associations (Hills 2013). However, we do endorse the view that distributional semantics *is* a theory of semantics, and that DSMs are an important part of the semantic component of an adult speaker's mental lexicon. In short, the claim is that a core aspect of the meaning of a word is given by (a function of) its distribution over the linguistic contexts (and possibly the non-linguistic ones, see next subsection) in which it occurs, encoded in a vector of real values that constitutes a feature-based semantic representation of the word.

2.5 The symbol grounding problem

Since DSMs represent the meaning of a symbol (a word) in terms of a set of other symbols (the words or other linguistic contexts it co-occurs with), they are subject to the lack-of-grounding criticism traditionally vented against symbolic models (Harnad 1990; from a philosophical perspective, the obvious reference is to the Chinese Room thought experiment of Searle 1980). If symbols are not grounded in the sensory-motor system and thus connected to the external world, they cannot really have "meaning". A good DSM might know about the linguistic contexts in which the word *daisy* occurs so well that it can fake human-like intuitions about which other words are most similar, or accurately predict which sentences could contain the word *daisy*. Still, since the DSM has never seen a daisy and so it has never experienced its color, its shape, etc., we might be reluctant to admit that the model truly "knows" the meaning of the word *daisy* (references for the grounding debate in relation to DSMs include Andrews et al. 2009; Burgess 2000; Glenberg and Robertson 2000; Louwerse 2011; Riordan and Jones 2011). It is indeed quite telling that DSMs have been applied with some success to the Voynich Manuscript, a 15th century text written in an unreadable script (Reddy and Knight 2011)—a case of 'semantic analysis' on a document of unknown content.

We believe that the current limitations of DSMs to *linguistic* contexts are more practical than theoretical. Indeed, by exploiting recent advances in image analysis, a new generation of DSMs integrates text data with visual features automatically extracted from pictures that co-occur with the target words, to attain a more perceptually grounded view of distributional word meaning (Bruni et al. 2011, 2012; Feng and

Lapata 2010; Leong and Mihalcea 2011; Silberer and Lapata 2012). With research continuing in this direction, DSMs might be the first symbolic semantic models (or even more generally the first fully implemented large-scale computational semantic models) to truly address the symbol grounding problem.

2.6 Meaning and reference

The symbol grounding challenge raised by philosophers and cognitive scientists pertains to the perceptual underpinnings of our generic knowledge of concepts (you need to have seen a dog to truly grasp the meaning of the word *dog*). The dominant tradition in formal semantics stresses instead another type of relation between linguistic signs and the external world, characterizing meaning in terms of reference to a specific state of the world, above and beyond our ability to perceive it. Knowing the meaning of the statement *Marco is a dog* is knowing under which outside-world conditions this statement would be true. To calculate this, standard *denotational semantics* takes as its primitives individuals (objects or events), truth values and propositions (possible worlds, states of affairs).

The focus of denotational semantics and DSMs is very different, and so are their strengths and weaknesses. In denotational semantics, proper names are the simple cases, those that directly point to individuals, unary predicates refer to sets of individuals having a certain property at a given time and world, binary ones refer to sets of ordered pairs of individuals, and so forth. In turn, quantifiers express relations between sets, modifiers typically reduce the size of sets, predicate conjunction intersects them, etc. (see, e.g., Heim and Kratzer 1998). This model of meaning has been designed to express *episodic knowledge*— facts that are true of specific individuals at specific places and times. Capturing the meaning of *generic sentences*—statements about laws, regularities or tendencies of whole classes of objects—requires a complex quantificational apparatus (Krifka et al. 1995; Cohen 2004) and is a widely debated but still ill-understood topic.

DSMs, on the other hand, are extracted from large corpora where proper names, common nouns and other predicates refer to states of the world and events spanning a large chunk of time and space, reflecting different points of view, etc. So, if they are able to extract any factual information at all, this is very likely to take the form of generic knowledge. Indeed, a typical application of corpus-based semantics is the extraction of commonsense-knowledge "factoids" that are generally useful while not universally true: bananas are yellow, birds fly, etc. (e.g., Eslick 2006; Schubert and Tong 2003). Statistical notions are simply not native to the formal semantics setup, but they are at the heart of the DSM approach. We will return to the issue of generic knowledge in Section 5.2 below. Two things should be noted here.

First, it is perfectly possible to give a reference-based interpretation of DSMs, the question is what it tells us.[17] Suppose we characterize the meaning of a word w in the corpus C in terms of its sentential context, expressed via a vector of *binary* values: for every word g, $\text{vector}_w(g) = 1$ if g appears along with w in some sentence in C, 0 otherwise. Suppose we now call S the set of all words for which vector_w gives 1, i.e. the set of all words that cooccur with w some sentence, and treat the lexicon L of C as our domain of reference. Now S, built as an approximation of the 'meaning of w' in a DSM, is at the same time the denotation in L of the expression *"the lexical sentential context of word w"* in denotational semantics. With some added complexity, it is straightforward to give a referential translation of vectors which do not contain just binary numbers, but any integer value. What this example shows is that the divide between DSM and denotational semantics is not reference/lack-of-reference, but rather reference to *linguistic strings* (which we can easily record) or to *objects* (which we cannot). The question becomes what the referential meaning of the noun phrase *the linguistic context of "dog"* can tell us about the referential meaning of *dog*. As we hope to show, quite a lot.

But now what about *the linguistic context of "John"*? How can DSMs deal with objects that are often described as being "purely referential", empty of descriptive content? (proper names, demonstratives, personal pronouns, etc.; Kripke 1980). We believe that in DSMs there is no *principled* distinction between proper names and common nouns, but there are very far-reaching *practical* ones. If we consider names like *Barack Obama* and bare nouns like *presidents*, the difference is small; both will appear in highly informative contexts; people will write contrasting things about *Barack Obama*, but so they will about *presidents* or just about any common noun. Jut like common nouns, proper names can be polysemous (*Italy lost to Spain*—the soccer team; *Italy is boot-shaped*— the land, etc.), and the same techniques mentioned above for common nouns can be used to make the right facets of meaning emerge in the proper combination. But moving on the scale of referential expressions from *Barack Obama* to *Obama*, then to *Barack*, to *that person*, to *him* (or *here*, *now*, any finite tense marker), the dimension of *homonymy* increases dramatically. Pure referential expressions are infinitely more

---

[17]Indeed, we recently became aware of the attempt of Copestake and Herbelot (2012) to provide an extensional semantics for DSMs along lines that are very similar to the ones we sketch here. See Section 6 for a brief review of their approach.

ambiguous than descriptive ones, and this causes a proliferation of apparent inconsistencies.

There are different strategies to cope with this problem. One is to abandon the attempt to distinguish one *John* from another and focus on what descriptive content remains to names and deictics, for instance the fact that *John* will appear in contexts suitable for an anglophone male human being. At the other end of the spectrum, one could preprocess the input corpus with a (cross-document) *anaphora resolution* system (Ng 2010; Poesio et al. 2010) to try to unify those names and deictics that are likely to be coreferential.[18]

At least for the time being, we will just treat denotational semantics and DSMs as covering complementary aspects of meaning. To exemplify, suppose we hear the sentence *A dog is barking*. Our distributional-feature-based representation of its constituents will provide us with a sketch of typical contexts in which it can be uttered truthfully, which can orient our perceptual system to pick up the relevant cues to determine if a dog is indeed barking right now, so that we can evaluate the referential meaning of the sentence. Indeed, to step into science fiction for a moment, given that state-of-the-art computational image analysis systems produce vectorial representations of objects (see, e.g., Grauman and Leibe 2011), the process of verifying the state of affairs described by an utterance against perceptual input could take the form of operations on distributional and perceptual vectors, the former representing the (parts of the) utterance, the second representing objects and possibly events in the perceived world. This idea gains further plausibility if we adopt distributional vectors that record perceptual information coming from vision and other senses, as briefly discussed at the end of the previous subsection.

Intriguingly, the view of the division of labour between DSMs and denotational semantics we just sketched is not too far from those interpretations of Frege's (1892) famous *sense* and *reference* distinction (e.g., Dummett 1981) that see the sense of a linguistic expression as the *manner* in which we determine the referent (this would be the job of its distributional representation), whereas the denotational meaning is the referent itself.

Bridging denotational and distributional semantics to account for the semantic interpretation of episodic statements is an exciting research program, but it is probably too early to pursue it. However,

---

[18] An exciting new development that might be useful for these purposes is that of distributional methods to *geo-locate* documents (Roller et al. 2012): The John Smith referred to in a document from Bakersfield is relatively unlikely to be the same John Smith mentioned in an article from Hyderabad.

there are many other aspects of semantics that can be captured independently of the ability to pick up reference from the current state of the world. We reviewed above the many lexical semantic tasks where DSMs representing single words have been very effective despite their lack of direct real-world referencing capabilities (spotting synonyms and other semantic relations, measuring verb-argument plausibility, etc.), and we will discuss in Section 5.2 below potential applications of non-real-world-referring DSMs to the semantics of phrases and sentences.

3 Composition by function application in distributional semantics

Given the success of distributional semantics in modeling the meaning of words (in isolation or in context), it is natural to ask whether this approach can be extended to account for the meaning of phrases and sentences as well. Some pursuers of distributional semantics think that the latter should be limited to modeling lexical meaning. We postpone to Section 5 below a discussion of our theoretical and practical motivations for constructing distributional representations of constituents above the word, since it will be easier to motivate phrasal/sentential distributional semantics after we have introduced (in this and the next section) how we intend to realize it and the current empirical support we have for our approach.

We suggested in the previous section that the (distributional) meaning of a word is a summary of the contexts in which the word can occur. We maintain a contextually-based meaning for phrases and sentences too. Since we typically use the other words in the same sentence as context for our lexical DSMs, many colleagues have asked us what we think the context for sentences should then be. There are many possibilities, and here are just a few: Since any sentence can be extended with adjuncts, coordinates, etc., the context of a sentence could be given by words that would naturally occur in its extensions. For *"the boy kissed the girl"*, context would include words occurring in *"the boy, being madly in love, passionately kissed the girl on her mouth in the park under the tree at midnight..."*. In alternatively or in addition, the sentence context could include words or fragments of the previous and following sentences. Another possibility for sentence contexts (in line with DSMs such as LSA and Topic Models) is that they are distributions over the possible documents in which a sentence is more or less likely to occur. Importantly, the approach to composition we will develop in this section allows us to postulate different distributional spaces for different types of linguistic expressions, since we are not

committed to the limiting view that word and sentence vectors must
live in the same contextual space (we return to this point in Section
3.4 below).

For both words and larger expressions, distributional semantics must
find ways to extract from finite evidence an estimate of how their distributional profile would look if we had an infinite corpus available.
For words, a large but finite corpus provides a sample of possible contexts of sufficient size to constitute a decent surrogate of infinity; for
most phrases and sentences, it does not (given that there is an infinite
number of possible phrases and sentences), and we need a different,
compositional strategy to come up with indirect estimates of their distributional profiles.

Building on what we originally proposed in Baroni and Zamparelli
(2010), we present an approach to compositional distributional semantics that relies on Frege's (1892) distinction between "complete" and
"incomplete" expressions. Specifically, we distinguish between words
whose meaning is directly determined by their distributional behaviour,
e.g. nouns, and words that act as functions transforming the distributional profile of other words (e.g., verbs). As discussed in Section 2, representations for the former can be directly induced from their patterns
of co-occurrence in a corpus. We add to this standard practice a new
view on the incomplete expressions and treat them as transformations,
the simplest case of which is a mapping between the corpus-derived
vector for a word to the corpus-derived vector for a larger constituent
that contains that word. While distributional vectors are extracted from
a corpus directly or are the result of a composition operation, distributional functions are induced from examples of their input and output representations, adopting regression techniques commonly used in
machine learning. Finally, like in formal semantics, we take syntactic
structure to constitute the backbone guiding the assembly of the semantic representations of phrases. In particular, following Montague
(e.g., Montague 1970b,a), we assume a categorial grammar and define
a correspondence between syntactic categories and *semantic types*. In
our case, the latter are the types of the semantic spaces where words
and other expressions live rather than their domain of denotation.

We first motivate the function-based approach comparing it to the
current mainstream "component mixture" view of composition in distributional semantics (Section 3.1). The idea of distributional functions is presented in Section 3.2. Section 3.3 provides mathematical
background for our concrete proposal concerning distributional functions, that is then introduced in Section 3.4. Section 3.5 describes how
distributional functions can be induced from corpus data. Section 3.6,

TABLE 2: Left: distributional vectors representing the words *dog, cat* and *old*. Center: adding the *old* vector to *dog* and *cat*, respectively, to derive *old dog* and *old cat* vectors. Right: The same derivations using component-wise multiplication.

	dog	cat	old	additive		multiplicative	
				old + dog	old + cat	old ⊙ dog	old ⊙ cat
runs	1	4	0	1	4	0	0
barks	5	0	7	12	7	35	0

finally, shows how our approach can be used together with a Categorial-Grammar-based syntactic analysis of sentences to account for the syntax and (distributional) semantics of an interesting fragment of English in parallel.

3.1   Composition by vector mixtures

Mitchell and Lapata (2010), in what is probably the most influential paper on the topic (see also Mitchell and Lapata 2008, 2009) have proposed two broad classes of composition models focusing on important special cases for each of the classes. These special cases are the additive and multiplicative models we discuss next.

If each word is represented by a vector, the most obvious way to "compose" two or more vectors is by summing them (that is, adding the values in each of their components), as illustrated by the center columns of Table 2. Indeed, this *additive* approach was also the most common one in the early literature on composition in distributional semantics (Foltz et al. 1998; Kintsch 2001; Landauer and Dumais 1997).

The other model studied in depth by Mitchell and Lapata adopts instead a *multiplicative* approach. The latter is exemplified by the rightmost columns of Table 2, in which the values in the components of the input vectors are multiplied to derive the composed representation.[19]

The components of additive vectors inherit the cumulative score mass from the corresponding input components, so if an input vector has a high value in a component, the same high value will appear in the composed vector, even if the same component was low or 0 in the other input vector(s): For example, **old+cat** inherits a relatively high *barks* score from **old**. Multiplication, on the other hand, captures the interaction between the values in the input components. For example, since **cat** has a 0 *barks* value, **old** ⊙ **cat** has 0 for this component

---

[19]Following Mitchell and Lapata, we use the ⊙ symbol for component-wise multiplication, since the standard product symbol ($\times$) is used in linear algebra for matrix multiplication, an operation that is not even defined for the pairs of column vectors in Table 2.

irrespective of **old**. When both input vectors have high values on a component, the composed vector will get a very high value out of their product, as illustrated for the second **old** ⊙ **dog** component in the table. Mitchell and Lapata characterize these interaction properties of the multiplicative model as a quantitative form of "feature intersection".

In these two models, the input vectors are perfectly symmetric: They contribute to the composed expression in the same way. However, linguistic intuition would suggest that the composition operation is asymmetric. For instance, in the composition of an adjective and a noun, the adjective modifies the noun that constitutes the head of the resulting phrase (an *old dog* is still a *dog*). The effect of syntactic constituency on composition is partially addressed by Mitchell and Lapata's *weighted additive model*, where the vectors are multiplied by different *scalar* values before summing.[20] For example, in an adjective-noun construction we might want the meaning of the noun head to have a stronger impact than that of the adjective modifier. We can then multiply the adjective vector by, say, 0.2 and the nominal one by 0.8 before summing them. In the example from Table 2, $(0.2 \times \mathbf{old}) + (0.8 \times \mathbf{dog}) = (0.8, 5.4)$, a vector that is considerably closer to **dog** than to **old**. Assigning different weights to vectors before summing can also address, to a certain extent, the problem that both addition and multiplication are commutative $(a + b = b + a; a \times b = b \times a)$, and they thus produce the same vector for, say, *dog trainer* and *trainer dog*, or *dogs chase cats* and *cats chase dogs*.[21]

Mitchell and Lapata show that the multiplicative and weighted additive models perform quite well in the task of predicting human similarity judgments about adjective-noun, noun-noun, verb-noun (Mitchell and Lapata 2010) and noun-verb (Mitchell and Lapata 2008) phrases.[22] They also show that these simpler models (that we will call, henceforth, the *ML models*) outperform approaches involving more sophisticated composition operations from the earlier literature, such as tensor products (Smolensky 1990; Clark and Pulman 2007).

---

[20] In linear algebra, single numbers such as 31 or 0.212 are referred to as scalars, to keep them apart from vectors and other multiple-component numerical structures.

[21] It can be shown that, as long as we use the cosine as similarity measure (see Section 2 above), the multiplicative model will not be affected by scalar weights. The effect of multiplying one or both vectors by a scalar before applying the component-wise product is that the resulting composed vector will change its length while pointing in the same direction. Thus, the (cosine of the) angle of the composed vector with any other vector will stay the same.

[22] The other successful model of Mitchell and Lapata (2010), namely the *dilation* model, can be seen as a special way to estimate the weights of the weighted additive model, and we consider it as a special case of the latter here.

Other studies have confirmed that the ML methods, in particular the multiplicative model, are very competitive in various composition tasks that involve simple phrases and do not test for word order or different syntactic structures (Erk and Padó 2008; Grefenstette and Sadrzadeh 2011a; Vecchi et al. 2011; Boleda et al. 2012b). Interestingly and surprisingly, Blacoe and Lapata (2012) recently found that the ML models reach performance close to the one of knowledge-intensive state-of-the-art systems on a full-sentence paraphrasing task. Given the weaknesses of the models we will present below, we can only conjecture that the sentences in this data set fail to test for some crucial syntactic aspects of language (a suspicion that is strengthened by the fact that Blacoe and Lapata obtain excellent results with versions of the additive and multiplicative models that ignore, if we understand correctly, all function words – determiners, negation, etc. – in the test sentences). The ML models are also very well-suited (and empirically effective) for tasks that we will not consider here under the rubric of compositionality but which do involve looking at sentences and larger passages, such as measuring textual coherence (Foltz et al. 1998) or predicting the next word that will be uttered (Mitchell and Lapata 2009). Besides their good empirical performance, the ML models are extremely easy to implement, which makes them, undoubtedly, the best current choice for practical applications.

Criticism of vector-mixture models

There are principled reasons, however, to believe that the ML models can only account for the simple phrases made of *content* words (nouns, verbs, adjectives) that they have been generally tested on, and that they will not scale up to represent the meanings of sentences, or even sub-sentential constituents with more complex internal structure.

One important limitation stems from the fact that both additive and multiplicative models take as input corpus-harvested distributional vectors representing the individual words that form a larger constituent, and produce a *mixture* of these vectors to represent the constituent.[23] The meaning of the phrase *old cat* might indeed be seen as a mixture of the features of *old* things and *cats*. Consider however a determiner phrase (DP) such as *some cat*: The mixture view is suddenly a lot less appealing. First, we face the empirical problem of extracting a

---

[23]Instead of mixtures, we could also speak of averages, since the ML models represent phrases as (functions of) averages of the vectors that compose them. The result of (weighted) addition is a vector pointing in the same direction as the (weighted) arithmetic average of the input vectors. The components in the vector resulting from component-wise multiplication are squares of the geometric average of the values in the corresponding components of the input vectors.

distributional vector for a *grammatical* word such as *some*.[24] Unlike the content word *cat*, *some* occurs all over the place in the corpus, without being associated to any specific domain or topic. It is unlikely that the corpus-based vector of *some* will provide meaningful distributional information about this word (and information that distinguishes it from other grammatical words such as *the*, *not* or *to*).[25] Even ignoring this issue, it is highly counter-intuitive to think of the features of *some cat* as a mixture of the features of "*some*" things and of the features of *cats*. Rather, as we will argue below, the role played by *some* and *cat* in composition is deeply asymmetric, with *some* acting like a function operating on the features of *cat*.[26]

The mixture models are moreover unable to capture the radical structural differences that depend on the choice of words in a phrase. Compare for example *lice on dogs* with *lice and dogs*. For the ML models, the two phrases only differ in that one contains *on*-vector-specific component values that are replaced by *and*-specific features in the other, in both cases mixed in the same way with the same *lice* and *dogs* vector components. This completely misses the fact that the two grammatical words reflect different semantic structures, with *on dogs* operating as a modifier of *lice* in the first, while *and* conjoins *lice* and *dogs* in the second. The ML models have no way to capture the different functional nature of words such as *on* (taking a DP to return a locative nominal modifier) or *and* (in this case, taking two DPs and returning a third one representing their conjunction).

Yet another reason to reject additive and especially multiplicative

---

[24]It might be tempting to get away from the thorny issue of representing grammatical words in distributional semantics by simply ignoring them. Indeed, the items in the Mitchell and Lapata (2008, 2010) and Grefenstette and Sadrzadeh (2011a) test sets we will partially introduce in Section 4 only contain content words: To tackle these tests, we are asked to model sentences and phrases such as *table shows results* or *lift hand*, rather than their more natural determiner-enhanced counterparts. This is convenient in the current early stages of compositional modeling, but eventually, even to capture similarity judgments about simple phrases, we will need to take grammatical words into account. For example, to model the intuition that *exterminating rats* is more similar to *killing many/all rats* than to *killing few rats*, you need to include the relevant quantifying determiners in the distributional representations you compare.

[25]If context is extracted from very narrow windows, the distributional vectors of function words might provide some useful information about their syntactic, rather than semantic, properties.

[26]The problem already arises with composition of certain content words, for example so-called "intensional" adjectives such as *former* (Kamp 1975): A *former owner* is not somebody with a mixture of properties of *former* things and *owners*. See Boleda et al. (2012b), shortly reviewed in Section 4.3 below, for an account of intensional adjectives in compositional distributional semantics.

models of composition comes from *recursion*, a crucial property of natural language. One of its consequences is that there is no fixed limit to the number of modifiers. Consider the expressions *cat, Siamese, spayed, toilette-trained* and *short-haired*. In a DSM, they are all likely to have high values for the component corresponding to *pet*. But now, if we mixed their vectors to build a *nice toilette-trained spayed short-haired Siamese cat*, the resulting value for the *pet* component will be astounding, dwarfing any component whose value is high just because it is high in *one* of these expressions.[27]

The problems arising in phrases of just a few words will compound when representing sentences, that are formed by combining these phrases. We just cannot see how, by combining with addition or multiplication the vectors of the words in *"many dogs and some cats have big lice on the back"* we could come up with a meaningful representation for this sentence.

3.2 Composition with distributional functions

To overcome the *a priori* limitations of the additive and multiplicative models, we adopt the view from formal semantics that composition is largely a matter of function application. We thus propose that the distributional meaning of certain words (and certain larger expressions) is not encoded in vectors, but in *distributional functions* that take distributional vectors (or other linear algebraic objects, as we will see) as input and return other vectors (or other objects) as output by operating on the input components. Nouns, DPs and sentences are still represented as vectors, but adjectives, verbs, determiners, prepositions, conjunctions and so forth are all modeled by distributional functions. An approximate geometric intuition for the difference between a mixture and a functional approach is given in Figure 2.[28]

Under the functional approach, we no longer treat grammatical words such as *many* and *some* as highly problematic corpus-harvested distributional vectors to be mixed with content word vectors, but rather as functions from and onto representations of phrases that also include content elements (e.g., from *dogs* to *some dogs*).

---

[27] On the other hand, this effect might be used to capture the Conjunction Fallacy (Tversky and Kahneman 1983). People might find it more probable that the concept of *pet* is instantiated by a *nice toilette-trained spayed short-haired Siamese cat* than by just a *cat*, despite the fact that the former is a subset of the latter. If what we are after is modeling human judgment, we should strive to preserve a small amount of the effect given by multiplicative models also in our functional approach to distributional semantics.

[28] The figure only illustrates the simple case of functions operating on vectors and generating outputs that live in the same semantic space of the inputs.

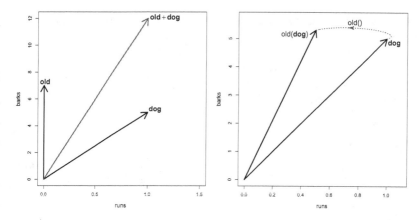

FIGURE 2: Mixture-based composition, such as the additive model illustrated in the left panel, takes distributional vectors representing two words and "mixes" them (e.g., adds their components) to obtain the representation of a phrase. In a function-based model, such as the one illustrated on the right, one of the two words is not a vector, but a function exerting an action on the argument vector to move it to a new position in semantic space.

Moreover, different grammatical words impose different compositional structures on phrases. Coming back to the *lice on dogs* vs. *lice and dogs* example, we would model *on* as a function from DPs onto distributional functions that, in turn, act as modifiers of nominal vectors: $(\mathcal{ON}(\mathbf{dogs}))(\mathbf{lice})$; whereas *and* could be an unary function from a pair of DP vectors onto one representing their conjunction: $\mathcal{AND}(\mathbf{lice}, \mathbf{dogs})$.[29]

The asymmetry between a noun modified by a prepositional phrase and a conjunction of DPs is seamlessly captured.

Anybody familiar with the classic treatment of compositionality in formal semantics will agree that the functional approach is more promising than vector-mixture methods. However, we must now spell out what it means, in concrete, to apply a function to a vector, and how we can come up with (i.e., in the jargon of machine learning, "learn") distributional functions that perform just the operations we want on their inputs. Before we discuss these issues, we introduce the relevant concepts from linear algebra.

---

[29]More precisely, in our approach we "curry" *and* into a unary function from DPs onto functions from other DPs onto the conjoined form.

3.3 Linear transformations, matrix-by-vector products and tensors

The class of functions on vectors known as *linear transformations* or *linear maps* plays a fundamental role in linear algebra, the branch of mathematics that studies the algebra of vectors (e.g., Axler 1997; Meyer 2000; Strang 2003). When looking for an equivalent to compositional function application in the vector-based distributional framework, it is thus natural to start with the hypothesis that the relevant functions are linear transformations. A linear transformation takes a vector of size J and returns a vector of size I (where J might equal I), where each output component is a linear combination of all input components, that is, each output component is a weighted sum of the input components.[30]

There is an important correspondence between linear transformations and matrices (we introduce matrices in the next paragraph). Recall from Section 2 above that the N-dimensional vector space is the set of all possible vectors of size N.[31] Given the J- and I-dimensional vector spaces, any linear transformation from the first onto the second is entirely characterized by a matrix of shape $I \times J$. The application of the corresponding linear transformation is given by the product of the matrix by an input vector from the J-dimensional space.

A *matrix* of *shape* $I \times J$ is an array of numbers whose components (or *cells*) are indexed by two integers i, ranging from 1 to I, and j, ranging from 1 to J.[32] An $I \times J$ matrix is naturally thought of as a rectangular

---

[30]The defining characteristics of a linear transformation are that (i) the linear transformation of the sum of two vectors must equal the sum of the linear transformations of the two vectors ($f(\mathbf{a} + \mathbf{b}) = f(\mathbf{a}) + f(\mathbf{b})$), and that (ii) the linear transformation of a vector multiplied by a scalar equals the product of the scalar by the linear transformation of the vector ($f(k\mathbf{a}) = kf(\mathbf{a})$). As a consequence of this latter property, if vectors are parallel in the input space, their linear transformations will stay parallel in the output space, since multiplying a vector by a scalar changes its length but not its direction.

[31]In this section, given the emphasis on vector algebra, we ignore the association of components to linguistic labels in distributional semantic spaces.

[32]We prefer the non-standard term *shape* to the more commonly used *size* to stress the fact that matrices and the other multi-index objects we will introduce next are not only characterized by the number of components they have, but also by how the latter are arranged according to their indices. Consider for example a 2×3 matrix. By interpreting the product symbol the usual way, we can correctly state that it is an object of size 2×3, in the sense that it has $2 \times 3 = 6$ components; but, using the term *shape*, we want to emphasize that the 6 components are arranged into a 2-by-3 array. When we say that two linear algebraic objects have the same shape, we mean that the objects have the same number of indices (below, we will call this quantity the *order* of the objects), *and* their indices have the same size (obviously, by "size of the index I" we mean I itself: the size of the first index of a 2×3 matrix is 2). A 2×3 matrix has a different shape from a 3×2 matrix,

object with I rows and J columns. When we multiply an $I \times J$ matrix by a vector of size J, we obtain a vector of size I whose i-th component is a weighted sum of all J input components, each multiplied by the value in the ij-th cell of the matrix. In mathematical notation, given a matrix $\mathbf{M}$ of shape $I \times J$ and a vector $\mathbf{v}$ of size J, each component w_i of the I-sized vector $\mathbf{w}$ resulting from the product $\mathbf{w} = \mathbf{M} \times \mathbf{v}$ is given by:

$$w_i = \sum_{j=1}^{j=J} M_{ij} \times v_j$$

For example, the following 3×2 matrix $\mathbf{M}$ encodes a linear transformation from the 2- onto the 3-dimensional space.

$$\mathbf{M} = \begin{pmatrix} 1 & 5 \\ 1 & 2 \\ 4 & 0 \end{pmatrix}$$

Let us apply the linear transformation encoded in $\mathbf{M}$ to the 2 component vector $\mathbf{v}$:

$$\mathbf{v} = \begin{pmatrix} 3.1 \\ 1 \end{pmatrix}$$

We obtain the 3 component vector $\mathbf{w}$ as illustrated in the following equation:

$$\mathbf{w} = \mathbf{M} \times \mathbf{v} = \begin{pmatrix} 1 & 5 \\ 1 & 2 \\ 4 & 0 \end{pmatrix} \times \begin{pmatrix} 3.1 \\ 1 \end{pmatrix} = \begin{pmatrix} 1 \times 3.1 + 5 \times 1 \\ 1 \times 3.1 + 2 \times 1 \\ 4 \times 3.1 + 0 \times 1 \end{pmatrix} = \begin{pmatrix} 8.1 \\ 5.1 \\ 12.4 \end{pmatrix}$$

Note how, for example, $w_1 = 8.1$ is given by the sum of the $\mathbf{v}$ components weighted by the 1st row of $\mathbf{M}$ ($v_1 = 3.1$ is multiplied by the value in the $(1,1)$-th cell of $\mathbf{M}$, that is, $M_{1,1} = 1$; $v_2 = 1$ by that in the $(1,2)$-th cell, that is, $M_{1,2} = 5$).

The notion of linear transformations extends to arrays with more than two indices, that in linear algebra are called tensors. A *tensor*, more precisely, is any numerical array $\mathcal{T}$ whose values are indexed by n indices (i.e., any object of shape $I_1 \times \ldots \times I_n$). The number of indices of a tensor is called the *order* of the tensor. A vector is a first-order tensor (components are addressed via a single index), matrices are second-order tensors (one index for the rows, one for the columns), the $I \times J \times K$ object mapping vectors to matrices we are about to discuss is a third-order tensor, and so on. In this article, depending on the context,

---

despite the fact that they have the same size (6 components) and number of indices (2 indices). Their indices, however, have different sizes (the first indices have sizes 2 and 3, the second indices sizes 3 and 2, respectively). Note that a vector with I components is, trivially, both an I-sized and an I-shaped object.

we might use the term tensor to refer to any indexed number array (including vectors and matrices), or, when contrasted with the vectors or matrices, to objects of order larger than second (the latter are also referred to as higher-order tensors).[33]

Coming back to linear transformations and how they extend to general tensors, suppose for example that we want to map from K-sized vectors onto $I \times J$-shaped matrices (since we just saw that matrices encode linear transformations, this is our equivalent of a function that returns a function). Again, each ij-indexed component of the output matrix will derive from a weighted sum of all K input vector components. A tensor $\mathcal{T}$ with shape $(I \times J) \times K$ stores the lists of K weights needed to derive each ij-th component, and the mapping is performed by the product of $\mathcal{T}$ with the input vector.[34] Similarly, if we want to map from $K \times L$ onto $I \times J$ matrices, the mapping tensor $\mathcal{T}$ will have shape $(I \times J) \times (K \times L)$, and the mapping will be performed by the product of $\mathcal{T}$ with the input matrix. In this case, the $ijkl$-th component of $\mathcal{T}$ will contain the weight that the kl-th cell of the input matrix must be multiplied by when computing the weighted sum of all input cells that generates the ij-th output cell. We refer to the product operation needed to map from and onto objects other than vectors as *generalized matrix-by-vector product*[35] (vanilla matrix-by-vector multiplication is

---

[33] Again, please pay attention to the terminology: The *size* of an index I is I; the *size* of a tensor is the total number of components it contains, that is, the product of the sizes of its indices; the *order* of a tensor is the number of indices used to arrange its cells; the *shape* of a tensor refers to both the number of indices and their respective sizes.

[34] Here and below, we add parentheses to the index structure of higher-order tensors, in order to emphasize their functional role. We might denote the shape of the same $I \times J \times K$ tensor with $(I \times J) \times K$ if we intend to use it to map from K-sized vectors onto $I \times J$ matrices (as in the main text), or with $I \times (J \times K)$ if we use it to map from $J \times K$ matrices onto I-sized vectors.

[35] We use this term to underline the fact that the general product operation we assume here is equivalent to unfolding both the input and the output tensors into vectors, applying standard matrix-by-vector multiplication, and then re-indexing the components of the output to give it the appropriate shape. For example, to multiply a $(I \times J) \times (K \times L)$ fourth-order tensor by a $K \times L$ matrix, we treat the first as a matrix with $I \times J$ rows and $K \times L$ columns and the second as a vector with $K \times L$ components (e.g., a $(2 \times 3) \times (3 \times 3)$ tensor can be multiplied with a (3×3) matrix by treating the latter as a 9 component vector and the former as a 6×9 matrix). We perform matrix-by-vector multiplication and then rearrange the resulting $I \times J$-sized vector into a matrix of shape $I \times J$ (continuing the example, the values in the 6 component output vector are re-arranged into a 2×3 matrix). This is a straightforward way to apply linear transformations to tensors (indeed, there is a precise sense in which all tensors with the same shape constitute a "vector" space). There are alternative ways to multiply tensors of various orders (including standard matrix-by-matrix multiplication) that are not relevant for our current

of course a special case of the generalized product).

The formula to compute each output component in generalized matrix-by-vector multiplication is as follows. Given input $\mathcal{V}$ with shape $J_1 \times \ldots \times J_n$ and components denoted by $V_{j_1\ldots j_n}$, and a linear transformation encoded in a tensor $\mathcal{M}$ with shape $(I_1 \times \ldots \times I_m) \times (J_1 \times \ldots \times J_n)$ and components denoted by $M_{i_1\ldots i_m j_1 \ldots j_n}$, each component $W_{i_1\ldots i_m}$ of the output tensor $\mathcal{W}$ (of shape $I_1 \times \ldots \times I_m$) is given by a weighted sum of all input components as follows:

$$W_{i_1\ldots i_m} = \sum_{j_1=1}^{j_1=J_1} \ldots \sum_{j_n=1}^{j_n=J_n} M_{i_1\ldots i_m j_1 \ldots j_n} V_{j_1\ldots j_n}$$

We conclude this brief survey of the linear algebra behind our approach by pointing out that there exists an operation of *tensor transposition* that, in the restricted version we need here,[36] swaps the last two indices of a tensor. Specifically, in the third-order case, each component of the transposed tensor $\mathcal{T}^T$ is given by: $T_{ijk}^T = T_{ikj}$. A useful property of transposition is that

$$(\mathcal{T} \times \mathbf{v}) \times \mathbf{w} = (\mathcal{T}^T \times \mathbf{w}) \times \mathbf{v}$$

That is, the result of multiplying a third-order tensor (in the generalized matrix-by-vector product sense) by one vector, and then the resulting matrix by another vector is the same as that of multiplying the tensor transpose by the two vectors in the opposite order. We will see a linguistic application of this property in Section 3.6 below.

3.4 Distributional functions as linear transformations

We propose that distributional functions are linear transformations on semantic vector (or more generally tensor) spaces. First-order one-argument distributional functions (such as adjectives or intransitive verbs) are encoded in matrices. The application of a first-order function to an argument is carried out via matrix-by-vector multiplication as follows:

$$f(a) =_{def} \mathbf{F} \times \mathbf{a} = \mathbf{b}$$

where $\mathbf{F}$ is the matrix encoding function f as a linear transformation, $\mathbf{a}$ is the vector denoting the argument a and $\mathbf{b}$ is the vector output to the composition process.

Let us take as an example the composition of an adjective with a noun. Let us assume, as we have done above, that nouns live in a 2-dimensional space. Hence the adjective, as a function from nouns to

---

purposes (Bader and Kolda 2006; Kolda and Bader 2009).

[36] See Bader and Kolda (2006, Section 3.3) for a more general and detailed discussion of various properties of tensors including transpositions.

TABLE 3: The adjective *old* as the distributional function encoded in the matrix on the left. The function is applied to the noun *dog* via matrix-by-vector multiplication to obtain a compositional distributional representation of *old dog* (right).

OLD	runs	barks			dog			OLD(dog)
runs	0.5	0	$\times$	runs	1	$=$	runs	$(0.5 \times 1) + (0 \times 5)$ $= 0.5$
barks	0.3	1		barks	5		barks	$(0.3 \times 1) + (5 \times 1)$ $= 5.3$

nouns, is a 2×2 matrix (it multiplies with a 2 component vector to return another 2 component vector). Suppose that *old* is associated to the toy matrix on the left of Table 3. Then, applying it to the usual *dog* vector returns the vector for *old dog* shown on the right of the same table.

The matrix labels illustrate the role played by each cell of the distributional function matrix in mapping from the input to the output vector: Namely, the ij-th cell contains the quantity determining how much the component corresponding to the j-th input context element contributes to the value assigned to the i-th context element in the output vector. For example, the first cell of the second row in the toy **OLD** matrix indicates that the *runs*-labeled component of the input noun will contribute 30% of its value to the *barks*-labeled component of the *old N* output.

In the case of *old*, we can imagine the adjective having a relatively small effect on the modified noun, not moving its vector too far from its original location (an *old dog* is still a *barking* creature). This will be reflected in a matrix that has values close to 1 on the diagonal cells (the ones whose weights govern the mapping between the same input and output components), and values close to 0 in the other cells (reflecting little "interference" from other features). On the other hand, an adjective such as *dead* that alters the nature of the noun it modifies more radically could have 0 or even negative values on the diagonal, and large negative or positive values in many non-diagonal cells, reflecting the stronger effect it has on the noun.

Table 3 also illustrates an important point about matrices and higher-order tensors when they are used as distributional functions. In Section 2, we remarked that a distributional semantic space is characterized not only by its mathematical properties. The linguistic tags associated to the components also matter. Similarly, when looking at matrices and tensors from the distributional point of view, the sets of labels associated to their cells also matter. Table 3 contains a 2×2 matrix with the same labels for rows and columns (this is not necessary: it happens here because adjectives, as we have already stated, map nouns onto the same nominal space), and where the first cell, for example, weights the mapping from and onto the *runs*-labeled components of the input and output vectors. A mathematically identical matrix where the first cell maps, say, from *banana* to *sympathy* components is a very different linguistic object. Just like for vectors, we can meaningfully speak of tensor spaces. Just like for vectors (that are of course a special case), a *distributional tensor space* is the space of all possible tensors with the same shape *and with the same associations of index elements to linguistic content labels* (that, ultimately, reflect information about possible context distributions).[37]

Different matrices can act differently on the same vectors, but also the same matrix can act differently on different vectors. Since a linear distributional function derives each component of the output vector by combining a set of input components with different weights, there is a lot of room for modeling varied semantic effects. Consider for example the case of *some* (that, in this paper for sake of simplicity, we assume to be a function taking a noun and returning a determiner phrase). *Some* should have a different effect depending on whether it is applied to a mass (*some coffee*) or count (*some cats*) noun. Consider another toy example where, for explanatory reasons, we promoted nouns from 2 to 3 components (with labels NMass, NCount1 and NCount2), and DPs are vectors with 4 components (DPOther, DPObj1, DPObj2, DP-Subst). Suppose moreover that mass nouns tend to have high values in the first component (NMass) and count nouns in the second and third (NCount1, NCount2). Similarly, say that the quantifying characteristics of a DP that would be relevant to a substance are expressed in the fourth component (DPSubst), whereas those that are relevant to countable objects are captured by the second and third components, DPObj1 and DPObj2 (with the first component, DPOther, expressing other properties). Then, *some* could be a matrix with the following form:

SOME	NMass	NCount1	NCount2
DPOther	1	1	0
DPObj1	0	3	2
DPObj2	0	2	3
DPSubst	5	0	0

---

[37]When we say that a component (or cell) of a tensor is associated to a (set of) linguistic label(s), we mean, more precisely, that the index element or set of index elements needed to uniquely address that component are associated to the label(s).

When the distributional *some* function is applied to a noun, that is, the **SOME** matrix is multiplied by the noun vector, the value in the first component of the resulting DP is determined, with equal weights, by both a mass and a count component of the input noun (since NMass and NCount1 have the same value and NCount2 is 0), reflecting the fact that this component expresses properties that are unrelated to the count/mass distinction. The second and third components of the DP (containing information about quantity characteristics of countable objects) will depend on the second and third components of the noun, that are high in count nouns only, with a strong positive dependence between the input and output components (the input values are multiplied by weights higher than 1 before summing them). The fourth component of the DP, encoding quantification information pertaining to substances, is just (positively) affected by the first component of the noun vector, the one that is high in mass nouns only.

This toy example should give an idea of the flexibility of the linear approach. With realistically sized vectors and matrices, it is possible to capture many more patterns, and in a more granular way (for example, including negative weights to capture inverse correlations between input and output components, and encoding semantic properties such as substance and objecthood as a distribution over a large set of input and output components, rather than just one or two).[38] Indeed, it is the flexibility given by the wealth of information that can be encoded in large matrices that makes us hopeful that the linear approach will be able to handle the regular polysemy phenomena we discussed in the introduction and in Section 2.3. Probably not by chance, in Baroni and Zamparelli (2010), we found that some of the adjectives that are best modeled by the linear approach are very polysemous terms such as *new*, *great* or *large*.

Before we move on to discuss various aspects of the linear-transformation-based composition framework, we will highlight two properties of the operation employed to perform linear transformations, namely (generalized) matrix-by-vector products, that have important consequences for how we use them in the linguistic composition framework.

First, generalized matrix-by-vector multiplication is only defined when the last indices of the first term have the same shape as the

---

[38]Speaking of flexibility, note that the multiplicative model is a special case of linear transformation where the matrix has as diagonal elements the components of a corpus-derived vector for one of the words in the phrase and 0s elsewhere. This matrix is then multiplied by the vector representing the other word. It is a bit more involved but also possible to encode the additive model as matrix-by-vector multiplication.

second term. For example, you cannot multiply an $I \times I$ matrix by a J component vector, or by an $I \times J \times K$ tensor.[39] This resonates with types in formal semantics, where you cannot apply, say, an $e \to t$ function to any argument but those of type e, a point we will return to multiple times below.

Second, the generalized matrix-by-vector product, unlike the product of scalars, is not commutative. For example, $\mathbf{OLD} \times \mathbf{FAST} \times \mathbf{car} \neq \mathbf{FAST} \times \mathbf{OLD} \times \mathbf{car}$, and $\mathcal{CHASE} \times \mathbf{cats} \times \mathbf{dogs} \neq \mathcal{CHASE} \times \mathbf{dogs} \times \mathbf{cats}$, in accordance with our linguistic expectations about the corresponding constructions.[40]

Mapping between different distributional semantic spaces

The toy **SOME** matrix we just discussed highlights another important novelty with respect to the ML mixture models. Addition and multiplication will create composed vectors that must live in the same vector space as their inputs. On the other hand, linear transformations can map onto different spaces from those of their domains. For example, **SOME** maps nominal vectors living in a 3-dimensional space to DP vectors that live in a 4-dimensional space, where the two spaces also differ in terms of the linguistic labels associated with the components. Linear transformations do not *need* to map vectors to an output space that differs from their domain (unlike earlier methods based on tensor operations where each composition step resulted in tensors of higher orders: see Mitchell and Lapata 2010 for discussion). For example, we have already seen that the **OLD** matrix in Table 3 above maps nouns onto adjective-noun phrase vectors that live in the same space, in accordance with the standard analysis of (attributive) adjectives as modifiers that take nouns as input and return other nouns as output.[41] However, in other cases the possibility of defining different distributional semantic spaces for different constituents gives us further flexibility for

---

[39] At least, you cannot do it using the generalized matrix-by-vector product operation we defined in Section 3.3.

[40] Treating nominal conjunctions as third order tensors, we predict inequalities of the sort: $\mathcal{AND} \times \mathbf{cats} \times \mathbf{dogs} \neq \mathcal{AND} \times \mathbf{dogs} \times \mathbf{cats}$ that are not intuitive from a truth-theoretical point of view. It remains to be seen if they are justifiable in a distributional perspective.

[41] Indeed, this property of attributive adjectives make them an ideal illustration of an important property of language, recursivity. Since the application of an adjective to a noun gives a result in the same space as the original noun, the operation can be easily repeated an indefinite number of times. That is, if we have matrices representing *large*, *old* and *brown* separately, we can easily apply them in sequence to generate a meaning for *"large old brown dog"* (however, see footnote 42 for an alternative). Ongoing work aims to uncover the semantic effects of various deviant adjectival sequences (e.g., contradictions like *"old young dog"* and redundancies such as *"brown brown dog"*).

encoding contextual information into features that are rich enough to capture different nuances of meaning. For example, nouns might live in a semantic space characterized by features (that is, linguistic labels associated to specific components) that are content words connected to the target nouns by interesting syntactic relations (along the lines of Curran and Moens 2002a, and many others), whereas sentences might be vectors living in a space of topics of conversation, à la Griffiths et al. (2007), or even in a space characterized by more abstract contextual cues to discourse structure and such (see the beginning of Section 3 above for some conjectures about the nature of sentence space).

Of course, if different spaces have to be handcrafted to suit the needs of different categories we would run against the objection that any semantic effects uncovered using them might be due to our specific choice of vector dimensions. Even with the best intentions, the selection of the ideal features for each space might be problematic, especially if spaces begin to multiply.[42] To address this potential criticism, we ultimately envision a fully automated labeled-component selection system. The general idea is that we should initially prepare a single huge semantic space whose components are associated with linguistic features at many different levels (lexical, categorial, syntactic-structural features, information-structural, topical, etc.), then extract the n features that are most informative in the representation of the various linguistic structures that we regard as non-functional (minimally Ns, DPs and S), e.g., features whose associated components exhibit the highest within-category variance.[43] These components and associated

---

[42] A case in point is that of recursive structures, which we just discussed in the context of adjectival modification. According to some authors, complements are the only truly recursive cases in languages, modifiers are not. In this view (see Cinque 2002, Cinque 2010, Scott 2002 and most representatives of the 'cartographic' approach to syntax), adjectives and adverbs follow a natural ordering, e.g., SIZE > COLOR > SHAPE, and there is a finite sequence of types of modifiers available for each noun. This view could be easily (if laboriously) accommodated within the present framework by assuming that in, say, *"large blue car"* the COLOR adjective *blue* does not project *car* back into its original noun-space, but into a slightly different space which is that of nouns-plus-COLOR-information. In turn, *large* would map elements from the nouns-plus-COLOR-information to the nouns-plus-COLOR-and-SIZE-information space, and so forth. This entails that *large* could not be directly applied to *car*; rather, one would have to first apply an invisible mapping from *car* to *car-with-unspecified-color* (to move the input to the correct space), then apply *large* to it. The oddness of applying multiple adjectives in the wrong order (*"red large car"*) would be the effect of applying a function to an input in the wrong space. It is an open question whether this additional complexity is justified. What matters here is that it would pose no special theoretical problems to our approach.

[43] Needless to say, the initial computation to calculate the most informative features for each primitive category will be humongous. But it needs to be carried out

features will then characterize the space where the distributional meanings of the individual expressions in each non-functional category reside (the labels of components of higher-order tensors are, deterministically, those of their input and output categories).

Modeling functions operating on functions

In Section 3.3 we showed how linear transformations by matrix-by-vector multiplication can be generalized to structures with an arbitrary number of indices. This is fundamental for their use in semantics, where functions must manipulate other functions both as input and as output. Let us start with an example of the second case. If nouns are I component vectors, DPs J component vectors and we adopt the standard analysis of a preposition such as *on* (in a noun-modifying context) as taking an input DP to return an adjective-like function that takes and returns a noun, in distributional terms we will treat *on* as an $(I \times I) \times J$ tensor. When this object is multiplied by a J-sized DP vector, it returns an $I \times I$ matrix (analogous to our representation of the adjective *old* above), that can then be multiplied by a noun, as in the following derivation of an I-sized vector for *louse on dogs*:

$$(\mathcal{ON}_{(I \times I) \times J} \times \mathbf{dogs}_J) \times \mathbf{louse}_I = [\mathcal{ON}(\mathbf{dogs})]_{I \times I} \times \mathbf{louse}_I$$
$$= \{[\mathcal{ON}(\mathbf{dogs})](\mathbf{louse})\}_I$$

In our running toy example, nouns are 3-component vectors and DPs have 4 components, so $\mathcal{ON}$ would be tensor of size $(3 \times 3) \times 4$ mapping from a 4-dimensional vector space onto a 3×3-dimensional tensor space.

Similarly, suppose that an intransitive verb is analyzed as a VP (verb phrase), that is, a function from DPs to sentences, and thus as a matrix of shape $K \times J$ mapping from the J-dimensional DP space (in which subject vectors live) onto the K-dimensional sentence space. A transitive verb will then be a third-order $(K \times J) \times J$ tensor mapping from the J-dimensional DP space (where of course also DPs that function as sentential objects live onto a VP, that is, an intransitive-verb-like $K \times J$ matrix.) If, to continue the toy example, DPs are vectors with 4 components and sentences vectors with, say, 2 components, then intransitive verbs would be 2×4 matrices and transitive verbs would be $(2 \times 4) \times 4$ tensors. Readers familiar with the standard theory of semantic types will recognize, again, the analogy between the role of denotation-based types in the standard theory and the shape of tensors (plus the associated index labels!) in the distributional approach, a point we return to more explicitly in Section 3.6.

Consider next the case of a higher-order function that takes other

---

only once.

functions as arguments. As we know from formal semantics (see, e.g., Heim and Kratzer 1998; Chapter 5), a relative pronoun acts as a bridge between a verb phrase and a noun: it modifies the noun with the verb phrase. In the denotational view, it is represented by the 2-argument function that takes a verb phrase (viz., a property) and a noun (viz., a property) to return a noun denoting the intersection of the two properties, for instance $[\![\text{dogs}]\!] \cap [\![\text{eat meat}]\!]$. Note that this is the semantics of intersective conjunction, as we see it in the examples in (6), applied to verbs, nouns, DPs and adjectives.

(6)   a. Bill [walked] and [talked].

    b. My [friend] and [colleague] gave me a long hug.

    c. As [a mother] and [a well-respect researcher], Sue has much to share with us.

    d. A [tall] and [handsome] gentleman

How can we capture the same intuition in distributional semantics? We do not have an overt *and* as in the examples above, so in first approximation we must capitalize on the presence of the relative pronoun, treated as a function that takes a VP such as *"eat meat"* as input and returns the noun modifier *"which eat meat"*.[44] What kind of linear algebraic object should *which* be to serve this role? Suppose, as before, that nouns live in 3-dimensional space, DPs in 4-dimensional space and sentences in 2-dimensional space. Consequently, VPs are 2×4 matrices and a noun modifier (such as an adjective) is a 3×3 matrix. It follows that *which* is a fourth-order tensor with shape $(3 \times 3) \times (2 \times 4)$ mapping from 2×4 input VP matrices to 3×3 output noun-modifier matrices. More generally, if the noun space is I-dimensional, the DP space is J-dimensional and the sentence space is K-dimensional, then a relative pronoun such as *which* is an $(I \times I) \times (K \times J)$ tensor.

Measuring similarity of tensors

In the same way that we can measure degrees of similarity (and other properties) of two or more vectors living in the same vector space, we can measure the similarity (and other properties) of matrices and higher-order tensors, as long as they have the same shape (as we remarked in footnote 35, the set of all same-shape tensors constitutes, indeed, a vector space).[45] In particular, we can always represent an

---

[44]In Section 3.6, we will handle the more difficult case in which the pronoun acts as object of the relative: *"meat which animals eat"*.

[45]In line with our idea of distributional space as a linear algebraic space enriched with linguistic index labels, a meaningful comparison will only be possible between identically shaped tensors that also share the same associations of index elements

n-th order tensor of shape $I_1 \times \ldots \times I_n$ as a vector with a number of components that equals the product $I_1 \times \ldots \times I_n$, and thus we can use exactly the same methods we adopt to measure the similarity of vectors (such as the cosine comparison introduced in Section 2) to measure the similarity of tensors of any order but with the same shape. Intuitively, the cells of a matrix (or higher-order tensor) contain weights specifying the impact that each component of the input has on each component of the output. Two matrices (or tensors) are similar when they have a similar weight distribution, i.e., they perform similar input-to-output component mappings (we might expect the **DECREPIT** matrix to dampen the *runs* component of an input noun just like the **OLD** matrix in Table 3 does).

On the other hand, there is no straightforward way to compare tensors of different orders or shapes. This entails that it is possible to compare all and only the linguistic structures that live in the same distributional semantic space, a limit which we regard as a positive feature, if the goal is a more constrained theory of language: In the ML models, all words and larger constituents live in the same space, so everything is directly comparable with everything else. This is too lax: asking for the degree of similarity between, say, *the* and *eating carrots* is asking an ill-conceived question. At the same time, we are aware that the ban imposed by our method can sometimes be too strong. In its pure form, it allows nouns to be compared to nouns, since they are represented by vectors with the same number of components, but not to adjectives, which are matrices. As a result, *Rome* and *Roman*, *Italy* and *Italian* cannot be declared similar, which is counter-intuitive. Even more counter-intuitively, *Roman* used as an adjective would not be comparable to *Roman* used as a noun.

We think that the best way to solve such apparent paradoxes is to look, on a case-by-case basis, at the linguistic structures involved, and to exploit them to develop specific solutions.[46] For example, a way to measure similarity between an adjective and a noun would be to apply the adjective matrix to a number of vectors representing nouns that are frequently modified by the adjective, average these adjective-noun vectors, and compare the resulting averaged vector (that, as a

---

to labels.

[46]One could also adopt purely mathematical methods to project tensors of different orders and sizes onto the same space. We doubt that such general methods would be very effective empirically (the naturalness of the task is cued by the fact that one of the methods to pursue it is called "Procrustes Analysis"; Wang and Mahadevan 2008), they are so general that they would then also allow the unconstrained similarity comparisons we want to avoid (e.g., the same method used to compare *Italy* and *Italian* could also be used to compare *the* to *eating carrots*).

sum of adjective-noun vectors, is still a vector living in nominal space) to the noun of interest. For example, *Italian* could be represented for these purposes by an average of the vectors of *Italian citizen*, *Italian flag*, *Italian government*, *Italian food*, etc. (Baroni and Zamparelli 2010, show that a similar method gives good results in an adjective clustering task).

In the case of pairs such as *Italy* and *Italian*, perhaps the right linguistic intuition to capture is not about similarity, but about the fact that these two forms are related by a morphological process of derivation, whereby the lexical function *-(i)an* is applied to nominal roots to obtain the corresponding denominal adjectives. As we discuss in Section 3.5 below, a nice feature of our approach to composition learning is that it naturally extends to lexical functions of this sort (in the case at hand, *-(i)an* would be a tensor mapping noun vectors to adjective matrices). Then, "similarity" of *Italy* and *Italian* could simply be modeled by observing that in our system the latter (at least when used with a transparent denominal meaning) is derived from the former.[47]

As intuitively clear, such special methods to capture similarity cannot be applied anywhere and for any category. Some cases are and will remain incomparable. It is an empirical issue whether this restriction is too severe, or if, on the contrary, our assumptions impose just the right constraints on the scope of similarity and related properties.

3.5 Inducing distributional functions from corpus data

We have argued that distributional functions might be a more appropriate representation to capture composition than vector mixtures. However, we have not yet addressed the fundamental issue of how the operations performed by the distributional composition functions corresponding to individual words and constructions are specified. Assuming that distributional functions are linear transformations, the question can be framed more precisely as: How do we determine the values to fill the cells of the tensor representing a distributional composition function?

Obviously, we do not want to fill them by hand. It would be highly impractical, since realistically-sized tensors will contain at least a few thousand cells, and a useful lexicon should contain thousands of such objects: one per adjective, one per verb, etc. The manual approach

---

[47] As a reviewer observed, as a model of word formation this would lead to overgeneration. However, the techniques described in Vecchi et al. (2011) for detecting semantically anomalous AN combinations might be applied to exclude, at least, semantically deviant root-affix combinations such as *first-er*.

would also be theoretically undesirable, since we are pursuing systems that, like humans, acquire semantic knowledge from naturally occurring data.

We propose instead to learn a distributional function by extracting examples of how its input and output tensors should look like from the corpus, and using standard machine learning methods to find the set of weights in the matrix that produce the best approximations to the corpus-extracted example output vectors when multiplied by the corresponding input vectors (the input and output vectors used to estimate the matrix weights are called *training examples* in the machine learning literature, and the estimation process *training*; we use the terms *training*, *learning* and *inducing* more or less as synonymous). Consider the case of the determiner *some*. The idea is to collect directly from the corpus pairs of distributional vectors matching the templates $<N,$ *some* $N>$ ($<dog,$ *some dog*$>$; $<cats,$ *some cats*$>$; $<coffee,$ *some coffee*$>$; etc.). We then use a statistical algorithm (regression) to find the sets of weights that, on average, provide the best approximation to each output component as a weighted sum of the corresponding input components across the training set. These weights will fill the **SOME** matrix.[48]

Clark (2013b) wonders if extracting composed vectors directly from the corpus is in the true spirit of compositional semantics. We think it is, since we only use these vectors in the learning phase as examples of how the output of compositional processes should look like: It is acceptable even to a Fregean compositionalist to try to find out what a compositional function does by comparing examples of its input and output. Less compositionally inclined researchers of language development, such as Tomasello 2003, actually view the acquisition process more as one of *decomposing* larger chunks by discovering their internal structure, than one of putting pieces together to build those chunks. Note that we can throw away the corpus-extracted examples of phrase vectors after learning, and use our fully compositional system to (re-)generate all phrases and sentences. But this might not always be a good move: As we briefly discuss at the end of Section 3.5 below, in some cases there might be good reasons to prefer a "dual-route" view where both compositionally-derived and directly corpus-induced phrase representations are available.

---

[48]Incidentally, the idea of using corpus-harvested phrase vectors as targets of learning is not restricted to our functional approach. We could for example use minimum distance between composed and corpus-derived vectors from a training set as the criterion to choose the best settings for the weighted additive model.

Learning by regression

Algorithms to predict a continuous numerical value (such as a the value in a component of the output vector) from a set of features (such as the input components) are called *regression* methods, and they are widely studied in statistics and machine learning (Hastie et al. 2009). We do not need to delve here into the complexities of regression algorithms. As linguists, we limit ourselves to borrow state-of-the-art methods from the relevant literature. Suffice to say that alternative regression algorithms mostly differ in how they find a trade-off between fitting the training data as best as possible (i.e., finding sets of weights that produce output values that are very similar to those in the example output vectors) and avoiding "overfitting", that is, avoiding very *ad-hoc* weight settings that might produce an excellent approximation of the training set, but won't generalize to new data, since they over-adapted to the random noise present in any set of examples, including the training set.

From a linguistic perspective, it is more interesting to ask whether distributional vectors, directly harvested from the corpus for the composed expressions we want to model, are a good target for function learning. Theoretically, since distributional vectors are summaries of the contexts in which a linguistic expression occurs, it is reasonable to expect that a vector directly constructed from corpus contexts is a good model of what we would like to learn by composition. If we want to define a composition function generating the distributional vector of *some coffee* from that of *coffee*, it stands to reason that we define a function that approximates the actual distributional vector of *some coffee*.

Of course, not many corpus-extracted phrases (and very few sentences) are common enough to find enough occurrences of them in a corpus to extract meaningful distributional vectors (that's why we want composition in the first place). However, we only need a few, reasonably frequent examples for each composition function to be learned by regression. In the transitive verb experiments of Grefenstette et al. (2013), good results were obtained with as little as 10 training examples per verb.

Corpus-extracted phrase vectors as targets of learning

Given the centrality of learning from phrase examples for our approach, we have collected various forms of empirical evidence that, at least for adjective-noun constructions (ANs) and DPs, phrase vectors directly extracted from the corpus make good semantic sense. It is thus reasonable to use them as our target of learning.

In Baroni and Zamparelli (2010), we have presented qualitative ev-

TABLE 4: The 3 nearest neighbours of the corpus-derived distributional vectors of 9 randomly selected ANs (from Baroni and Zamparelli 2010).

bad luck	electronic communities	historical map
bad	electronic storage	topographical
bad weekend	electronic transmission	atlas
good spirit	purpose	historical material
important route	nice girl	little war
important transport	good girl	great war
important road	big girl	major war
major road	guy	small war
red cover	special collection	young husband
black cover	general collection	small son
hardback	small collection	small daughter
red label	archives	mistress

idence that the nearest neighbours (the nearest vectors in semantic space) of the corpus-derived AN vectors are reasonable. See Table 4 (taken from Baroni and Zamparelli 2010) for examples of nearest neighbours of nine randomly selected ANs.

A series of recent unpublished experiments provided quantitative support for the intuition about the good quality of corpus-derived ANs suggested by the data in Table 4. The experiments showed that the nearest neighbour in distributional semantic space of a corpus-derived AN vector is systematically picked by subjects as its most closely semantically related term over other plausible alternatives.[49] Subjects were presented with an AN (e.g., *serious decision*), the nearest neighbour of the corresponding distributional vector in semantic space (*crucial decision*), and another relevant term, for example the nearest neighbour of another AN sharing the same head noun (e.g., *wrong decision*, which is the nearest neighbour of *correct decision*). Subjects were asked which of the two terms they found most closely related in meaning to the target AN (without, of course, being aware of how the two terms were selected). Overall, 5,000 distinct triples were evaluated, with the alternative foils including, besides random terms, nearest neighbours of the adjective, of the noun, of ANs sharing the same noun and of ANs sharing the same adjective. In all settings, subjects showed a strong, statistically significant preference for the true nearest neighbour (in the running example, *crucial decision* was picked over *wrong decision*

---

[49]These experiments and the *some N* nearest neighbour examples in Table 5 are based on DSMs similar to those described in Section 4.1 below.

Table 5: A choice of nearest neighbours (among top 20) of the corpus-derived vectors for *some cats* and *some coffee*.

some cats	*some coffee*
some dogs	some tea
most cats	some breakfast
most dogs	some dinner
many cats	some chocolate
many dogs	another bottle
most rabbits	some beer
some breeds	another drink
most animals	some cake
some horses	some toast
some babies	more beer

as the term most related to *serious decision*).

Note that, differently from the ML models, our approach to distributional function induction does not require harvesting vectors for grammatical words such as prepositions or determiners. Instead, we collect vectors for *phrases* that contain such words combined with content words. We do not extract a (presumably uninformative) vector from all contexts in which *some* occurs, but pairs of example vectors such as <*cats, some cats*> and <*coffee, some coffee*>. A choice of nearest neighbours of the corpus-harvested vectors for *some cats* and *some coffee* is presented in Table 5.

Note first in Table 5 how all the neighbours are intuitively semantically close to the target DPs, involving nouns from the same domain and mostly the same or a related quantifying determiner. Note moreover how the neighbours of the count usage of *some* in *some cats* are, consistently, other expressions involving counting of distinct individuals. The mass usage with *coffee*, on the other hand, tends to attract other constructions involving quantifying amounts of substances. It should be possible to learn, by regressing on training examples of this sort, that *some* has a different meaning when modifying a count or a mass noun, as illustrated in the toy **SOME** matrix in the Section 3.4 above.

In Baroni et al. (2012), we have shown that corpus-harvested distributional vectors for DPs with a quantifying determiner contain enough information for a statistical algorithm to correctly learn and generalize the entailment status of pairs of DPs represented distributionally. For example, if we extract from the corpus distributional vectors for a few thousand entailing (*each dog*$\models$*some dog*) and non-entailing (*many cats*$\not\models$*all cats*) pairs, and we feed them as labeled training data to a machine learning program, the program is then able, given an arbitrary pair of DP vectors, to tell whether the pair is entailing or not, with accuracy significantly above chance. Generalization works even in the case in which the test pairs contain determiners that were not in the training data. That is, the program correctly predicts that, say, *several snakes* $\not\models$ *every snake* even if it did not see any phrase containing *several* in the training data.

Further support for the hypothesis that corpus-harvested distributional vectors for phrases are high-quality examples of the composite meaning they represent come from Boleda et al. (2012b) and Turney (2012). Boleda and colleagues show that corpus-harvested vectors representing AN constructions instantiating different kinds of modification (intersective, subsective, intensional) display global patterns of similarity that reflect linguistic intuitions about adjectival modification (see also Section 4.3 below). Turney reports that corpus-harvested phrase vectors (which he calls "holistic" vectors) reach excellent performance when used in the task of finding the best single-word paraphrase for a noun phrase.

Together, these results suggest that, at least for simple phrases, we can indeed harvest meaningful examples of how we would want the output of composition to look like directly from the corpus. The relative success of our method in predicting human intuitions about full sentences (see Section 4.2 below) suggests that meaningful training vectors can also be harvested for simple sentential constructions, since inducing representations for verbs (necessary to handle sentences) involves extracting example subject-verb and subject-verb-object vectors. Although the relevant techniques are introduced below, we discuss some issues raised by these "bare-bone" sentence vectors here, since they pertain to the general topic of the current section, namely the role played by corpus-extracted examples in our approach.

First, some have objected that our method might work for *simple* instantiations of a target construction, but how about complex ones? We might be right, the objection goes, that large corpora contain enough informative examples of *"spiders chase ladybugs"* to build a meaningful example vector for this bare-bone subject-verb-object construction. However, how would you ever expect to extract a meaningful corpus-based vector for *"sneaky black spiders quietly chase cute little ladybugs in the midnight garden"*? This objection forgets the very mechanisms of compositionality our entire framework rests upon, and confuses the corpus-extracted phrase vectors needed for learning (that only requires a small set of bare-bone instantiations of the target construction) with the vectors representing arbitrarily complex structures we can derive once our compositional system has been trained. After the system has been trained, a complex sentence like the one above can be constructed in steps by applying the relevant composition rules: recursive adjective modification to build *"sneaky black spiders"* and *"cute little ladybugs"* vectors, adverbial modification to derive a *quietly chase* tensor from *chase*, multiplication of the resulting transitive verb tensor by the object and subject vectors to derive the basic transitive sentence (see below), etc. Each of these rules can be trained from the simplest instantiations of the corresponding constructions, for which we should be able to find a sufficient number of training examples in the corpus: For example, the *chase* tensor will be learned from simple example subject-*chase*-object vectors such as the one for *"spiders chase ladybugs"*. There will never be the need to extract vectors directly from the corpus for complicated but composite structures such as the larger *"sneaky black spiders"* sentence above. It only makes sense to derive the latter compositionally.[50]

A related objection is that the corpus will contain few bare-bone sentences of the *"dogs bark"* or *"spiders chase ladybugs"* kind, that we need to learn verbs by regression, since real-life sentences are typically more complex than this (again, see below for the actual learning procedure). This objection overlooks the fact that a *"spiders chase ladybugs"* example vector can be extracted from sentences of *any* complexity, as long as they contain *spiders* as subject, *chase* as (main) verb and *ladybugs* as object, with all other lexical material in the sentence potentially treated as context for the target phrase. For example, if *"sneaky black spiders quietly chase cute little ladybugs in the midnight garden"* does occur in our training corpus, then during training we will treat it as a context in which *"spiders chase ladybugs"* occurs, and as evidence that it co-occurs with *sneaky, black, quietly, cute*, etc., which is precious information for constructing the corpus-based *"spiders chase ladybugs"* vector (see also the analogous *"boy kissed girl"* example we discussed at the beginning of Section 3).

We conclude our discussion of the corpus-extracted phrases we use in learning with some conjectures about the role of such example phrases once the compositional system has been trained. After learning, should we throw the example phrase vectors away, and prefer the compositional route in any case? To take a simple case, suppose we use the *red car* vector as training example to learn the *red* function. Given that we have extracted the vector during training, if we later need to use a dis-

---

[50]Still, we do not want to deny that even for skeletal sentences with a subject-verb-object structure, we might incur into data sparseness problems. We briefly address the issue towards the end of this section.

288 / Marco Baroni, Raffaella Bernardi and Roberto Zamparelli

tributional representation for *red car*, should we use the training vector directly extracted from the corpus or generate it anew by multiplying the estimated **RED** matrix by **car**? This is an open question.

Note that, although we use corpus-extracted phrase and sentence vectors to train distributional functions (and we just argued that they are of sufficient good quality to motivate this choice), it is not the case that corpus-extracted vectors (when available at all) are necessarily of a better quality than their composed counterparts. In Baroni and Zamparelli (2010), we have shown examples where the nearest neighbour of a composed AN vector is more reasonable than that of the corresponding corpus-derived vector. For example, the nearest neighbour of composed *special something* is *special thing*, that of corpus-derived *special something* is *little animal*; the nearest neighbour of composed *historical thing* is *historical reality*, the one of its corpus-derived counterpart is *different today*. We hypothesize that, in such cases, the corpus did not contain sufficient information to create a good representation of the phrase (e.g., because the phrase is too rare). Thus, applying the distributional adjective function, that has been trained on many more examples, to the noun vector produces a better approximation to the meaning of the phrase than the one we get out of direct evidence (in the limit, the claim becomes trivial; a corpus-extracted vector representing a phrase that never occurs in the corpus, that is, a vector of 0s, will certainly be worse than its compositionally derived counterpart).

On the other hand, at least in certain cases both corpus-derived and composed vectors have a role to play. An obvious case is that of idioms.[51] A corpus-derived vector for *red herring* will probably have neighbours related to its "misleading cue" sense. On the other hand, the output of **RED** × **herring** will probably be a vector for the literal colored-fish meaning. An English speaker will be aware of the idiom, but she can also compositionally understand *red herring* as referring to the colored fish (indeed, the general consensus in psycholinguistics is that whenever an idiom is encountered, it is also automatically processed via a compositional route; see Cacciari 2012). By providing (where possible) both directly corpus-derived and composed representations of the same phrases, our approach can capture the same dichotomy.[52]

---

[51] Note that we are speaking here of completely opaque idioms of the *red herring* and *kick the bucket* sort. We expect corpus-derived examples to provide enough evidence for our approach to pick up any systematic semi-lexicalized or metaphorical pattern, such as the political usage of the adjective *red* to refer to socialism. Indeed, as mentioned above, the compositional system for AN meanings of Baroni and Zamparelli (2010) performed particularly well with highly polysemous adjectives.

[52] Relatedly, automatically scoring the degree of semantic opaqueness of a phrase

Learning higher-order tensors

Having shown how regression can be used to estimate the weights of matrices (second-order tensors) and argued that corpus-extracted examples of the relevant output constructions are a suitable target for regression learning, we turn now to how this approach can be extended to functions of more than one argument. Recall that such functions are encoded in higher-order tensors (an n-argument function is encoded in an $n + 1$-th order tensor), and thus the goal of regression is to estimate the values to be stored in the cells of such tensors.

In particular, when a function returns another function as output, e.g. when it acts on a vector and generates a matrix, we need to apply a two-step regression learning method, inducing representations of example matrices in a first round of regressions, and then using regression again to learn the higher-order function.[53]

Grefenstette et al. (2013) illustrated this for transitive verbs. An intransitive verb is naturally modeled as a VP, that is, a function from a DP (the subject) to a sentence. A transitive verb, then, is a function from a DP (the object) to a VP, i.e., to a function from DPs to sentences.[54] Let's go back to our toy DP semantic space of 4 dimensions (as in the "some" example of the previous subsection) and let's take sentences to live in 2-dimensional space. Hence, a VP is a 2×4 matrix. For example, both *jump* and *"eat cake"* are matrices of this shape.[55] A transitive verb such as *eat* is then a third-order $(2 \times 4) \times 4$ tensor, that takes an object DP vector (e.g., *cake*) to return the corresponding 2×4 VP matrix (*"eat cake"*).

To learn the weights in such tensor, we first use regression to obtain examples of matrices representing verb-object constructions with a specific verb. These matrices are estimated from corpus-extracted examples of $<subject, subject\ verb\ object>$ vector pairs (picking, of course, subject-verb-object structures that occur with a certain frequency in the corpus, in order to be able to extract meaningful distributional vectors for them). After estimating a suitable number of such matrices for a variety of objects of the same verb (e.g., *"eat cake"*, *"eat meat"*, *"eat snacks"*), we use pairs of corpus-derived object vectors and the

---

has recently been proposed as a benchmarking task for distributional semantic models (Biemann and Giesbrecht 2011).

[53] Georgiana Dinu (p.c.) has developed a method to estimate higher-order tensors in just one step: However, the method requires the same training data as the multi-step method, that is conceptually simpler.

[54] In the conclusion, we will come back to some important issues pertaining to this treatment of verbs, such as how to handle changes in argument structure.

[55] Like Grefenstette et al. (2013), we ignore for purposes of all examples discussed in this subsection the inflection of the verb and number of nouns and DPs.

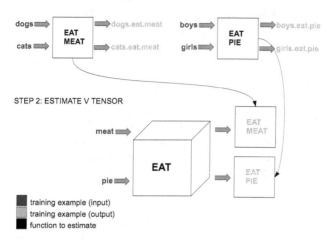

STEP 1: ESTIMATE VP MATRICES

STEP 2: ESTIMATE V TENSOR

■ training example (input)
▨ training example (output)
■ function to estimate

FIGURE 3: Estimating a tensor for *eat* in two steps. We first estimate matrices for *eat meat, eat pie*, etc., by regression on input subject and output subject-*eat*-object vector pairs (directly extracted from the corpus). We then estimate the tensor for *eat* by regression with the matrices estimated in the first step as output examples, and the vectors for the corresponding objects as input examples (from Grefenstette et al. 2013).

corresponding verb-object matrices estimated in the first step as input-output examples in a second regression step, where we determine the verb tensor components. The two-step estimation procedure is schematically illustrated for *eat* in Figure 3 (from Grefenstette et al. 2013). Of course, after the *eat* tensor has been estimated, it can be used to generate transitive sentences with subjects and objects that were not used in the training phase.

Next, let us consider the most complex case, that is, that of a higher-order function that takes other functions both as input and as output. In this case, we will first use regression to construct examples of both the input and output functions (e.g., matrices), and then use these examples to train the higher-order tensor we are interested in. Let's go back to the example of the relative pronoun *which* that we discussed in Section 3.4 above. We concluded there that *which*, as a function from VPs onto noun modifiers, is a fourth-order tensor mapping input VP matrices onto output noun-modifier matrices. In particular, in our toy lexicon we took *which* to be a third-order tensor with shape (3 × 3) × (2 × 4) mapping from 2 × 4 input VP matrices to 3 × 3 output noun-modifier matrices.

In this case, the first training step will generate examples of both the input and the output matrices. For the input VPs, training will proceed exactly like with transitive verbs (see Figure 3) to derive a set of VP matrices (2×4), that in this case can contain different verbs and be both transitive and intransitive (*"eat meat"*, *"chase cats"*, *sing*, *jump*, ...). The training of output noun modifiers (3 × 3) is similar, but here the corpus-extracted example vectors will be pairs of <*noun, noun which VP*>. For example, the *"which eat meat"* matrix will be trained from corpus-extracted vectors of pairs such as <*dog, dog which eats meat*>, <*cat, cat which eats meat*>, etc. In the second phase, we estimate the *which* tensor by optimizing, via regression, the mappings between VP-matched input-output matrix pairs trained in the first phase, e.g., <*eat meat, which eat meat*>, <*sing, which sing*>, and so on.

Two problems loom ahead: data scarcity and computational load. Consider the first. As the complexity of the structures to be learned grows, it becomes increasingly difficult to find a sufficient number of frequent examples of their inputs and outputs in order to obtain meaningful training vectors from the corpus. In pursuing our regression-based program for learning compositional semantics, it will thus be crucial to devise ways to harvest and optimally exploit high-quality training examples for all structures of interest. This might involve, on the one hand, using regression methods that can learn successfully from very few examples, and on the other, coming up with ways to extend the training sets exploiting similarities between linguistic expressions to 'share' training examples across distributional functions. Intuitively, good training examples for the *"which eat pie"* matrix could also be recycled as training examples when learning *"which eat cake"*. We envision the use of clustering methods to discover when two forms are sufficiently close to be pooled together in the training phase.

A second problem is computing power and storage needs. Given realistically-sized input vectors, the number of components to estimate in the corresponding higher-order tensors is humongous. If we assume (like Grefenstette et al. 2013 did, see Section 4.1 below) that nouns, DPs and sentences live in 300-dimensional spaces, a transitive verb is a (300 × 300) × 300 tensor, that is, it contains 27 million components. A relative pronoun, being a (300 × 300) × (300 × 300) tensor, contains 8.1 billion components. Luckily, there aren't as many relative pronouns as there are transitive verbs, since structures of this size are pushing the boundary of what can be stored and manipulated with reasonable efficiency given our (and we suppose most linguists') computational power. However, a somewhat technical but important consideration must be made here. The giant tensor is derived from training examples of much smaller sizes and often correlated with each other. Hence, by using algorithms that might exploit similarities in input and output components to effectively reduce the dimensionality of the problem, there will be a lot of "redundancy" in its cells. Furthermore, it will be probably possible to express the values they contain as weighted combinations of a much smaller set of vectors. Thus, a careful implementation of both learning and generalized matrix-by-vector product application might be able to sidestep some of the worse computational issues.

Learning functions that are not triggered by words

Since our learning procedure only requires examples of the input and output to a composition function, our system can also be extended to learning composition processes where the functional element is not an autonomous word. For example, the semantics of an affix such as -ment can be learned from training pairs such as <contain, containment>, <endorse, endorsement>, etc. (the derivation of Italian from Italy discussed in Section 3.4 above works analogously).[56] In the ML models, on the other hand, one would need to extract a vector for -ment or -(i)an, which is very problematic.

Actually, composition is not even constrained to be associated to any phonological material at all. A simple case is that of "null determiners", needed to account for the fact that dogs and meat are nouns, but in "dogs eat meat" they are used as full noun phrases (DPs, in our notation). Again, this is not a problem for our approach, where we can train a null determiner function that takes as input noun vectors (extracted from all contexts in which the nouns occur) and, as output, vectors for the same nouns constructed from those contexts only where they are used as full DPs.[57] A similar strategy can be followed for the "invisible" relative pronoun in constructions such as "the meat dogs eat (is very fat)". We do not see how composition triggered by phonologically empty elements (equivalently: purely structural configurations) could be handled by the ML approaches.

Of course, for such cases to work properly within our framework, we will need to make sure that the relevant rules are automatically

---

[56] This approach to the semantics of affixes was in fact already proposed in Guevara (2009).

[57] In the fragment of grammar to be presented next, we instead adopt the simpler and less linguistically informed strategy to treat bare plurals, such as dogs in "dogs bark", as primitive elements —corpus-extracted vectors— of category DP.

triggered in the appropriate contexts by specific structures produced by the syntactic parser.

3.6   Syntax-semantics interface

So far we have presented the general intuitions and the technical aspects behind our proposal on the semantic modeling of natural language expressions. Now, we will look at how our semantic model interacts with syntactic analysis to scale up to account for sentence structure. We base our proposal on Montague's lessons and on the type-logical view of the syntax-semantics interface that has been developed starting from his Universal Grammar (Montague 1970b). Following this tradition, we will adopt Categorial Grammar (CG) to account for syntactic constructions and employ the formal techniques of the type-logical view to define a tight connection between syntax and semantics. Note that the same syntactic structures can also be used as the basis to construct standard referential representation of meaning, in a parallel distributional/referential approach to semantics.

To capture the relation between the syntax and the semantic level, the type-logical view uses the following steps: define an atomic set of syntactic categories and of semantic types based on which functional syntactic categories and complex semantic types are built; define a recursive mapping between the syntactic categories and the semantic types; assign typed meaning representations to each lexical entry, where the types are those of the corresponding domain of interpretation; assign to the lexical entries syntactic categories that correspond to their semantic types. This procedure allows one to proceed in parallel in the composition of the syntactic and semantic constructions.

Besides this theoretical advantage, employing a CG framework has practical benefits, because of the existence of a fast and wide-coverage syntactic parser, namely C&C parser(Clark and Curran 2007), based on (Combinatory) Categorial Grammar(Steedman 2000). This parser is also integrated with Boxer, a system that builds a referential semantic tier using Discourse Representation Structures (Curran et al. 2007), thus allowing us to maintain the same large-scale approach that characterizes lexical DSMs in our compositional component, and providing a concrete infrastructure for the possibility of parallel distributional/referential representations built from the same semantic structures. Of course, other lexicalized formal grammars could also be considered; CG is just the one that might allow the integration in the most straightforward way.[58]

---

[58] Our choice of CG (and in particular Combinatory CG) over Dependency Gram-

In denotational semantics the semantic types give the type of the domain of denotation (e.g., the domain of entities D_e, containing the denotation of proper names, or the domain of functions from entities to truth values, $D_{(e \to t)}$, used for intransitive verbs, verb phrases, and nouns). In a DSM, we take domains to stand for the distributional semantic spaces in which the expressions live, and, as in denotational semantics, we take these semantic spaces to be typed. The type records the shape of the tensors in the space (plus the associated index labels) as discussed in Sections 3.3 and 3.4. We mark atomic types with subscript indices standing for the shape of the items in the corresponding semantic space. Suppose, for example, that the noun *dog* lives in a 10,000-dimensional nominal space; then, its distributional representation will be a vector in this space and will have type $C_{n_{10000}}$, where we use C to remind ourselves that this is a type based on *C*ontextual information, the subscript n points to the *n*ominal space (characterized by a specific index-to-labels mapping) and the subsubscript to the dimensionality of the space.

Similarly, functional types will correspond to space mappings (linear transformations) and will be represented by different tensors: matrices (that is, second order tensors) for first order 1-argument functions, third order tensors for first order 2-argument functions, etc. In general, we assume that words of different syntactic categories live in different semantic spaces. Note that we are *not* assuming that the complexity of the formal semantic type must correspond to a corresponding complexity in the shape and order of the corresponding DSM structure. A salient case is that of nominals. In Montague Grammar proper names are of type e (entities), but quantified DPs are of type $(e \to t) \to t$ (sets of properties). In our current experiments we do not cover proper names, due to the ambiguity issues pointed out in Section 2.6, but we treat quantificational DPs as first order tensors, i.e., vectors, albeit potentially living in a different space from that of nouns.[59] Note,

---

mar, another widely-used parsing framework in computational linguistics (Kübler et al. 2009; Mel'chuk 1987), was also motivated by the fact that dependency-parsed structures are not binary, and do not make explicit the mutual scope of modifiers (in a parse of *"the hypothetical high percentage of voters"*, *the*, *hypothetical* and *high* would all be dependent on *percentage*, without any indication but word order that *hypothetical* scopes over *high*, but not vice-versa.)

[59]This might seem untenable in a view of semantics in which determiners are diadic functions over a restrictor and a predicate. As we have seen in Section 3.4, our determiners are unary functions over Ns, while VPs are unary functions over DPs. This approach is not feasible in Montague Grammar because the operation VPs perform on their subject is extremely simple: set membership. Thus, *John runs* will be true in a model M iff it is true that j' $\in$ [[run]]^M. In our approach, a VP function can be far more sophisticated (like the determiner, it takes an input vector,

moreover, that in denotational semantics the domain of interpretation is partially ordered by the inclusion relation ($\subseteq$) holding within the denotational sets. It is on the basis of this order that the logical entailment of phrases and sentences is computed; in our case semantic similarities are computed based on similarities of tensors living in the same space, as discussed in Section 3.4. Thanks to this notion of "typed similarity", once the whole framework is implemented, we believe that we can arrive to draw richer (or more "natural") kinds of reasoning based on distributional representations plus logical entailment, rather than on logical entailment alone.

Given the programmatic nature of this paper, we have touched upon many constructions for which a full computationally viable analysis is still underspecified. However, following the Montagovian tradition, we also want to give the reader a precise idea of how our system could handle a fragment of English. In the lexicalized view of CG, this means defining the lexicon out of which sentences of the fragment are built.

The lexicon we chose is a representative sample, in that it includes expressions with primitive types, functions over primitive types and functions over functions.

Most compositions in natural language are 'local', in that they take place between adjacent expressions, and involve first order n-functional categories. However, all human languages have instances of non-local dependencies. In some of these, the elements that should combine are not adjacent, but still within the same tensed sentence ("clause-bound dependencies"); in others, the dependency is between elements that can be separated by arbitrary amount of material ("long-distance dependencies"). In our fragment we will consider a single, syntactically simple but semantically challenging case of clause-bound non-local dependency, that of relative clauses with object gap and an overt relative pronoun.

In an object relative, like *"a cat which dogs chase runs away"*, the noun *cat* plays the double role of being the subject of the main clause and the object of the relative clause. As an object, it depends on the verb *chase* to which it is not juxtaposed. From a formal semantic viewpoint, the relative pronoun is represented by the lambda expression in (7)which intersects two properties, e.g., [[cat]] $\cap$ [[dogs chase]] (as we have seen in Section 3.4), (8)[a] gives the type for *which* and (8)[b] spells out how *which* combines with the property denoted by the gapped clause

---

but of course it does not return just a binary value, "true" or "false"). So, while it is an empirical question whether our current approach is tenable in the long run, we do not see strong theoretical motivations against it.

it C-commands[60] (*"dogs chase"*), then with the property denoted by *cats* in a sister node, to yield the property denoted by *"cat which dogs chase"*.

(7) $\lambda X_{(e \to t)}.\lambda Y_{(e \to t)}.\lambda x_e[X(x) \wedge Y(x)]$

(8) a. which $\in (e \to t) \to ((e \to t) \to (e \to t))$

  b. (**which**($[\![$dogs chase$]\!]$)($[\![$cats$]\!]$)

Now that we have laid the ground, we can start introducing the syntactic categories, the semantic types, and the fragment we will be dealing with.

We use small letters (e.g., a) for atomic syntactic categories, capital letters (e.g., A and B) for complex syntactic categories, and Type for the function mapping syntactic categories to semantic types:[61]

$$\begin{aligned} \text{Type}(a) &= C_a \text{ (for } a \text{ atomic)} \\ \text{Type}(B\backslash A) = \text{Type}(B/A) &= C_A \to C_B \end{aligned}$$

N (noun), DP (determiner phrase) and S (sentence) are our atomic syntactic categories, mapped to indexed types as follows: $\text{Type}(N) = C_{n_i}, \text{Type}(DP) = C_{dp_j}, \text{Type}(S) = C_{s_k}$. The types of the complex categories are obtained by the definition above. We use a fragment of English whose vocabulary consists only of words in the syntactic categories listed in Table 6, which are representative of the varieties of functional categories we have discussed above. For sake of clarity, in the table, next to the syntactic category, we indicate both the corresponding distributional semantic type, as well as the shape of the corresponding distributional representation.

Relative pronouns (RelPr) in subject or object relatives should ideally receive the same syntactic category in CG. This can be done using other connectives besides the traditional functional ones ($\backslash$ and $/$), but since our interest is in the syntax-semantics interface rather than in syntactic issues per se, we adopt the easiest CG solution and consider two syntactic categories: $(N\backslash N)/(S\backslash DP)$ for subject gap and $(N\backslash N)/(S/DP)$ for object gap, both mapping to the same semantic type.

While many constructions are not captured in the fragment, given that we can harvest thousands of distributional representations for lexical items from corpora, the fragment actually covers a huge amount of sentences, including the following:

---

[60]A node N *C-commands* another node M if it does not dominate it nor it is dominated by, and the first branching node that dominates N also dominates M (Reinhart 1976).

[61]We are adopting Steedman's (2000) CG notation.

TABLE 6: Syntax-Semantics interface for a fragment of English

Syn Cat	Lexicon		Tensor shape
	CG Cat	Semantic Type	
N	N	C_{n_i}	I vector (1st ord.)
NNS[a]	DP	C_{dp_j}	J vector (1st ord.)
ADJ	N/N	$C_{n_i} \to C_{n_i}$	$I \times I$ matrix (2nd ord.)
DET	DP/N	$C_{n_i} \to C_{dp_j}$	$J \times I$ matrix (2nd ord.)
IV	$S\backslash DP$	$C_{dp_j} \to C_{s_k}$	$K \times J$ matrix (2nd ord.)
TV	$(S\backslash DP)/DP$	$C_{dp_j} \to (C_{dp_j} \to C_{s_k})$	$(K \times J) \times J$ (3rd ord.)
Pre	$(N\backslash N)/DP$	$C_{dp_j} \to (C_{n_i} \to C_{n_i})$	$(I \times I) \times J$ (3rd ord.)
CONJ	$(N\backslash N)/N$	$C_{n_i} \to (C_{n_i} \to C_{n_i})$	$(I \times I) \times I$ (3rd ord.)
CONJ	$(DP\backslash DP)/DP$	$C_{dp_j} \to (C_{dp_j} \to C_{dp_j})$	$(J \times J) \times J$ (3rd ord.)
RelPr	$(N\backslash N)/(S\backslash DP)$ $(N\backslash N)/(S/DP)$	$(C_{dp_j} \to C_{s_k}) \to (C_{n_i} \to C_{n_i})$	$(I \times I) \times (K \times J)$ (higher ord.)

[a] Plural nouns phrases. In the fragment, we will be assuming that they can be directly mapped onto full DPs ("Bare plurals").

(9)   The sneaky black spiders with long hairy legs that the boys love ate the cute little guinea-pig that the girls bought.

Expressions are composed by using the CG syntactic tree (or derivation) as the backbone and by defining a correspondence between syntactic and semantic rules. In Montague Grammar, two main types of semantic rules are used: function application and abstraction. The syntactic correspondence of abstraction is also used in the logic version of CG, namely in the Lambek calculi (Lambek 1961; Moortgat 1997), and a restricted instance of it (type raising) is also present in CCG, the combinatory version of CG (Steedman 2000). In short, abstraction is used mostly for two cases: non-local dependency and inverse scope. In the current study, we are not interested in scope ambiguities since we believe that they are a challenge for syntacticians rather than semanticists; once the grammar provides the right representation for an ambiguous sentence (i.e., a disambiguated 'logical form') the semantic operations should be able to compute the proper meaning straightforwardly. Hence, in what follows we will only look at abstraction cases motivated by non-local dependencies, and in particular at the case of relative pronouns that extract an object from relative clause.

Local dependencies

Since in natural language function-argument order matters, CG has two function application rules: backward (when the argument is on the left of its function) and forward (when the argument is on the right of its function.)

On the DSM side, the sentences in the fragment we are considering require the following function application cases.

(10)   a. A matrix (2nd order tensor) composes with a vector (ADJ N e.g., *"red dog"*; DET N e.g., *"the dog"*; DP IV e.g., *"the dog barks"*, *"dogs bark"*);

       b. A 3rd order tensor composes with two vectors (DP TV DP, *"dogs chase cats"*; N Pre DP, *"dog with tails"*; DP CONJ DP, *"dogs and cats"*);

       c. A higher-order tensor composes with a matrix ((c1) Rel IV, e.g., *"which barks"*; Rel TV DP, *"which chases cats"*; and (c2) Rel DP TV, *"which dogs chase"*)

To emphasize the relation with the Montagovian framework, we begin by building a labeled syntactic tree. The labels record the operational steps and are therefore called *proof terms* or "derivation terms". A proof term can then be replaced with the appropriate corresponding semantic representation. Under the classic Montagovian view, it will be replaced by λ-terms standing for the meaning of the words (like the lambda terms discussed before for the relative pronoun). In a Continuation Semantics, it would be replaced by λ-terms that take the context into account (see Bernardi and Moortgat 2010; Barker and Shan 2006). In our setting, we replace proof terms with the corresponding tensors. To help reading the proof terms, we use the @ symbol to indicate the application of a function to an argument ($f@a$). For instance, when parsing the expressions *"dogs bark"*, *"dogs chase cats"* and *"which chase cats"*, CG produces the structures and terms in the trees in (11)and (12).

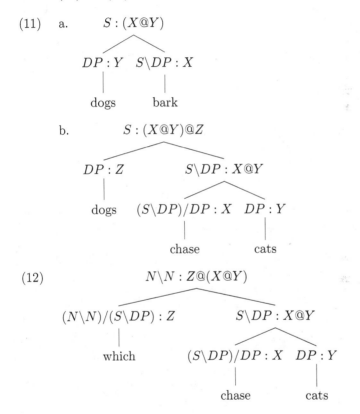

(11)   a. $S : (X@Y)$

        $DP : Y$ $S \backslash DP : X$

        dogs   bark

   b. $S : (X@Y)@Z$

      $DP : Z$ $S \backslash DP : X@Y$

      dogs $(S \backslash DP)/DP : X$ $DP : Y$

            chase   cats

(12) $N \backslash N : Z@(X@Y)$

   $(N \backslash N)/(S \backslash DP) : Z$ $S \backslash DP : X@Y$

      which $(S \backslash DP)/DP : X$ $DP : Y$

           chase   cats

We replace the variables with the corresponding DSM representations obtained from corpora and compute the vectors representing the sentences. In particular, in (11)[a] the labels X and Y are replaced with the matrix **BARK** and the vector **dogs**, respectively, giving **BARK** $\times$ **dogs**; whereas in (11)[b] X is replaced by the 3rd order tensor representing the meaning of *chase*, and Y and Z are replaced with the vectors representing the meaning of *dogs* and *cats*, respectively. Hence, we obtain ($\mathcal{CHASE}$ × **cats**) × **dogs**. Similarly for (12), where we obtain $\mathcal{WHICH}$ × ($\mathcal{CHASE}$ × **cats**). Once we have built this sort of representation of the sentence, we can compute its meaning using the generalized matrix-by-vector product introduced in Section 3.3.

Crucially, our vectorial representations have been built on the output of a CG parse of the sentence, a representation commonly used in formal semantics as input to build the logical form of sentences compositionally (van Benthem 1986; Moortgat 1997; Steedman 2000). Indeed, as we have mentioned above, the same CCG parser that produces the trees we use for our compositional operations is integrated with the logic-based Boxer system (Curran et al. 2007). Thus, we offer a clean and practical implementation of the parallel construction of logical and distributional semantic representations of sentences. A representation that, as we are about to see, also extends to the non-local dependency case we handle in our fragment.

Non-local dependencies

So far we have been dealing with local dependencies: the dependent element was always juxtaposed to the head. In CG terms, we can say that the function always found its syntactic argument next to it. We will consider the case of non-local dependency that is part of our fragment of English, namely the one of relative clauses with object gap and an overt relative pronoun, introduced above. As an example of this clause-bound dependency, we consider the sentence *"a cat which dogs chase runs away"* in which the object position of *chase* is missing, and *dog* plays the role of the object of the relative clause verb *chase* while being the subject of the main clause verb *runs*.

Besides the forward and backward rules used so far, CG (or more exactly, the logical version of it) is endowed with another kind of rule. We have seen that the forward and backward rules correspond to the application of a function to an argument; the third rule type corresponds to the abstraction of a variable from a term, in other words, to *hypothetical reasoning*. In the parsed linguistic structure we are considering, the verb *chase* requires an object (a DP) to its right, but no object is provided next to it.The parser, reasoning by hypothesis, assumes there is a DP juxtaposed to *chase* and composes the verb with this hypothetical DP, then it continues its composition process by composing the verb phrase thus obtained with the subject *dogs* found to its left. These steps are represented in (13), where we mark the hypothetical object by *hyp*, and we label the nodes with proof terms as done so far. The clause with the hypothetical object, *"dogs chase hyp"*, is represented by the proof term $(Z@X)@Y$.

(13)
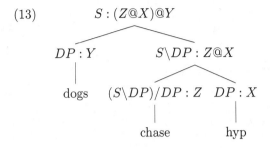

$$S : (Z@X)@Y$$

$$DP : Y \qquad S \backslash DP : Z@X$$

dogs $\qquad (S \backslash DP)/DP : Z \quad DP : X$

chase $\qquad$ hyp

As explained above, in denotational semantics the relative pronoun *which* acts as a modifier of the noun *cat*, restricting the set of cats to those that dogs chase. Hence, it composes first with the property *"dogs chase"* and then with the noun *cat*. As we have already seen, it has semantic type $(e \to t) \to ((e \to t) \to t)$—a function from properties to properties to truth values. The CG category that expresses the same behaviour at the syntactic level is the higher-order two-argument category (N\N)/(S/DP) which requires a sentence missing a DP on the rightmost position to return the category N\N. Hence, the parser encounters a category mismatch: It has the task of composing (N\N)/(S/DP) (*which*) with the tree of category S corresponding to *"dogs chase hyp"*. The tree of category S, however, contains an hypothesis of category DP—it would be a sentence if a DP had been provided. The parser can now withdraw the hypothetical DP, as illustrated in (14), and build the tree of category S/DP. The rule that allows this step is the one-branch rule encoding hypothetical reasoning. The lambda calculus goes step by step with this hypothetical reasoning process. Besides the function application rules we have used so far, it consists of the *abstraction* rule that abstracts from the term $(Z@X)@Y$ (namely the term assigned to the S tree –hence, a term of type t), the variable X assigned to the hypothetical DP (hence, a term of type e), building the lambda term $\lambda X.(Z@X)@Y$ (a term of type $(e \to t)$). The next step is again the application of a function (W of type $(e \to t) \to ((e \to t) \to t)$) to an argument (the lambda term of type $(e \to t)$ we have just built).

(14)

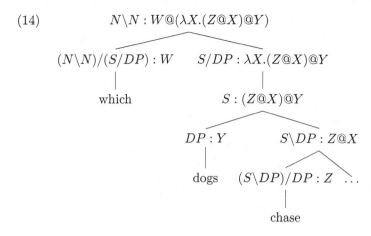

$$N \backslash N : W@(\lambda X.(Z@X)@Y)$$

$(N \backslash N)/(S/DP) : W \qquad S/DP : \lambda X.(Z@X)@Y$

which

$S : (Z@X)@Y$

$DP : Y \qquad S \backslash DP : Z@X$

dogs $\qquad (S \backslash DP)/DP : Z \;\; \ldots$

chase

How do we deal with the lambda abstraction step if we replace proof terms with DSM representations instead of their denotational counterparts? We sidestep this question by suggesting a solution that implicitly employs the rule of *associativity*. Through this rule, when the parser fails to find the DP object on the right of the relative clause verb, it can replace the category of the verb $(S \backslash DP)/DP$ with $(S/DP) \backslash DP$ since the two categories are equivalent *modulo* associativity.[62] This change of the category allows the verb to combine first with the subject on its left to return a predicate that looks for the object to its right. As a consequence, the tree corresponding to *"dog chase"* is already of the correct S/DP category to be taken as argument by the relative pronoun *which*.

One reason for suggesting this solution is that we have a nice, ready-to-use solution on the tensor composition side. The proof term recording the steps of the tree structure assigned to *which dogs chase* (15) mostly consists of function applications of the kinds discussed so far; the 'one branch step', which changes the category of the transitive verb, is the only new one. This syntactic step has a natural distributional semantic counterpart in the tensor transposition operation introduced at the end of Section 3.3, which gives a general procedure to generate a transposed tensor such that:

$$(\mathcal{T} \times \mathbf{v}) \times \mathbf{w} = (\mathcal{T}^T \times \mathbf{w}) \times \mathbf{v}$$

---

[62] Associativity causes over-generation problems. However, its application could be controlled by employing the multi-modal version of CG (Moortgat 1997). Since our focus is on the composition of the distributional semantic representations involved in such constructions, we will overlook the syntactic issues. Our semantic analysis or a close variation of it could be connected to different syntactic proposals in the literature.

This comes in very handy, since it allows us to transform a (pretrained) transitive verb tensor that would normally be multiplied by an object and then a subject into the transposed form, that can take the subject first, and the object later, producing the same result. In the tree, we represent this semantic rule as taking the term X and yielding the term X^T. Now we can replace the proof term with the actual distributional representation, obtaining $\mathcal{WHICH} \times (\mathcal{CHASE}^T \times$ **dogs**). This can later modify the vector representing *cat*.

(15)
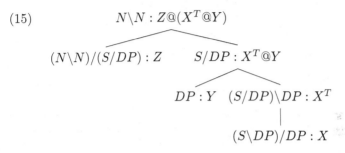

$$N \backslash N : Z@(X^T @Y)$$

$$(N \backslash N)/(S/DP) : Z \qquad S/DP : X^T @Y$$

$$DP : Y \quad (S/DP) \backslash DP : X^T$$

$$(S \backslash DP)/DP : X$$

Among the challenging class of non-local phenomena, we have restricted our attention to relative clauses involving object abstraction from its outmost position to the main sentence that immediately dominates the relative, a phenomenon that, as far as we are aware, is already more linguistically complex than anything studied so far by the compositional distributional semantics research community. We will of course have to verify whether our current solution, besides being conceptually simple, is also supported by empirical evidence, and whether it can be extended to other non-local dependencies. Note that in this transposition-based approach the relative clause changes its shape as a result of abstraction: it goes from being a vector to being a matrix, so the heads that could subcategorize for it in one shape cannot straightforwardly do so in the other. This means, for instance, that the *that* in (16)[a] cannot have the same type as the one in (16)[b] (the first would take a sentence vector, the second a matrix, from the transposed verb). The grammatical rules used so far (function application, abstraction and associativity) derive the type-shifting rule that maps the first *that* into the second (syntactically, from an (S/S) to an $((S/DP)/(S/DP))$). They derive also the rules needed for the verb *claim* in (16)[b] to take a clause missing the object instead of the complete sentence it takes in (16)[a]. The derived shifting of types would allow *who* in (16)[b] to work just as *which* in 14. We have not investigated whether for these type-shifting rules there exists a ready transformation as for the case discussed above, if this is the case, we will consider extending our fragment to these more complex long-distance dependencies.[63]

(16)　a. People claim that [girls love this boy].

　　　b. A boy who people claim that [girls love __] arrived.

It is also possible that a general solution for long-distance cases will come not from the pure DSM composition and transposition rules, but by reconstructing the arguments in their base position and calculating 'localized' vectors to be used as modifiers. For instance, the long distance relative in (16)[b] could be rendered by first computing the vector for those tokens of the lemma *boy* which appear in the context of (17)(and possibly, related sentences, to ease data sparcity).

(17)　People claim that girls love DET **boy(s)**

Next, this localized vector would be combined (e.g., by intersective modification) with the general vector for *boy* in the sentence *a boy arrived*, yielding an approximation of the meaning of (16)[b]. Exploring this and similar mechanisms will be a task for future research.

4　Current empirical support for the functional approach to distributional semantics

The aim of this paper is to sketch a program for compositional distributional semantics based on function application and to show how it could be applied to an extended fragment of English that includes grammatical words. But there is already evidence that the approach is empirically feasible, at least when it comes to modeling phrases and simple sentences made of content words. In this section, we briefly review the relevant empirical work.

4.1　DSM implementation and composition methods

We start by providing a succinct summary of the technical aspects of the compositional DSMs used in the experiments that follow; please refer to the original publications for more detail. These DSMs are harvested from a corpus of almost 3 billion running words containing all the documents from the British National Corpus (see Section 2.1 above), a dump of the English Wikipedia and a large sample of other Web documents. The distributional space in which the vectors live is defined by

---

[63]Although our transposition approach could be a solution for relatives with a gap in an *argument* position, as far as we can see, it would not work when all the arguments of the verb are saturated. For instance, it would be insufficient to deal with, e.g., *the way in which Marco runs*, where the pronoun is extracted from a manner modifier. A conceivable solution would be to take modifiers to be additional arguments of the verb. A verb with a missing "manner argument" would in this case be transposable, though its dimensionality would increase.

co-occurrence within sentence boundaries with the 10,000 most common lemmatized content words in the corpora (Baroni and Zamparelli 2010, and Vecchi et al. 2011, include nouns, adjectives and verbs; Grefenstette et al. 2013, and Boleda et al. 2012b, also include adverbs). The raw counts are transformed into Mutual-Information-based association scores (see Section 2.1) and the 10,000 original components are compressed into 300 with dimensionality reduction techniques (again, refer to Section 2.1 above).[64]

Across all experiments, the functional model we are proposing is contrasted with the (unweighted) additive and multiplicative models of Mitchell and Lapata. Vecchi et al. (2011) and Boleda et al. (2012b) also test the model proposed by Guevara (2010) (see Section 6 below). Boleda et al. (2012b) also implement the dilation model of Mitchell and Lapata (2010) (see footnote 22 above). Grefenstette et al. (2013) include, in the transitive tests, the Kronecker model that was the best performer in Grefenstette and Sadrzadeh (2011b) (and that is not defined for intransitive verbs).

4.2   Intransitive and transitive sentences

Mitchell and Lapata (2008) introduced a data set of similarity judgments for 120 intransitive sentence pairs. The pairs, rated by 49 subjects on a 1-7 scale, were constructed to maximize the similarity or dissimilarity between the sentences by exploiting verb ambiguity. For example, one of the pairs that received high similarity ratings was *"the child strayed"–"the child roamed"*; one pair with low ratings was *"the child strayed"–"the child digressed"*. By replacing *child* with *discussion*, the opposite intuitions are obtained. As already discussed in Section 2.3 above, these stimuli tap into systematic polysemy, and in particular co-compositional aspects of verb meaning. All sentences were presented with the definite determiner and in simple past format to the subjects, but the constant determiner and tense are ignored by the composition models.[65] Grefenstette et al. (2013) implemented the approach to composition with intransitive verbs that we sketched in Section 3.4 above. Given the concrete DSM we described in the previous subsection, in which all vectors live in 300-dimensional space, they derived 300-component sentence vectors by multiplying 300×300 ma-

---

[64]For technical reasons, the multiplicative model requires a different method of dimensionality reduction than the other models (Grefenstette et al. 2013), or no reduction at all (the other studies except Vecchi et al. 2011).

[65]Given how this and the following task are set up, we ignore the distinction between nouns and DPs, and, following Grefenstette and colleagues, we speak of nouns when it would be probably more appropriate to speak of DPs.

trices representing the verbs by the 300-component vectors representing the subject nouns (verb matrices were trained on example input and output vector pairs as illustrated in Section 3.5 above). Performance was measured by the correlation of the cosines (see Section 2 above) between sentence vectors produced by a model with the subjects' rating for the corresponding sentence pairs (if the model is good, when subjects assign high ratings the cosine should be high, indicating high sentence similarity, and *vice versa* for low ratings). Correlation scores range from 0 for no correlation whatsoever to 1 for perfect correlation (or -1 for a perfect *inverse* correlation). To put things into perspective, the inter-subject correlation is of 0.40; and measuring the similarity between corpus-extracted vectors representing the verbs only (thus ignoring the contribution of subject nouns to meaning) achieves a correlation of 0.06. The functional model outperformed all other composition methods with a correlation of 0.23 (still well below that of human beings), with the multiplicative model coming a close second with a correlation of 0.19.

Turning to transitive cases, Grefenstette and Sadrzadeh (2011a) constructed a data set of simple transitive sentences with criteria similar to those used by Mitchell and Lapata for intransitives. Their data set contains 200 subject-verb-object sentences rated by 25 subjects. An example of a high-similarity pair is *"map shows location"–"map pictures location"*, whereas *"map shows location"–"map expresses location"* is low-similarity (compare to: *"table shows/expresses results"*). Grefenstette et al. (2013), following the functional approach, model transitive verbs as third-order $300\times300\times300$ tensors, estimated from example data using the procedure illustrated in Figure 3 above. The tensor is first multiplied by a 300-component object vector, giving a matrix corresponding to the VP, which is then multipled by a 300-component subject vector, to return the 300-component vector representing the sentence. In this task, inter-subject correlation is at 0.62, and using verb vectors only achieves a correlation of 0.08. Again, the functional model outperforms all the rivals, with a correlation of 0.32. The second best is Grefenstette and Sadrzadeh's state-of-the-art Kronecker model (0.25) followed by the multiplicative approach (0.23).

4.3   Adjective-noun constructions

Vecchi et al. (2011) studied a sample of the adjective-noun constructions (ANs) that never occur in the 3 billion word corpus we described above. These were rated as semantically acceptable or not by two linguists, resulting in a data set containing 280 acceptable and 413 "deviant" ANs (examples of acceptable: *blind trader, coastal mosquito, eth-*

ical trademark; example of deviant: *blind numeral, coastal subtitle, ethical sunset*). Vecchi and colleagues hypothesize that the (model-derived) vectors representing acceptable ANs will inhabit areas of the semantic space that are more densely populated (with vectors of nouns, adjectives and corpus-attested ANs) than those inhabited by the deviant ANs: We might have not encountered *coastal mosquitoes* yet, since this is a sensible concept, there are many close concepts (*river mosquitoes, coastal bugs...*) that we are familiar with. Consequently, the model-derived vector for the *coastal mosquitoes* AN should be close to many corpus-derived vectors. On the other hand, *coastal subtitles* are not just unheard of, it is not even clear what a related concept should be. Operationally, Vecchi and colleagues measure the *neighborhood density* of a vector as the average cosine of the vector with its 10 nearest neighbours in distributional space (the denser the neighborhood, the higher this average cosine). Under the functional view, ANs are 300-component vectors derived by multiplying a 300×300 adjective matrix (trained from corpus examples) by a 300-component noun vector. Vecchi and colleagues found that the functional method, as well as the additive and multiplicative models (but not Guevara's method), correctly predicted a significant difference in density between acceptable and deviant ANs. The functional method, moreover, predicts the largest difference.[66]

As discussed in Section 3.4, it is possible to measure the similarity of matrices and higher-order tensors just like we compare vectors, e.g., using the cosine method. Do these higher-order representations capture lexical similarity as well as traditional distributional vectors do? A small experiment reported by Baroni and Zamparelli (2010) looks at the specific case of (attributive) adjectives (that, in their implementation, are, again, 300×300 matrices mapping noun vectors to AN vectors). The results suggest that the higher-order representations of adjectives derived by matrix estimation are comparable and even *better* than vector representations directly extracted from the corpus. The task is to group 19 adjectives into 4 classes: color (*white, red...*), positive evaluation (*nice, excellent...*), time (*recent, new...*) and size (*big, small*). Baroni and Zamparelli use a standard clustering algorithm that assigns the adjectives to classes based on the similarity of their matrix or vector representations. Both the traditional vector-based and the matrix-based representations of adjectives achieve clustering per-

---

[66]Vecchi and colleagues also consider a length-based heuristic to measure acceptability. However, they estimate the adjective matrices with a length-insensitive criterion of fit between predicted and example output vectors. Not surprisingly, the length-based cue (that works for the additive and multiplicative methods) does not produce good results when using functional composition.

formance significantly above chance, with matrices being better than vectors (0.74 vs. 0.68 in *purity*, a measure of how good the automated clustering is compared to the real classification, ranging from 1 for perfect clusters to values centered at 0.46 for random clustering).

Boleda et al. (2012b) tackle what is probably the most sophisticated linguistic issue that has been addressed with compositional DSMs until now, namely that of characterizing three kinds of adjectival modification: intersective (*white dress*), subsective (*white wine*) and intensional (*former criminal*) modification. Both intersective and subsective constructions are restricted to those involving color terms. From a denotational perspective, intersective adjectives (more precisely: intersectively-used adjectives) are those that produce the intersection of the set of entities defined by the adjective with the set of entities defined by the noun (a *white dress* is a *dress* and a *white thing*). Subsective (subsectively-used) adjectives cause the inference that the property denoted by the noun holds of the entities being described, whereas the property denoted by the adjective is just a proxy for a more descriptive property, and might or might not hold in a literal sense, with the resulting AN denoting a subset of the noun set (a *white wine* is a yellow-ish sort of *wine*; *brown bear* refers to the species *Ursus arctos*, not to just any type of bear which is brown; a *white paper* is an exhaustive report, which might or might not be white). Intensional adjectives do not describe entities but rather complex operations that act on the intension of the noun they modify (a *former criminal* was a *criminal* in a past state of the world, but not in the current one). Boleda and colleagues first show that corpus-extracted vectors for ANs instantiating the different kinds of modification show global patterns in accordance with linguistic intuition. For example, intensional AN vectors tend to be significantly closer than the other types to their head noun vectors, since "intensional adjectives do not restrict the descriptive content of the noun they modify, in contrast to both the intersective and subsective [adjectives]" (Boleda et al. 2012b; p. 1230). Boleda and colleagues then proceed to test how well the compositional models mimic linguistically sensible patterns displayed by corpus-extracted ANs. They find that the functional approach (where, again, adjectives are 300×300 matrices estimated from corpus examples) provides the best approximation (the multiplicative method also does fairly well). Moreover, the functional approach produces composed vectors that are nearest their corpus-extracted counterparts, not only in the case of intersective and subsective ANs (where the additive model also does well), but also for the more difficult intensional adjectives (that is, only the functional approach is able to compositionally predict the corpus-attested distribution of, say, *former criminal*). Finally, qualitatively, the functional approach generates vectors that have the most sensible nearest neighbors. For example, the nearest neighbours of the functionally composed *artificial leg* vector include *artificial limb*, *artificial joint* and *scar*.

The experiments we reviewed, taken together, confirm that the functional approach to composition is empirically viable, and better than the ML mixture models and other state-of-the-art methods (although the multiplicative model performs fairly well across the board). Still, current data sets do not allow us to test some of the most important predictions we made in the previous section, for example that the functional model will be able to handle composition involving grammatical words, to take word order into account and to rightly compare full sentences with different structures (the intransitive and transitive sentences in the pairs used in the reviewed experiments have always exactly the same structure, and indeed share the same subject and object, with only the verb changing). Clearly, a high priority for the field – and one we are actively pursuing – is to build larger and more varied test sets, to truly explore the potential of more advanced compositional models. For the time being, equipped with the theoretical framework we developed in the previous sections and the empirical results just discussed, we move on to motivating the compositional aspect of the distributional semantics enterprise.

5 Motivating compositional distributional semantics

The previous sections have laid out a method to go from distributional representations of words to distributional representations of phrases and sentences, and presented preliminary evidence of the empirical viability of this method. We have however not yet sufficiently motivated *why* we would need distributional representations of *phrases* and *sentences*, as opposed to just *words*. We are now in the position to take this step with the proper background.

There is ample evidence that distributional vectors capture many aspects of word meaning and play an important role in lexical semantics. Should we also expect that larger constituents are represented in distributional space? We will start by arguing that, once you assume that words have distributional representations, it is hard to avoid the conclusion that phrases and sentences have distributional representations as well. We will then proceed to discuss some semantic challenges where such representations might prove their worth, showing that they are not only "unavoidable", but also very useful.

5.1 The unavoidability of vector representations of constituents above the word

One could take the view that distributional semantics is a theory of *lexical* semantics, and compositional semantics should be handled by other means. A nicely spelled-out proposal of this sort was recently presented by Garrette et al. (2013). Garrette and colleagues assign vectors to content words (nouns, verbs, adjectives, some adverbs), but use a (probabilistic) logical formalism to capture sentential aspects of meaning, such as entailment between utterances. The vectors representing content words (contextualized using word-meaning-in-context techniques along the lines of those presented in Section 2.3) provide evidence exploited by inferential processes involving the sentences containing them, but no distributional representation of constituents above the word level is constructed. Grammatical words are seen as logical operators and they are not provided with a distributional representation, neither as part of phrases –since phrases are not distributionally represented– nor by themselves. Garrette and colleagues use, for example, distributional vectors to compute the contextualized similarity between *sweeping* in "*A stadium craze is sweeping the country*" and *covering* in "*A craze is covering the nation*", and feed the resulting similarity score, together with Discourse Representation Theory representations of the sentences, to their probabilistic logical inference system, that uses these various sources of evidence to decide if there is entailment.

While the approach of Garrette et al. (2013) is extremely interesting, we find the restriction of distributional semantics to the representation of content words too limiting. First, if we assume a distributional representation for single words, it is strange that combinations of such words would have just a completely different logical-form representation. It would mean, for example, that it is meaningful to measure the degree of similarity between, say, *showering* and *bathing* (two content words, both with distributional representations enabling the similarity comparison), but not between *showering* and *taking a shower* (a content word, with distributional representation, and a phrase, not represented distributionally).

Indeed, the standard analysis of idioms as "phrases that behave as words", in the sense that they are stored in the lexicon with their compositionally unpredictable meaning, comes very natural if we assign distributional representations to phrases: An idiomatic phrase such as *red herring* is stored in the lexicon with a special vector that is different from the one that can be obtained compositionally. On the other hand, if phrases do not normally have distributional representations, the birth of an idiom would correspond to a big shift in the representation of the corresponding phrase, from logical form to vectorial representation. This "catastrophic" view of idiom formation does not sit well with the common observation that idiom formation is a gradual process, with different kinds of multiword expressions spread on a cline of idiosyncrasy: Compare the perfectly transparent *kick the ball* to the semi-opaque *kick the habit* to the completely idiomatic *kick the bucket* (see, e.g., Sag et al. 2002; and references there). While the details remain to be worked out, a view in which words and phrases have the same kind of semantic representation promises to handle the lexicalization cline of semantically opaque phrases better than a view in which words and phrases are very different objects, semantically speaking.

Garrette and colleagues limit distributional representations not only to *single* words, but to single *content* words. This is also problematic, given the fuzziness of the boundary between content and grammatical words. Everybody agrees that *car* is content and *the* is grammatical. But how about *several* and *various*? Syntactic tests suggest that *several* is a determiner (**the several friends*) –and hence a grammatical word– and *various* an adjective (*the various friends*) –and hence a content word. However, the meaning of the two terms does not look dramatically different and, again, it seems artificial to assume that *several* is (only) a logical operator, while *various* comes with a distributional vector.

Or think of adverbs. It seems reasonable to consider *very* a grammatical word, perhaps to be formalized as an intensifying logical operator. However, take a *-ly* adverb such as *massively*. Intuitively, we want to assign similar analyses to *a very dirty look* and *a massively dirty look*, so *-ly* adverbs should also be treated as logical operators. But then, should we provide a (manually crafted?) interpretation for the potentially infinite set of *-ly* adverbs seen as logical operators? Alternatively, if their semantics is to be derived from the corresponding adjectives (that are certainly content words with distributional representations), how does the process of taking a vector and returning a logical operator work?

Another argument to treat content and grammatical words in the same way comes from the fact that often the meaning of a single content word is synonymous of a phrase containing one or more grammatical terms: e.g., *bachelor* can be paraphrased with *man and not married*. Note that we are not making the controversial claim that *not* is part of the semantic representation of *bachelor* (Fodor et al. 1980), but simply observing that it is meaningful to compare a content word (*bachelor*) to a phrase containing grammatical words (*not married*), which is problematic if grammatical words are just logical operators working above the lexical level.

Finally, consider the historical process of *grammaticalization* (Hopper and Traugott 1990), whereby the same word starts its life as a full content word and progresses to become a grammatical element: Again, such gradual progression is hard to account for if content and grammatical terms have completely different semantic representations. Once more, it is simpler to assume that *all* words have (also) distributional representations.[67]

We have an argument, then, for the view that all words, including grammatical elements, have (also) distributional representations. In Section 3, we have argued at length that the right way to handle (most) grammatical words in distributional terms is as distributional composition functions. Putting the two conclusions together, if grammatical words have distributional representations, they are distributional composition functions, which in turn implies distributional representations for the phrases they construct.[68]

We conclude from the previous arguments that the position of Garrette et al. (2013) that only single (content) words, and not phrases of any complexity, have distributional representations is not tenable. Another very interesting recent contribution that promotes distributional semantics while rejecting composed vectors is that of Turney (2012). Although it is not directly relevant to compositionality, to fully

---

[67]The same fuzzy-boundary arguments can be used to argue that, if there are reasons to represent grammatical elements in a logical formalism, then content words should also have a logical-form representation. We have no qualms about this conclusion. More specifically, we find it appealing to conjecture that the logical representations of content words are radically underspecified, with details about the conceptual knowledge they convey encoded in their distributional vectors.

[68]In the approach sketched in Section 3 above, there is a clear-cut distinction between words that act as *arguments* (vectors) and *functions* (matrices or higher-order tensors). This is a different cutoff from the one between content and grammatical words. For example, adjectives and verbs are content words that act as functions, and pronouns, being DPs, are grammatical words that should be treated as arguments. Just as in formal semantics, it might be difficult for specific combinations to decide which element acts as the functor and which as the argument (with type shifting operations possibly allowing both analyses for the same word), but the resulting competing theoretical proposals will still have a clear separation between functions and arguments, there is no "argument-function continuum". More importantly, all linguistic objects, whether functions or arguments, are represented by distributional tensors, so that there is not a big ontological leap from one type to the other. For example, a change-of-category rule, e.g., the one associated to a nominalizing suffix such as *-ness*, is easily modeled as a function from matrices (adjectives) to vectors (nouns).

understand Turney's account of the latter we must first introduce his domain and function spaces.[69] Turney represents the meaning of each word in *two* distributional semantic spaces, whose dimensions are populated with different kinds of co-occurrence counts. The dimensions of the *domain* space are meant to capture domain similarity: *Carpenter* is domain-similar to *wood* because both concepts belong to the domain of *carpentry*. The dimensions of the *function* space capture function similarity: *Carpenter* is functionally similar to *mason* because the two roles have the same function within different domains. Consequently, for each word pair we can compute two separate similarity scores.

Turney's proposal regarding phrases and sentences is that, instead of composing vectors representing these larger constituents and then measuring their similarity, we should first compute similarities between the words in the phrase (or in the sentence), and then *compose the similarities* to derive a single similarity score comparing the larger constituents. For example, to measure the similarity of *dog house* to *kennel*, Turney first computes the domain similarity of *dog* to *kennel*, and both the domain and function similarities of *house* and *kennel*. Then, Turney uses the geometric average of the resulting scores as his estimate of the similarity between the phrases. Different similarity composition functions are employed for phrases or sentences with different syntactic structures. For example, to compare *dog house* to *shelter for cats*, we would use a function that takes into account the fact that in this case we want to measure, among other things, both the function similarity between *dog* and *cats* and the one of *house* with *shelter*. Clearly, there is an explosion of possible similarity composition functions (we need to define, at least, a distinct function for each pairing of possible syntactic structures). Turney speculates that automated methods could be used to discover the right function for a certain pair of sentences or phrases (or, more generally, for a pair of syntactic structures, we suppose).

Turney's method is competitive against Mitchell and Lapata's additive and multiplicative models on the tasks of picking the right paraphrase for a composite nominal expression (e.g., *kennel* as the right paraphrase of *dog house*) and predicting similarity judgments about pairs of noun, verb and adjective-noun phrases. Turney's approach dramatically outperforms the Mitchell and Lapata models if the tasks are run on modified versions of the evaluation sets that take word order into account: Addition and multiplication will assign the same similarity to the pairs *dog house–kennel* and *house dog–kennel*, which is obviously

---

[69] Turney's study also connects compositionality and relation analogy modeling. We do not discuss this aspect of his work here.

wrong. In Turney's approach, on the other hand, similarity is sensitive to order (in one case, the overall similarity is a function of the domain similarity of *dog–kennel* and of both domain and function similarities of *house–kennel*; in the other, of the domain similarity of *house–kennel* and of domain and function similarity of *dog–kennel*).

The "dual space" idea is certainly worth exploring, and we also find the proposal of composing similarity scores very appealing. However, we do not see why the input to similarity composition should be limited to single word comparisons. Besides the huge number of similarity functions that need to be defined, this misses obvious generalizations. For example, different similarity functions are required to compare *"dogs sleep in kennels"* with *"dogs sleep in woody kennels"* vs. *"dogs sleep in kennels made of wood"*, and yet another set of functions are required if the first sentence is replaced by *"domestic dogs sleep in kennels"*. In an approach in which phrases have also distributional representations, we could instead define a single similarity composition function accounting for the previous sentences and many other structures by comparing, in each case, the subject noun phrase, verb and prepositional phrase vectors (and/or directly verb phrase vectors, that include the prepositional phases).

Turney conjectures that grammatical words could be either treated just like content words, and incorporated in the similarity calculations, or used as cues to guide the derivation of the right similarity composition functions. Regarding the first option, just as with the ML vector mixture approaches discussed in Section 3.1 above, it is not clear that vectors extracted from all contexts in which words such as *a* or *in* occur will carry any distinctive information. Moreover, we do not see, in most cases, how they would enter the similarity computations: When comparing *the dog sleeps in a kennel* to *dogs sleep in kennels*, which element of the second sentence should *a* be compared against? If we construct phrasal vectors, we can instead incorporate the contribution of the determiner in the computation of the similarity between the prepositional phrases *in a kennel* and *in kennels*.

But the second route (grammatical words guiding the construction of similarity composition functions) is even less appealing, since the contribution of grammatical words to meaning is reduced to signaling which content words are compared to which, and in which of the two spaces, and this is a very limited contribution. A reasonable role for *with* in the pairwise comparison N_1 *with* N_2–N_3 N_4 (e.g., *mansion with windows–terrace house*) would be to tell us that we must compare, domain- and function-wise, N_1 to N_4 and N_2 to N_3. However, when comparing N_1 *without* N_2 to N_3 N_4, all we can say about *without* is that it leads to exactly the same comparisons as *with*, which makes the two prepositions identical! Again, an approach in which *with* and *without* act as distinct distributional functions used to construct the distributional representations of different prepositional phrases is more appealing.

Turney also presents and extends an argument originally put forth by Erk and Padó (2008) against using vectors of the same size to represent sentences of all possible lengths. While the following is not quite the same argument that Turney presents (that is somewhat more technical and based on information-theoretic considerations), we think it captures its main point. In abstract mathematical terms, each component of a vector can contain an infinite number of real numerical values, and hence there is an infinite number of distinct vectors. However, when vectors are encoded on a psychical device such as a computer or a brain, the range of possible values that can be distinguished in a single component is finite, which makes the number of possible distinct vectors also finite. But a finite set of vectors cannot represent the meaning of the infinite number of possible sentences in a language.

In replying to this argument, we contend, first, that, just as vectors are infinite *in theory*, so sentence meanings are infinite *in theory*. No single brain (or computer) will ever be capable or need to encode anything but a small finite subset of this infinity of possible meanings. Indeed, humans have problems keeping distinct, in their heads, the meanings of very long sentences that differ in just a few words. Second and more importantly, the argument is based on the unwarranted inference from the premise that sentences have vector representations to the conclusion that sentence meaning is represented by these vectors and these vectors *only*. We (and, we suspect, most proponents of compositional DSMs) agree with the premise, but strongly disagree with the conclusion. If we build the sentence vector compositionally from distributional representations of its parts, we do not see why these intermediate representations should be thrown away once the top node is reached. We find it more natural to assume that any semantic operation that refers to the distributional meaning of a sentence can access the vector representing the whole sentence as well as the vectors (or tensors) representing all its sub-constituents, down to the word level. And, going beyond distributional meaning, we do not dispute either that sentences will also have one, or indeed many, logical-form representations (a point we shall shortly return to in the conclusion). Thus, we are interested in arguments against distributional representations of sentences (and long phrases) that show that such vectors are not *necessary*; we do not need to be persuaded of the fact that they are not *sufficient.*

We conclude this section by observing that, while we hope to have argued convincingly for the extension of distributional representations beyond single content words, we do not know whether *every* word, phrase and sentence should have a distributional representation. There might be good reasons to represent determiner and verb phrases distributionally (e.g., to insure that phrases such as *dog house* and *kennel* or *taking a shower* and *bathing* are directly comparable), but the motivations to assign distributional representations to larger expressions are not so clear (for example, when discussing Turney's "composition of similarity scores" idea above, we suggested to replace the comparison of single words with the comparison of *phrases*, rather than whole sentences). It's far from clear where the line between the constituents that need distributional representations and those that don't should be drawn. Ideally, we will want to strike an acceptable balance between what DSM representations "do for you", and what they cost (in time spent creating and applying them). Perhaps the distributional representation for some or even most sentences will be something vague, perhaps just a hint that the sentence sounds "formal", "threatening", "odd", "funny" or "positive". Knowing this much would be useless for drawing inferences, but it would be valuable information if the task is to decide whether the sentence can be embedded under *complained that*, *boasted that* or *joked that*. So, for some purposes, there could be reason enough to keep around even vague DSM representations for higher constituents, for others there might not. For the time being, we assume that all linguistic constituents up to sentence nodes have a distributional representation, and leave it to future work to look for principled ways to determine the upper syntactic bound on distributional representations, possibly on a task-dependent basis.

5.2 The usefulness of vector representations of constituents above the word

The arguments we presented in the previous section in favour of distributional representations for larger constituents are negative in nature: If you accept that content words are associated to distributional vectors (and there is ample lexical-semantic evidence for the usefulness of the distributional representation of content words), then it's difficult to deny distributional representations to function words and larger constituents. However, once we have such representations, what can we do with them? How can distributional representations of phrases and sentences aid and/or complement the classic truth-functional representation of utterances?

Note that this is a more specific question with respect to the more general issue of whether distributional semantics can help (compositional) formal semantics, a topic we briefly addressed in Section 2.6. For example, in formal semantics it is typically (tacitly) assumed that word meanings are disambiguated before composition applies. Contextually disambiguated vectors (see discussion and references in Section 2.3 above) can help solve the mystery of how such disambiguation takes place. This is a way in which distributional semantics can help compositional semantics, but it does not require distributional representations above words and perhaps simple phrases.[70] Similarly, in Section 2.6 we (very tentatively) hypothesized that the distributional representation of a sentence might help to pick up the right reference for the sentence in the outside world. This would be of great help to compositional semantics, but we suspect that the level of words or simple phrases is better suited to perform the matching with real-world percepts than full sentences. The anchoring of sentence *"a black dog is barking"* to the outside world might proceed by matching a (multimodally-enhanced) *black dog* vector to vectors representing objects in the current scene, in order to scan for candidate black dogs, and a (multimodally-enhanced) *barking* vector to current auditory events, in order to scan for candidate barkings, rather than by matching a single holistic vectorial representation of the sentence to a holistic vector representing all the current percepts together.

We focus here on the usefulness of *compositional distributional semantics*, and not on the just discussed potential contributions of word-level distributional models to compositional semantics. We want, moreover, to look at uses of phrasal and sentential vectors that should be of direct interest to purveyors of semantic theory, rather than aimed at engineering applications, although effective distributional representations of sentences *are* of considerable practical interest. In particular, such representations can be employed to measure sentence similarity in order to detect paraphrases (informally, paraphrases are sentences that mean approximately the same thing: we will get back to them shortly). Paraphrase detection, in turn, is useful for information retrieval tasks such as finding semantically equivalent ways to query a data-base or the Web, or avoiding search results that overlap with the

---

[70]Note, however, that, as we conjectured in Section 2.3, a compositional DSM might largely sidestep issues of polysemy and disambiguation by implicitly disambiguating terms as part of the composition process. The (relative) success of the intransitive and transitive sentence experiments reported in Section 4.2 above, where handling verb ambiguity plays a crucial role in getting the right similarity scores, suggests that this is an empirically viable approach to polysemy.

query in lexical terms but have very different meanings. Another natural application for paraphrase detection[71] pertains to the evaluation of machine translation systems, where we must check if the translation provided by a system is just a rephrasing or it is significantly different from a benchmark manual translation. Other practical tasks helped by paraphrase detection include text summarization, question answering and shallow forms of text understanding, such as recognizing whether a short text entails a certain conclusion (Dagan et al. 2009). Another application domain where compositional distributional semantics has already proved its worth is in predicting degrees of positive or negative evaluation expressed by sentences, where it is important to look not just at single words, but also at how they are combined: *Very bad* is a more negative assessment than *bad*, but *very good* is more positive than *good* (Socher et al. 2012).

Assessing sentence similarity

After the previous brief excursus on applications, which we included for the benefit of potential industrial funders, let us turn to more theoretical concerns. Just as with words, the main function of sentential (or phrasal) vectors is to measure the degree of semantic similarity between sentences (or phrases). This is probably not of immediate help to determine the truth conditions of sentences. To know that *"a dog is barking"* is very similar to *"one canine creature arfs"* won't (directly) help you establish under which conditions the first utterance is true. However, there are other important aspects of meaning that similarity might be better suited to handle than truth conditions.

First and most obviously, humans do have strong and reasonably consistent intuitions about phrase and (simple) sentence similarities (as shown, for example, by the relatively high inter-subject sentence similarity correlations in the benchmark of Grefenstette and Sadrzadeh 2011a discussed in Section 4.2 above). The notion of a *paraphrase*, in particular, seems psychological robust, and difficult to capture in truth-functional terms.[72] The *"one canine creature arfs"* sentence above strikes us as a rather close paraphrase of *"a dog is barking"*, but it's hard to characterize this intuition in terms of truth conditions. The sentences are not tautologies (the canine creature could be

---

[71]Suggested to us by Stephen Clark.

[72]Note that paraphrasing is not just a metalinguistic ability, but it's likely to play a role in many unconscious everyday linguistic tasks, such as deciding the best way to communicate a thought or quickly determining whether a piece of news brings new information. More speculatively, paraphrasing could be used as a fast surface-y way to reformulate a statement in a form that is better suited for deeper logico-semantic analysis.

a coyote, arfing is not quite barking), and to simply claim that they are not contradictory is too weak a condition for paraphrase status. It might be possible to capture paraphrasing in terms of possible worlds (something along the lines of a requirement that paraphrases must share truth values in a certain proportion of worlds of a certain kind), but this seems a rather torturous way to account for something that can be modeled very straightforwardly by compositional distributional semantics, as already shown empirically by the studies we reviewed in Section 4.2. Moreover, the very notion of "close paraphrasing" (as used, for example, by lawyers to assess plagiarism claims) suggests that being a paraphrase is not an all-or-nothing property: There exist closer ("*a dog is barking*"–"*one canine creature arfs*") and more distant paraphrases ("*a dog is barking*"–"*a small mammal is making sounds*"). This gradient property follows naturally from the view that paraphrases are neighboring sentences in distributional space, but it is difficult to capture in a logical formalism.

Semantic anomaly detection

Semantic anomaly is another important aspect of meaning that, we believe, can be captured more appropriately using distributional representations of sentences.[73] Chomsky's (1957) famous "*colorless green ideas sleep furiously*" example demonstrates how a sentence can be at the same time perfectly grammatical and completely nonsensical. Chomsky used the sentence as part of an argument against statistical models of language (that would fail to distinguish between this unattested but syntactically well-formed sentence and equally unattested but grammatically ill-formed ones).[74] However, ironically, the kind of purely semantic ill-formedness illustrated by this sentence resists an account in terms of the formal models of meaning developed within the paradigm of generative grammar. The natural way to tackle semantic ill-formedness with the classic apparatus of formal semantics is by adopting a very rich and granular inventory of semantic types (see Asher 2011; for a very interesting recent proposal in this direction). However, to capture violations such as that ideas cannot be green or that sleeping cannot be performed in a furious manner, one would need a very rich ontology made of thousands of types, and it is not clear how such ontology could be learned from data (recall that the logical

---

[73]A system able to predict degrees of semantic anomaly will be able to perform many linguistically and practically important tasks, such as checking if an argument satisfies the selectional preference of the verb it depends from.

[74]See Pereira (2000) for an interesting discussion of how modern statistical models can address Chomsky's challenge.

approach, unlike distributional semantics, lacks practical algorithms for large-scale induction of semantic knowledge from naturally occurring data). But even with a rich type ontology, the extended theory of semantic types might not be the right instrument to characterize semantic anomaly. First, anomaly is highly context-dependent (*green ideas* sound good in *"green ideas are dominating the global warming debate"*), and accounting for context-dependency will make the theory of types even more complex. Second, semantic ill-formedness judgments are not sharp like syntactic ones, but are rather spread on a cline of acceptability from the completely natural (*"dogs bark"*) to the utterly nonsensical (the Chomsky sentence) via various degrees of semantic plausibility: *"?cats bark"*, *"??closets bark"*, *"???preferences bark"*.

Collecting large amounts of lexico-semantic knowledge from data, handling context dependency and modeling graded judgments are, however, core properties of the distributional approach to meaning. And this is clearly a job for *compositional* distributional semantics: We cannot see how you could measure the semantic plausibility of a sentence or a phrase using just the distributional representations of the component words, without combining them. In Vecchi et al. (2011) (briefly reviewed in Section 4.3 above), we implemented and tested simple methods to measure the degree of semantic acceptability of phrases using compositional DSMs. Extending ideas from that work to sentences, we hypothesize that properties of the semantic space neighborhood inhabited by a sentence will provide us with information about the plausibility of the sentence. One simple hypothesis in this direction (with preliminary support from the work by Vecchi and colleagues) is that semantic acceptability correlates with the density of a sentence neighborhood. Figure 4 is a cartoon illustration of this hypothesis. A meaningful sentence such as *"some ideas are dangerous"* will have many neighbours, that is, sentences that state related things. On the other hand, the nonsensical *"green ideas"* sentence will be out there in semantic space, without any (meaningful) sentence stating related facts to keep it company.

An approximation to this approach would involve constructing a large set of (meaningful) sentence vectors (e.g., taking relatively frequent sentences from a corpus), and measuring how populated the area surrounding an arbitrary point (corresponding to a compositionally-derived sentence) is, or what are the closest neighbours of a given point. Yet, if we want to follow this idea to its full consequences we will need a different, more ambitious and more interesting method, which at present we can just sketch.

The compositional DSM enterprise, if fully successful, would allow us to build a meaningful vector for any meaningful and syntactically

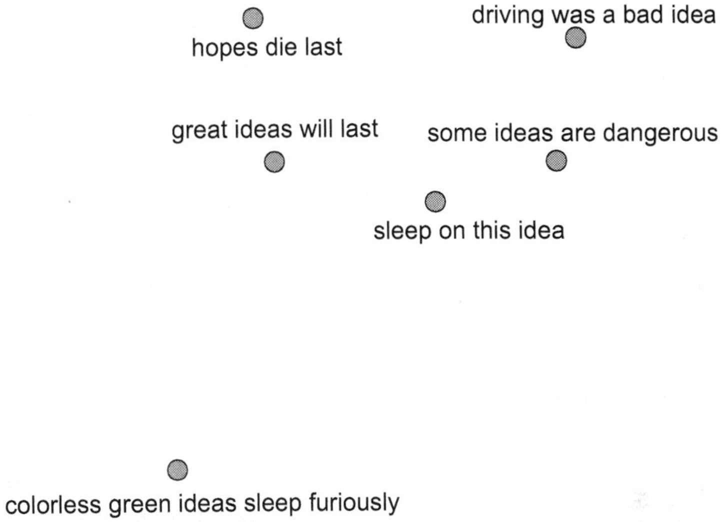

driving was a bad idea

hopes die last

great ideas will last   some ideas are dangerous

sleep on this idea

colorless green ideas sleep furiously

FIGURE 4: Nonsensical sentences might be isolated in semantic space.

correct sentence. The motivation for doing this compositionally is by now very familiar: the space of possible sentences is infinite. Suppose, now, that we want to reverse our task: Given a vector **s** produced by the distributional composition of a sentence, we want to ask which are the sentences that, if fed through the same process, would produce the vectors closest to **s**. In the best of possible worlds, if **s** has been created from S (let's say that **s** is a 'distributional composition' of S, **s** =CO(S)), the "noisy" inverse function GEN[75] applied to **s** should give back a set containing the closest paraphrases of S within certain bounds of length, complexity, etc. (including S itself). The distance of the generated phrases to S would then be measured by applying CO to them to obtain the corresponding vectors, and measuring the cosines of the latter to **s**. In particular, it should be the case that $\cos(\mathrm{CO(S)}, \mathbf{b}) \approx 1$.

An empirically effective formulation of GEN would have great practical importance, since without it we can only ask whether two candidate phrases are similar, but we have no way to *generate* similar cases,

---

[75]The name "GEN" should remind familiar readers of the formally similar problem of *candidate generation* in Optimality Theory (OT, Prince and Smolensky 2004). In OT, a set of ordered violable constraints can decide which of a set of candidates 'wins', i.e., satisfies the most important constraints. OT has no independent way of generating the candidates to be evaluated, and this task is left to an unspecified function also named GEN.

which is a fundamental step of the approach to semantic anomaly we just sketched and for some of the linguistic applications discussed below. We must however leave the construction of (approximations to) GEN to further work.

Alternative classes

There are several phenomena in formal semantics where the truth of a statement can be established only on the basis of a set of alternatives. The best-known case is probably Mats Rooth's (1985; 1995) seminal analysis of *association with focus*. Consider (18), where uppercased represents sentential stress and square brackets the focused constituent.[76]

(18) The candidate only [shared a CAB]$_F$ with the mafia boss.

For this sentence to be true, the candidate must have, of course, shared a cab with the mafia boss, and, to capture the semantics of *only*, he must have not done any of a set of alternative possible things he could have done with the mafia boss.

The problem is what the set of 'alternative possible things' amounts to. Obviously, (18)cannot be saying that the candidate could not have, say, shared a restaurant with a boss, or seen the mafia boss on TV. Intuitively, we understand the sentence as claiming that the most compromising relation the candidate had with the mafia boss was sharing a cab, which is maybe not particularly compromising. (18)thus excludes relations like 'being friend' or 'going on vacation' with him, 'paying him regular visits' and the like.

Unfortunately, formal semantics has very little to say on what the alternative set actually contains: Its content is assumed to be dependent on context, and is typically left to an underspecified 'pragmatic module'. However, without knowing the actual content of the alternative set, and indeed without having a measure of the extent to which an assertion counts as a valid alternative to the focused constituent, we have no way to explain why the replies in (19)[a-e] sound progressively less convincing as rejections of (18).

(19) a. That's false: he also worked for the mafia boss!

  b. That's false: he also shared a house with the mafia boss!

  c. That's false: he also ate in the same pizzeria as the mafia boss!

  d. That's false: he also ate at the same time as the mafia boss!

---

[76]Due to the mechanism of focus percolation, the area affected by focus is typically larger than the stressed (sub)constituent.

e. That's false: he also lived in the same country as the mafia boss!

The problem is pervasive since alternative sets are part and parcel of many semantic operations. They appear with what is sometimes called metalinguistic negation (20); in generic sentences (21); with scalar operators like *even* 21c, etc.

(20)   John didn't just [play a PRACtical joke]$_F$ on his colleague! He positively TERRified her!

(21)   a. In San Petersburg, [OFFicers]$_F$ always escort ballerinas (not low-rank military personnel)

b. In San Petersburg, officers always escort [balleRInas]$_F$ (but not other artists)

c. John even [SANG]$_F$ at the party (not just took part in it)

The problem is always the same: not all possible alternatives count (for instance if a ballerina is sometimes escorted by her husband, this doesn't seem to contradict (20)[a]; but if she was escorted by simple soldiers, it does.).

We believe that DSMs could actually offer a principled way to address this problem.[77] Very sketchily, the idea is to produce a tensor for the focused constituent in context, then use this tensor to decide which constituents would be sufficiently similar, i.e., which one would produce similar-enough tensors. The acceptability of the cases in 19 would thus have to be evaluated by computing the tensors for the constituents corresponding to the focus element of 18 (*"share a cab"*) and measuring the distance from its tensor. In other cases, e.g., to generate the continuation *"not low-rank military personnel"* in (20)[a], we would need to use the function GEN to produce examples of actual close alternatives (excluding, of course, those that are entailed by the focused assertion, like *"officers escort ballerinas"*).

Note, finally, that while focus on single elements (e.g., *John didn't actually [KISS]$_F$ Mary*) could still be handled by word-level DSMs, any case in which focus spans a VP or a complex nominal would require the full power of compositional DSMs.

Generic information

We already discussed in Section 2.6 how DSMs, reflecting statistical trends from large corpora, will capture generic rather than episodic knowledge. Indeed, modeling the acceptability of *generic sentences* is

---

[77]The relevance of compositional DSMs for the creation of alternative sets was first pointed out to us by Jacopo Romoli (p.c.).

another big challenge for a truth-functional view of meaning (Krifka et al. 1995; Cohen 2004) where distributional semantics might help. Generic statements about regularities in whole classes of objects, such as *"birds fly"*, *"mammals do not fly"* or *"lions have a mane"* are found acceptable despite the presence of (sometimes large and systematic) exceptions (*penguins, bats, lionesses*), which makes them difficult to handle in straightforward logical quantification terms.

Two aspects of generics suggest that distributional semantics might have something to contribute to this task. First, sentences such as *"lions have a mane"* express a facet of our general knowledge about a concept – in this case, that of a lion (Carlson 2009; draws an explicit connection between generics and conceptual knowledge). Not surprisingly, DSMs derived from large corpora are good at extracting general world knowledge about concepts (Almuhareb and Poesio 2005; Baroni et al. 2010; Kelly et al. 2012), so it is reasonable to expect their compositional extension to capture valid statements about properties of concepts.

Second, acceptability judgments about generic statements are not sharp. *"Lions live in Africa"* is perfect, *"lions live in Europe"* sounds funny but it is not nearly as bizarre and obviously false as *"lions live on the moon"*. Again, it is easier to model this sort of gradience in the geometric framework of distributional semantics than in truth-functional terms. In particular, there might be a relation between the way in which we just proposed to handle semantic acceptability and anomaly in general and the case of generics in particular. Not by chance, Chomsky's *"green ideas"* and almost all the examples we discussed above when speaking of semantic anomaly are in the form of generic sentences with bare plural subjects. And, again, density and other properties of the neighborhood of a generic statement might turn out to predict its degree of acceptability.[78]

6 A cursory look at some further relevant work

The last years have seen an enormous increase in the amount of published work on how distributional meanings can be composed; we refer to Clark (2013b), Erk (2012) and Mitchell and Lapata (2010) for

---

[78] A proper characterization of generics must take into account not only conceptual mismatches and world knowledge, such as the incompatibility of the class denoted by the subject with the property denoted by the predicate (lions are not the sort of things that live on the moon), but also grammatical aspects, such as the way in which the subject is overtly quantified: *"lions live in Africa"* sounds "true", but *"all lions live in Africa"* isn't; *"lions live in Europe"* sounds "false", but it is certainly the case that *"some lions live in Europe"*.

overviews. In previous sections, we have already discussed in depth some of the closest related work (see in particular Section 3.1 for a discussion of Mitchell and Lapata 2008, and Section 5.1 for our view of Garrette et al. 2013 and Turney 2012). Here, we limit our discussion to work that share our goal and that uses approaches either very close or radically different from ours.

Before going into the details of this work, it is worth mentioning that there is a rich tradition of corpus-based statistical semantics methods producing compositional representations that are different from the classic logic-based ones, but are not distributional in our sense. This line of research includes the corpus-based induction of semantic parsers suitable for question answering (Liang et al. 2011), role labeling (Titov and Klementiev 2012) and modeling semantic and syntactic acquisition (Kwiatkowski et al. 2012). The output of such semantic parsers could be tried as an alternative to the purely syntactic CG input used in our current work.

Recently, there also has been much interest in higher-order tensors for distributional semantics (e.g., Baroni and Lenci 2010; Giesbrecht 2010; Turney 2007; Van de Cruys 2010; Widdows 2008). However, even when this line of work tackles the issue of compositionality, it looks at tensors as a way to represent larger structures that result from composition, rather than taking the view we propose here of using tensors to encode composition functions.

Our view on the syntax-semantics relations traces back to the traditional type-logical approach introduced by van Benthem in 1986, following which we have exploited the Curry-Howard correspondence between logical rules and lambda-calculus rules to obtain a proof term for a parsed structure. The proof-term gives the backbone to be filled in with the interpretation of the linguistic signs composed. In our case, we have a clear-cut division of the workload. The grammar and the Curry-Howard correspondence with the lambda-calculus take care of building the proper structure by taking into account the expressivity issues, over-generation and under-generation problems as well as the scope possibilities that sentences with logical operators may display, and the distributional model accounts for lexical meaning and meaning composition.

Clarke (2011) studies the algebraic properties a vector space used for representing natural language meaning needs to have; the author claims the composition operation has to be bilinear (components of meaning persist or diminish but do not spontaneously appear; e.g., both *red* and *herring* must contain some components relating to the meaning of *red herring* which only come into play when these two words are combined in this particular order), associative and distributive. By taking this abstract view, Clarke manages to define a general framework that covers under its umbrella our approach together with, for instance, the one of Mitchell and Lapata (2008), discussed in Section 3.1, and Clark et al. (2008), which we discuss below. Moreover, the author identifies possible ways to account for degree of entailment between distributional representations, proposing to exploit the partial order of the defined algebraic structure.

Besides the general abstract framework, Clark et al. (2008) (and the extended version in Coecke et al. 2010) share also our view of the syntax-semantics interface of natural language and of its formal models. Similarly to us, they capture compositionality by exploiting a morphism between the syntactic and semantic building systems. Differently from us, they define a morphism directly between a grammar (a pre-group) and a vector space model without going through the intermediate step of the lambda-calculus. The choice of the pre-group is due to the authors interest in the category-theoretic perspective under which pre-groups share a common structure with vector spaces and tensor products. A different view is taken in Clark (2013a) where the author discusses the framework in terms of multi-linear algebra providing a more concrete and intuitive view for those readers not familiar with category theory. At the level of lexical and phrasal interpretation, Clark et al. (2008), Coecke et al. (2010) and Clark (2013a) import Frege's distinction into DSMs by representing "complete" and "incomplete" expressions as vectors and as higher-order tensors, respectively, and consider the syntax-semantics link established between syntactic categories and semantic types. For instance, a transitive verb has syntactic category $DP^r \cdot S \cdot DP^l$ (that corresponds to the functional CG category $(DP \backslash S)/DP)$ and semantic type $N \otimes S \otimes N$, since expressions in DP and S are taken to live in the semantic space of type N and S, respectively, and the transitive verb relates these vector spaces via the tensor product ($\otimes$): its dimensions are combinations of those of the vectors it relates. As explained in Clark (2013a), the verb vector can be thought of as encoding all the ways in which the verb could interact with a subject and object in order to produce a sentence, and the composition (via inner product) with a particular subject and object reduces those possibilities to a single vector in the sentence space. Different implementations of this framework have been proposed by, e.g., Grefenstette and Sadrzadeh (2011a), Grefenstette and Sadrzadeh (2011b), Coecke et al. (2013), Kartsaklis et al. (2013). The one closest to us is the one by Grefenstette et al. (2013), where the authors further develop the framework discussed above. In particular, they exploit a tensor contraction operation that guarantees an equivalence between tensor order and semantic type. Tensor contraction is closely related to our generalized matrix-by-vector product and indeed, the framework of Grefenstette and his colleagues can be seen as an abstract formalization of the one we are proposing here. Grefenstette and his colleagues (that, not by chance, include one of the authors of the current paper) also bring together the Coecke et al. formalism with ours by adopting the regression-based learning method we explained in this article (the empirical results of Grefenstette et al. 2013, are reviewed in Section 4.2 above).

We share the idea of learning composition functions by regression on corpus-extracted examples of their inputs and outputs with Guevara (2010), who, however, treats all linguistic expressions as vectors without distinguishing them into atomic and functional types. The importance of exploiting input and output training data for building compositional distributional semantic models is also stressed by Zanzotto et al. (2010), who present a model similar to the one of Guevara, but cleverly exploit dictionary definitions to extract both positive and negative training examples.

Another model that is closely related to ours is that of Socher et al. (2012), who also implement function application in terms of operations on matrices and vectors. However, differently from us, they treat each word equally, as both a vector and a matrix. Distributional composition is doubled – each word matrix is composed with the lexical vector of the other word in a phrase – and the result is still a pair of a vector and a matrix. Since Socher et al. (2012) do not use tensors higher than matrices, all composition is pairwise, whereas we have presented a model of composition permitting functions of larger arity. Finally, Socher and colleagues estimate the weights of their models by direct optimization of a specific semantic task, thus requiring hand-labeled examples of the intended output of the task, and producing different representations of the same linguistic expressions depending on the intended task. Direct empirical comparison of our approach to the one of Socher and colleagues is an important item in our future work agenda.

Rather different and quite interesting points of view are assumed in Garrette et al. (2013) (already discussed in Section 5.1) and Copestake and Herbelot (2012). Garrette et al. (2013) adopt a formal semantics framework to build First Order Logic (FoL) representations of sentences, lexical distributional semantic representation for computing word similarities and weighting FoL clauses, and Markov Logic Networks for reasoning on such clauses. Hence, they exploit the FoL logical operators, like negation, existential and universal quantifiers, to draw inferences involving their relations, and DSM representations to draw inferences involving lexical information.

The integration of logical and distributional models is studied in Copestake and Herbelot (2012). Here too, the authors distinguish the interpretation of closed and open class words by adopting a view closer to the logical one for the former and the distributional one for the latter, but they propose more drastic changes and an integration of the two models. On the one hand, they import in the logical model the idea that the meaning of a content word is given by the contexts in which it occurs, hence they replace the denotational sets of entities with distributional sets of contexts. On the other, they take the contexts to be logical rather than linguistic ones, namely the semantic space components are not words, but their logical representation. For instance, *jiggle* would be said to co-occur with the logical representation `table'(x)` if the corpus, from which co-occurrence information is extracted, contains the sentence *"the ball on the table jiggled"*. As in standard distributional semantics, here too there are different possibilities for choosing the logical context to be considered. For instance, logical contexts can be those predicated of the same entities of the target word, or those related by paths of a certain length to it, reaching sets of logical contexts corresponding to a very fine-grained notation of semantic features. Finally, each distributional set records also the connection of the formal logic representation of the sentence to the situation in which the sentence was uttered, as well as the entities that are arguments of the logical forms in it. This rich information allows to preserve the idea of extension as well as to distinguish words' intensions (sets of logical forms) even when their extension is the same.

7 Open issues and conclusions

In closing this paper, we want to touch on some of the open issues we see along the road to a full-sized DSM semantics, and return to the general system architecture.

One of the great advantages of DSMs is that they hold the promise to handle *polysemy* gracefully. We do not need to have a separate entry for *brown* in each of the *brown N* phrases cited in the Introduction (*"brown cow"*, *"brown book"*, etc.): The *brown* matrix will produce a sensible semantic value for (almost) all the nouns it is applied to. *Homonymy*, like the fact that *page* refers to a piece of paper or a person, is a different matter. The difference between polysemy and homonymy is notoriously difficult to draw, but the existence of a distinction seems indisputable. For instance, most people need some linguistic training to note that in co-predication cases like (22)*lunch* must mean different things (an object can be tasty, an event cannot), but any speaker is aware of the fact that *page, bank* or *bass* can each mean very different things.[79] With true homonyms co-predication is impossible (*"*the page was written in Latin and knew this language"*).

(22) Lunch was tasty but lasted forever.

Based as they are on word forms, DSMs tend to overlook homonymy, resulting in vectors that conflate all the different senses of a lexical expression. This is certainly a problem, but one which has been amply addressed at the lexical level in the computational community (see McCarthy 2009, and Navigli 2009, for recent surveys, and the discussion in Section 2.3). Word sense disambiguation techniques have limited success in fine-grained sense distinctions—fortunately, those that a DSM approach seems to be best at handling—but perform well on true homonymy, where there is no (synchronic) relation between the various senses. The output of these algorithms could thus be a semantic tagging of words in context, which distinguishes, say, between $page_{paper}$ and $page_{person}$. Suppose that tokens that cannot be disambiguated with confidence are left unlabeled, and that each labeled sense receives its own vector. When a compositional function like the adjectives *written* encounters an unlabeled ambiguous noun like *page* it could look up the vector for each of its possible meanings, then apply semantic anomaly detection, described in Section 5.2, applied to the output of $written(page_{person})$ and $written(page_{paper})$, to guess which meaning is probably correct for *"written page"*. If the ambiguity cannot be resolved locally it will be carried up the tree until it can be resolved by further compositions, up to the sentence (and potentially, the discourse) level. This will require a mechanism for storing multiple disjunctive meanings, but such a system would also be necessary if we want to store both compositional and idiosyncratic DSM-meaning for a constituent (to be able to process idioms in their literal and figurative use; see discussion in Section 3.5). It will make the system more complex, but it should not pose any special theoretical challenge, except for the general problem of deciding which words should be treated as homonyms. In the worst case, we run the risk of incorrectly treating a polysemous word as

---

[79]Words can be both polysemous and homonymous: *page* in the paper sense could refer to the object or the text in it, in the human sense, to the person or the position (*"he was nominated page"*). This suggests that homonymy and at least regular polysemy should not be seen as opposite values on a single scale. See Copestake and Briscoe (1995); Boleda et al. (2012a) for discussion of various approaches and Frisson (2009) and Klepousniotou and Baum (2007) for experimental results on the psychology of this distinction.

a case of homonymy, creating n possible lexical items with n vectors, where one should have been sufficient. Note however that in this case the vectors for the various senses will be quite similar, so even if the disambiguation system fails to distinguish one sense from the other, the harm done to the global system should be very limited.

A boundary case of 'lexical ambiguity' to which we will need to devote special attention is that of words with multiple argument structures. Recall that in our compositional DSMs the number of argument a word takes determines its shape, and that objects of different shapes cannot be directly compared (see Section 3.4). But many nouns can optionally take arguments: we have *mother*, but also *mother of twins*. Most nouns derived from transitive verbs can take PP arguments that correspond to the direct object of the verb (*"the end (of the paper) is near"*; *"the discovery (of America) was surprising"*, etc.).[80] Thus, it would appear that the same nouns are sometimes vectors, sometimes tensors, i.e., functions from the space of their arguments to nominal vectors.[81] The problem is also found with those verbs that have a transitive and an intransitive version (*John ate his lunch/John ate*): the VPs would be comparable (both matrices), the Vs would not. We reach the counterintuitive conclusion that the *end* in *"the end is near"* and *"the end of the paper is near"*, or the transitive and intransitive usages of *eating* are completely different and incomparable linguistic objects.

We see two linguistically informed solutions for this problem. First, we could treat verbs like *run* or *eat* as uniformly transitive, training them on their objects when they have one; when they do not, we could apply the transitive function to an 'internal object', built by averaging the vectors of the most frequent actual objects of the transitive version.[82] We surmise that the same approach could be applied to nouns.

---

[80]Treating all these cases as PP-adjuncts, i.e., cases where the preposition *of* takes the DP and the N to form a modified N, i.e., $(N\backslash N)/DP$, does not capture the fact that these are true arguments of the nouns, as they are of the corresponding verbs. Adjuncts are not selected; they can be attached to any noun, not just to relational ones. Moreover, arguments and adjuncts can combine, but only in one order (in *"a mother of twins of high social status"* only the second *of*-PP is an adjunct; *"*a mother of high social status of twins"* is impossible, at least with a neutral intonation).

[81]Following an old but still popular analysis (Stowell 1981), we could simplify things a bit taking the *of* that introduces nominal arguments to be a pure case marker. Semantically, this *of* would denote the identity function, which simply returns the vector of its DP argument. Relational nouns would then be matrices that map vectors in DP-space to vectors in N-space.

[82]This would attempt to capture the common observation that the understood object of the intransitive versions has to be somehow prototypical. If John is *"eating the dust"*, *"running a risk"* or *"drinking poison"*, it is odd to say that he is *eating*,

A second approach would be to use corpora to learn a mapping from the version of a word with an argument to the version without, or vice-versa. In this case, we would collect vectors for occurrences of *eat* or *end* without complements, vectors for occurrences of the same words when they have arguments, then use regression to establish a mapping (a third-order tensor if we map from a matrix to a vector). This approach might be feasible, but it is too general: nothing would prevent the function from being applied also to nouns that never take arguments.

Both routes are worth exploring if we want to handle a different and more productive case, that of *active/passive* alternations (23). In passives, the external argument of a transitive verb becomes syntactically optional and can be expressed by a *by*-phrase.

(23)   a. Mary kissed John.

        b. John was kissed (by Mary).

The two approaches (providing a null, 'average' argument, or learning a transitive-intransitive mapping) have different strengths and weaknesses. The first essentially reduces (23)[b] to *"someone kissed John"*, but is computationally straightforward (after training *kiss* on active sentences alone one would be able to compose the DSM for a passive sentence with no additional training). The second (learning from the corpus a mapping from active to passive verbs or vice-versa) seems potentially superior at capturing the fact that active and passive voice might be used in different contexts—their information structure is not the same (see, e.g., Lambrecht 1996). Neither methods, however, could recover the agent within *by*-phrases; this would probably require a more structural approach, akin to the tensor transposition we saw for relative clauses. In principle, cases like the causative alternation (*"the missile sank the ship"* / *"the ship sank"*) or the middle construction (*"the shop sells the book"* / *"the book sells well"*) could be handled in a similar way, though note that in these cases, unlike in passives, the necessary DSM-manipulations could not be associated with the presence of an affix (this was the spirit of the decompositional morphology hinted at in Section 3.4).

Operations that take existing forms and generate variations would be the DSM-equivalent of *lexical redundancy rules* in transformational syntax (Chomsky 1970): *if* a certain linguistic item has been observed with a certain argument structure, *then* we can generate a new argument structure for it according to the functions we have learned. De-

---

running or *drinking*.

spite the potential risk of overgeneration, the opportunity to establish interesting mappings for a large set of constructions is wide open: For instance, we could easily imagine a rule, triggered by Subject-Aux inversion, which maps a declarative-sentence vector into a yes/no-question vector.

As discussed in Section 3.5, a key ingredient for the success of a full-scale DSM-distributional approach is representational efficiency. This means, among other things, having more compact and efficient methods for representing and learning tensors, as well as the possibility to recognize and exploit the similarity of different linguistic objects in the learning phase. The latter would be crucial at the lexical and phrasal level, to learn rare forms. Recognizing, for instance, that *indigo* names a color, we could use whatever knowledge we have about other colors to extrapolate a part of its semantics.

A different case in which similarity of structures might play a role is the way we could handle generalized *coordination*. This extremely pervasive operation has many properties that set it aside from other constructions in grammar (see, e.g., Zamparelli 2011, for a review). One is its promiscuous categorial behavior: *and* can join any pair of syntactic categories (in CG, we can define the type of *and* as $((X\backslash X)/X)$, X a variable over categories). Since these categories can themselves be quite complex (e.g., transitive verbs or VP modifiers, higher-order tensors), a potential objection to our approach is that conjunction of all but the most basic cases will be impossible to implement, or train.

We believe that the situation is actually a lot better than it seems. Even setting aside the discussion at the end of Section 3.5, which suggests that the computational problem could be reduced by a careful implementation, we could follow the approach in Rooth and Partee (1983) and propose that conjunction never applies to higher-order tensors. In this influential approach (see also Winter 1996, 2001) the scope of coordination is not what it appears to be: V-conjunction in (24)[a] is semantically converted into sentential conjunction (24)[b], an operation on vectors in our system. Similarly, (25)[a] would become (24)[b], again vector conjunction.

(24) a. Dogs [chase and pester] cats.

     b. [Dogs chase cats and dogs pester cats]

(25) a. A [long and fat] hot dog.

     b. A [long hot dog and fat hot dog]

Additional reasons for optimism come from the observation that, when applied to predicates, conjunction in formal semantics boils down to a very simple operation—set intersection.[83] The DSM version of co-ordination could be equally simple; so simple, in fact, that we might discover that (some variation on) Mitchell and Lapata's componentwise vector multiplication might approximate it well enough to make train-ing superfluous for those coordinated categories that do not involve tensed elements.[84]

If coordination became, in fact, an 'easy' case, the road would be open to a *decompositional approach* to those constructions that have conjunction as one of their subcomponents (examples are relative clauses, correlatives, adpositional structures), factoring out conjunc-tion and dealing with the hopefully straightforward residual part. For instance, consider a relative clause, as in (26): in formal semantics, the brackets in this example would denote the intersection between the set of dogs and the set of cat-chasers.

(26)   The [dogs which chase cats] barked.

Now, in many languages, relative clauses can function as full nomi-nals ("free relatives", e.g., the constituents marked in (27)).

(27)   Whoever came k
        new [what Bill feared most].

This suggests an alternative treatment for *which* with respect to the one we propose in Section 3, where this word is a function from matrices (verb plus object or transposed verb plus subject) to N vectors. To deal with free relatives, the same operation that in *"dogs chase cats"* applies to the nouns *dogs* and *cats*, turning them into full DPs (see Section 3.6), would now map the free relatives in (27)onto the DPs needed by *knew*. But (26)would involve combining the noun *dog* with the "pseudo-noun" *"which chase cats"* by means of a standard N conjunction (which in this case would be entirely structure-driven: no *and* is present between *dogs*

---

[83]By predicates we mean, pretheoretically, any category that can appear after a copula (adjectives and non-quantificational noun phrases), and modifiers (attribu-tive adjectives, PPs). The behavior of conjunction with DPs is more complex, and has prompted some linguists to distinguish between an intersective (Boolean) and a non-intersective (non-Boolean) conjunction. Again, see Zamparelli (2011) for ref-erences.

[84]As Mitchell and Lapata discuss, componentwise vector multiplication produces a sort of "component intersection" —only those dimensions that are significantly different from 0 in both input vectors will be significantly different from 0 in the out-put. Tensed cases like *"John arrived and Mary left"*, or *"John took the car and went to school"* imply a temporal sequence of two events, while conjunction of statives do not: *"John likes spaghetti and Mary loves sushi"*. We do not see how vector-mixture models could approximate these cases, and especially their difference: if they are symmetrical, they might at best get the second, if not, the first.

and *"which chase cats"*). The DSM meaning of the relative pronoun would be quite simpler and the conjunction could be the same as the one trained for, say, *"a friend and colleague"*. The same *divide et impera* methodology could be applied to other cases, e.g., adverbial modifiers.

When DSMs were first developed for single words, they were tested on fairly basic lexical tasks, such as simulating word similarity judgments or spotting synonyms. However, in the two decades since these first experiments, the very same models have been applied to much more complex and arguably linguistically interesting tasks, such as predicting the selectional preferences of verbs or the qualia roles of nominal concepts (see Section 2.2). Analogously, we are currently testing our early compositional DSMs on relatively 'simple-minded' tasks such as paraphrase detection, but we are confident that the imagination of future researchers will find applications for these models in increasingly ambitious and linguistically interesting domains of semantics.

This paper is the beginning of a long journey. We hope that you, patient reader, will forgive us if its ambitious course still rests on empirical foundations that we and many others are just starting to verify. In the years to come, we will devote our energies to chart the land and to trim the paths, many of which undoubtedly lead nowhere. We hope that if you found the ideas presented here stimulating enough to accompany us until this last paragraph, you will also join us in the exploration of this brave new world.

Acknowledgments

We owe some fundamental ideas to Edward Grefenstette and Emiliano Guevara. Edward came up with the stepwise method to estimate higher-order tensors and suggested tensor transposition to implement the rule we use for relative clauses in Section 3.6. Emiliano first proposed to use regression to learn compositional functions. We also thank Chris Barker, Gemma Boleda, Johan Bos, Peter Bosch, Stephen Clark, Georgiana Dinu, Katrin Erk, Stefan Evert, Eugenie Giesbrecht, Dimitri Kartsaklis, Graham Katz, Alessandro Lenci, Louise McNally, Stefano Menini, Ray Mooney, Sebastian Padó, Massimo Poesio, Martha Palmer, Denis Paperno, Jacopo Romoli, Chung-chieh Shan, Mark Steedman, Anna Szabolcsi, Peter Turney, Dominic Widdows, Fabio Massimo Zanzotto, the LILT editor and reviewers, the members of the inter-continental FLOSS reading group, the audience at CLIN 2012, Linguistic Evidence 2012, the UCL Cognition, Perceptual and Brain Sciences seminar, the EACL 2012 Compositionality in Distributional Semantics tutorial, LSD 2012 and KONVENS 2012 for a mixture of ideas, stimulating discussions, constructive criticism, implementation help and feedback on earlier versions of this paper. Of course, we thank also all the COMPOSES group for so many engaging discussions. Last but not least, we thank Annie Zaenen for her careful proof-reading of our draft. The work described in the article is currently being funded by the ERC 2011 Starting Independent Research Grant nr. 283554 (COMPOSES project).

References

Aitchison, Jean. 1993. *Words in the Mind*. Malden, MA: Blackwell.

Almuhareb, Abdulrahman and Massimo Poesio. 2005. Concept learning and categorization from the web. In *Proceedings of CogSci*, pages 103–108. Stresa, Italy.

Andrews, Mark, Gabriella Vigliocco, and David Vinson. 2009. Integrating experiential and distributional data to learn semantic representations. *Psychological Review* 116(3):463–498.

Apresjan, Yuri. 1974. Regular polysemy. *Linguistics* 142:5–32.

Asher, Nicholas. 2011. *Lexical Meaning in Context: A Web of Words*. Cambridge, UK: Cambridge University Press.

Axler, Sheldon. 1997. *Linear algebra done right, 2nd ed*. New York: Springer.

Bader, Brett and Tamara Kolda. 2006. Algorithm 862: MATLAB tensor classes for fast algorithm prototyping. *ACM Trans. Math. Software* 32:635–653.

Baker, Collin, Charles Fillmore, and John Lowe. 1998. The Berkeley FrameNet Project. In *Proceedings of COLING*, pages 86–90. Montreal, Canada.

Barker, Chris and Chung-Chieh Shan. 2006. Types as graphs: Continuations in type logical grammar. *Journal of Logic, Language and Information* 15:331–370.

Baroni, Marco, Eduard Barbu, Brian Murphy, and Massimo Poesio. 2010. Strudel: A distributional semantic model based on properties and types. *Cognitive Science* 34(2):222–254.

Baroni, Marco, Raffaella Bernardi, Ngoc-Quynh Do, and Chung-Chieh Shan. 2012. Entailment above the word level in distributional semantics. In *Proceedings of EACL*, pages 23–32. Avignon, France.

Baroni, Marco and Alessandro Lenci. 2010. Distributional Memory: A general framework for corpus-based semantics. *Computational Linguistics* 36(4):673–721.

Baroni, Marco and Roberto Zamparelli. 2010. Nouns are vectors, adjectives are matrices: Representing adjective-noun constructions in semantic space. In *Proceedings of EMNLP*, pages 1183–1193. Boston, MA.

Basile, Valerio, Johan Bos, Kilian Evang, and Noortje Venhuizen. 2012. Developing a large semantically annotated corpus. In *Proceedings of LREC*, pages 3196–3200. Istanbul, Turkey.

Bernardi, Raffaella and Michael Moortgat. 2010. Continuation semantics for the Lambek-Grishin calculus. *Information and Computation* 208(5):397–416.

Biemann, Chris and Eugenie Giesbrecht. 2011. Distributional semantics and compositionality 2011: Shared task description and results. In *Proceedings of the ACL Workshop on Distributional Semantics and Compositionality*, pages 21–28. Portland, Oregon.

Blacoe, William and Mirella Lapata. 2012. A comparison of vector-based representations for semantic composition. In *Proceedings of EMNLP*, pages 546–556. Jeju Island, Korea.

Blei, David, Andrew Ng, and Michael Jordan. 2003. Latent Dirichlet allocation. *Journal of Machine Learning Research* 3:993–1022.

Bloom, Paul. 2000. *How Children Learn the Meanings of Words*. Cambridge, MA: MIT Press.

Boleda, Gemma, Sebastian Padó, and Jason Utt. 2012a. Regular polysemy: A distributional model. In *Proceedings of *SEM*, pages 151–160. Montreal, Canada.

Boleda, Gemma, Eva Maria Vecchi, Miquel Cornudella, and Louise McNally. 2012b. First order vs. higher order modification in distributional semantics. In *Proceedings of EMNLP*, pages 1223–1233. Jeju Island, Korea.

Boole, George. 1854. *An Investigation of the Laws of Thought*. London: Walton and Maberly.

Bruni, Elia, Giang Binh Tran, and Marco Baroni. 2011. Distributional semantics from text and images. In *Proceedings of GEMS*, pages 22–32. Edinburgh, UK.

Bruni, Elia, Jasper Uijlings, Marco Baroni, and Nicu Sebe. 2012. Distributional semantics with eyes: Using image analysis to improve computational representations of word meaning. In *Proceedings of ACM Multimedia*, pages 1219–1228. Nara, Japan.

Budanitsky, Alexander and Graeme Hirst. 2006. Evaluating WordNet-based measures of lexical semantic relatedness. *Computational Linguistics* 32(1):13–47.

Bullinaria, John and Joseph Levy. 2007. Extracting semantic representations from word co-occurrence statistics: A computational study. *Behavior Research Methods* 39:510–526.

Bullinaria, John and Joseph Levy. 2012. Extracting semantic representations from word co-occurrence statistics: Stop-lists, stemming and SVD. *Behavior Research Methods* 44:890–907.

Burgess, Curt. 2000. Theory and operational definitions in computational memory models: A response to Glenberg and Robertson. *Journal of Memory and Language* 43(3):402–408.

Cacciari, Cristina. 2012. Multiword idiomatic string processing: Many words in one? In J. Järviki, P. Pyykkönen, and R. Laine, eds., *From Words to Constructions: Structural and Semantic Complexity in Representation and Processing*. Berlin, Germany: Mouton de Gruyter. In press.

Carey, Susan and Elsa Bartlett. 1978. Acquiring a single new word. *Papers and Reports on Child Language Development* 15:17–29.

Carlson, Greg. 2009. Generics and concepts. In J. Pelletier, ed., *Kinds, Things and Stuff*, pages 16–35. Oxford, UK: Oxford University Press.

Chomsky, Noam. 1957. *Syntactic Structures*. Berlin, Germany: Mouton.

Chomsky, Noam. 1970. Remarks on nominalization. In R. Jacobs and P. Rosenbaum, eds., *Readings in English Trasformational Grammar*. Waltham, MA: Ginn-Blaisdell.

Cinque, Guglielmo, ed. 2002. *Functional Structure in DP and IP - The Carthography of Syntactic Structures*, vol. 1. Oxford University Press.

Cinque, Guglielmo. 2010. *The Syntax of Adjectives. A Comparative Study*. Cambridge, MA: MIT Press.

Clark, Stephen. 2013a. Type-driven syntax and semantics for composing meaning vectors. In C. Heunen, M. Sadrzadeh, and E. Grefenstette, eds., *Quantum Physics and Linguistics: A Compositional, Diagrammatic Discourse*, pages 359–377. Oxford, UK: Oxford University Press.

Clark, Stephen. 2013b. Vector space models of lexical meaning. In S. Lappin and C. Fox, eds., *Handbook of Contemporary Semantics, 2nd ed.*. Malden, MA: Blackwell. In press; http://www.cl.cam.ac.uk/~sc609/pubs/sem_handbook.pdf.

Clark, Stephen, Bob Coecke, and Mehrnoosh Sadrzadeh. 2008. A compositional distributional model of meaning. In *Proceedings of the Second Symposium on Quantum Interaction*, pages 133–140. Oxford, UK.

Clark, Stephen and James Curran. 2007. Wide-coverage efficient statistical parsing with CCG and log-linear models. *Computational Linguistics* 33(4):493–552.

Clark, Stephen and Stephen Pulman. 2007. Combining symbolic and distributional models of meaning. In *Proceedings of the First Symposium on Quantum Interaction*, pages 52–55. Stanford, CA.

Clarke, Daoud. 2011. A context-theoretic framework for compositionality in distributional semantics. *Computational Linguistics* 1(54).

Coecke, Bob, Edward Grefenstette, and Mehrnoosh Sadrzadeh. 2013. Lambek vs. Lambek: Vector space semantics and string diagrams for Lambek Calculus. *Ann. Pure Appl. Logic* 164(11):1079–1100.

Coecke, Bob, Mehrnoosh Sadrzadeh, and Stephen Clark. 2010. Mathematical foundations for a compositional distributional model of meaning. *Linguistic Analysis* 36:345–384.

Cohen, Ariel. 2004. Generics and mental representations. *Linguistics and Philosophy* 27:529–556.

Copestake, Ann and Ted Briscoe. 1995. Semi-productive polysemy and sense extension. *Journal of Semantics* 12:15–67.

Copestake, Ann and Aurelie Herbelot. 2012. Lexicalised compositionality. http://www.cl.cam.ac.uk/~ah433/lc-semprag.pdf.

Curran, James, Stephen Clark, and Johan Bos. 2007. Linguistically motivated large-scale NLP with C&C and Boxer. In *Proceedings of ACL (Demo and Poster Sessions)*, pages 33–36. Prague, Czech Republic.

Curran, James and Marc Moens. 2002a. Improvements in automatic thesaurus extraction. In *Proceedings of the ACL Workshop on Unsupervised Lexical Acquisition*, pages 59–66. Philadelphia, PA.

Curran, James and Marc Moens. 2002b. Scaling context space. In *Proceedings of ACL*, pages 231–238. Philadelphia, PA.

Dagan, Ido, Bill Dolan, Bernardo Magnini, and Dan Roth. 2009. Recognizing textual entailment: rationale, evaluation and approaches. *Natural Language Engineering* 15:459–476.

Dinu, Georgiana and Mirella Lapata. 2010. Measuring distributional similarity in context. In *Proceedings of EMNLP*, pages 1162–1172. Cambridge, MA.

Dumais, Susan. 2003. Data-driven approaches to information access. *Cognitive Science* 27:491–524.

Dummett, Michael. 1981. *Frege: Philosophy of language, 2nd ed.* Cambridge, MA: Harvard University Press.

Erk, Katrin. 2010. What is word meaning, really? (and how can distributional models help us describe it?). In *Proceedings of GEMS*, pages 17–26. Uppsala, Sweden.

Erk, Katrin. 2012. Vector space models of word meaning and phrase meaning: A survey. *Language and Linguistics Compass* 6(10):635–653.

Erk, Katrin and Sebastian Padó. 2008. A structured vector space model for word meaning in context. In *Proceedings of EMNLP*, pages 897–906. Honolulu, HI.

Erk, Katrin and Sebastian Padó. 2010. Exemplar-based models for word meaning in context. In *Proceedings ACL*, pages 92–97. Uppsala, Sweden.

Eslick, Ian. 2006. *Searching for Commonsense*. Ms thesis, MIT, Cambridge, MA.

Evert, Stefan. 2005. *The Statistics of Word Cooccurrences*. Ph.D dissertation, Stuttgart University.

Fellbaum, Christiane, ed. 1998. *WordNet: An Electronic Lexical Database*. Cambridge, MA: MIT Press.

Feng, Yansong and Mirella Lapata. 2010. Visual information in semantic representation. In *Proceedings of HLT-NAACL*, pages 91–99. Los Angeles, CA.

Firth, John R. 1957. *Papers in Linguistics, 1934-1951*. Oxford, UK: Oxford University Press.

Fletcher, William. 2004. Making the web more useful as a source for linguistic corpora. In *Corpus Linguistics in North America*, pages 191–205. Rodopi.

Fletcher, William. 2012. Corpus analysis of the World Wide Web. In C. Chapelle, ed., *Encyclopedia of Applied Linguistics*. Hoboken, NJ: Wiley-Blackwell.

Fodor, Jerry, Merrill Garrett, Edward Walker, and Cornelia Parkes. 1980. Against definitions. *Cognition* 8:263–367.

Foltz, Peter, Walter Kintsch, and Thomas Landauer. 1998. The measurement of textual coherence with Latent Semantic Analysis. *Discourse Processes* 25:285–307.

Frege, Gottlob. 1892. Über Sinn und Bedeutung. *Zeitschrift für Philosophie und philosophische Kritik* 100:25–50.

Frisson, Steven. 2009. Semantic underspecification in language processing. *Language and Linguistics Compass* 3(1):111–127.

Garrette, Dan, Katrin Erk, and Ray Mooney. 2013. A formal approach to linking logical form and vector-space lexical semantics. In H. Bunt, J. Bos, and S. Pulman, eds., *Computing Meaning, Vol. 4*, pages 27–48. Berlin: Springer.

Giesbrecht, Eugenie. 2010. Towards a matrix-based distributional model of meaning. In *Proceedings of the NAACL HLT 2010 Student Research Workshop*, pages 23–28. Los Angeles, CA.

Glenberg, Arthur and David Robertson. 2000. Symbol grounding and meaning: A comparison of high-dimensional and embodied theories of meaning. *Journal of Memory and Language* 3(43):379–401.

Grauman, Kristen and Bastian Leibe. 2011. *Visual Object Recognition*. San Francisco: Morgan & Claypool.

Grefenstette, Edward, Georgiana Dinu, Yao-Zhong Zhang, Mehrnoosh Sadrzadeh, and Marco Baroni. 2013. Multi-step regression learning for compositional distributional semantics. In *Proceedings of IWCS*, pages 131–142. Potsdam, Germany.

Grefenstette, Edward and Mehrnoosh Sadrzadeh. 2011a. Experimental support for a categorical compositional distributional model of meaning. In *Proceedings of EMNLP*, pages 1394–1404. Edinburgh, UK.

Grefenstette, Edward and Mehrnoosh Sadrzadeh. 2011b. Experimenting with transitive verbs in a DisCoCat. In *Proceedings of GEMS*, pages 62–66. Edinburgh, UK.

Grefenstette, Gregory. 1994. *Explorations in Automatic Thesaurus Discovery*. Boston, MA: Kluwer.

Griffiths, Tom, Mark Steyvers, and Josh Tenenbaum. 2007. Topics in semantic representation. *Psychological Review* 114:211–244.

Guevara, Emiliano. 2009. Compositionality in distributional semantics: Derivational affixes. In *Proceedings of the Words in Action Workshop*. Pisa, Italy.

Guevara, Emiliano. 2010. A regression model of adjective-noun composition-ality in distributional semantics. In *Proceedings of GEMS*, pages 33–37. Uppsala, Sweden.

Harnad, Stevan. 1990. The symbol grounding problem. *Physica D: Nonlinear Phenomena* 42(1-3):335–346.

Harris, Zellig. 1954. Distributional structure. *Word* 10(2-3):1456–1162.

Hastie, Trevor, Robert Tibshirani, and Jerome Friedman. 2009. *The Elements of Statistical Learning, 2nd edition*. New York: Springer.

Haxby, James, Ida Gobbini, Maura Furey, Alumit Ishai, Jennifer Schouten, and Pietro Pietrini. 2001. Distributed and overlapping representations of faces and objects in ventral temporal cortex. *Science* 293:2425–2430.

Heim, Irene and Angelika Kratzer. 1998. *Semantics in Generative Grammar*. Malden, MA: Blackwell.

Hills, Thomas. 2013. The company that words keep: comparing the statis-tical structure of child- versus adult-directed language. *Journal of Child Language* 40(03):586–604.

Hopper, Paul and Elizabeth Traugott. 1990. *Grammaticalization*. Cam-bridge, UK: Cambridge University Press.

Huth, Alexander, Shinji Nishimoto, An Vu, and Jack Gallant. 2012. A con-tinuous semantic space describes the representation of thousands of object and action categories across the human brain. *Neuron* 76(6):1210–1224.

Jackendoff, Ray. 1990. *Semantic Structures*. Cambridge, MA: MIT Press.

Kamp, Hans. 1975. Two theories about adjectives. In E. Keenan, ed., *Formal Semantics of Natural Languages*, pages 123–155. Cambridge, UK: Cam-bridge University Press.

Kamp, Hans and Barbara Partee. 1995. Prototype theory and composition-ality. *Cognition* 57(2):129–191.

Kartsaklis, Dimitri, Mehrnoosh Sadrzadeh, Stephen Pulman, and Bob Co-ecke. 2013. Reasoning about meaning in natural language with compact closed categories and frobenius algebras. In *Logic and Algebraic Structures in Quantum Computing and Information*. Cambridge University Press. To appear.

Kelly, Colin, Barry Devereux, and Anna Korhonen. 2012. Semi-supervised learning for automatic conceptual property extraction. In *Proceedings of the 3rd Workshop on Cognitive Modeling and Computational Linguistics*, pages 11–20. Montreal, Canada.

Kintsch, Walter. 2001. Predication. *Cognitive Science* 25(2):173–202.

Kipper, Karin, Anna Korhonen, Neville Ryant, and Martha Palmer. 2008. A large-scale classification of English verbs. *Language Resources and Evalu-ation* 42(1):21–40.

Klepousniotou, Ekaterini and Shari Baum. 2007. Disambiguating the ambi-guity advantage effect in word recognition: An advantage for polysemous but not homonymous words. *Journal of Neurolinguistics* 20:1–24.

Kolda, Tamara and Brett Bader. 2009. Tensor decompositions and applications. *SIAM Review* 51(3):455–500.

Kotlerman, Lili, Ido Dagan, Idan Szpektor, and Maayan Zhitomirsky-Geffet. 2010. Directional distributional similarity for lexical inference. *Natural Language Engineering* 16(4):359–389.

Krifka, Manfred, Francis Pelletier, Gregory Carlson, Alice ter Meulen, Godehard Ling, and Gennaro Chierchia. 1995. Genericity: An introduction. In G. Carlson and F. Pelletier, eds., *The Generic Book*, pages 1–124. Chicago, IL: University of Chicago Press.

Kripke, Saul A. 1980. *Naming and Necessity*. Cambridge, Mass: Harvard University Press.

Kübler, Sandra, Ryan McDonald, and Joakim Nivre. 2009. *Dependency Parsing*. San Francisco: Morgan & Claypool.

Kwiatkowski, Tom, Sharon Goldwater, Luke Zettelmoyer, and Mark Steedman. 2012. A probabilistic model of syntactic and semantic acquisition from child-directed utterances and their meanings. In *Proceedings of EACL*.

Lahav, Ran. 1993. The combinatorial-connectionist debate and the pragmatics of adjectives. *Pragmatics and Cognition* 1:71–88.

Lambek, Jim. 1961. On the calculus of syntactic types. In R. Jakobson, ed., *Structure of Languages and its Mathematical Aspects*, pages 166–178. American Mathematical Society.

Lambrecht, Knud. 1996. *Information Structure and Sentence Form: Topic, Focus, and the Mental Representations of Discourse Referents*. Cambridge, UK: Cambridge University Press.

Landauer, Thomas and Susan Dumais. 1997. A solution to Plato's problem: The latent semantic analysis theory of acquisition, induction, and representation of knowledge. *Psychological Review* 104(2):211–240.

Lenci, Alessandro. 2008. Distributional approaches in linguistic and cognitive research. *Italian Journal of Linguistics* 20(1):1–31.

Lenci, Alessandro. 2011. Composing and updating verb argument expectations: A distributional semantic model. In *Proceedings of the 2nd Workshop on Cognitive Modeling and Computational Linguistics*, pages 58–66. Portland, OR.

Leong, Chee Wee and Rada Mihalcea. 2011. Going beyond text: A hybrid image-text approach for measuring word relatedness. In *Proceedings of IJCNLP*, pages 1403–1407.

Liang, Percy, Michael Jordan, and Dan Klein. 2011. Learning dependency-based compositional semantics. In *Proceedings of ACL)*, pages 590–599.

Louwerse, Max. 2011. Symbol interdependency in symbolic and embodied cognition. *Topics in Cognitive Science* 3:273–302.

Lund, Kevin and Curt Burgess. 1996. Producing high-dimensional semantic spaces from lexical co-occurrence. *Behavior Research Methods* 28:203–208.

Manning, Christopher. 2011. Part-of-speech tagging from 97% to 100%: Is it time for some linguistics? In *Proceedings of CICLing*, pages 171–189. Waseda, Japan.

Marcus, Mitchell, Mary Ann Marcinkiewicz, and Beatrice Santorini. 1993. Building a large annotated corpus of english: the Penn Treebank. *Computational Linguistics* 19(2):313–330.

McCarthy, Diana. 2009. Word Sense Disambiguation: An overview. *Language and Linguistics Compass* 3(2):537–558.

McDonald, Scott and Chris Brew. 2004. A distributional model of semantic context effects in lexical processing. In *Proceedings of ACL*, pages 17–24. Barcelona, Spain.

McDonald, Scott and Michael Ramscar. 2001. Testing the distributional hypothesis: The influence of context on judgements of semantic similarity. In *Proceedings of CogSci*, pages 611–616.

Mel'chuk, Igor A. 1987. *Dependency Syntax: Theory and Practice*. Albany: State University Press of New York.

Meyer, Carl. 2000. *Matrix Analysis and Applied Linear Algebra*. Philadelphia, PA: SIAM.

Miller, George and Walter Charles. 1991. Contextual correlates of semantic similarity. *Language and Cognitive Processes* 6(1):1–28.

Mitchell, Jeff and Mirella Lapata. 2008. Vector-based models of semantic composition. In *Proceedings of ACL*, pages 236–244. Columbus, OH.

Mitchell, Jeff and Mirella Lapata. 2009. Language models based on semantic composition. In *Proceedings of EMNLP*, pages 430–439. Singapore.

Mitchell, Jeff and Mirella Lapata. 2010. Composition in distributional models of semantics. *Cognitive Science* 34(8):1388–1429.

Mitchell, Tom, Svetlana Shinkareva, Andrew Carlson, Kai-Min Chang, Vincente Malave, Robert Mason, and Marcel Just. 2008. Predicting human brain activity associated with the meanings of nouns. *Science* 320:1191–1195.

Montague, Richard. 1970a. English as a Formal Language. In B. V. et al., ed., *Linguaggi nella Societaà e nella Tecnica*, pages 189–224. Edizioni di Comunità. Reprinted in Montague (1974), 188–221.

Montague, Richard. 1970b. Universal Grammar. *Theoria* 36:373–398.

Montague, Richard. 1973. The proper treatment of quantification in English. In K. e. a. Hintikka, ed., *Approaches to Natural Language*, pages 221–242. Dordrecht: D. Reidel.

Moortgat, Michael. 1997. Categorial Type Logics. In J. van Benthem and A. ter Meulen, eds., *Handbook of Logic and Language*, pages 93–178. Cambridge, MA: The MIT Press.

Murphy, Brian, Partha Talukdar, and Tom Mitchell. 2012. Selecting corpus-semantic models for neurolinguistic decoding. In *Proceedings of *SEM*, pages 114–123. Montreal, Canada.

Murphy, Gregory. 2002. *The Big Book of Concepts*. Cambridge, MA: MIT Press.

Navigli, Roberto. 2009. Word Sense Disambiguation: A survey. *ACM Computing Surveys* 41(2):1–69.

Newport, Elissa, Henry Gleitman, and Lila Gleitman. 1977. Mother, I'd rather do it myself: Some effects and non-effects of maternal speech style. In C. E. Snow and C. A. Ferguson, eds., *Talking to children : Language input and acquisition*, pages 109–150. Cambrdige: Cambridge University Press.

Ng, Vincent. 2010. Supervised noun phrase coreference research: The first fifteen years. In *Proceedings of ACL*, pages 1396–1411. Uppsala, Sweden.

Nivre, Joakim. 2003. An efficient algorithm for projective dependency parsing. In *Proceedings of IWPT*, pages 149–160. Nancy, France.

Padó, Sebastian and Mirella Lapata. 2007. Dependency-based construction of semantic space models. *Computational Linguistics* 33(2):161–199.

Padó, Ulrike, Sebastian Padó, and Katrin Erk. 2007. Flexible, corpus-based modelling of human plausibility judgements. In *Proceedings of EMNLP*, pages 400–409. Prague, Czech Republic.

Pantel, Patrick and Dekang Lin. 2002. Discovering word senses from text. In *Proceedings of KDD*, pages 613–619. Edmonton, Canada.

Partee, Barbara. 2004. *Compositionality in Formal Semantics*. Malden, MA: Blackwell.

Pelletier, Francis Jeffry. 2001. Did Frege believe Frege's principle? *Journal of Logic, Language, and Information* 10:87–114.

Pereira, Fernando. 2000. Formal grammar and information theory: Together again? *Philosophical Transactions of the Royal Society* 385:1239–1253.

Poesio, Massimo, Simone Ponzetto, and Yannick Versley. 2010. Computational models of anaphora resolution: A survey. http://clic.cimec.unitn.it/massimo/Publications/lilt.pdf.

Prince, Alan and Paul Smolensky. 2004. *Optimality Theory*. Malden, MA: Blackwell.

Pustejovsky, James. 1995. *The Generative Lexicon*. Cambridge, MA: MIT Press.

Rapp, Reinhard. 2004. A freely available automatically generated thesaurus of related words. In *Proceedings of LREC*, pages 395–398. Lisbon, Portugal.

Reddy, Sravana and Kevin Knight. 2011. What we know about the Voynich manuscript. In *Proceedings of ACL Workshop on Language Technology for Cultural Heritage, Social Sciences, and Humanities (LaTeCH)*, pages 78–86. Stroudsburg, PA, USA: Association for Computational Linguistics.

Reinhart, Tanya. 1976. *The Syntactic Domain of Anaphora*. Ph.D dissertation, Massachusetts Institute of Technology.

Reisinger, Joseph and Raymond Mooney. 2010. Multi-prototype vector-space models of word meaning. In *Proceedings of NAACL*, pages 109–117. Los Angeles, CA.

Riordan, Brian and Michael Jones. 2011. Redundancy in perceptual and linguistic experience: Comparing feature-based and distributional models of semantic representation. *Topics in Cognitive Science* 3(2):1–43.

Roller, Stephen, Michael Speriosu, Sarat Rallapalli, Benjamin Wing, and Jason Baldridge. 2012. Supervised text-based geolocation using language models on an adaptive grid. In *Proceedings of EMNLP*, pages 1500–1510. Jeju Island, Korea.

Rooth, Mats. 1985. *Associations with Focus*. Ph.D. thesis, University of Massachusetts at Amherst.

Rooth, Mats. 1995. A theory of focus interpretation. *Natural Language Semantics* 4.

Rooth, Mats and Barbara Partee. 1983. Conjunction, type ambiguity and wide scope *or*. In D. Flickenger, M. Macken, and N. Wiegand, eds., *Proceedings of WCCFL1*. Stanford, CA: Stanford Linguistic Association.

Sag, Ivan, Timothy Baldwin, Francis Bond, Ann Copestake, and Dan Flickinger. 2002. Multiword expressions: A pain in the neck for NLP. In A. Gelbukh, ed., *Computational Linguistics and Intelligent Text Processing*, pages 189–206. Berlin: Springer.

Sahlgren, Magnus. 2005. An introduction to random indexing. http://www.sics.se/~mange/papers/RI_intro.pdf.

Sahlgren, Magnus. 2006. *The Word-Space Model*. Ph.D dissertation, Stockholm University.

Sahlgren, Magnus. 2008. The distributional hypothesis. *Italian Journal of Linguistics* 20(1):33–53.

Schubert, Lenhart and Matthew Tong. 2003. Extracting and evaluating general world knowledge from the Brown corpus. In *Proceedings of the HLT-NAACL 2003 workshop on Text Meaning*, pages 7–13. Morristown, NJ.

Schütze, Hinrich. 1997. *Ambiguity Resolution in Natural Language Learning*. Stanford, CA: CSLI.

Schütze, Hinrich. 1998. Automatic word sense discrimination. *Computational Linguistics* 24(1):97–123.

Scott, Gary-John. 2002. Stacked adjectival modification and the structure of nominal phrases. In G. Cinque, ed., *Functional Structure in DP and IP. The Cartography of Syntactic Structures*, vol. 1. Oxford, UK: Oxford University Press.

Searle, John. 1980. Minds, brains and programs. *Behavioral and Brain Sciences* 3(3):417–457.

Silberer, Carina and Mirella Lapata. 2012. Grounded models of semantic representation. In *Proceedings of EMNLP*, pages 1423–1433. Jeju, Korea.

Smolensky, Paul. 1990. Tensor product variable binding and the representation of symbolic structures in connectionist networks. *Artificial Intelligence* 46:159–216.

Socher, Richard, Brody Huval, Christopher Manning, and Andrew Ng. 2012. Semantic compositionality through recursive matrix-vector spaces. In *Proceedings of EMNLP*, pages 1201–1211. Jeju Island, Korea.

Steedman, Mark. 2000. *The Syntactic Process*. Cambridge, MA: MIT Press.

Stowell, Timothy. 1981. *Origins of Phrase Structure*. Ph.D. thesis, MIT.

Strang, Gilbert. 2003. *Introduction to linear algebra, 3d edition*. Wellesley, MA: Wellesley-Cambridge Press.

Thater, Stefan, Georgiana Dinu, and Manfred Pinkal. 2009. Ranking paraphrases in context. In *Proceedings of the 2009 Workshop on Applied Textual Inference*, pages 44–47. Suntec, Singapore.

Titov, Ivan and Alexandre Klementiev. 2012. A Bayesian approach to unsupervised semantic role induction. In *Proceedings of the Conference of the European Chapter of the Association for Computational Linguistics*. Avignon, France.

Tomasello, Michael. 2003. *Constructing a Language: A Usage-Based Theory of Language Acquisition*. Cambridge, MA: Harvard University Press.

Turney, Peter. 2007. Empirical evaluation of four tensor decomposition algorithms. Tech. Rep. ERB-1152, NRC.

Turney, Peter. 2012. Domain and function: A dual-space model of semantic relations and compositions. *Journal of Artificial Intelligence Research* 44:533–585.

Turney, Peter and Patrick Pantel. 2010. From frequency to meaning: Vector space models of semantics. *Journal of Artificial Intelligence Research* 37:141–188.

Tversky, Amos and Daniel Kahneman. 1983. Extension versus intuitive reasoning: The conjunction fallacy in probability judgment. *Psychological Review* 90(4):293–315.

van Benthem, Johan. 1986. *Essays in Logical Semantics*. Dordrecht: Reidel Publishing Company.

Van de Cruys, Tim. 2010. A non-negative tensor factorization model for selectional preference induction. *Natural Language Engineering* 16(4):417–437.

Vecchi, Eva Maria, Marco Baroni, and Roberto Zamparelli. 2011. (Linear) maps of the impossible: Capturing semantic anomalies in distributional space. In *Proceedings of the ACL Workshop on Distributional Semantics and Compositionality*, pages 1–9. Portland, OR.

Wang, Chang and Sridhar Mahadevan. 2008. Manifold alignment using Procrustes analysis. In *Proceedings of ICML*, pages 1120–1127. Helsinki, Finland.

Werning, Markus, Wolfram Hinzen, and Edouard Machery, eds. 2012. *The Oxford Handbook of Compositionality*. Oxford University Press.

Widdows, Dominic. 2008. Semantic vector products: Some initial investigations. In *Proceedings of the Second Symposium on Quantum Interaction*. Oxford, UK.

Winter, Yoad. 1996. A unified semantic treatment of singular NP coordination. *Linguistics and Philosophy* 19:337–391.

Winter, Yoad. 2001. *Flexible Principles in Boolean Semantics*. The MIT Press.

Wittgenstein, Ludwig. 1953. *Philosophical Investigations*. Oxford, UK: Blackwell. Translated by G.E.M. Anscombe.

Zamparelli, Roberto. 2011. Coordination. In K. von Heusinger, C. Maienborn, and P. Portner, eds., *Semantics : an international handbook of natural language meaning*, pages 1713–1741. De Gruyter Mouton.

Zanzotto, Fabio M., Ioannis Korkontzelos, Francesca Falucchi, and Suresh Manandhar. 2010. Estimating linear models for compositional distributional semantics. In *Proceedings of COLING*, pages 1263–1271. Beijing, China.